The Adobe® Photoshop® Album 2 Book

Enjoying Digital Photography

Michael Slater

Adobe Press
Berkeley, California

The Adobe Photoshop Album 2.0 Book
Enjoying Digital Photography

Michael Slater

Adobe Press books are published by Peachpit Press.

Peachpit Press
1249 Eighth Street
Berkeley, CA 94710
510/524-2178
800/283-9444
510/524-2221 (fax)

Peachpit Press is a division of Pearson Education
To report errors, please send a note to errata@peachpit.com

For the latest on Adobe Press books go to www.adobepress.com

Editors: Nancy Peterson, Becky Morgan
Production Editors: Myrna Vladic, Gloria Marquez
Copyeditor: Elissa Rabellino
Compositor: David Van Ness
Indexer: FireCrystal Communications
Cover design: Alan Clements
Interior design: Maureen Forys

ISBN 0-321-22055-2

9 8 7 6 5 4 3 2 1

Printed and bound in the United States of America

For my family—Irene, Gregory, and Amanda

Acknowledgments

Many people have made invaluable contributions to this book—directly or indirectly. And the book is possible, in turn, because of three years of teamwork that led to Photoshop Album 2.0.

The Making of This Book

My wife, Irene, and my children, Gregory and Amanda, contributed in numerous ways both to Photoshop Album and to this book. Without their loving support through the many evenings and weekends I spent writing, this book would not have been possible.

My family has not only put up with the many long days a startup requires, but they have also served as my primary photo subjects and tolerated—sometimes unwittingly—being featured in thousands of photos used in experimentation as Photoshop Album evolved.

As I considered writing this book, agent Matt Wagner, of Waterside Associates, put me together with the right publisher. At Peachpit Press, editors Becky Morgan and Nancy Peterson, along with copy editor Elissa Rabellino, worked tirelessly to improve the organization and clarity of the book. If you find it easy to read, as I hope you will, they deserve much of the credit.

Valuable comments on drafts of this book were provided by Greg Beddow, Jim Jütte, Dick Sites, and Kakul Srivastava.

I've tried to create an accurate book, but no doubt some errors have slipped through. Please visit the book's Web site, Enjoying Digital Photography (www.enjoyingdp.com), for the latest updates and to report any errors you find.

The Making of Photoshop Album

This book has its origins in the frustrations I experienced when switching from film to digital photography in 1999. I was exasperated with the quality of the experience on the PC and inspired to create a better solution.

This led to my cofounding PhotoTablet, later renamed Fotiva. The company was acquired by Adobe Systems in late 2001, and Fotiva's software formed the core of Photoshop Album.

The central concepts behind Photoshop Album were developed by Fotiva cofounder Ken Rothmuller and Laurie Vertelney. Their original thinking is responsible for many of the product's innovations. Cofounder Bernard Peuto was instrumental in Fotiva's financing and business planning.

Many thanks must go to Stewart Alsop, of New Enterprise Associates. Without his belief in the PhotoTablet team, we would not have had the financial resources to succeed. Fotiva's CEO, Jim Heeger, and VP of marketing, Tanya Roberts, each contributed greatly. Loralee Denny was an invaluable part of Fotiva, running administration and helping me stay sane. Board members Scott Briggs and Pierluigi Zappacosta also made critical contributions.

At Adobe, it was the support of Greg Gilley, Bryan Lamkin, and Rajiv Mehta that made the acquisition of Fotiva possible. Without their vision, Photoshop Album (at least in this form) would not exist.

Many insights, as well as all the early implementation work, came from members of Fotiva's engineering team, most of whom continue at Adobe today: Greg Beddow, Barry Burris, Mike DePaoli, Tony Fardella, Scott Geiger, Lance Groody, Eric LaFranchi, Steve Rossi, Claire Schendel, and Allan Young.

Many people have played a part in making Photoshop Album what it is today. The Album engineering team has grown to include Doug Ahmann, Mark Crowley, Alan Dixon, Jeff Garner, Bruce Hunt, Peter Johnson, Glenn Larson, Mark Maguire, and Vasile Nedelcu. Along the way, Rich Dermer, Jon Ferraiolo, Rick Gordon, Paton Lewis, Bob Reents, Dick Sites, Gregg Wilensky, Ric Wright, and Bill Wyman have all made significant contributions. The breadth and depth of Album's capabilities are a testament to this team's abilities.

Johnnie Manzari and Michael Mueller are largely responsible for Album's elegant user interface, Wayne Jiang created most of the template designs, and Mary Van Riper helped refine the program with user feedback. Quality engineering was led by Barry Burris, Chris Gonzales, Anand Kamat, Kaori Mikawa, Doug Musto, Adriana Ohlmeyer, Danny Pampel, Mark Sgarlato, Jun Shim, Michael Sobiesky, and Chad Watson.

Product and program managers who made major contributions to Photoshop Album include Rod Alligood, Tapan Bhat, Marci Hildt, Barry Hills, Dave Klaphaak, Jim Mohan, Yoko Nakagawa, Atsushi Yoshida, and Asako Yoshimura.

Contents

Introduction

People are making the switch to digital cameras in droves. Digital cameras now account for the majority of cameras sold. For most people, taking digital photos is fun, but organizing, sharing, and printing them remains complex and often frustrating.

It doesn't have to be that way. Your experience with digital pictures can be as easy and enjoyable as it's been with your film photos, and you can do more with your pictures than ever before.

I've spent the past three years helping create Photoshop Album—a program that enables you to organize, fix, share, and preserve your digital photos painlessly. With this book, I hope to show how to spend more time enjoying your photos and less time dealing with unnecessary complexities.

Who Should Read This Book

If you have a digital camera but aren't entirely satisfied with your experience storing, finding, editing, printing, and sharing your photos—or if you've just purchased your first digital camera and are trying to figure out how to do all these things—then this book is for you. It's designed to tell you all you need to know for an easy, fun, and satisfying digital photo experience, without burdening you with more detail than you need.

This book assumes that you're using a digital camera, a Windows PC, and Photoshop Album. My goal is to enable you to use Album to change the way you think about and interact with your photos.

As you read the book, you'll follow a straightforward path to get up to speed with a minimum of complexity. Most of this book centers on Photoshop Album—which lets you do nearly everything most people do with their photos. I'll also delve briefly into Photoshop Elements and Photoshop CS to show you how to take the next steps in photo editing.

How to Read This Book

The first half of this book—Chapters 1 through 5—describes the core of Photoshop Album. I recommend that you read these chapters first to gain a solid foundation in how Album works and how to make the most of it. Chapters 6 through 10 cover editing, making creations, printing, and sharing—and you can read these in any order, as you have need for those features.

I've included background sections between chapters and in appendixes that go beyond using Album to discussing some key pieces of technology, as well as how to select your camera, PC, and printer. This background information will help you choose better equipment and will remove some of the mystery from digital photography. You can, however, skip these background sections without missing anything about using Photoshop Album.

Within each chapter there are sidebars that, like the background sections between the chapters, are not essential to using Photoshop Album. They do, however, explain how the software works in more detail.

By the time you finish this book, you'll be an expert user of Photoshop Album—and you'll be able to do more with your photos with less hassle than ever before. Enjoy!

1 Getting Started

Taking pictures is easier than it's ever been. Now that inexpensive digital cameras capture high quality photos, you can snap away to your heart's content.

The problem is the proliferation of digital photos on our hard drives and the difficulty of doing anything with them. The more photos you add, the tougher it is to organize them and find the ones you're looking for. And since there are so many ways to use them—from emailing them, to making Web pages, to creating slideshows, albums, and greeting cards—the number of programs you have to use can make life complex.

Now, thankfully, there's a better way: Adobe Photoshop Album puts everything you need into one application that's centered around your photo collection. In this chapter, you'll see how Album can transform a clunky workflow into a smooth one. You'll get insight into how Album works and get an overview of all that it can help you do. Finally, I'll introduce you to Photoshop Elements and Photoshop, programs you may want to use to extend beyond Album.

Note: *If you're using Photoshop Album Starter Edition (the free version of Album) parts of this book will be confusing—the two programs have many differences. (If you want to introduce a friend to the free version, direct them to www.adobe.com/products/photoshopalbum/starter.html.)*

Photoshop Album: The Center of Your Photo World

Photoshop Album makes it easy to collect and organize all your photos. It lets you:

- Copy photos and video clips from your camera or memory card to the hard disk and delete them from the memory card
- Scan photos
- Consolidate photos and video clips from your camera, scanner, CDs, email, hard disk, and elsewhere into one unified collection
- Quickly find photos by the date they were taken, regardless of what folder (or even what disk) you store them in
- Organize photos by who is in them, where they were taken, what events they were associated with, and any other categorization you want
- Keep your entire collection safe by copying it to CD, DVD, or an external hard disk

Once you've collected and organized your photos with Album, it's easy to find the ones you want and then enhance and share them. You can:

- Fix common photo problems, such as poor lighting or unbalanced color, with a single click
- Display slide shows on your PC that include photos, video, audio captions, and background music
- Print photos, one or more per page, in any common size on your home printer—or order prints from an Internet photofinisher
- Make slide shows, albums, greeting cards, and calendars, and print them either on your home printer or via an Internet service
- Create CDs that will play a slide show on a PC or a DVD player
- Share photos by email, on a commercial Web site, or by creating Web pages for your own Web site—even Web pages that display a virtual 3D gallery

Making Life Simpler

Photoshop Album can make your life—at least the part of it that revolves around digital photos—a lot simpler. The typical methods for handling digital photos involve a great deal of complexity. One of the most confounding aspects is that you have to use the Windows file system to organize your photos. You must rename and sort photos yourself in Windows, and then you have to remember the names and locations days, weeks, and years from now. This situation only gets more complicated every time you edit or resize a photo and create more copies.

Besides the challenge of organizing photos through the file system, the usual approach also requires using a multitude of programs. You might use software that came with your camera to copy photos to your PC; a thumbnail browser to find the ones you want; an editor to fix photos and resize them for sharing; a utility program to print photos in various arrangements; another to burn a CD, or to make a slideshow that you can play on a DVD player; and yet another to create Web pages.

If you're lucky, you may have found programs that can do several of these tasks, but you probably still need at least two or three programs for everything you do (or wish you could do) with your photos.

Album simplifies the process by letting you perform all of these tasks and more from within just one streamlined environment.

A Catalog, Not a File-System Browser

With Photoshop Album, you don't have to find files in Windows. Instead, you can see all your photos in one window and search for photos based on any category you create, such as the subject of the photo, the date, or an event (**Figure 1.1**). Album finds them for you no matter what folder you've stored them in. You can view photos from many different folders, yet see them in chronological sequence.

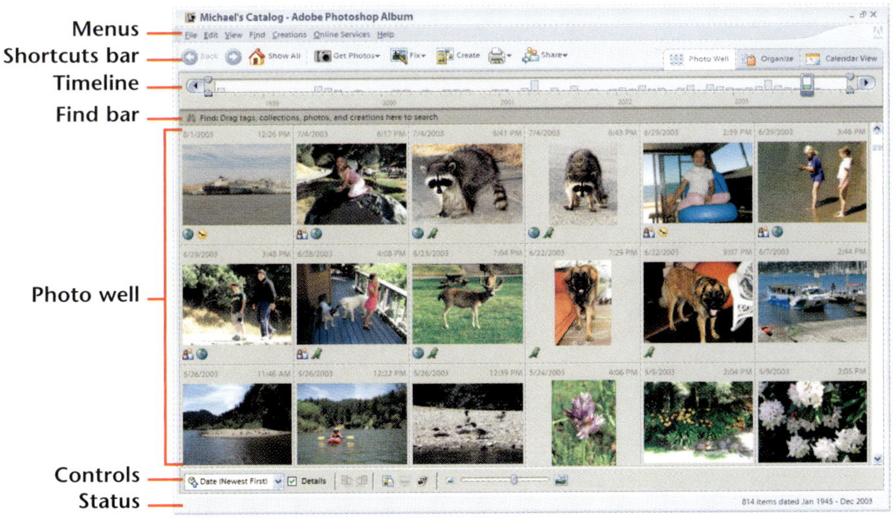

Figure 1.1 Photoshop Album's main window shows all your photos, regardless of where they are stored on the disk.

The reason Album can show photos regardless of where they're stored is that it's based around a *catalog*, a special database that tracks all your photos, video clips, and audio clips. Before you can work with any of these items in Album, you must import them into a catalog. The original files remain in the file system; the catalog simply creates a link to each item and provides a place to store additional information (such as a caption). You can still access your photos in the file system, but you'll rarely need to.

If you've been using photo applications that are file-system oriented, such as ACDSee or ThumbsPlus, it's important to realize that Album works in a different way. Those programs provide a view into a part of the file system. Photoshop Album instead lets you see all the photos in your catalog, independent of where they are in the file system.

If you've already developed ways to manage your digital photos without Album, you're accustomed to doing things in a different way. Album offers a new way of working with your photos that may seem unfamiliar at first and requires that you change some habits. If you make the shift, though, you'll probably find that many tasks become simpler.

A Quick Tour of Photoshop Album

In this book you'll learn about all that Photoshop Album can do, and the many tasks you can do with it. To get an overview of Album, let's look at some of its key features.

***Note** This book assumes that you're running Windows XP. Almost all features should work the same under Windows Me or Windows 2000, but some details of dialogs and file paths may be different.*

The Quick Guide

When you first open Album, the Quick Guide is displayed (**Figure 1.2**). The Quick Guide is a set of visual shortcuts to common operations. You might find the Quick Guide helpful if you aren't sure how to access a given function, but you can access the same functions by selecting the appropriate menu items or buttons on the shortcuts bar.

Since the Quick Guide duplicates the usual ways of accessing each function, I'm going to skip it and instead describe the direct method, which is more efficient. I suggest that you click the "Show this window at startup" box at the bottom of the Quick Guide window to deselect it, and you'll never see the Quick Guide again. If you miss it, choose Help > Quick Guide to view it.

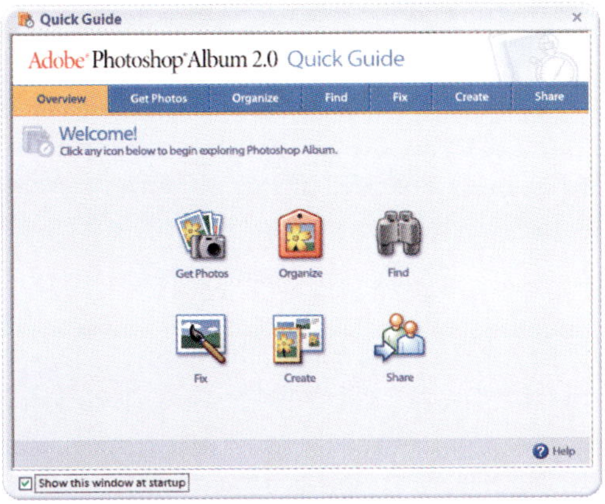

Figure 1.2 The Quick Guide provides visual shortcuts to common functions, but the regular menus and shortcut buttons provide more direct paths to every function.

The photo well

The central area of Album's main window, the photo well, can show your photos in a range of sizes—from lots of small thumbnails to one large photo at a time (**Figure 1.3**). It normally shows all your photos, regardless of where they are on your disk (even if they're stored on CDs), arranged in one of several ways.

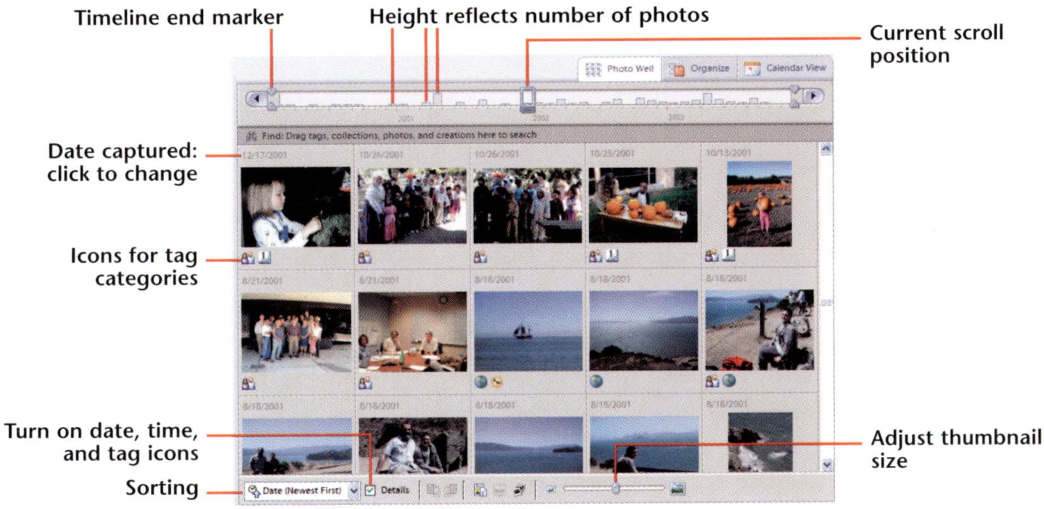

Figure 1.3 The photo well and timeline work together to help you find photos quickly.

Normally they're arranged by time. Within a day they go into chronological order, but you can choose whether to put the most recent or the oldest day first. You can also arrange the photo well by folder location or by import batch (in groups according to when you imported them rather than when you took them). You can use the pop-up menu at the bottom left to select the arrangement. (Chapter 5 describes how to use the photo well in detail.)

The slider at the bottom of the photo well allows you to control the size of the thumbnails. Small thumbnails work well for an overview of lots of photos, when you don't need to see detail; larger thumbnails are better when you're selecting photos or tagging them.

If you select the largest size—with one photo filling the frame—you can move from one photo to the next using either the scroll bar or the left and right arrow keys. This is a great mode for scrutinizing your photos to select favorites. You can also enter captions in this view by typing them in the space provided below the photo.

Getting Help

Any time you're wondering what an icon means, or you want more information about an object, try pausing the mouse over it (this is called hovering). In most cases, a tool tip (descriptive text in a small pop-up box) providing more information will appear.

To access Album's Help text, choose Help > Adobe Photoshop Album Help. If you don't find what you need there (or in this book), choose Help > Support to access Adobe's support Web site. You may want to check the FAQ (frequently asked questions) available there, or join the user-to-user forum to post your questions. One other source is the Web site that supports this book (www.enjoyingdp.com).

You can also find phone numbers on the support site for technical support, should you have an installation problem or encounter a program bug. Support for these kinds of problems is free, but assistance with using the program is not.

Feel free to experiment, because Album tries very hard to be forgiving. You can almost always press Ctrl-Z (or choose Edit > Undo) to reverse your last action. In fact, you can step back ten actions by repeatedly pressing Ctrl-Z.

You'll also find that Album often displays informational dialogs to make clear what is happening. Almost all of them have a "Don't show again" check box you can select. Once you've seen one of these dialogs a couple of times and understand what it's explaining, click the check box to make it stop popping up. (Each dialog has a separate control, so selecting the check box affects only that dialog.) If you want to make these dialogs come back, choose Help > Reset "Don't Show Again" Settings, and they'll all return.

You can choose whether to show photos only, or to also show the date, time, and tags. Check the Details box at the bottom of the photo well to display this information. Album automatically changes the amount of information shown to make the best use of the available space. It's a good idea to leave details on, except for rare occasions when you want every bit of the available space for the photos themselves.

The timeline

Above the photo well, the timeline has a bar for each month in which you took photos. The height of each bar indicates the relative number of photos you took that month. You can instantly scroll to photos in a particular month by clicking the bar for that month.

If you have photos covering more years than will fit in the timeline, buttons with side-facing triangles at each end allow you to scroll the timeline. You can drag the markers at each end of the timeline (the up and down triangles) toward the center to restrict the range of photos that appear in the well.

The shortcuts bar

Above the timeline, the shortcuts bar has buttons for many common functions (**Figure 1.4**). The three tabs at the right let you select different modes of the main window: photo well, organize (a variation of the photo well), and calendar view (described later).

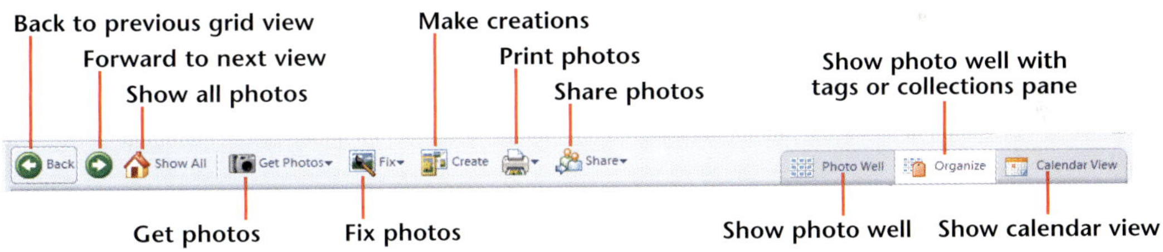

Figure 1.4 The shortcuts bar provides quick access to many commonly used functions.

The two arrow buttons at the far left allow you to go back to the previous view and then forward to restore the more recent view. The Show All button will become useful after you learn how to restrict the photos shown in the photo well (in Chapter 5). You can click the Show All button at any time to see all your photos.

The other buttons in the shortcuts bar provide quick access to frequent commands, such as fixing, printing, and sharing photos.

***Note** All functions are also available via menu items, and most have shortcut keys as well, so you can choose which method is easiest for you. Shortcut keys are the fastest—if you can remember them. Some functions are available only through the menus, so be sure to peruse them. The menus also show the shortcut keys, so you can learn the ones for functions you use frequently. (See Appendix B for a list of common shortcut keys.)*

In Photoshop Album you always select the photos you want to work with first, and then choose what you want to do with them. When you choose a command, it operates on the photos you have selected. You select photos by clicking them. A yellow outline around a photo shows that you have selected it.

***Note** If you don't select any photos, most of Album's functions will apply to all photos.*

Other photo well controls

Two buttons to the right of the Details check box at the bottom of the photo well allow you to easily rotate the selected photo(s) by 90 degrees in either direction (**Figure 1.5**). The button to the right of the rotate buttons lets you open and close the Properties palette, which provides detailed information about a photo.

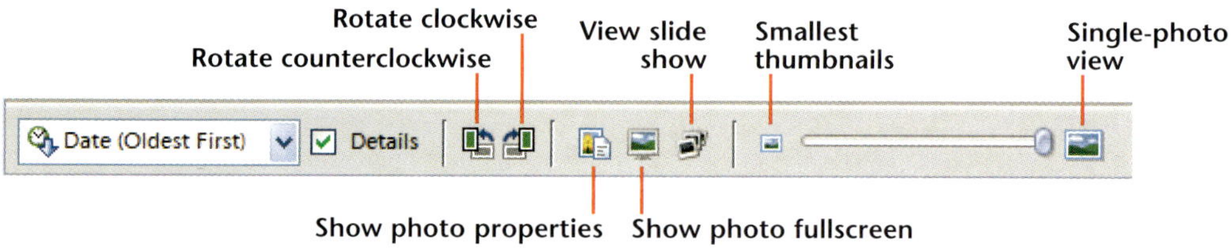

Figure 1.5 **The controls at the bottom of the photo well make it easy to rotate photos and control how you're viewing them.**

You can easily view photos full screen, completely hiding the Photoshop Album user interface. The Full Screen Preview button displays a single photo full screen; you can use the left and right arrow keys to move to other photos. Click anywhere on the screen to go back to thumbnail view.

The Slideshow button starts an automatically advancing slide show; you can control its timing and other features by choosing Edit > Preferences to bring up the Preferences dialog and choosing Slideshow from the list on the left side of the dialog.

Many functions are also available from a menu that appears when you right-click a photo (**Figure 1.6**). If more than one photo is selected, you can right-click any of them, and the selected command will apply to all of them. This is a quick way to access many functions, such as editing or rotating photos.

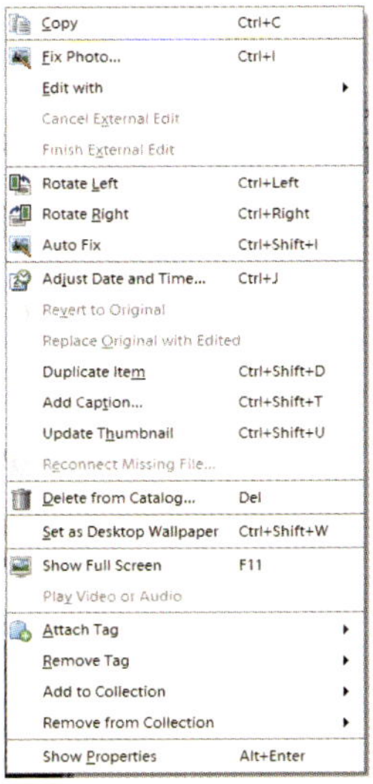

Figure 1.6 **This menu, which gives quick access to common operations, appears when you right-click a photo in any view.**

The calendar view

Selecting the Calendar View tab at the right of the shortcuts bar gives you a great way to find photos by the date they were taken (**Figure 1.7**). (The photo well can also show photos in calendar order, but it doesn't group them by day or format the display like a calendar.) After all, most of us organize our lives with the calendar, so it's a natural tool for organizing photos.

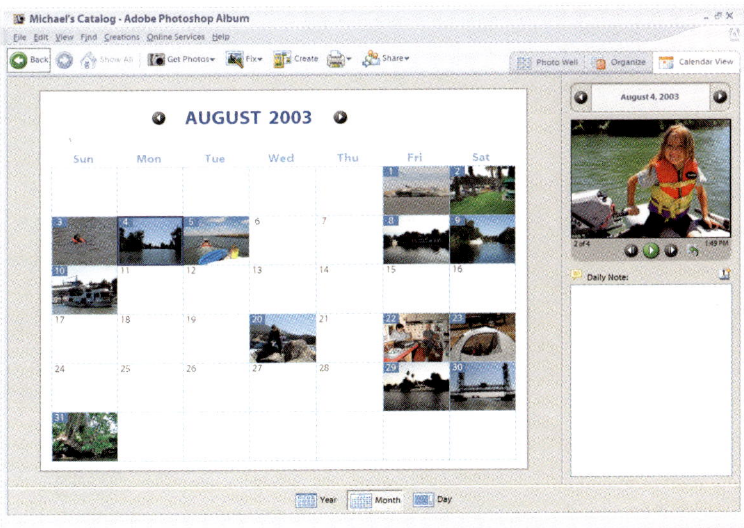

Figure 1.7 **Photoshop Album's calendar view shows how your photos are distributed in time.**

The calendar has year, month, and day views (which you can select at the bottom of the window); the month view is generally the most useful. It shows the first photo taken on each day as part of the calendar itself. To see all the photos taken on any day, just click that day, and you can see a mini–slide show of all the photos in the right-hand pane. You can also enter notes for the day. (See Chapter 5 for full details on using the calendar view.)

The calendar view is different from the photo well in that you can't make a selection. The photo you are viewing is automatically selected, and there is no way to select multiple photos. As a result, the photo well view is more powerful; use the calendar view to browse photos by day or month, but return to the photo well to take action on the photo, such as printing it or making a creation (see "Sharing photos and making creations"). If you want to do something with a single photo, you can do it from the calendar view, but you can't select more than one photo in this view.

Note *The calendar view always shows all your photos. Even if you have done a search in the photo well, the calendar shows everything in your catalog (except items marked as hidden). When you switch back to the photo well, your search results will still be there.*

A Better Way to Organize

If you're like most people, organizing isn't something you do for fun. You probably do as little of it as possible, but enough so that you can (hopefully) find your photos when you want them. Photoshop Album makes it far easier and more satisfying—even fun—to keep your photos organized.

Photoshop Album overcomes the limitations of organizing in the file system. The breakthrough is the use of tags, which are like keywords in a database. Unlike keywords, however, tags are visual and easier to use (**Figure 1.8**). You apply tags by simply dragging them onto a photo. Each photo can have dozens of tags.

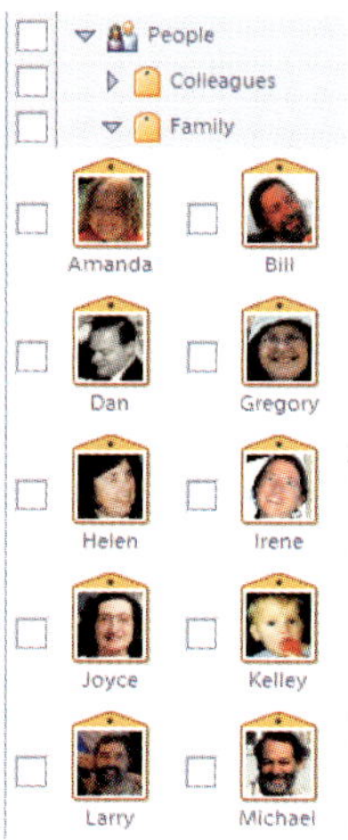

Figure 1.8 Tags are an easy, visual way to identify who is in a photo, where it was taken, or other aspects of it.

Disadvantages of Organizing in the File System

If you manage your photos in the Windows file system, you have to use folders to organize them. If you're really organized, you could rename photos so that you can find them. This approach has several serious drawbacks, however:

- Renaming photos is tedious, so it just doesn't happen for most photos. And coming up with unique names is a real challenge as a collection grows.
- Many people organize folders by the date when the photos were taken or copied from the camera. This is easy to do, but it gives you no simple way to find photos by subject.
- You can create folders by subject, but then you have to decide which folder to put each photo in. Do the photos of Gregory and Amanda in Hawaii go in the Gregory folder, the Amanda folder, the Hawaii folder—or the Spring 2003 Vacation folder? Will you remember which one you put it in when you go to find it?
- There is no way within Windows to scroll through more than one folder of photos at a time. If you organize your folders by subject, then there's no way to see all the photos from a particular date.
- The dates normally shown in Windows are the dates when the file was modified, not the date when the photo was taken—even though the capture date is stored in the file for any photo from a digital camera.

Once you assign tags to photos, you can find all the photos that have a particular tag or any combination of tags. Applying tags takes only a few minutes if you do it each time you import photos. And since it's so rewarding to be able to locate exactly the photos you're looking for, you'll probably find tagging addictive.

If you want to keep things simple, you can ignore tagging entirely and just search for photos by date. Album automatically organizes your photos by date and time, so you don't have to do anything to create this type of organization (assuming that the photos are from a digital camera and that you set the camera's clock correctly). Using only this organization works well as long as the number of photos remains modest (in the hundreds). When you get ready to put some effort into organization, you can begin tagging.

Use tags to describe your photos

Click the Organize tab at the right of the shortcuts bar to display the organizing pane at the right side of the photo well (**Figure 1.9**). Within the organizing pane, two tabs allow you to choose between organizing by tags and organizing by collections. The two methods are similar, but each is designed to help you do different things.

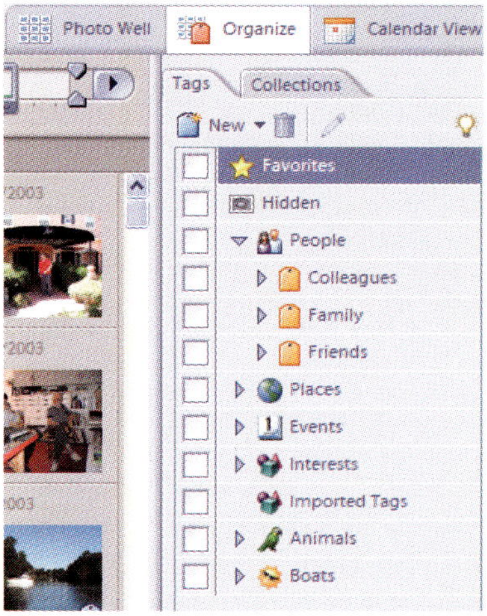

Figure 1.9 With the Tags tab selected, you can either apply tags to organize your photos or use the tags to search for photos.

Tags provide a very powerful and easy-to-use mechanism for organizing your photos. You'll use tags to mark photos according to the people who are in them, where they were taken, what event they are associated with, and so forth. Tags are divided into categories, and within each category you can have any number of subcategories. This makes it easy to organize your tags so that you can find the ones you want.

The categories set up for you automatically are People, Places, Events, and Other. You can rename these and add your own as well. (Organizing with tags is described in detail in Chapter 4, and finding photos with tags is covered in Chapter 5.)

To apply a tag to a photo, just drag it from the Tags pane to the photo. You can select multiple tags and multiple photos, and apply all the tags to all the photos with one action.

To find photos according to their tags, just click the check box to the left of a tag—or double-click the tag, which is a shortcut for clearing an existing search and performing a new one. To search on multiple tags, select more than one by clicking the box to its left. You can also search with tags by dragging the tags you want to search with to the gray find bar at the top of the photo well.

Make collections to assemble and sort photos

Collections provide another dimension for organizing your photos. You'll use collections to gather photos for a particular purpose, such as making a slide show or album, or to print or share.

To work with collections, choose the Collections tab in the organizing pane (**Figure 1.10**). Putting photos in a collection is similar to applying a tag to them, with one critical difference: within a collection you can set the organization of the photos manually, in any order you want; you aren't constrained to a chronological order.

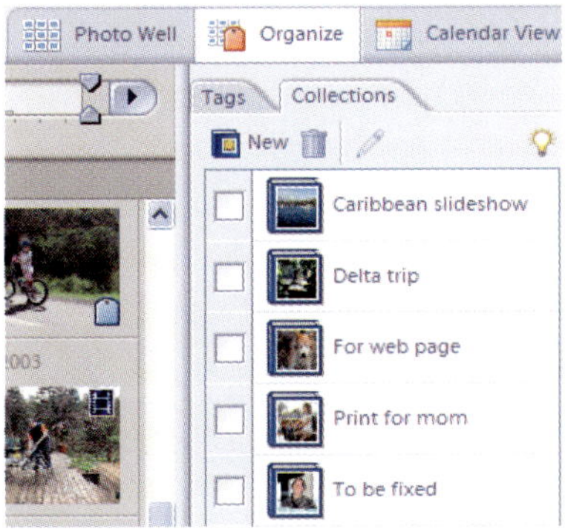

Figure 1.10 When the Collections tab is selected, you can add photos to a collection or show only photos that are in a collection.

Use tags to describe attributes of your photos: who is in them, where they were taken, and so on. Use collections to put together a group of photos for a specific purpose. For example, you might have hundreds of photos with the Hawaii tag, but the Hawaii Slide Show collection would contain only the photos you want to share, in the order in which you want to show them.

To make a new collection, click the New button at the top left of the Collections tab. To add photos to the collection, drag the collection icon to the photos, just as with tagging. (You can also drag the photo to the collection icon, if that feels more natural.)

To display a collection, double-click the collection's icon. When the collection is displayed, a small number appears in the upper-left corner of each thumbnail that shows the order of the photos. You can rearrange photos in the collection by simply dragging and dropping them. You can view only one collection at a time.

Note *You can also make an album or slide show as a creation (as described in Chapter 8) without making a collection first. Like collections, creations save the order of the photos. Collections are more general purpose, though: when making a collection, you don't have to decide whether to make an album or a slide show, or what template to use.*

Chapter 4 describes how to use collections in more detail.

Fixing and Sharing Your Photos

Organizing your photos is just a means to an end: sharing and enjoying them. Photoshop Album does more than help you find your photos easily—it also enables you to easily fix common photo problems, share your photos, and make slide shows, albums, and more.

Fixing photos

You can quickly and easily fix common photo problems in Photoshop Album's Fix Photo window (**Figure 1.11**). Unlike photo editors such as Photoshop Elements, Fix Photo involves virtually no learning curve—just click the appropriate button to get the results you want. You can fix lighting and color problems, sharpen, fix red-eye, crop, and convert to black-and-white or sepia. (See Chapter 6 for details on fixing photos.)

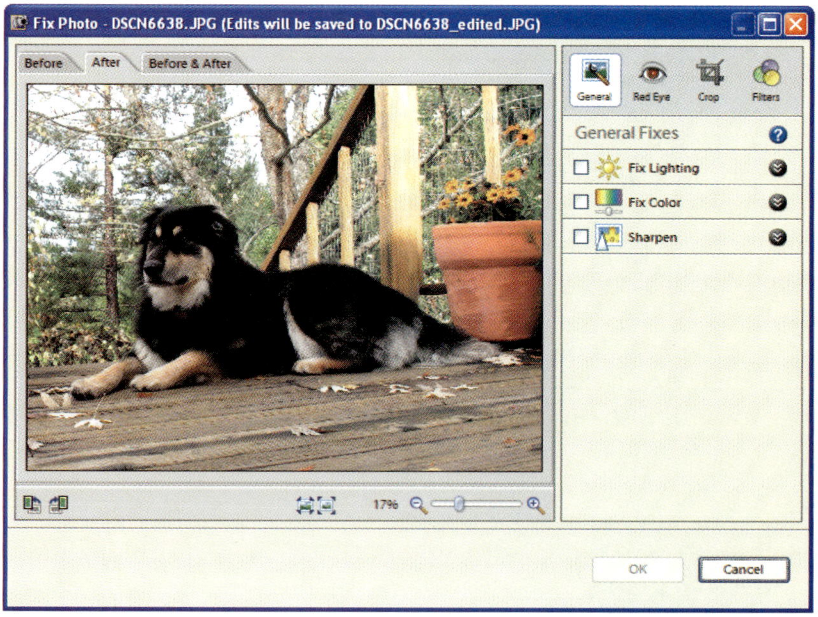

Figure 1.11 **The Fix Photo window makes it easy to improve your photos.**

Album eliminates the need to keep track of multiple versions of the same photo that can clutter up your disk and create confusion. When you edit a photo in Album, the original is always preserved (unless you explicitly ask to overwrite it), and the edited version is stored as a copy. A single thumbnail, which shows the edited version, represents the original version as well. You can always revert to the original.

Sharing photos and making creations

The ease of sharing photos is one of the greatest benefits of going digital. Photoshop Album makes it easy to share just a photo or two, or complete albums or slide shows.

Emailing photos is as simple as choosing the photos you want to email from the photo well, clicking the Share button, and choosing E-mail from the Share drop-down list. Album automatically makes reduced-size versions of your photos for emailing and then deletes them after the message is sent. If you choose, Album will automatically combine all your photos into a single PDF file so that the recipient will have a slide show rather than just a collection of photo files. (See Chapter 10 for details on sharing.)

Slide shows, albums, calendars, cards, and the like are called *creations* in Album. You can choose from a variety of templates that provide different designs. The layout is fully automated, so making creations is quick and painless. (See Chapter 8 for details on making creations.)

When you make a creation, it's saved as a description in your catalog, with links to the photos that are in it. Like a photo, it is represented in the photo well by a thumbnail. You can view the creation in Album, and you can change it at any time.

To share a creation, you publish it—to a printer, a PDF file, or an online printing service. You can email creations in PDF format to anyone who has Adobe Reader, and they'll see it just as you intended—complete with any video clips and background music you include. You can also write slide show creations to CDs for playback on either a computer or a DVD player.

If you have your own Web site, you can use Album to create Web photo galleries. You only have to pick a style and Album generates all the HTML pages, automatically creating lower-resolution copies of your photos. You can even make 3D photo galleries, in which your photos appear on the walls of a virtual gallery.

Beyond Photoshop Album

As comprehensive as Album is, it won't let you do everything you might ever want to do with your photos. It's designed to provide a quick, simple set of tools for common tasks, but for any given task there are specialized programs that will give you more flexibility, but you'll give up some of the simplicity (and, of course, you'll have to buy and learn another program).

You may want to use other programs to do the following:

- Edit your photos in more sophisticated ways than Album's Fix Photo window provides
- Combine several photos into one, to create a montage or a composite image
- Trim video clips, leaving only the best parts
- Make albums, greeting cards, and other creations that are more elaborate than Album supports
- Create slide shows with greater control over timing, or with more complex, synchronized audio tracks
- Create Video CDs or DVDs with more elaborate menus, variable timing, or synchronized sound tracks
- Have more flexibility in designing Web pages than Album's built-in Web-page creator provides

For more sophisticated photo fixing, editing, and compositing, Album integrates smoothly with Adobe's photo editors: Photoshop and Photoshop Elements. The following sections provide a brief overview of those products, and Chapter 7 provides a few tips on using them. These programs provide tremendous depth, and many books describe how to use them; see Appendix A for recommended reading.

You can also set Album to link to any other photo editor, but the integration will not be as smooth because the programs were not designed to work together.

If you want to use other programs to make creations, the easiest approach generally is to use Album to locate the photos you want and then export a copy of those photos to a folder you create for this purpose. You can then easily find all the photos you need from within the other program by simply going to that folder. Alternatively, you can drag and drop photos from Album into most other applications. You can also rename photos within Album to make them easier to find in the file system, and then browse the file system from the other application, but this is more complicated (see "Behind the Scenes: Working with Windows," which follows Chapter 4).

Photoshop Elements

Photoshop Elements is a great complement to Album for users who want more editing power than Album's Fix Photo. Photoshop Elements was designed for hobbyists, as opposed to Photoshop (the high-end photo editor, such as Photoshop CS), which is aimed at professionals. It lacks a few of Photoshop's features, such as support for CMYK files (needed for offset printing), complex color management, and some enhancement and automation tools. But it's less than one-sixth the price, and it's easier to use.

Figure 1.12 shows the Photoshop Elements user interface. You select tools from the tool palette on the left. The palette at the top right provides integrated help for the selected tool, and the Recipes pane below it guides you through common tasks. You can select other palettes from the tabs at the upper right.

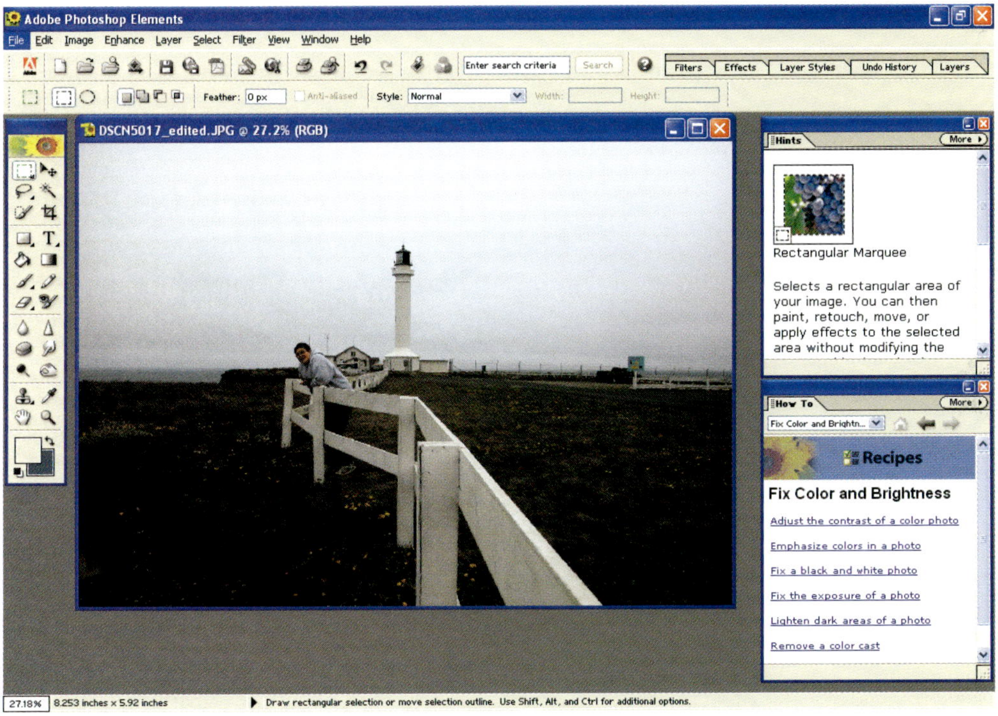

Figure 1.12 Photoshop Elements provides a simplified version of the Photoshop user interface, with added assistance in the form of hints and recipes.

You might need Photoshop Elements to read certain types of files that Album can't process, such as Kodak's Photo CD, and save those in a form that Album can use (see Chapter 2).

Album's Fix Photo window enables you to make one-click fixes and to adjust those fixes using simple sliders. In Photoshop Elements you can do much more, once you learn how. Here are some ways in which you might want to take advantage of Photoshop Elements:

- Make precise color corrections
- Add special effects via filters, such as a blur or a painted look
- Touch up blemishes or dust from scanning, and even give people a variety of "slimming" adjustments
- Erase distracting objects or backgrounds from photos, or remove one or more people from a group photo
- Combine elements from multiple photos into a single composite, such as using the background from one photo and the foreground from another, to create a single, realistic image

Photoshop and Photoshop Elements are both primarily tools for working with one photo at a time. As you do with a word processor, you open a file, work on it, and then save it. These programs will do a few multiphoto tasks, however.

Photoshop Elements includes a feature called Photo Merge, which combines multiple, overlapping photos into a seamless panorama (see Chapter 8). You can also create PDF slide shows in Photoshop and Photoshop Elements, but in general you'll find Photoshop Album to be a better tool for this. Photoshop and Photoshop Elements have "picture package" multiphoto layouts that are in some ways more flexible than those in Album (see Chapter 9).

I describe how to do some of these tasks using Photoshop Elements in Chapters 7 and 8. For the more advanced tasks, refer to the books listed in Appendix A.

Photoshop: the Pro Tool

Relatively few Photoshop Album users are likely to need the professional level of capability that Photoshop provides. (The latest version of Photoshop is called Photoshop CS—the successor to Photoshop 7.) Indeed, Photoshop Elements is easier to use, and it will meet the needs of most consumers for a fraction of the price of Photoshop. But if you simply want the most capable tool available, Photoshop is it.

You'll notice that the user interfaces of Photoshop (**Figure 1.13**) and Photoshop Elements are very similar. Photoshop has far more options, however, which are represented by more menu items, more palettes, and more tools.

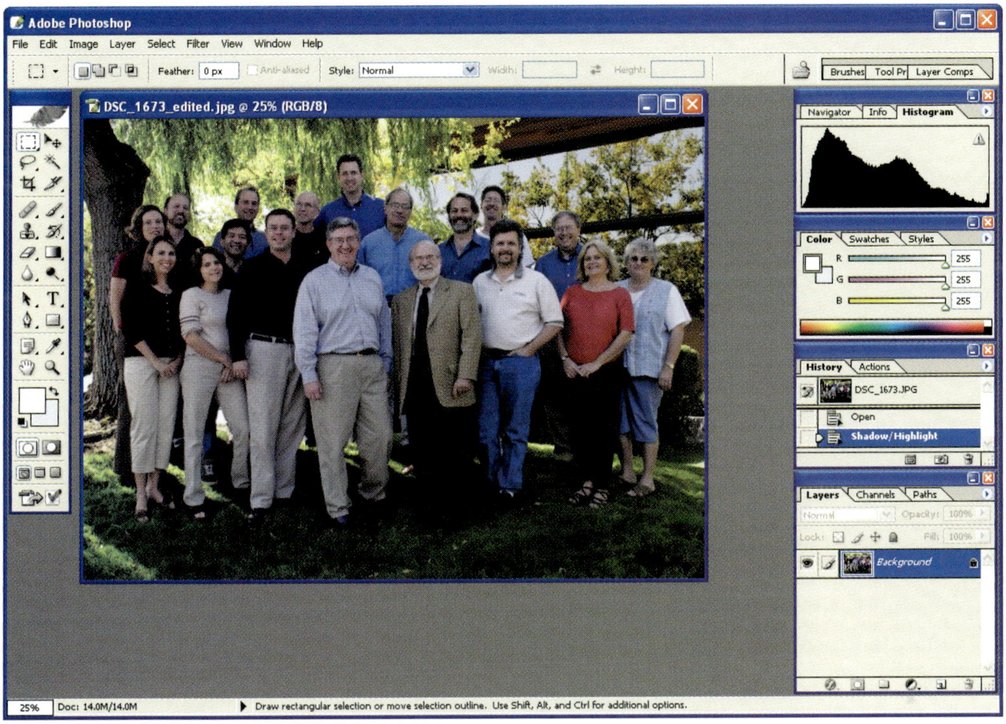

Figure 1.13 **Photoshop gives you many different palettes that offer tremendous control over editing functions and information about the photo you're using.**

Photoshop has a fantastic, easy-to-use tool that may be the strongest single reason for a Photoshop Album user to consider buying it: the *healing brush*. This tool makes it easy to remove blemishes from faces, delete scratches from scanned prints or negatives, and make a variety of other fixes. It allows you to paint over a section of a photo, blending the color and texture and feathering the edges automatically. You'll find a brief example of what this tool can do in Chapter 7.

If you want to go deep into image enhancement, Photoshop offers a tool called *curves*. It gives you a sophisticated way of making color corrections that isn't available in Photoshop Elements.

Photoshop also offers better type handling, which helps if you're adding text to your photos. And it comes with Image Ready, a powerful tool for optimizing photos and other graphics for the Web.

BEHIND THE SCENES: What You Need in a PC

To use Photoshop Album effectively, you need to have a capable PC. If you have an older system, you may need some upgrades to optimize it for digital photography. In the past few years, PCs have become so fast, and their disk drives so large, that you really can't buy an underpowered new PC for digital photography, but you still need to pay attention to the peripherals.

If you have an older system, you may find that it takes a long time to scroll in the photo well or to move from one photo to another in single-photo view. Other tasks that may be slow are making photo fixes and creating PDFs. A faster processor can help a lot. First, however, make sure you have enough memory; if you're short on RAM, the PC will spend a lot of time swapping parts of the program in and out of memory, which will make things go slowly no matter how fast the processor.

Note ***Prices given here are as of late 2003. Memory prices have been falling steadily, as have LCD-monitor prices. Hard disks often retain their price but increase in capacity.***

Consider a Notebook PC

If you travel and can afford the extra expense, consider a notebook PC—ideally one with a separate keyboard and monitor (and, optionally, a docking station) for use at home. This way you still have a great setup at home, but you can carry the PC with you and enjoy your photos the day you take them. You can also take it to a friend's house to share photos.

You will pay a considerable premium for such a setup, though, and you won't get the fastest processor or the largest hard drive (which is fine). You can get by without the home keyboard and monitor, but your hands and eyes might suffer strain from extended notebook use.

Caution ***Photoshop Album is designed for use on a single system. It is not easy to synchronize your catalog and photos between two PCs. If you do use a notebook PC, get one capable enough that it can be your primary photo PC so you aren't always moving files to a desktop system.***

Evaluating a PC

Whether you're thinking of upgrading your existing PC or buying a new one, it's important to know which features matter and which ones don't. The features that the dealer and PC maker try to sell you aren't always the ones that matter most—high-speed microprocessors being a striking case in point.

If your PC is only a year or two old, it's probably perfectly capable of doing everything you want with Photoshop Album. A faster system will make photo-handling processes go a little quicker, but with a little patience most recent PCs are fine. If you're still running Windows 98 (not supported by Album), Windows Me, or Windows 2000, however, it's well worth it to upgrade to Windows XP—and by far the easiest way to do so is to buy a new PC.

The heart of the system: processor and RAM

As a former microprocessor expert, I'd like to say that you should pay attention to what microprocessor is in the machine you get, but I'm afraid I can no longer find much justification for that. Everything today is plenty fast for most of what you'll do, and most of the delays you experience will be limited by the speed of the disk drive, your Internet connection, and your printer.

A faster processor will make some things a little snappier, especially when editing high-resolution images, so if you can afford it, buy a midrange system. In a high-end system you'll pay a big premium for a modest gain. Even the least-expensive new system will be perfectly adequate.

Upgrading the processor in an existing PC is almost never worthwhile; if your system is old enough to need a processor upgrade, the rest of it probably needs an upgrade, too. Any Pentium III or Pentium 4 processor is fine, as is any Celeron, Athlon, or Duron processor with a clock speed of 1 GHz or higher. Photoshop Album doesn't officially support Pentium II systems, and they may strain your patience, but the program should run if your system meets the other requirements.

RAM (memory), on the other hand, is inexpensive and well worth upgrading. If your existing system has available memory slots, more RAM is an inexpensive and very worthwhile upgrade. A 256 MB memory upgrade costs only $50 to $100.

Photoshop Album requires lots of memory to run well, especially if you are using it with Photoshop or Photoshop Elements for editing. I'd consider 256 MB a realistic minimum; 512 MB is better. And if you want to run multiple applications at the same time and use large images, 1 GB will allow you to do so without a long wait. You'll also be able to import larger photos into Album if you have 512 MB or more of RAM (see Chapter 2).

Storage options

For easy access, you want to be able to store your entire photo and music collection on your hard disk. Video clips should all fit, too, unless you have a tremendous number of them. (Hour long videos are still a stretch, however.)

Unless you have a voracious appetite for software, your programs won't occupy more than 10 to 20 GB. As for photos, even if you store high-quality 5-megapixel images of perhaps 6 MB each, every 10 GB chunk will hold 1,600 of them; if you store more-common JPEG files of 2.5 MB each (plenty for very high quality), you'll get 4,000 of them in 10 GB.

So the 80 GB and larger drives that are widely available for less than $100 (and are included in many new PCs) should last you a long time, unless you get into collecting video or lots of music. If you're looking to extend the life of an older PC, consider buying a new hard disk—they're inexpensive and can be well worth it. New desktop systems all have ample hard drives. If you're buying a new notebook, the drives are smaller than in desktop PCs, and you may want to pay the premium for a larger drive.

A CD-R/RW drive is essential; you'll want one for backing up your photos and making slide show discs to share with friends and family. A writable DVD drive is even better, especially if you have or plan to take lots of photos, because you can back up so much more on the disc. (Even with only a CD-R/RW drive, you can make slide show discs that will play in most DVD players, however.)

You can add a CD or DVD burner to a desktop PC by adding an internal drive, in many cases; you may need to have someone at the computer store install it. You can also buy a CD or DVD burner with a USB or IEEE-1394 interface, so that you can plug it in externally.

You might want an external hard disk with a USB or IEEE 1394 connection, because it makes a great backup device. You can get a 120 GB external drive for less than $200 or an 80 GB external drive for around $150. It is far faster to copy your files to this type of hard disk than to burn CDs or DVDs, which means that you'll do it more often and you'll be less likely to lose anything.

You can add an external disk to any PC as long as the system has the required USB or IEEE 1394 interface. And when you change PCs later, you can copy everything to the external disk and then plug it into the new PC, simplifying the transfer. If you get a USB disk, make sure it is USB 2.0, not USB 1.1 (which is much slower).

Don't scrimp on the monitor

You're going to spend a lot of time looking at your monitor, and its size and resolution will determine the quality of the photos you see, so this is the place to use your extra cash. Buying a new monitor can be a perfect way to enhance an older system, and when you later replace the system, you can keep the monitor.

If you're buying a desktop PC, I recommend spending as much or more on the monitor. Don't consider anything smaller than 17 inches, and if you can, get a 19-inch or larger monitor. The minimum resolution you'll want is 1280 by 1024, and 1600 by 1200 is very nice.

LCD (Liquid Crystal Display) monitors are a lot lighter and take a lot less space than CRTs (Cathode Ray Tubes), and they are nice and bright. They are considerably more expensive than CRTs, however; a good 19-inch LCD will set you back about $700, whereas a great 21-inch CRT can be had for under $500. A good CRT will deliver a great image, and many photo perfectionists still prefer them because of their ability to deliver accurate color. Also, if you want to be able to run the monitor at a variety of resolutions, CRTs handle this much better than LCDs. The best LCDs have a digital connection to the PC (called DVI), but make sure the PC is compatible with the LCD.

Connecting to the outside world

USB ports are invaluable for connecting to your camera, card reader, scanner, printer, and so forth. Every PC today comes with USB 2.0 ports, which are very fast and work with older USB devices as well. If you have an older PC, you probably have USB 1.1 ports, which are workable but much slower. If you don't have enough ports and find you're always swapping cables around, you can add more ports inexpensively with a USB hub. You can get a four-port USB 2.0 hub for less than $30.

If you are using a digital camcorder as well, you'll need an IEEE 1394 port (also called FireWire); many new consumer-oriented PCs, except at the low end, include this. If you're upgrading, you can buy an IEEE 1394 card inexpensively (you can buy either a PCI card for a desktop system or a PC Card for a notebook PC for less than $50). Some higher-end scanners and printers, and even a few cameras, use IEEE 1394 ports.

2 Getting Your Photos into Photoshop Album

Now that you know the basics of how Photoshop Album works, you're almost ready to begin enjoying your photos with it. First, however, you need to *import* your photos into Album. Once you've done this, you'll be able to find your photos quickly without having to deal with Windows' folders and filenames.

Importing photos is straightforward, but you must choose from several import functions. The right one depends on whether this is your first import and you want to find all the photos on your disk, or whether you want to import photos from a specific folder or disk. It also depends on where you're importing the photos from, such as your hard disk, your camera, or a CD. This chapter will help you decide which function to use and will also offer tips on how to work with photos that you don't want to store on your hard drive, how to import audio and video clips, and how to enhance your collection with scanned images.

Before you perform your first import, though, let's take a look at Album's catalog, which keeps track of all your photos. You don't have to deal with the catalog itself, but it's such an essential part of Album that understanding some basics will enable you to work more easily with the program and could help you avoid some common mistakes.

Setting Up Your Catalog

Think of the catalog as an index to your complete collection of photos. For each photo, Photoshop Album's catalog tracks its location, any changes you've made to it, and how you've used it—saving you the trouble of having to do all this yourself.

Album automatically creates a catalog for you when you first run the program, and one catalog will probably be sufficient most of the time. However, you might want to create additional catalogs if, for example, you have distinct collections of photos, or your kids take their own digital photos and they each want to have their own catalog (and you'd rather they didn't mess with yours).

The catalog that Album creates for you automatically is called My Catalog. If you plan to create multiple catalogs, you'll probably want to ignore this catalog and make new ones, so that you can name them all. To make a new catalog, choose File > Catalog, and in the Catalog dialog click New (**Figure 2.1**). In the New Catalog dialog, enter the name you want to give the catalog and click Save.

Tip ***You can't rename or delete a catalog from within Album. You can use File > Catalog > Save As to make a copy with a new name (and just abandon or delete the old one). To delete it, you must first find it in Windows. The default location is Documents and Settings/All Users/Application Data/Adobe/Photoshop Album/Catalogs.***

Photoshop Album always launches with the catalog you had open when you last closed the program. If you have more than one catalog, be sure the right catalog is open before you add photos or make changes. If you hold down Shift while Photoshop Album is starting, it will ask which catalog you want to open.

Catalogs: One or Many?

Don't divide your photos among multiple catalogs unless there's a very good reason to do so. Although it's easy to switch from one catalog to another, you can work with only one at a time. For example, you can search within only a single catalog, and you can make a slide show or album from photos in only a single catalog. You can't move or copy photos between catalogs, so they represent fairly rigid boundaries.

You can have the same items in more than one catalog, but this can get confusing and can cause problems—if you import the same photo into two catalogs, for instance, and then edit the photo in one catalog, the other catalog won't have any link to the edited copy.

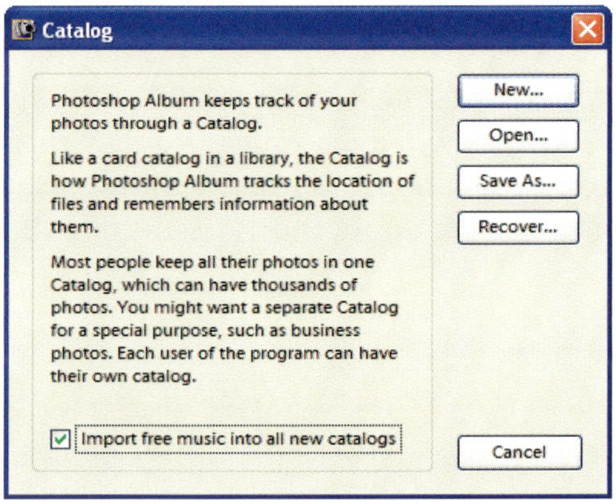

Figure 2.1 In the Catalog dialog, you can make new catalogs, open or recover existing ones, or save the current catalog under a new name.

When you create a new catalog, Album automatically imports into the catalog the standard background music files that come with the program. You don't see these files in the photo well by default, but they appear in the pop-up list of background-music files when you make a slide show.

If you don't plan to use any of this background music, you can delete it from your catalog later; or you can unselect the box next to "Import free music into all new catalogs" in the Catalog dialog (**Figure 2.1**), and the music files will not be imported when you make a new catalog.

Compacting and Repairing Catalogs

Under rare circumstances, such as a power failure while you're updating the catalog, the catalog file can be damaged. In addition, with normal use, catalogs can accumulate blank space that causes them to occupy more space than necessary on your hard disk.

It's a good idea every month or two to open the Catalog dialog (File > Catalog) and click Recover. This will fix any errors in your catalog and compress it to eliminate wasted space.

If the catalog is badly damaged and you can't open it in Photoshop Album, hold down Ctrl while Album is starting up; a dialog will appear, asking if you'd like to perform a recovery on the current catalog.

You can also trigger a catalog recovery when opening a catalog. Choose File > Catalog to open the Catalog dialog, click the name of the catalog you want to recover, and then hold down Ctrl while clicking OK.

Getting Photos from Your Hard Disk

Once you decide whether to go with Album's default catalog or create your own, your next step is to import all the photos that you have on your hard disk into a catalog. There are two ways to do this: have Photoshop Album search the disk for all your photos, or select specific folders. The searching method is generally the best way to get started.

Searching for All Your Photos

To have Album find all the photos on your hard disk, choose File > Get Photos > By Searching (**Figure 2.2**). If you don't change any of the settings in the Get Photos By Searching for Folders dialog (**Figure 2.3**), Photoshop Album will search all your hard disks, skipping system and program folders, and it will exclude files smaller than 100 Kbytes (since these are probably low-resolution photos).

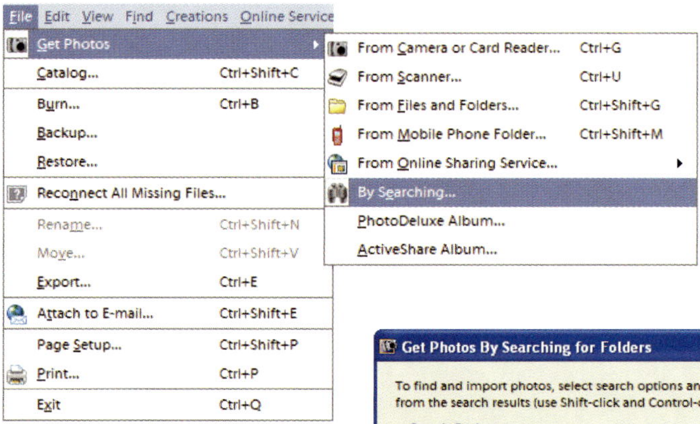

Figure 2.2 When you're getting started with Photoshop Album, By Searching is the best option for importing photos.

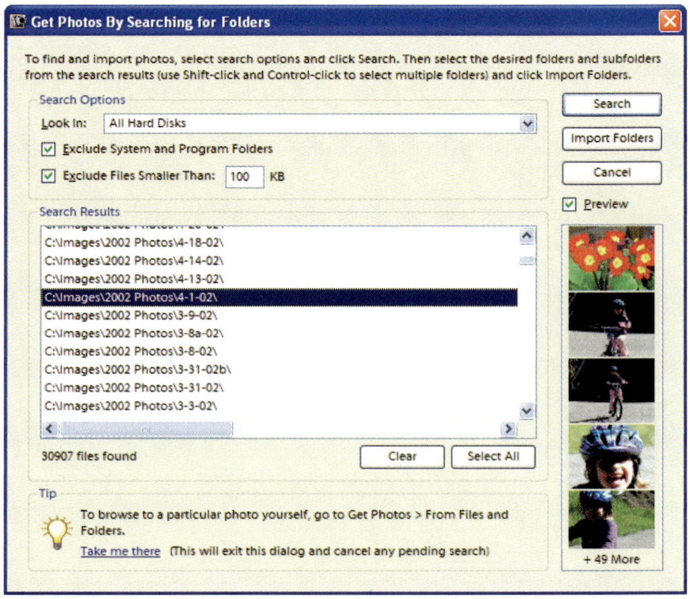

Figure 2.3 To import photos you've found on your hard drive, select the folders you want to import, and then click Import Folders.

What Files Can You Import?

Album can import most photo files, video clips, and audio files. The formats it supports are:

- Standard photos: JPEG, TIFF, PSD, PDD, PNG, GIF, and BMP. Files that use transparency are only partially supported; transparent areas appear as white.
- RAW format photos: CRW (Canon), NEF (Nikon), MRW (Minolta), RAF (Fuji), and ORF (Olympus).
- Video clips: MOV (QuickTime), AVI (Windows Audio/Video), MPG (MPEG-1), and 3GP (cell phone video). You must install QuickTime to use MOV and 3GP formats.
- Audio files: MP3 and WAV.

Note that there are many variations of these formats; for example, NEF files are a little different for each camera model; MOV files use a variety of compression schemes; and MP3 files can be encoded at different bit rates and use different types of metadata. So you may find that some files aren't compatible even if the file type is supported.

Album can import JPEG photos from PDF files, but it doesn't import the PDF file itself, just the photos within it.

Some formats you may encounter that Album cannot read include PCD (Kodak's Photo CD), WMV (Windows Media Video), and MP4 (MPEG 4 video).

Photo Size Limits

There is a limit of 12 megapixels for all photos imported into Album, unless you have 512 MB or more of RAM. With 512 MB, you can import photos up to 24 megapixels, and with 1 GB you can import photos up to 36 megapixels. Note that this limit doesn't have to do with the size of the file; it's a megapixel limit, not a megabyte limit. (If you know a photo's horizontal and vertical dimension in pixels, multiply them together to find the megapixel value.)

Even with less than 512 MB of RAM, you won't encounter this limit if you're using photos from digital cameras, unless you have a very expensive professional camera. If you scan photos at 300 dpi, you won't have problems with scans of up to 8.5 by 11 inches. You will run into this limit if you scan prints larger than 5 by 7 at 600 dpi (which is unnecessary; 300 dpi captures all the useful information), or if you use a film scanner. If you do encounter the limit, you'll have to either add memory or reduce the resolution of the photos using Photoshop or Photoshop Elements.

These settings will meet most people's needs, but you may want to change them in the following situations:

- You want to include low-resolution photos (less than 1 megapixel). Unselect the box next to Exclude Files Smaller Than, or lower the limit to perhaps 20 Kbytes.
- You have multiple hard disks but all your photos are on one of them. You can restrict the search to that drive to speed it up. If you have a backup drive with copies of the photos, be sure *not* to include it in the search, or you may get everything twice.
- You have photos in system or program folders. Either move them to a folder within My Pictures (a good place to keep all photos) or unselect the box next to Exclude System and Program Folders. Most people don't have photos stored in these folders, and Photoshop Album doesn't search them by default because it would typically find lots of screen graphics and other files you wouldn't want to include in your catalog.

Once you've made any changes you want to the settings, click Search. If you're searching an entire disk or have many photos, go take a coffee break.

When the search is done, the dialog lists all the folders containing photos. If you click any folder name, a preview of the first few photos in the folder appears on the right. This preview is not for browsing , as you can see only the first few photos, but rather to help you decide whether to import from the folder. If in doubt about a photo, import it; you can always remove it from the catalog later.

If you want to import photos from all the folders listed, just click Select All and then Import Folders. To import only selected folders, Shift-click the first and last folders to select all the folders in a range, and Control-click to select folders that are noncontiguous.

If you have multiple versions of your photos in various resolutions on your hard disk—say, you made lower-resolution versions for posting on the Web, or maybe you have a CD that has multiple resolutions on it—it's generally best to import only the original, highest-resolution version into Album. You can delete the others, since it's easy to make lower-resolution versions in Photoshop Album when you need them.

***Note** The searching import method is designed primarily for one-time use when you first set up Photoshop Album. It does not allow you to select specific photos. It ignores music files (since you probably don't want to import most of them) and .gif files (which are more likely to be Web graphics than photos).*

Photoshop Album has special search functions to find photos you have previously managed with Adobe ActiveShare or PhotoDeluxe. These functions are listed below By Searching in the File > Get Photos submenu.

Photoshop Album is not able to import information from other photo organizers, except for captions stored in the photo file itself.

How Photoshop Album Treats Duplicates

If you've been working with digital photos for long, you might have multiple copies of some photos on your disk. There's no point in importing multiple identical copies into Album, since they just clutter up your photo well and can cause confusion if you make changes or add a caption to one copy but not the other.

Photoshop Album helps you eliminate duplicates by checking photos you're importing against those already in the catalog. If you try to import a photo that is the same in all respects as one that's already in the catalog, Photoshop Album assumes it's a duplicate and does not import it. This is true even if the photo is in a different folder.

If Photoshop Album rejects as a duplicate a file that you want to import, just make a small change to its name and try the import again.

You can make a duplicate copy of a photo from within Photoshop Album. In this case, Photoshop Album appends "-copy" to the name to distinguish the new version. This can be useful if you want to create two differently edited versions from the same original.

Getting Photos from Particular Folders

After your first-time import of all the photos on your hard disk, you won't generally need to repeat the search—it would find all the photos you've already imported, as well as any new ones. Instead, choose File > Get Photos > From Files and Folders (**Figure 2.4**) to select a specific folder (or folders). (You can also access this function from the Get Photos button on the shortcuts bar.)

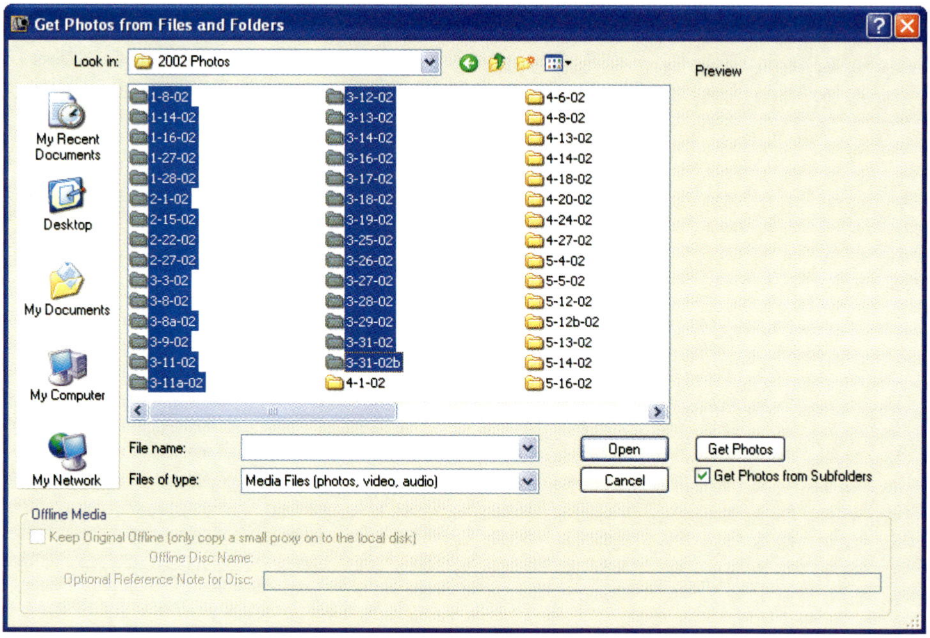

Figure 2.4 **When importing photos (or audio or video) from the hard disk, you can select an entire folder, multiple folders, or one or more photos within the folder in the Get Photos from Files and Folders dialog.**

To import all the photos in a certain folder, in the Get Photos from Files and Folders dialog select the folder and click Get Photos. If you don't want to import photos in subfolders as well, unselect the box next to Get Photos from Subfolders. To import only selected photos, open the folder in the dialog and select the photos you want to import. (Use Shift-click to choose two photos and all of the photos in between them in a group; use Ctrl-click to select discontinuous photos.)

Note *When this book, and Photoshop Album itself, refers to "photos," the idea is often equally applicable to video clips and audio files. Photoshop Album uses the term photos to avoid the awkwardness of more general and potentially confusing terms, such as* **media** *and* **items**. *But this in itself can be confusing if you're looking for the menu item for importing video or audio clips; use Get Photos, even though it's not photos you're getting.*

If you make Photoshop Album the center of your photo handling process, you may not need to import photos from your hard disk often, as you can get them directly from your camera (Get Photos > From Camera) or scanner (Get Photos > From Scanner). But from time to time you may get photos via email, or you may choose to import from a camera or other device to the hard disk (using Windows or software that came with that device). In these cases, use File > Get Photos > From Files and Folders to import the photos.

If you've added new photos to a folder from which you have previously imported photos, don't worry about selecting only the new photos. Just select the folder, and Album will ignore the ones that have been previously imported.

Another way to import individual photos into Photoshop Album is to drag them into the photo well and drop them there. If you drag them from a location that appears to be temporary, such as the system temp folder, Album will automatically copy the photos to a folder within My Pictures/Adobe/Other Photos; otherwise, it will leave them in place.

Getting Photos from Network Drives

You can also import photos from network drives—that is, disk drives connected to computers on your network. This is useful if you have a server on which you store all your photos, or if you want to include photos stored on another PC. Note, however, that Photoshop Album treats network drives just like local drives—it expects them to always be there.

If you try to view a photo stored on a network drive when the drive is not available, Album will begin searching for the file. If you know the disk is not available, just click Cancel in the search dialog. An icon will appear on the photo to show that Photoshop Album can't access the file (**Figure 2.5**). The next time you access that photo with the network drive available, Album will automatically reconnect the file.

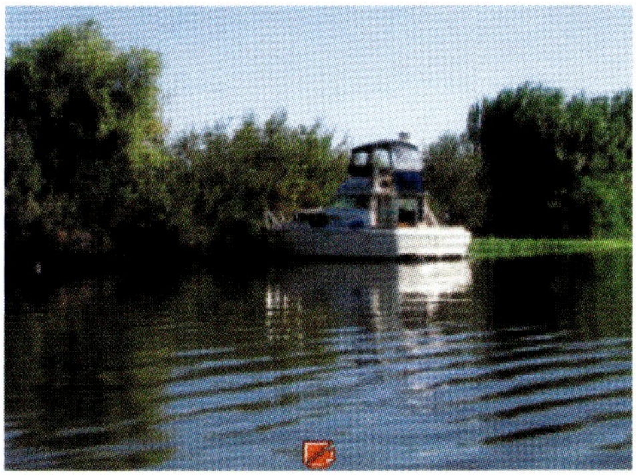

Figure 2.5 The broken red rectangle icon in the bottom center of the thumbnail indicates that Photoshop Album could not access the photo's file.

Getting Photos from CDs and DVDs

If you've accumulated too many images to store on your hard drive, it's quite possible that you've burned CDs to store them on. Or you might have CDs containing photos that either were scanned in from film or originated as digital photos. When you import them, you have the option to have Album copy them automatically to the hard disk.

Note ***Most references to CDs in this book apply equally to data DVDs.***

Unless you choose the Keep Original Offline option in the Get Photos from Files and Folders dialog (**Figure 2.6**), the photos will be copied from the CD to the hard drive. Once this is done, Photoshop Album does not maintain any link to the CD. As long as you have enough hard-disk space, this is the best method to use because your photos are always available.

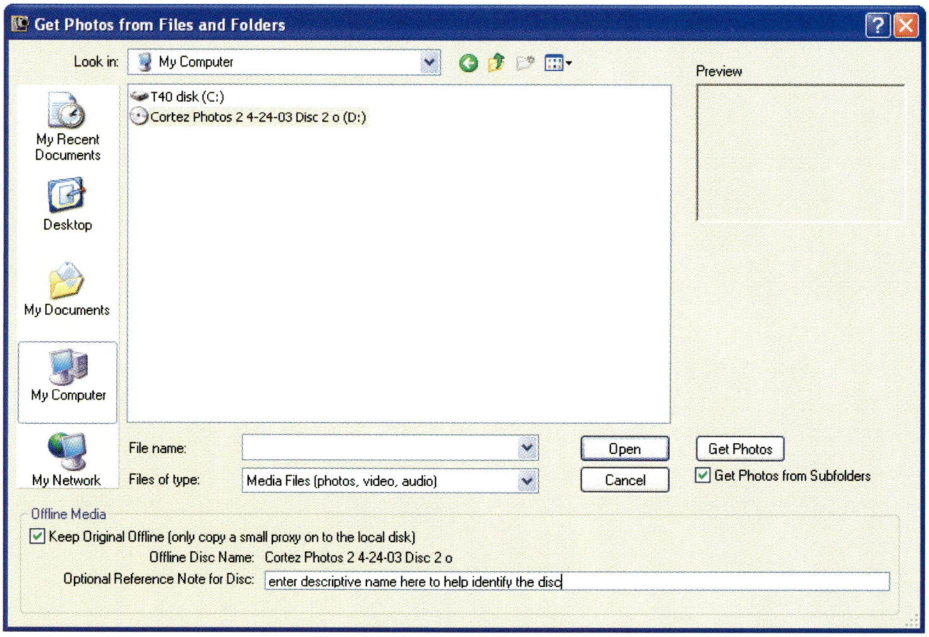

Figure 2.6 If you do *not* want photos copied to the hard disk, be sure the check box in the Offline Media section next to Keep Original Offline is selected.

Tip *If you're using a desktop computer, I don't recommend keeping any photos offline unless you have an old computer or a tremendous number of CDs with photos on them. New PCs typically have hard disks of at least 80 GB. Using half of this space for photos from CDs would provide room for more than 60 CDs full of photos.*

If you need more space, you can add a 120 GB hard disk just for photos—enough for more than 180 CDs—for about $100. The convenience of having all your photos immediately available makes it far more likely that you'll find opportunities to enjoy your older photos.

If you select the Keep Original Offline option, Album remembers that the original photo is stored on the CD. This is called an *offline master*. In this case, Photoshop Album creates a lower-resolution version, called a *proxy*, and stores it on the hard disk. A disc icon on the thumbnail indicates that the master is offline (**Figure 2.7**).

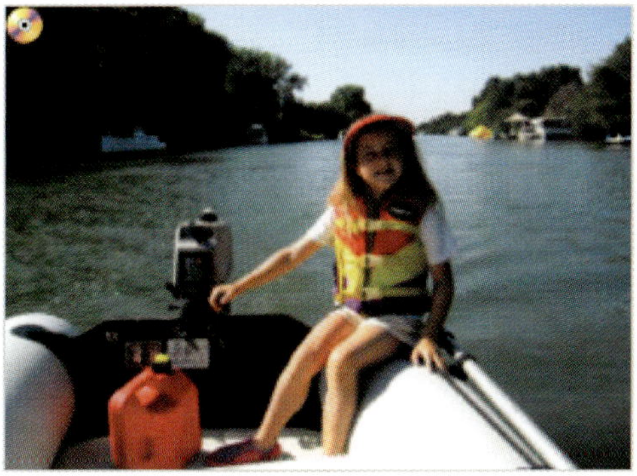

Figure 2.7 The gold disc icon in the upper-left corner indicates that the photo is offline—that is, the full-resolution file is stored on a CD.

Working with Offline Masters

If you're using a laptop computer and have many photos on CD, you may have a genuine lack of disk space. In this case, keeping the masters offline is a good idea.

When you import photos and select the Keep Original Offline option, you can enter a name for the CD in the import dialog (in addition to the volume name that is fixed on the disc itself) to help you remember which CD the photos are on. If you enter a name here, be sure to write it on the CD as well.

Besides controlling where you store photos from CDs, you may want to control where you store *all* of your photos. Photoshop Album has default settings for storing various files, but you don't have to use them. The most common reason to change the location is if you have multiple disk drives (or partitions) and want Photoshop Album to put its files on a drive other than the C drive. Most people don't need to change any of the default locations, but it's still helpful to understand what goes where.

Default Locations

When Photoshop Album imports photos from your camera, a memory card, a CD, or a temporary location on your hard disk, it copies the files to one of several subfolders within the folder My Pictures/Adobe. Among these folders are the following:

- Digital Camera Photos: All photos imported from cameras and memory cards go here, by default in a subfolder named with the date and time.
- Scanned Photos: Just what you'd think, all photos from scanners go here. No subfolders are created automatically.
- Photos from Removable Media: This contains photos imported from CDs, DVDs, Zip disks, or other removable media for which "keep offline" has *not* been selected. Photos are in subfolders named by the removable media volume and serial number.
- Other Photos: A catch-all for photos imported from various places that require the photos to be moved, such as the Windows temp folder.

Changing the Defaults

You can tell Photoshop Album to put files in other locations in two ways:

1. In the Files pane of the Preferences dialog (Edit > Preferences), you can change the location for the My Pictures/Adobe folder and all of its subfolders. To do so, choose Files in the list at the left of the Preferences dialog and click the Browse button next to Folders for Saved Files. In the Browse for Folder dialog, navigate to the spot where you'd like to store the subfolders that are normally in the My Pictures/Adobe folder and click OK.

2. In the Camera or Card Reader and the Scanner Preferences panes, you can change the location of the Digital Camera Photos and Scanned Photos folders independently of the other folders in the My Pictures/Adobe folder. To change the location, first open the appropriate pane (Camera or Card Reader, or Scanner), then click the Browse button in the Files section of that pane. In the Browse for Folder dialog, select the new location, and click OK.

You can also use the Files pane to change the folder where Photoshop Album stores its catalog files, though there's generally no reason to move them unless you have a very large catalog and want to store it on a volume other than C:. To change the location of future new catalogs, use the Save Catalogs In setting of the Files Preferences pane.

Changing any of these settings affects only files created in the future; *it does not cause existing files to be moved.*

Moving Existing Files

To move existing catalogs, you must move the appropriate folders using Windows. There are two folders you need to move: one called Catalogs, and another called Catalog Folders.

Exit Photoshop Album, and open in Windows the folder Documents and Settings/All Users/Application Data/Adobe/Photoshop Album. To do so, you may have to change your Windows settings because Application Data is a hidden folder. In any Windows folder window, select Tools > Folder Options, click the View tab, and click the button labeled "Show hidden files and folders." Then click OK.

Then drag the folders called Catalogs and Catalog Folders to the location to which you want to move them. Restart Album, choose File > Catalog > Open, navigate to the new catalog location, and click Open. (If you want future new catalogs to be stored in the new location, be sure to change the Preferences setting as described earlier.)

If you want to move the photo folders within My Pictures/Adobe to another location, you can do so using Windows. When you restart Album, choose File > Reconnect All Missing Files, and Album will search for the moved files and update the links in the catalog.

In general, however, it's better to move photo files using the File > Move command, as described in "Behind the Scenes: Working with Windows," which follows Chapter 4.

You can set the resolution of the proxy file in the Preferences dialog (**Figure 2.8**). By default, it's set to 640 by 480 to keep the file size to a minimum. Unless you have a great number of offline photos and very limited disk space, increase the proxy size to the resolution of your display. (To find out what your display resolution is, right-click on the desktop, choose Properties, and click on the Settings tab.) That way you can see the photos on screen with all the resolution your display is capable of, even though the full-resolution images are offline.

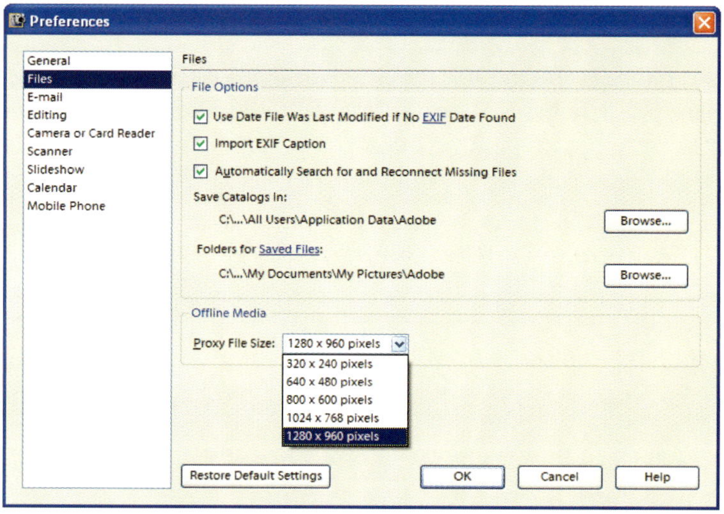

Figure 2.8 **Set the proxy file size before you import any images that you want to keep offline. A larger proxy size gives a better display without inserting the CD but takes up more hard-disk space.**

Caution *You cannot change the proxy resolution for files after you import them, so be sure to make this change before importing from CDs.*

When Album shows offline photos in the photo well, it uses the proxy image. If you edit an offline photo, use it in a creation (such as a slide show or calendar), or print it, Photoshop Album prompts you for the disc with the master (**Figure 2.9**). You can choose at this point to proceed with the proxy, but the results may not be pleasing if the proxy provides inadequate resolution for what you're doing.

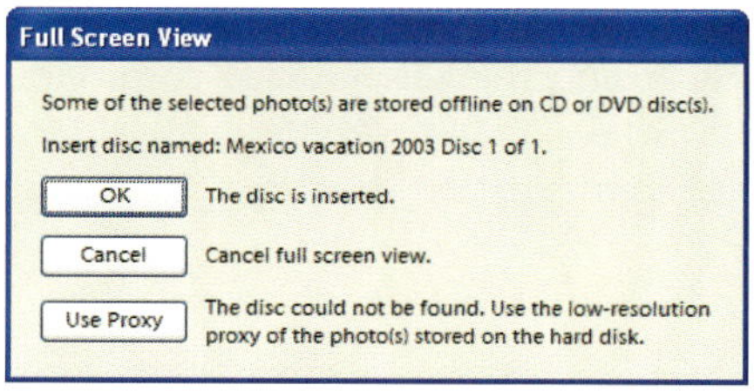

Figure 2.9 **If you take any action that requires access to the full-resolution file for a photo that is stored offline, this dialog (in this example, for viewing full screen) prompts you to insert the CD.**

When you edit a photo that's offline, Album must copy the photo to the hard disk, since it cannot write to the CD. Both the original and the edited copy will be stored on the hard disk, and the photo will no longer be offline.

Caution *If you're editing a photo and choose to work with the proxy rather than insert the CD, the proxy becomes the master, and the link to the original on the CD is lost. You should do this only if you have lost the CD. (You won't have this problem if you're printing or making a creation and choose to use the proxy; only that print job or creation will be affected and the catalog will continue to link to the CD.)*

If you've imported photos from your hard disk and want to store them offline, you can do so by burning an archive CD (see Chapter 3). This is especially useful if you're running out of disk space and can't get a bigger hard disk.

Note *If you want to later convert offline photos to online by copying them to the hard disk, use the Move Files function described in "Behind the Scenes: Working with Windows," which follows Chapter 4.*

Photoshop Album supports only photos as offline media; proxies are not available for video clips and audio, so these items must be copied to the hard disk to import them.

Getting Photos from Your Camera into Your PC

After you have imported your existing collection of photos into Photoshop Album, you'll probably add photos primarily from your digital camera. You don't have to use Album to get photos directly from your camera or memory card; you could use Windows or software that came with your camera to copy photos to the hard disk, and then import from the disk. But that process is more complex than it needs to be, and it forces you to deal with the file system and folder naming.

There are two ways to move photos from your camera to your PC: connect the camera to the PC, typically via a USB cable (or a dock connected to a USB cable); or remove the memory card from the camera and plug it into a card reader attached to the PC.

Each method has its pros and cons. Connecting the camera directly to the PC has the advantage of requiring no extra hardware, other than the cable that comes with the camera. One disadvantage, though, is that since you have to use the camera's battery during the transfer process, it's possible to lose photos if the battery runs out. Using a card reader is more reliable, especially because it provides independence from the vagaries of your camera's software.

Connecting Your Camera and PC

When your camera is connected to your PC (and turned on), the PC should be able to read the images from the camera. Depending on the specific camera and camera software, this might work in a number of different ways:

- Many cameras look like a disk drive to Windows. An icon appears in the My Computer window in the Devices with Removable Storage section (**Figure 2.10**), and you can double-click the icon to "open" the memory card in the camera just as you would any other disk.
- Even if your camera does not appear as a disk drive, it might not need any driver software to work with Windows Me or XP. Some cameras use an interface approach called Picture Transfer Protocol (PTP), and support for it is built into Windows Me and XP.
- Some cameras come with a WIA (Windows Imaging Architecture) driver, which other software can use to access the camera. If your camera offers both TWAIN (software most appropriate for scanners) and WIA drivers, be sure to use the WIA driver. (WIA is not supported on Windows 2000; if you're still running this OS, now is a good time to switch to Windows XP.)

Caution ***Don't use a TWAIN driver for cameras. (It's fine for scanners.) If you import from the camera using a TWAIN driver, you may lose metadata (such as the capture date and time), and JPEG files may be converted to much larger TIFF files. Look for a WIA driver, rather than a TWAIN driver, if you're running Windows Me or XP. If you can't find one, or if you're running Windows 2000, move the memory card to a card reader instead of using a direct camera-to-PC connection.***

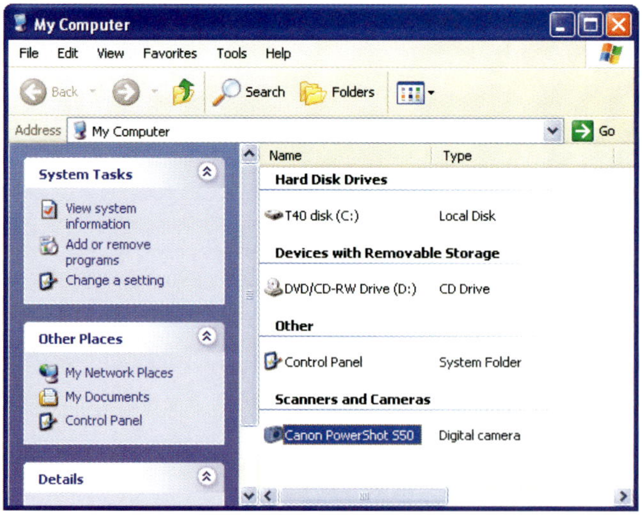

Figure 2.10 When you connect your camera to your PC via USB, it should show up in the My Computer window. If it does not, Photoshop Album will not be able to access it. (It may appear in the Devices with Removable Storage section.)

- Some older cameras use proprietary protocols for the computer and camera to communicate. In this case, you'll probably need to use the software that came with your camera to transfer the photos. If you have such a camera, move the memory card to a card reader, rather than connecting the camera to the PC.

In general, life will be simpler if you can avoid using the camera maker's software (other than drivers, if necessary). The camera-connection approach is best when either the camera mounts as a disk drive, Windows Me or XP automatically recognizes the camera, or you have a WIA driver for the camera.

Using a Card Reader

If you remove the memory card from the camera and plug it into a card reader, the process is the same regardless of what camera you're using. The transfer is also generally faster and more reliable; you don't have to use the camera's battery; and if you have more than one memory card, you can keep using the camera while waiting to transfer the photos.

The way you plug the memory card into the PC depends on the type of memory card and whether you have a notebook or a desktop PC. Let's look first at notebook PCs.

If you have a Sony camera and a Sony notebook, then you can simply remove the Memory Stick from the camera and plug it into the Memory Stick slot on the notebook. (Some Sony desktop systems have Memory Stick slots as well.)

If your camera uses any other type of memory card, your notebook probably doesn't have a place to plug in the card directly. But almost all notebooks have one or more PC Card slots, which will accommodate an inexpensive adapter that accepts the memory card (**Figure 2.11**). This is a great approach because the adapter sits inside your notebook computer.

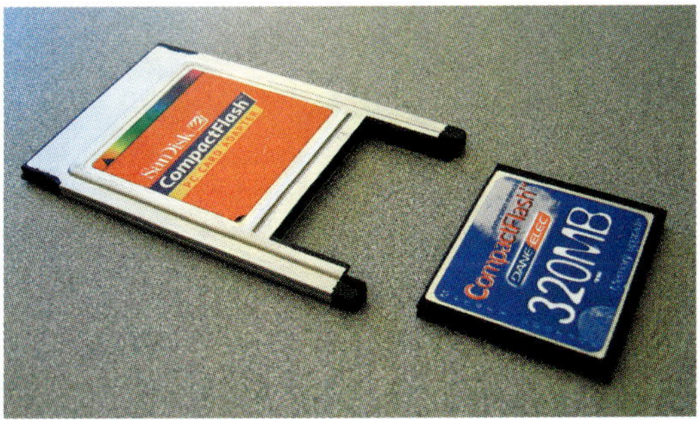

Figure 2.11 A PC Card adapter allows you to insert your memory card into a notebook PC. This adapter is for CompactFlash cards; adapters are also available for other memory-card types.

Most desktop PCs have neither memory card slots nor PC Card slots. There is a simple solution, however: purchase a memory-card reader (typically $20 to $50) that connects to the PC via a USB or IEEE 1394 cable (**Figure 2.12**). When you plug the memory card into the card reader, it appears as a disk drive on your PC. You can even get card readers that have slots for multiple types of memory cards, which is handy if you use more than one camera and they have different memory-card types.

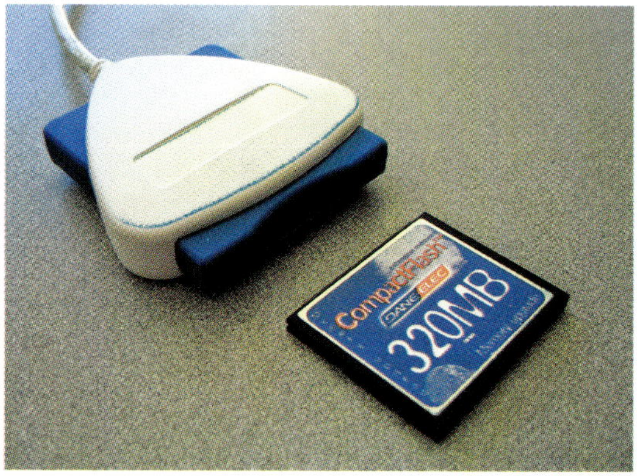

Figure 2.12 Memory-card readers that plug into a USB port allow any desktop PC to access memory cards directly. This is generally a better approach than connecting the camera via USB.

Using Album to Get Photos

To import photos from your camera, choose File > Get Photos > From Camera. In the resulting dialog, click Get Photos in the shortcut bar, and select From Camera or Card Reader (**Figure 2.13**) or press Ctrl-G. The first time you access this function, the settings you select in the Get Photos from Camera or Card Reader dialog will be saved in preferences, so from then on you shouldn't have to do anything except click OK or press Enter (**Figure 2.14**).

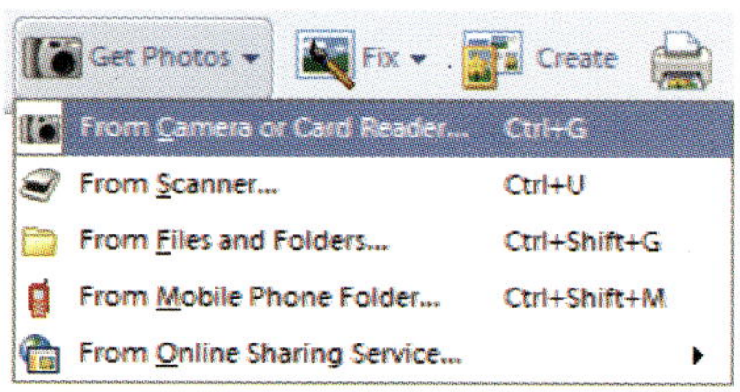

Figure 2.13 To get photos from a camera or memory card, use the Get Photos button in the shortcuts bar (if Windows has not triggered the import automatically).

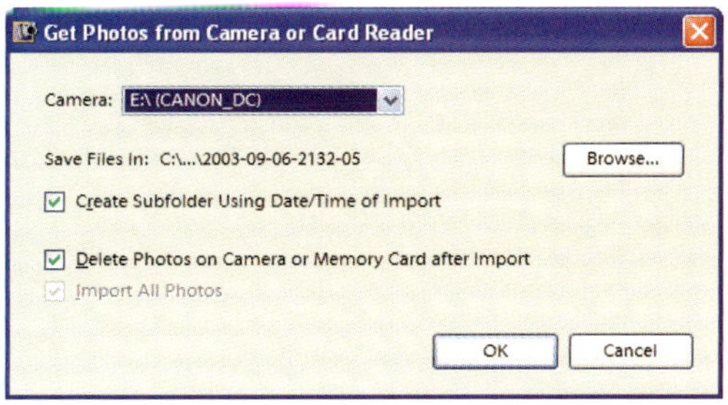

Figure 2.14 The first time you choose Get Photos > From Camera, the settings you choose in the Get Photos from Camera or Card Reader dialog are saved in preferences.

Note *If you choose From Camera or Card Reader via the Get Photos button in the shortcuts bar, the Get Photos from Camera or Card Reader dialog will not appear after the first time; the import will simply proceed with the default settings. If you choose it from the File > Get Photos menu, then the dialog is always displayed, and you can change the settings for an individual import operation. To change the settings for all future imports, go to Edit > Preferences, select Camera or Card Reader from the Preferences dialog, and change the settings.*

In the Camera pop-up menu, select your camera or memory-card reader, if it's not already selected. Note that you must have the camera connected and turned on, or a card inserted in the card reader, for it to appear on this list.

By default, each time you get photos from your camera or card reader, Photoshop Album creates a new folder inside My Pictures/Adobe/Digital Camera Photos and names this folder with the date and time. If you want to change this, click the Browse button and navigate to the folder you want to use. Letting Photoshop Album create and name the folder for you automatically makes the process easier, however.

If you unselect the box next to Create Subfolder Using Date/Time of Import, then all your photos will go into a single folder—not a good approach unless you're explicitly creating a new folder using the Browse function each time. And you'll find that this is more trouble than it's worth unless for some reason you're really attached to naming folders. In the long run, folder names won't matter at all, because you'll be finding photos using Photoshop Album, not the file system.

In general, it's easiest just to import everything into Photoshop Album and then delete anything you don't want. But if you're reading photos from a connected camera using a WIA driver, you have the option of selecting photos to import. If you unselect the Import All Photos option, the Windows camera wizard will show thumbnails of all the photos in the camera. You can then select the photos you want to import. This can save time if you are using a USB-connected camera and there are lots of photos you don't want to import.

Importing Automatically upon Connection

When you connect your camera via USB or insert your memory card into a card reader, Windows presents a dialog containing a list of options for what to do (**Figure 2.15**). One of the choices on this list is Find, Fix, and Share Photos using Photoshop Album.

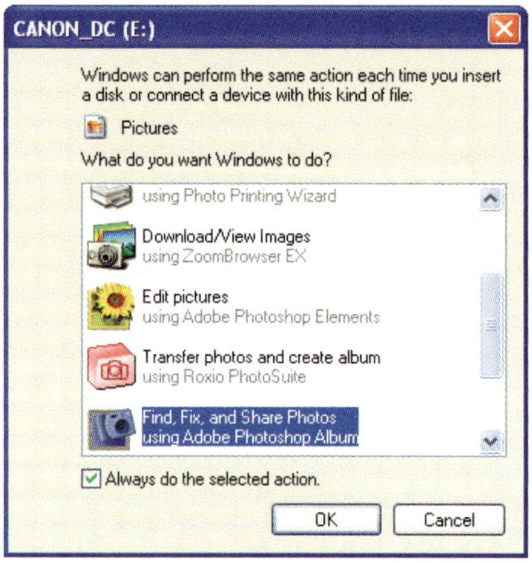

Figure 2.15 The first time you insert a memory card (or connect a camera that appears as a disk drive), Windows displays this dialog. Choose the Photoshop Album option, select the box next to "Always do the selected action," and click OK.

If you choose this option and check the box next to "Always do the selected action," then in the future this dialog shouldn't appear again. Windows will automatically launch Album (if it is not already running) and initiate an import operation. If you have already set your preferences and are letting Photoshop Album handle folder naming and deletion, then all you'll have to do is press Enter a few times to acknowledge the dialogs, and your photos will be imported and your card emptied for the next use.

Windows maintains separate lists of actions for what to do upon insertion of cards (or connection of cameras) with photos, video clips, audio files, or mixed content. So if you have only photos at first, and then later import from a camera or memory card with only video clips, or with a mix of photos and video clips, you'll have to make the selection from the Windows dialog again and check the "Always do the selected action" box. You may also find that these dialogs reappear after some applications are installed, or if you change memory cards or the connection method.

Deleting Photos from Your Camera or Memory Card

For the easiest import process, click the box next to Delete Photos on Camera or Memory Card after Import either in the import dialog (Figure 2.14) or in the camera preferences dialog (Edit > Preferences > Camera or Card Reader). Photoshop

Album will delete the photos only after it has confirmed that it has successfully copied all of them to the hard disk. This way your memory card will be empty and ready for your next photo session. If you select this by default (by setting it the first time this dialog appears, or in preferences), then all you need to do after selecting Get Photos > From Camera or Card Reader is press Enter twice (once for each dialog), and all your photos will be imported and your card erased and ready for more.

If you're the extra-cautious type, however, or if a particular set of photos is especially precious, leave the Delete Photos box unchecked. If you do so, it's up to you to clear out the memory card using Windows (with the camera connected or the memory card in the card reader) or using the camera itself.

***Tip** Erasing the card in the camera, a function usually called Format in a camera menu, is the most reliable approach. It's easier to erase the card from the computer, but if you have problems with a card, format it in the camera.*

If you don't erase the card and add more photos to it, Photoshop Album will ignore the ones it has already imported.

For maximum security, burn the photos to CD (or DVD) before erasing the card. This ensures that you always have a backup copy. Until you burn the CD and erase the card, the card itself serves as your backup. (See Chapter 3 for details.)

Removing Your Memory Card

If you're using a card reader, it's all too easy to forget to take the memory card out and put it back in your camera. Taking your camera off to an event and finding that you left the memory card in the computer can be very frustrating.

To be sure that Windows is done accessing the card before you remove it, click the Safely Remove Hardware icon at the right of the Windows task bar, and select the letter of the drive containing the card you want to remove. Windows displays a message when it is safe to remove the card.

***Tip** You can bypass this Windows function and just eject the card, but problems can occur if the software is still accessing the card. (Delete operations, for example, can be queued up even after you've finished copying photos from the card.) It's possible to ruin a card if you remove it from the PC or camera at just the wrong moment while it's being accessed.*

If the camera does not recognize the card after you have reinserted it, select the camera's format-card command. If formatting doesn't work, your card may be permanently damaged.

Getting Photos from Mobile Phone Cameras

If you have a mobile phone that includes a camera, you can use Photoshop Album to organize the photos you take with it. These photos won't generally be good enough to print (because of the low quality of the cameras in mobile phones), but they can be fun to share.

You can import photos from your mobile phone into your PC in three ways:

- Email them to yourself from your mobile phone. This doesn't require any special cables or software, but it can be slow and may result in additional charges on your mobile phone bill.
- Connect your mobile phone to your PC with a special cable, which you'll probably have to purchase separately. You'll also need special software for your PC that works with your mobile phone; it should come with the cable.
- If your phone has a removable card, you can insert the card in a card reader and import photos from it.

If you use the first approach, you can add photos from your email to Photoshop Album as described in the section "Photos That Others Share with You" later in this chapter.

In the second approach, once you transfer the photos from the phone to a folder on your PC, Photoshop Album can import photos from that folder. To get photos from this folder, choose File > Get Photos > From Mobile Phone Folder, or click the Get Photos button in the shortcuts bar and choose From Mobile Phone Folder.

The first time you use this feature, you have to tell Photoshop Album what folder the photos are in; you do this in the Specify Mobile Phone Folder dialog (**Figure 2.16**). Click Browse and select the folder in which your mobile phone software places the photos.

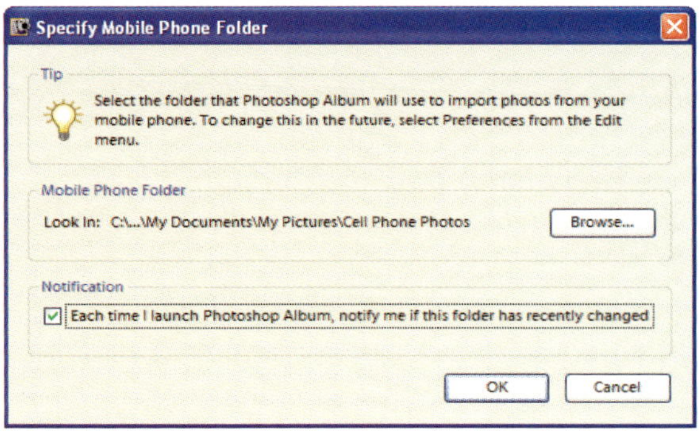

Figure 2.16 The first time you choose Get Photos from the Mobile Phone Folder, you must specify which folder you want to associate with your mobile phone.

If you click the box next to "Each time I launch Photoshop Album, notify me if this folder has recently changed," Photoshop Album will check the contents of this folder each time you start the program to see if there are any new photos there, and it will give you the chance to import any that are (**Figure 2.17**). Any photos that have previously been imported will be ignored, and any new photos will be imported.

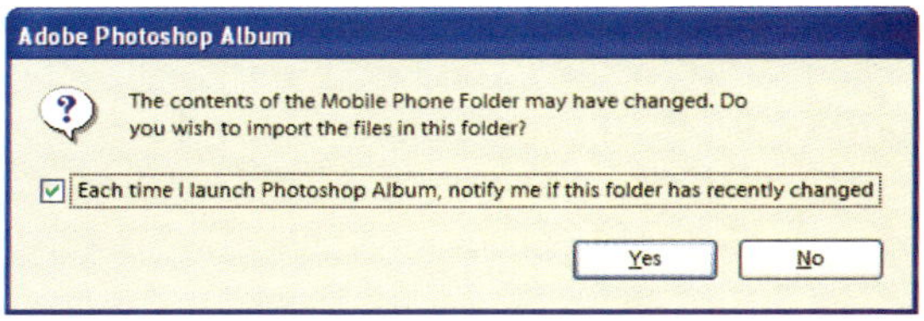

Figure 2.17 If you have enabled this option, Photoshop Album checks for new photos in the mobile phone folder every time you start the program.

***Tip** You can put photos you receive by any method in this folder, if you want Photoshop Album to import them automatically each time it starts. There is nothing specific to mobile phones about this process.*

Getting Audio and Video Clips

Album is not just for photos; you can also use it to manage video clips you've captured with your digital camera. It can also manage audio files, including audio that some cameras can capture as annotations to photos, and music files that you want to use as background music for slide shows.

Despite its name, you can use the Get Photos from Files and Folders dialog to get audio and video clips as well as photos.

Importing Video Clips

The video-management functions in Photoshop Album are designed to deal with video clips that come from digital still cameras. These clips are typically AVI or MOV files. Within these file types, however, there are many variations; many different codecs, or compression methods, can be used. Photoshop Album is compatible with most, but not all, such files. Photoshop Album first tries to use Microsoft's Windows Media Player to process video files. If this player cannot handle the format, then Photoshop Album checks to see if QuickTime is installed, and if so, it uses that program to decode the file.

Pictures That Move

In the film world, stills and video live in separate universes, with different cameras, film (or tape), and viewing methods. But in the realm of digital cameras, the divisions are not so sharp. Most digital "still" cameras can capture video clips, and many can record sound annotations for still photos in addition to sound tracks for the video clips.

Video clips are not yet of the same quality as camcorder video. The resolution is typically 320 by 240 or less, with a rate of only 15 frames per second (fps), and there is often a lot of random noise in the color information. Camcorder digital video, on the other hand, generally captures 30 fps with a resolution of 720 by 480. A few still cameras can capture video with a resolution of 640 by 480 at 30 fps, which makes it comparable to analog videotape (VHS).

Motion makes up for a multitude of sins, and even low-resolution video clips can be surprisingly satisfying. Not having to carry a separate video camera makes it far more likely that you'll be able to capture a video of a special moment while taking mostly stills.

The other limitation of using a still camera to capture video is the length of the video you can store. Video takes lots of memory, and most cameras limit the length of a video clip to between 30 seconds and 3 minutes. Video will also fill up your memory card quickly: a typical 15 fps 320 by 240 video clip consumes about 1 MB every 3 seconds, or 20 MB for a 1-minute clip. Higher-quality video takes much more space.

***Tip** In too many cameras, changing from still to video mode is a multistep operation. If you're buying a new camera, look for one in which it's easy to switch in and out of movie mode. Also look for video with a resolution of 640 by 480 if you want better video quality—and are willing to buy a high-capacity memory card.*

Most cameras that can capture video record an audio sound track along with the video. Some cameras also allow you to store an audio note, sometimes called a *sound caption* or *audio annotation,* along with a still photo. This can be very useful, but it is a hard habit to get into; with film cameras, there is no such thing as a still picture with sound.

You can use audio annotations to record your own comments about the photo or to record ambient sound (like the sound of a waterfall). Audio notes can consume lots of storage space, so use them sparingly unless you have ample space on your memory card.

Many camcorders are capable of capturing stills, providing another type of single device that can capture photos or video. The difference is that camcorders store the video on tape (or discs) rather than on a memory card. This allows them to store much more video, but the video is also harder to access. The still photos captured by camcorders are generally of lower resolution than those from still cameras, so your choice of a still camera or a camcorder is a matter of deciding which is your priority: stills or video.

Tip ***If you have problems with your video files, try installing or updating QuickTime or updating your version of Windows Media Player. If Album is still unable to process your video, you may be able to rectify the problem by installing a third-party codec. Figuring out what you need can be challenging; try checking with your camera manufacturer, or look on the Photoshop Album support site to see if others are having similar issues.***

Album cannot manage video files from your camcorder or other sources unless they are in AVI or MOV format. Large video files can be managed, but Photoshop Album is not designed for this use. If you use Photoshop Album's backup function, for example, it will copy all your media files—including video files of any length—as part of the backup operation. If any single video file is larger than the media you are using (typically 700 MB for CD or 4.7 GB for DVD), then the backup will fail; it cannot split a single file across multiple discs.

Importing Audio Files

Album supports audio files in the MP3 or WAV formats, primarily for the purpose of providing background music for slide shows. To appear in the pop-up lists for background music (in creations; see Chapter 8), audio files must be imported into your catalog. Because audio files are just represented by a generic icon (**Figure 2.18**), however, you generally will not want them cluttering up your photo well. Thus, display of audio files in the well is disabled by default. You can enable it via View > Media Types.

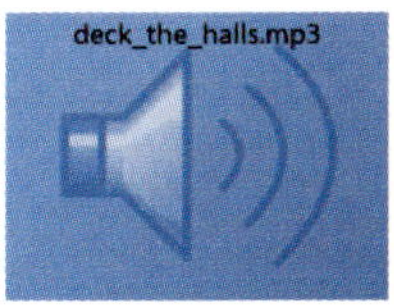

Figure 2.18 Audio files are represented in the photo well by this icon.

Even if display of audio files in the well is normally disabled, the files will be shown immediately after they are imported, and they will also appear if you search for them via Find > By Media Type > Audio.

Working with Scanners

If you take all your photos with a digital camera or use a service to scan your film, you may not need a scanner. But it's a great tool to bring all your older photos into the digital realm, so that you can use and enjoy them along with your digital photos. You can also scan in ticket stubs, maps, and other memorabilia that you might want to add to your photo albums.

Choosing a Scanner

Scanners span a wide range of prices, quality, and capabilities, so first you need to consider how you're going to use a scanner and how much you're willing to spend. There are three basic types of consumer-level scanners:

- Sheet fed
- Flatbed
- Transparency

A sheet-fed scanner moves the paper through the scanner. These scanners are generally better for documents than for photos.

Flatbed scanners are the most common. Some of them have paper-feeder options, allowing them to operate like a sheet-fed scanner as well. Some models will feed from a stack of 4-by-6 prints, which is a convenient way to scan in your old photos—though not the highest-quality method. Some models can also scan negatives and slides, but they do not do as good a job as dedicated transparency scanners.

Flatbed scanners have become amazingly inexpensive, and even the least-expensive scanners do a good job of scanning documents and low-quality photos. But if you're concerned about the quality of your scanned images, don't buy a $99 scanner. Flatbed scanners in the $300 range deliver significantly higher quality and offer more features.

If you have negatives or slides to scan, film scanners can deliver better results. By scanning the film or slide, you eliminate the significant loss of tonal range and color that occurs when a print is made, and you avoid all the imperfections in the print. Such scanners must operate at higher resolution than print scanners, however, since they are working from a much smaller area. Dust can also be a problem, since the amount of the image covered by a dust particle on a negative or slide is much greater than on a 4-by-6 print.

For lots of slides, or prints and negatives, if you want the best quality, go with a film scanner if you can afford it. But if you have boxes of 4-by-6 prints and want the quickest way to make them digital, get a flatbed scanner, perhaps with a feeder.

A good film scanner will set you back more than $500, and the higher-quality models are more than $1,000. In addition to delivering better image quality, the more expensive models are faster. Some also have optional auto-loaders that feed slides in automatically, which makes the process a lot less painful. Some of the more expensive film scanners eliminate the effects of small dust particles by using special lighting.

If you're trying to evaluate the image quality delivered by a scanner, the key is to look at shadow detail; this is one area where the low-cost scanners really fall down. You'll also notice differences in color fidelity and speed.

Scanning with Photoshop Album

As in getting photos from your camera, you can scan photos in two ways:

- Use Photoshop Album to manage the entire process.
- Scan to the hard disk and import into Photoshop Album from there.

With the first approach, you avoid having to worry about filenames and locations. Photoshop Album creates a name for each scanned photo, and they are all stored in the folder My Pictures/Adobe/Scanned Photos. If you organize them using tags (see Chapter 4), then you can always find them independently of their folder locations.

Unlike imports from a camera, all scans go into the same folder. Unless you are scanning hundreds of photos, putting them all in one folder is fine.

***Tip** If you scan many hundreds of photos, you may want to periodically change the folder into which the photos go to make them easier to locate should you ever want to find them using Windows. To do this, click the Browse button in the scanner preferences dialog (Edit > Preferences > Scanner). A good time to do this is at the start of any major scanning project. You can make a series of folders, one for each project, all within the Scanned Photos folder.*

You can scan into Album either by using the Get Photos from Scanner dialog (File > Get Photos > From Scanner) or by clicking the Get Photos button on the shortcuts bar and selecting From Scanner. In the Get Photos from Scanner dialog (**Figure 2.19**) you can change the scanner selection and settings; if you use the Get Photos button, the defaults are always in place. You can set the defaults in Scanner section of the Preferences dialog (Edit > Preferences), which provides the same set of controls.

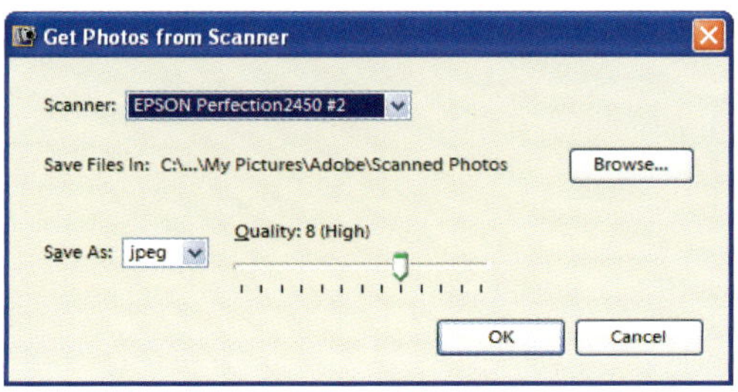

Figure 2.19 The Get Photos from Scanner dialog is initially set to the defaults from preferences, but you can override those settings here for a particular scan operation.

Storing your scans as JPEG files will keep the file sizes down and should be fine unless you're doing extremely critical work, in which case you could choose TIFF or PNG to store uncompressed files. A good compromise is to increase the JPEG-quality slider setting to 10 or so (make this change in preferences, not in the Get Photos from Scanner dialog, so it will be persistent). This reduces the file size significantly while maintaining very high image quality. (See "Behind the Scenes: Choosing File Types" at the end of this chapter.)

Once the scan operation is initiated, the scanner driver provided by either your scanner maker or by Windows takes over. (Exactly what happens depends on which version of Windows you are using and what type of driver is installed for your scanner.) The user interface you see during scanning operations is not controlled by Photoshop Album and will vary considerably from one scanner to another. **Figure 2.20** shows the dialog that appears if I select the TWAIN driver for my Epson 2450; **Figure 2.21** shows the simpler user interface presented if I select the WIA driver for the same scanner.

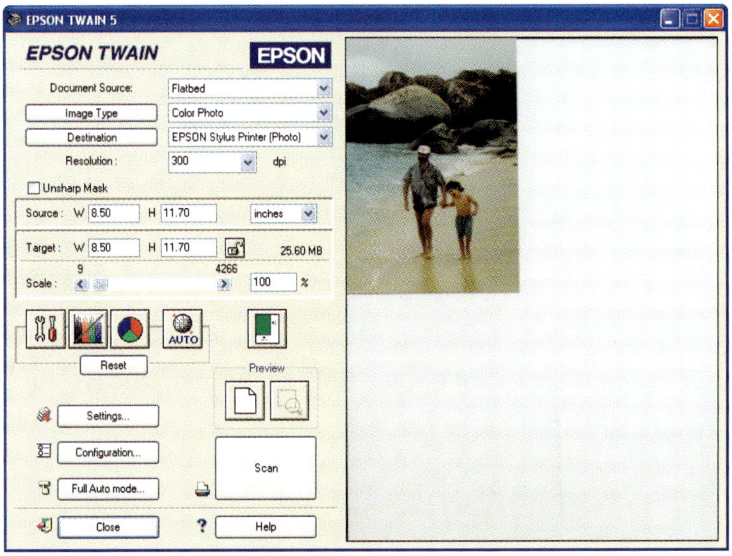

Figure 2.20 The user interface that appears after you click OK in the Get Photos From Scanner dialog depends on the scanner you are using and which interface software you have selected. The TWAIN driver interface for Epson's 2450 is shown here.

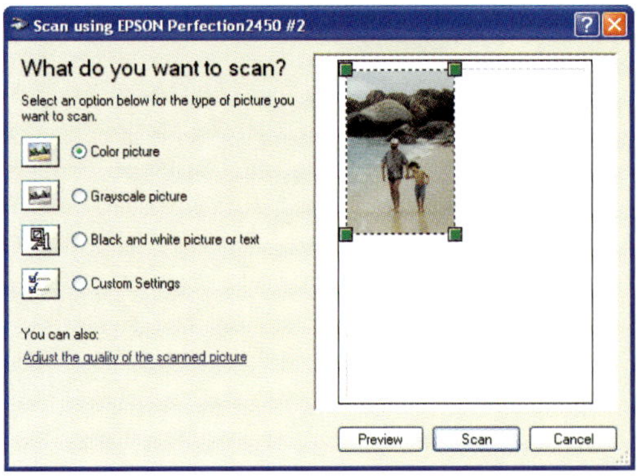

Figure 2.21 If I select the WIA driver instead of the TWAIN driver, I get this simplified interface for my Epson 2450 scanner.

***Tip** If you are scanning photo prints, there is rarely any value in scanning at resolutions higher than 300 dpi. Higher resolutions just give you bigger files and show more dirt and other defects. (When scanning film, however, much higher resolutions are necessary.)*

With most scanners, you have to scan photos one at a time. Some scanners include in their driver software the ability to split multiple photos apart into separate photos, so that you can put several smaller pictures on your flatbed scanner and scan them all together. If your scanner's driver software provides this capability, then the pictures will be automatically imported into Photoshop Album as separate photos.

***Tip** If your scanner comes with a TWAIN driver and a WIA driver, as many do, you can try both of them; although the WIA interface is the newer technology, some scanners actually provide more features in the TWAIN drivers.*

Using Other Scanning Software

The alternative approach—using other software to scan your photos and store them on disk, and importing them into Photoshop Album from there—is more trouble, but it gives you more control.

If you scan into Photoshop, for example, you can make enhancements and greatly improve color accuracy (see "Calibrating Your Scanner") and then import the final version into Photoshop Album.

There are also specialized scanning programs, including some inexpensive ones such as Hamrick Software's VueScan (www.hamrick.com), that operate independently and allow more control over the scanning process.

Calibrating Your Scanner

If you are scanning lots of photos, you may want to consider calibrating your scanner by creating an ICC (International Color Consortium) profile. You'll have to buy special software, such as Monaco's EZcolor (www.monacosys.com) to do this.

Although profiling your scanner can significantly improve the color accuracy of your scans, for most consumers it's more trouble and expense than it's worth. If you want to go down this path, start with the color-management references listed in Appendix A.

Having Your Film Scanned

If you're still shooting film as well as digital photos, you can include your film pictures in your digital collection by ordering a CD along with your photo processing. You can generally get this for a modest additional cost, and it is both easier and less expensive than getting the film scanned later. If you have a choice of scanning resolutions, pick the highest one available, and make sure the file format is JPEG. (Kodak's Picture CD and most others use JPEG.)

One format to avoid is Kodak's Photo CD (not to be confused with Kodak's Picture CD). Photo CD is an older format, which is still offered primarily for professionals. It provides higher-resolution scans than Picture CD, but the files are in a Kodak proprietary format that Photoshop Album cannot read.

Tip *You can read Photo CD format with Photoshop Elements, so if you do have Photo CDs, you can use that program to convert the files to the JPEG or TIFF format.*

If the CD has multiple copies of each photo in different resolutions, you only need to import the highest-resolution ones. The photos will generally be in different folders on the CD, and you can just ignore the lower-resolution folders. (Photoshop Album makes it easy to create lower-resolution versions on demand when you need them, so there's no need to clutter up your hard disk and your photo collection with them.)

Tip *When having your film developed, you may also have the option of having your photos posted on the Web, instead of or in addition to getting a CD. You may find this useful if you want other people to be able to see the photos right away, but in general you're better off just getting the CD and then posting online those photos you want to share.*

For more information on importing photos from CDs, see the section "Getting Photos from CDs and DVDs" earlier in this chapter. Unless you are short on hard-disk space, I recommend that you copy the photos to your hard disk rather than keeping them offline.

Photos That Others Share with You

Since one of the joys of digital photography is sharing photos, you're likely to receive photos from friends and family as well as to send them. By adding these photos to your Photoshop Album catalog, you'll be able to easily view or print them—and find them later.

To add photos you've received as email attachments, you can either use drag and drop or save the photos from your email program to a folder and then import the photos from that folder.

Drag and Drop from Email

Using drag and drop is the simplest approach once you get accustomed to it, provided that you're willing to let Album put the photos in its generic Other Photos folder. First, you must have Album running. Then, in your email program drag the icon for the photo file from the email message into Photoshop Album's photo well.

If the email program window is covering up the Photoshop Album window and preventing you from doing this directly, drag the photo from the email message to the Photoshop Album icon in the Windows taskbar, but don't release the mouse button. The Photoshop Album window will open and you can drop the photo into it.

Album automatically copies the photo file from your email program's attachments folder to a folder within My Pictures/Adobe/Other Photos.

Note ***If you use an uncommon email program, it's possible that Photoshop Album won't recognize the attachments folder as a temporary location and will leave the photo files there. You might then lose the photos if the contents of that folder are ever deleted. Check the photo properties (by selecting a photo and pressing Alt-Enter) after importing from your email program to make sure the photos are being copied to a permanent location. If not, use the "importing via the file system" method described later in this chapter.***

Importing Tags with Shared Photos

If you're receiving photos from other Photoshop Album 2.0 users, you can import the tags along with the photos if the sender includes tags (**Figure 2.22**). To do that, begin the import using the drag and drop method or File > Get Photos > From Files and Folders. In the Import Tags dialog check the boxes next to the tags you want to import. If any of the tag names match the names of tags already in your catalog, they will be noted with an asterisk.

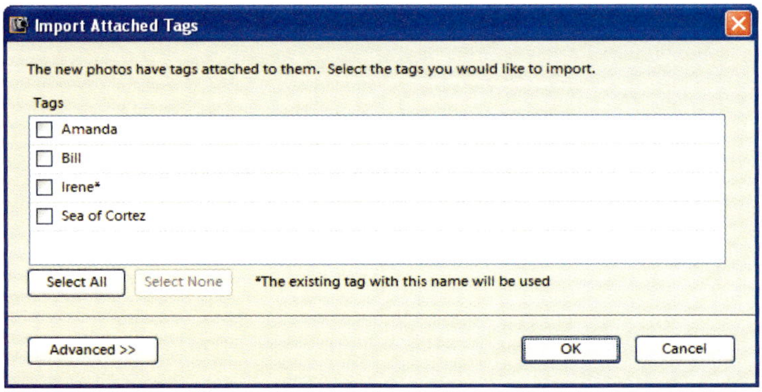

Figure 2.22 When Photoshop Album 2.0 users share photos with you via email, they can include their tags and you can import them.

If you don't want to use the sender's tags, leave all the boxes unchecked and click OK. If you want to use all of them, click Select All and then OK. If there is a matching tag name in your catalog, that tag will be used. If not, a new tag will be created.

If you want complete control over how the imported tags are used, click the Advanced button. In the Import Attached Tags (Advanced) dialog, you can choose which new tags are created, and how imported tags are mapped to existing tags (**Figure 2.23**). For example, as the figure shows, you may have a tag named Aunt Irene, and the sender may have called the tag simply Irene. The selection shown in the figure will make the translation so that you don't end up with both Irene and Aunt Irene tags.

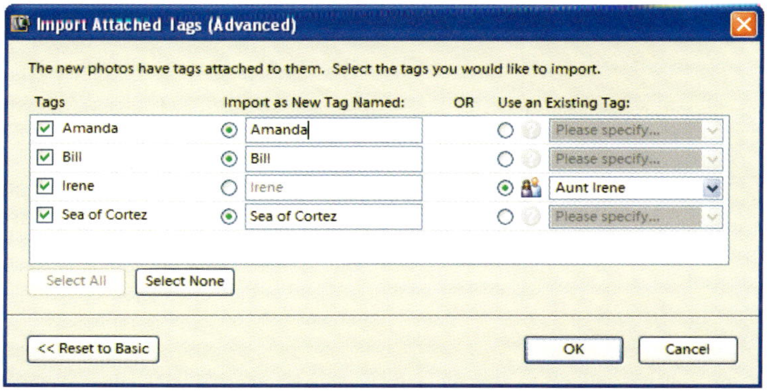

Figure 2.23 **If you select the Advanced option, you can map any of the tags in the shared photos to any of your existing tags, or choose to create new ones.**

Importing via the File System

If you save the files from your email program to your hard disk, you can import them as you would any other file from the hard disk. You might be tempted to create a folder organization, putting photos from various people into their own folders, but it's unnecessary. Just put all the photos that have been shared with you into one folder (Photoshop Album's My Pictures/Adobe/Other Photos is as good a place as any) and then import them from there. After importing, use tags (as described in Chapter 4) to organize them.

When you get photos from the file system, Photoshop Album generally leaves them in their existing location. The one exception to this is if they are in a location that Album believes to be temporary, such as C:/Windows/Temp, or, in some cases, an email program's attachments folder. In that case, they will be copied to the My Pictures/Adobe/Other Photos folder.

Tip *You can drag and drop photos from any Windows folder. You can also right-click a file in Windows and select Import into Adobe Photoshop Album from the contextual menu.*

You can select multiple items in Windows and then right-click any of them to access this function. This works correctly as long as Photoshop Album is running when you do it. If it is not, Album will be launched, but only the first of all the selected items will be imported.

You can store digital photos using several different formats, but how do you know which one you need? It's a tricky balancing act between two opposing forces: high-quality images and small file sizes. Knowing when to use which format, and the advantages of each, will help you decide whether to use JPEG, TIFF, or RAW format settings on your camera or scanner, as well as what JPEG quality settings to use when choosing your camera's settings, when exporting files from Album, and when saving files in Photoshop Elements.

Reducing File Size with JPEG Compression

A 5-megapixel image, in its uncompressed form, requires 15 MB on your memory card or hard disk. That's a lot of memory to store just one image.

Fortunately, there are ways to dramatically reduce the size of a file. Of the many different compression methods, by far the most common is that used in JPEG (which stands for Joint Photographic Experts Group, the name of the international organization that defined the standard).

All consumer digital cameras normally perform JPEG compression each time they store a photo on the memory card. This greatly increases the number of pictures you can fit on a card. Most cameras give you a choice of how aggressive you want the compression to be. The best setting, typically called *fine* or *superfine,* might compress by a factor of 5 to 8 (making the file one-fifth to one-eighth of its uncompressed size), while the lowest-quality setting might compress by a factor of 25 or more.

In the early days of digital cameras, when memory cards were small and expensive, the higher-compression settings were valuable; now I always use the best-quality setting. If you need to fit lots of pictures in the available memory and are willing to accept a modest compromise in quality, you can choose the next-lower setting. The lowest-quality setting is of little use.

Why Does File Size Vary?

You can't predict exactly how many pictures you can fit on your camera's memory card if you're using compression, such as JPEG. That's because compressed images vary in size depending on the content of the image. A forest scene typically results in a relatively large file because the tree leaves contain a great deal of detail. The same scene in winter, when the leaves have fallen and the ground is covered in snow, will result in a noticeably smaller file. You may find, for example, that 5-megapixel images at the highest-quality setting range from 1.5 to 2.5 MB.

Compression takes advantage of the fact that extremely fine details in an image aren't noticeable to the eye, and that there are often areas of the same color. If, for example, there's an area of nearly solid color, that area can be encoded in the file much more compactly by storing only its outline and color. In an uncompressed file, by contrast, the color value for every single pixel is stored.

You can compress most images to about one-fifth of their original size with almost no visible degradation. A 5-megapixel, 15 MB uncompressed image can be reduced to about 2.5 MB and remain high quality. With more aggressive compression you can reduce the same image to a much smaller size, but you'll get *artifacts*—undesirable side effects of the compression process (see Chapter 7, Figure 7.13 for an example). Artifacts are especially apparent if you view or print the image at a large size.

Using RAW Files for Maximum Quality

There are times when you don't want to lose any image quality to compression and you're willing to pay the price in file size. In such cases, you can store the image using *TIFF* (Tagged Image File Format). Less-expensive digital cameras store only JPEGs, but most higher-end cameras provide the option to store images in TIFF format.

It's unlikely, however, that you'll ever want to choose this option. The much-larger TIFF files will fill up your memory card more quickly, and your camera will operate more slowly. In the vast majority of cases, it's hard to tell the difference between a high-quality JPEG and a TIFF image.

A better option, offered by all prosumer cameras and an increasing number of consumer cameras, is the *RAW* format. (Despite the fact that it's typically in all caps, this is not an acronym; it means just what it says, raw.) The RAW format is not a single, standard format like JPEG, but rather the name for a class of formats proprietary to each camera manufacturer. Thus, Canon's RAW files (which have the .crw file extension) are different from Nikon's RAW files (with a .nef extension).

RAW files, as the name suggests, represent the raw information from the camera's image sensor. Because of the way the image sensors work, RAW files are much smaller than TIFF files but still preserve all the detail and use no compression.

RAW files must be processed in the PC before they can be viewed, and because each camera manufacturer uses a proprietary RAW format, each manufacturer provides its own software to process and view RAW-format images. Adobe offers a plug-in for

(continues)

Why Go RAW?

How can RAW files contain the same detail as TIFFs while being much smaller? The answer lies in how the camera detects images. Digital cameras use image sensors made up of millions of tiny light sensors. Each tiny sensor detects only one color: red, blue, or green, so a 4-megapixel camera has only 4 million sensors *total* (rather than 4 million of each color).

When you're not shooting in RAW mode, the software and processor in the camera convert the sensor information into an image with a red, green, and blue value for each spot. For each spot, even though the sensor detects only one color, the camera's software must compute values for all three colors. To estimate the level of blue at a spot that only detects red, for example, the software will consider the levels detected by the nearest blue sensors and use a sort of average.

When you shoot in RAW format, the camera doesn't do this processing; it just stores the raw data from the sensor. This makes a much smaller file than TIFF format, since each dot is represented by information about only one color, not all three.

To use a RAW file, you must have software on your PC that can convert it to the complete red, blue, and green image data you need to display or print it. Album does this automatically for the supported RAW formats.

Photoshop and Photoshop Elements that can process many RAW formats, making these files much easier to use. (You can buy this plug-in for Photoshop 7 and Photoshop Elements, but it's included in Photoshop CS.)

When a RAW file is processed, parameters like white balance and exposure can be adjusted by the software, providing additional flexibility that isn't available for JPEG or TIFF images that are processed in the camera. Photoshop Album can read common RAW file formats, but it doesn't provide the options to adjust them that Photoshop and Photoshop Elements do.

Because of the flexibility to make more adjustments to the image, and because no detail is lost to compression, many prosumer and professional photographers shoot primarily in RAW mode. RAW files are typically two to three times the size of a high-quality JPEG file but less than half the size of a TIFF file.

Other File Formats

Another important image file format is PSD, the Photoshop file format. PSD files are uncompressed, like TIFF and RAW files, and they can store multiple layers. If you add text to an image in Photoshop Elements, for example, the text is stored in a separate layer, which allows you to edit the text independently of the image. When you do sophisticated editing tasks in Photoshop or Photoshop Elements, you can use multiple layers for various elements of the image, and the PSD format can store all this information. As a result, PSD files are relatively large.

There are many other image formats, but you aren't likely to need any of them. These are a few of the most common:

- PNG (Portable Network Graphics) compresses data without any loss and is an alternative to TIFF and GIF.
- BMP (Bit MaP) is the native Windows format for uncompressed images.
- GIF is a compressed graphics format widely used on the Web. Because of its limited range of colors, it's better suited for graphics than for photographic images.

3 Keeping Your Photos Safe

In the world of film cameras, your master copies of your photos are probably in a shoebox. If you're really careful, you might keep this in a fire safe or other protected location. If you have a burglary, your negatives aren't likely to be stolen. Your PC, on the other hand, is a very likely target—even more so if it's a notebook computer.

Furthermore, one of the nasty realities of personal computers is that disk drives can fail. In addition to being subject to hardware failures, the contents of the disk can be lost or damaged by errant programs, viruses, or user error. So your precious photos are now stored in a location that is a likely target for thieves and that can self-destruct at any time.

Obviously, this is not a situation you should accept. Don't count on your PC's hard disk as the only storage location for anything important. Photos are among the most irreplaceable items you may have stored there, so they deserve special protection. Your Photoshop Album catalog, while not as irreplaceable, may represent many hours of work organizing your photos and making creations with them, so you'll want to ensure that it's safe, too. After you import your full collection of photos into Album, it's an ideal time to do a backup.

If you regularly back up your entire hard disk, then this backup will preserve your photos and catalog as well. Make sure the backup is stored in a location where it would not be likely to get stolen along with your PC, and where it is protected from fire. Always verify your backups to make sure they work correctly, and keep more than one backup set in case something goes wrong with the most recent one.

CDs and DVDs

Flash memory cards are great for storing pictures in your camera: they're tiny and robust, and they require no mechanical parts. They are far too expensive, however, to use for permanent photo storage.

On the other hand, CDs and DVDs are relatively large (especially compared with memory cards) and they require complex and delicate mechanical drives to access them. Their enormous advantage is that they are very cheap, making them the best way to store your photos for the long term.

A few digital cameras include writable CD or DVD drives and store photos directly on them, but these cameras are bulky and not very popular. A far better approach for most consumers is to use a camera that stores the pictures on flash memory cards: you transfer the photos from the memory card to the PC's hard disk and then copy them to a CD or DVD for backup and long-term storage.

CDs and DVDs look the same, but DVDs hold much more data. CDs are available in capacities of 650 or 700 MB, whereas DVDs store 4.7 GB—about seven times as much. As of late 2003, bulk CD-R (compact disc recordable) discs cost about 30 cents each, and bulk DVD-R (DVD-recordable) discs are about $1. At roughly three times the price for seven times the capacity, they are a great deal.

(You may notice that the word *disc,* with a *c,* is used to describe CDs and DVDs, whereas the word *disk* is used to describe the hard drive in your computer. This trivial but annoying distinction is a legacy of the trademark name for audio CDs, Compact Disc.)

Most DVD drives cannot write to DVDs, however, but only read them; DVD drives that can write to discs are still relatively expensive and not nearly as common as writable CD drives. As long as your photo collection is modest, CDs are adequate, but when your collection grows large enough, you'll want to switch to DVDs to archive it.

Understanding CD and DVD Varieties

There's a confusing array of CD and DVD types, plus a variety of formats for organizing the information on each of them.

CDs

For CDs, the situation is reasonably simple—there are three types:

- CD-ROM (compact disc read-only memory) discs, like the ones your software and music comes on, are manufactured with the information already on them, and are not writable.
- CD-R (compact disc recordable) discs are the most common media for preserving your photos. They can be "burned" (written) in your PC, assuming that you have a CD-R or CD-RW drive and not the more basic CD-ROM drive, but once written, they cannot be erased.
- CD-RW (compact disc rewritable) discs can be erased as well as written. The blank discs are more expensive than CD-R discs and are not as widely used.

The information on a CD can be formatted in several ways, using any of the disc types listed above:

- Data CDs are used for storing your photos, backing up other computer information, and making slide-show CDs to share (via playback on a PC). The PC accesses a data CD as files, just like it does with any disk drive.
- Video CDs contain slide shows or movies that are recorded on CD but played back on a DVD player. A higher-quality version is called Super Video CD.
- Audio CDs contain digital music for playback on a CD player (they're not relevant to photos).

DVDs

For DVDs, the situation is more complicated. As with CDs, there are DVDs on which the information is written when the disc is manufactured, and R and RW discs that can be written once (R) or written and erased (RW). Unfortunately, however, two competing manufacturer camps chose two different ways to make these discs, so there are two confusingly named versions of each: DVD-R and DVD-RW, and DVD+R and DVD+RW.

(continued)

Understanding CD and DVD Varieties *(continued)*

Most writable DVD drives are limited to one type of media or the other (plus or minus). If you're shopping for a writable DVD drive, look for one of the newer "universal" models that can work with either type. (There is yet another type of writable DVD disc called DVD-RAM, but it is much less common.)

DVD discs can be formatted in two primary ways:

- DVD-video is the format used for DVD movies. It contains an MPEG-2 video stream with menu-based navigation. It can also be used for slide shows (though Photoshop Album doesn't support it).
- Data DVDs are just like big CDs, giving you 4.7 GB in which to store lots of photos and other information from your computer's hard disk.

Using Album's Backup Function

Photoshop Album has built-in backup and restore functions that you can use instead of a full system backup. If you're only backing up selected information from your PC, instead of the entire disk, use Photoshop Album's backup function to ensure that you've saved everything needed to re-create your photos and the catalog. You access the backup function, and the related archive function, through the Burn option in the File menu.

If you have an external hard-disk drive, you can back up to it. (Note that this function can be accessed via File > Burn, even though you aren't actually burning an optical disc.) This is the easiest and fastest approach, since you don't have to feed in a series of discs, and writing to a hard drive is faster than writing to a CD or DVD. But unless you're willing to devote an external hard disk to this, and move it to a more secure location after the backup, it is likely to get stolen along with your computer, should you have a burglary. Unlikely as that may be, you don't want to take chances with your precious photos.

The most common way to back up is to use writable CDs or DVDs. You can easily hide or store these discs in a fire safe or safe deposit box, or even take them with you if you're going away on vacation and leaving the computer at home.

If you have more than a few hundred photos, a writable DVD drive is a good investment. You can back up even a large collection onto CDs, but it will take many discs and is quite tedious. If you have more than one writable CD or DVD drive, they will be listed in the Backup dialog, and you can select the one you want to use.

***Note** Keep in mind that the backup function operates on a single catalog—whichever catalog is open when you select the command. So if you have multiple catalogs, be sure the one you want to back up is open before you start the process. If you want to back up multiple catalogs, you'll have to handle them individually.*

After you select File > Burn, you have to choose the type of files you want to burn in Step 1 of the Burn/Backup dialog (**Figure 3.1**). To make a backup, select the second option, Backup the Catalog. (You can also choose File > Backup instead of File > Burn, which will bring you to this same dialog with the backup option already chosen.)

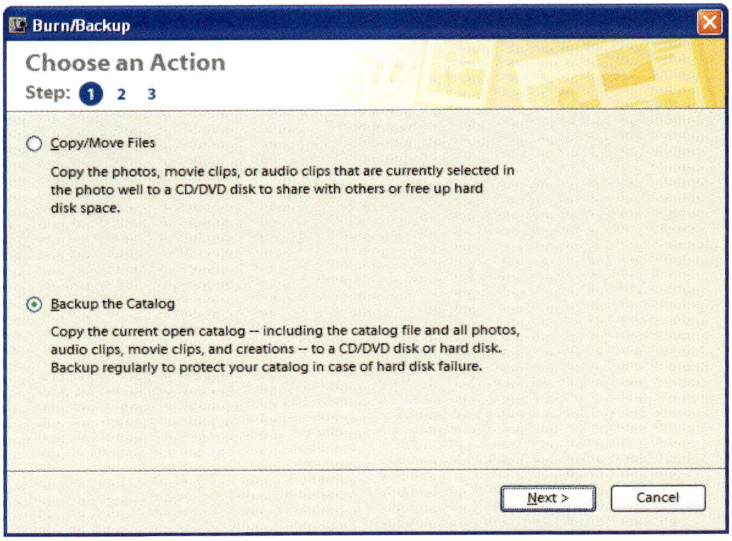

Figure 3.1 In the Burn/Backup dialog you can access two different functions: Copy/Move Files, which creates discs with selected photos only, and Backup the Catalog, which copies the catalog and all your photos.

When you click Next, Photoshop Album asks if you want to check for missing files. It is a good idea to do this now (by clicking the Reconnect button), because missing files (those that are not in the location where the catalog says they are) won't be backed up. If you don't want this reminder in the future, just click the Don't Show Again box and you will be reminded no longer. If you want to skip the reconnection step, click the Continue button.

Next, choose whether to make an incremental or a full backup in Step 2 of the Burn/Backup dialog (**Figure 3.2**). The first time you make a backup, choose Full Backup. Photoshop Album will copy your catalog and every item to which the catalog points (that is, all the photos, video clips, and audio clips in the catalog). It will tell you how many discs you'll need and prompt you when you need to insert another.

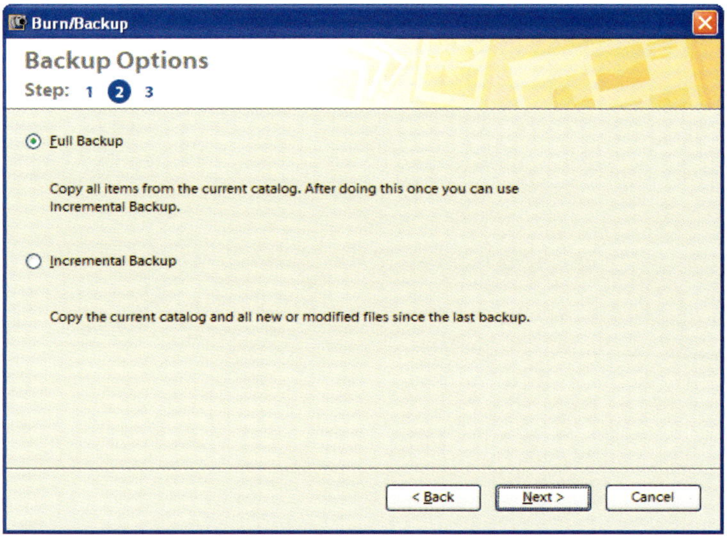

Figure 3.2 When creating a backup for the first time, use Full Backup; use Incremental Backup to add to that backup later.

Once you have a full backup set, you can update the backup without having to burn all the discs again, by selecting Incremental Backup. You need to use a blank disc for the incremental backup, but it only backs up things that have changed (it adds to the set of discs in the prior backup set, but does not physically add to the last disc). Incremental backups include the full catalog but only the new photos.

After you've chosen an incremental or full backup and clicked the Next button, you can choose which drive to use in Step 3 (**Figure 3.3**). If you've selected a CD or DVD drive, you can also select the write speed. If you have a well-designed system, a good CD or DVD burner, and high-quality blank media, you should be able to use the maximum speed listed, which will minimize the burn time. If you encounter errors, however, try lowering the write speed (see the sidebar "Solving Disc Burning Problems").

Click Done, and the backup will begin. A couple hundred photos may take only 10 minutes to back up to CD, but if you're backing up a catalog with thousands of high-resolution photos to multiple DVDs, it can take an hour or longer. You'll need to be present to change discs if the backup doesn't all fit on one, otherwise you can let the backup run unattended until it's time to verify the discs.

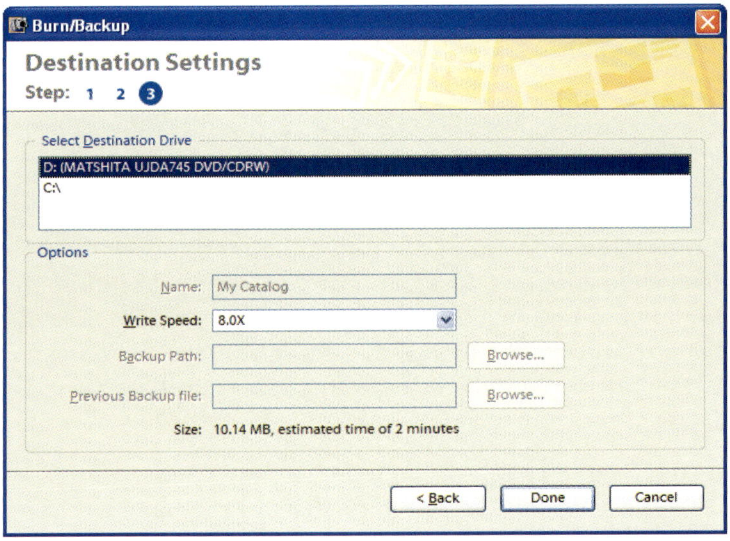

Figure 3.3 You can choose which drive to write to, as well as the write speed, if you've selected a CD or DVD drive.

Note *All discs in a backup set must have the same capacity to avoid problems. Album assumes the capacity of every disk is that of the first one you use. So if you start with a 650 MB CD, you'll only get 650 MB per disc, even if you use 700 MB CDs later in the series. And you cannot use a CD to add to a backup set that started with a DVD (or vice versa).*

Solving Disc-Burning Problems

When burning a CD or DVD, your computer must provide the drive with a long, fast, uninterrupted stream of data. Some of the newer drives include a technology called BurnProof, which ensures that other computer activity doesn't cause burning to fail. If your drive doesn't have this technology, and especially if you have any older system, don't try to use the computer for anything else while burning is in progress, or errors may occur.

The quality of blank CD and DVD media varies greatly. If you encounter lots of problems with one brand, don't buy it anymore. For the best chance of burning at the maximum rate, make sure the media is rated for a burn speed at least as high as your drive's. For instance, if your drive is rated at 32X speed, Album will try to write at that speed. But you may find writing is more reliable if you reduce the speed to 16X.

You can use CD-RW or DVD-RW (or +RW) media if you want to be able to erase it. It is more expensive, however, and there is something reassuring about *not* being able to erase your backup discs! If you do use an RW disc, you need to erase it (if it is not already blank) before using it with Photoshop Album; Album cannot add to a disc that already has other information on it.

Conflicts with other CD- and DVD-writing programs can also cause problems writing to CDs and DVDs; this is one area where Windows does not provide a clean set of mechanisms to coordinate programs. If Photoshop Album does not recognize your CD or DVD drive, or if it crashes when trying to write to the media, make sure you have no other CD- or DVD-writing software running—including programs that run in the background and may show up in the tool tray at the right of the task bar.

If you're having problems burning disks, choose Run from the Windows Start menu, type `msconfig`, and click OK. This utility will enable you to disable any programs or services that automatically run at startup. Click the Selective Startup radio button, then select the Startup tab, and look for any items related to disc burning. Uncheck their boxes to disable them, and reboot the system. If this resolves the problem, then there is a conflict between the software you disabled and Photoshop Album, and you'll have to decide whether to leave the other software disabled or forgo using Photoshop Album's disc-burning features. (You may be able to find updates to either the conflicting software or Photoshop Album that can resolve the issue.)

If you're still having trouble burning discs, check Adobe's Photoshop Album support Web site for tips (www.adobe.com/support/products/photoshopalbum.html), or call Adobe's technical support (206-675-6323 in the U.S.).

When all the discs have been burned, Album asks if you want to verify them (**Figure 3.4**). It is tempting to skip this step, but *don't!* You're depending on these discs in case anything goes wrong with your PC's hard disk. If one of the CDs was not written properly for any reason, you won't know until it is too late if you don't verify.

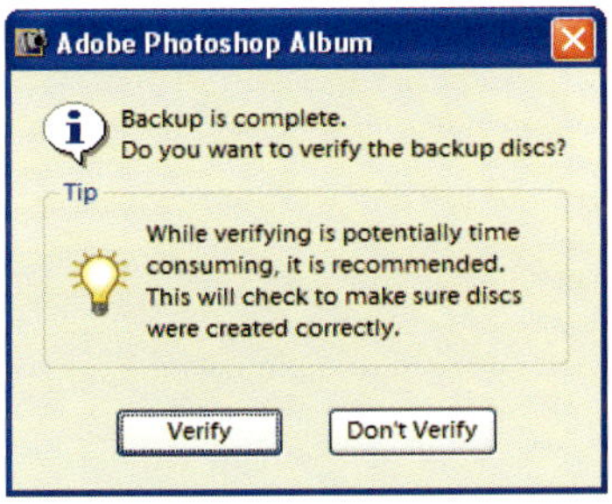

Figure 3.4 You can save time by skipping the verify step, but then you'll have no way of knowing if your backup discs are usable.

***Note** Backup discs are intended to be accessed only with Photoshop Album's File > Restore command. The files on the backup discs will not be organized into folders, and they will not have their original names (but all this information will be restored on the hard disk if you use Album's Restore function). If you want to make discs for other purposes, make archive discs instead, as described later in this chapter.*

Backing Up Your Offline Masters

If you have photos whose masters are offline—that is, the masters are on a CD or DVD—then your master copy of these files exists only on that CD or DVD. When you perform a backup, the proxy file (a lower-resolution copy stored on the hard disk) is written to the backup set, but the master is not (since the masters are not available without inserting the discs where they are stored).

Thus, you need to be sure to back up your offline masters separately. Since they are already on removable optical media, you don't have to worry about disk crashes or accidental deletion (unless you use RW discs), and you can store them in a safe place—but you should never depend on any single copy of important photos. (If you lose the master disc, you'll still be able to access the proxy file in Photoshop Album, but it won't have the full resolution.) Discs can get lost, broken, stolen, or scratched—and eventually they can fail from old age.

Once your photos are offline, you can't use Photoshop Album to make an extra backup copy; you'll need to use a CD-burning utility to make copies of the discs. Then put the copies away in a separate, safe location with your other backup discs.

Note *Photoshop Album stores in the catalog the serial number of the disc for each offline photo. When it asks you to insert the disc (if you're printing the photo, for example), it checks the serial number. If you copy the files to a new disc, the copy may have a new serial number, depending on how you do it.*

If the serial numbers do not match, Photoshop Album will display a warning that the disc may not be the correct one. You can proceed anyway, which of course you should do. Just be sure that it is a copy of the correct disc.

Restoring Backups

If that fateful day comes when something has gone wrong with your hard disk, you'll be glad that you have your backups and they're up to date. Just reinstall Photoshop Album (if necessary), and select File > Restore, which brings up the Restore dialog (**Figure 3.5**). Click the Restore button and feed in the discs as requested (**Figure 3.6**). Photoshop Album will restore the catalog and all the files that it references.

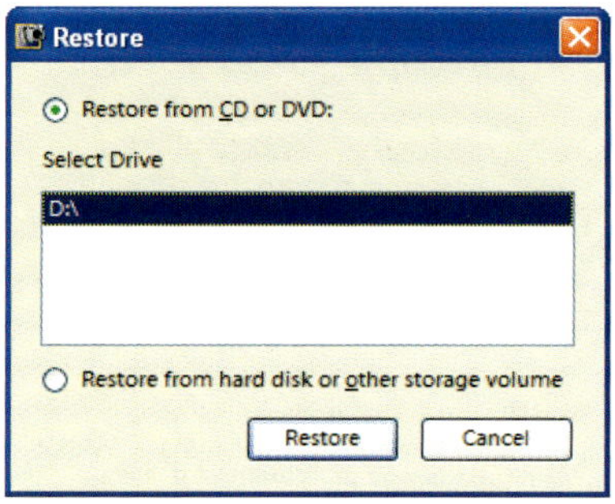

Figure 3.5 To restore a backup set, first indicate what drive it is on. If you select "Restore from hard disk or other storage volume," you'll be able to navigate to the folder with the backup files.

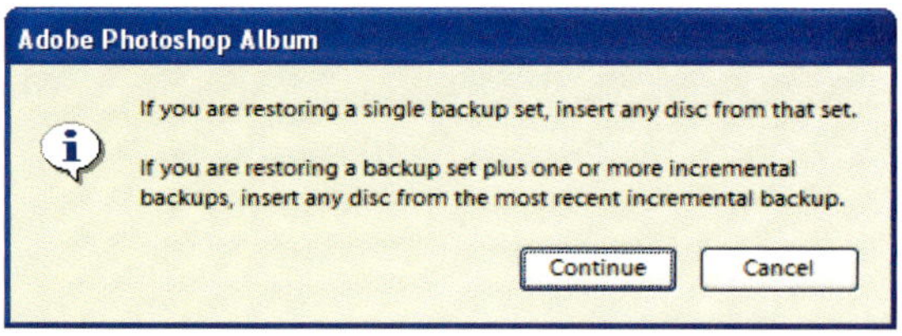

Figure 3.6 You don't have to put in the backup discs in order.

You may also want to use the restore function if you switch to a new PC. Make sure your backups are up to date on your old system, install Photoshop Album on the new system, select File > Restore, and feed in the discs as requested.

When you restore a catalog, Photoshop Album will overwrite any existing catalog of the same name (after warning you). If you have used the default My Catalog name, and you restore to a new installation of Photoshop Album, the program will warn you that you are about to overwrite an existing catalog (**Figure 3.7**). This is what you want—as long as you haven't added anything to the new My Catalog. If you want to avoid overwriting, cancel the restore operation and select File > Catalog > Save As to save the existing catalog under a new name. Then restart the restore. You'll still get the overwrite warning, since the copy under the old name is still there, but that's OK, since you now have a second copy of it.

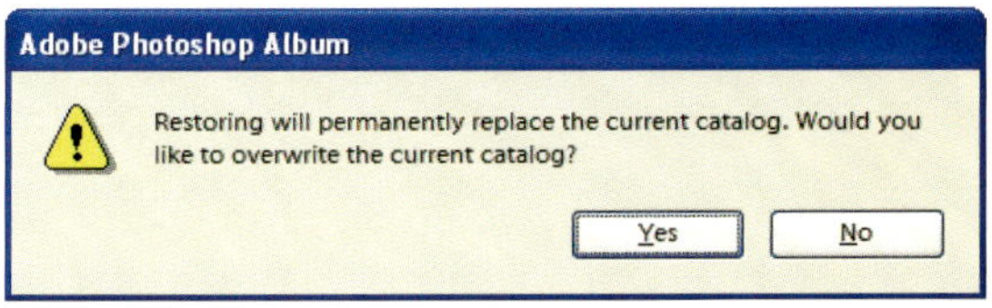

Figure 3.7 Photoshop Album warns you if there is an existing catalog of the same name as the one you're restoring.

In the process of restoring the photo files themselves, each time Album finds a photo in the backup set that is already present on the hard disk, it presents you with a dialog asking if you want to overwrite the file (**Figure 3.8**). If you want to replace everything on the hard disk with the contents of the backup set, click Yes to All the first time this dialog appears. If you want to restore only the catalog and photos that aren't already on the hard disk, choose No to All. (You can also choose on a photo-by-photo basis, but this gets tedious quickly and is generally unnecessary.)

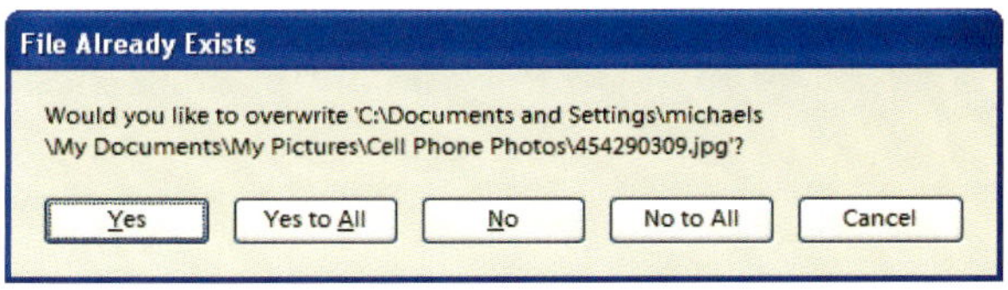

Figure 3.8 Each time Album tries to restore a file that already exists on the hard disk, it asks if you want to overwrite the file.

Where Do the Files Go?

When Photoshop Album restores photo, video, and audio files that are linked to your catalog, it attempts to put them in their original location, creating folders as needed. So no matter how you have your files arranged on your hard disk, if you use backup and restore to switch to a new system, Photoshop Album will re-create the same arrangement.

The restore function will automatically make changes to folder locations under two circumstances. First, any folders in the My Pictures folder on the system where the backup was created will be restored to the corresponding location within the My Pictures folder on the system on which you are restoring. From the perspective of the My Pictures folder, they are in the same location. But the full path to the My Pictures folder may be different from one system to another, depending on the operating-system version and the user name (if any) under which you are logged in. Photoshop Album will automatically adjust for these differences, correcting the file paths in the catalog so that the files will be found in their new location.

Restore will also change the location of a file if the drive volume from which it was backed up does not exist on the system to which you are restoring. If you back up a system that had photos stored on the D drive, for example, and then restore to a system that has no D drive, Photoshop Album needs to create a place to put these photos. It will create a folder, named Drive D in this case, within the folder My Pictures/Adobe/Photos from Backup, and put all the folders from the old D drive in that folder.

There is not, unfortunately, any way to control where the restore function puts the photos. If all the photos were on the C drive in the system being backed up, they will be written to the C drive in the system being restored to. If the C drive doesn't have enough room for this, you will not be able to complete the restore. If you can free up enough space to complete the restore, you can then move the files to another drive (by using File > Move, or by moving the files using Windows and then using File > Reconnect All Missing Files to fix up the links in the catalog).

Making Archive Discs

Back in the first dialog that appears when you select File > Burn (Figure 3.1), if you select the Copy/Move Files option, you'll be making archive discs instead of backup discs. The distinction is more than semantic: archive discs serve different purposes. You might want to make archive discs for any of the following reasons:

- To make a copy of selected photos (rather than the full collection) to ensure their safety
- To remove full-resolution files from your hard disk to free up disk space
- To make copies of selected photos to give to someone or to take into a retail store to get prints made

***Note** The restore function cannot use archive discs, and they do not contain any catalog information; they are simply copies of the photo files. Backup discs, on the other hand, include the catalog and all your files, but they do not show your original filenames and are intended only for use by Album's restore function.*

To make an archive disc, choose File > Burn; select Copy/Move Files in the first pane of the Burn/Backup dialog, and click Next. In the lower section of the second pane, you can choose whether to burn both the original and the edited copy (if any), or just the newest version (the edited copy if there is one, otherwise the original) (**Figure 3.9**).

***Tip** The first option is best if you're making an archive disc to preserve the photos. Be sure to use the second option if you're making a disc to share with someone, or to send to a service or take to a store to get photos printed.*

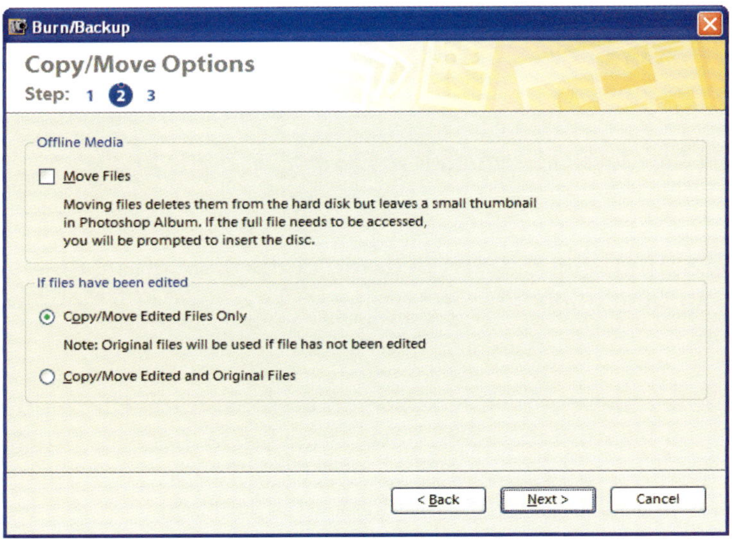

Figure 3.9 If you check the Move Files option, Album first writes your files to an archive disk. Then it removes the original files from the hard disk and creates low-resolution proxy files.

You have a *very important* choice to make in the upper section of the second pane: whether or not you want the files removed from the hard disk. If you choose the Move Files option, only a proxy—a lower-resolution copy—will be left on the hard disk, and you will have to insert the disc with the full-resolution master file when you want to view the photo full screen, print it, edit it, or make a creation with it (**Figure 3.10**).

Tip ***Before moving any photos offline, check the proxy setting in preferences, as discussed in Chapter 2, to make sure you have chosen the proxy size you want; you can't change it later. Use the maximum proxy size unless you are very short on hard-disk space.***

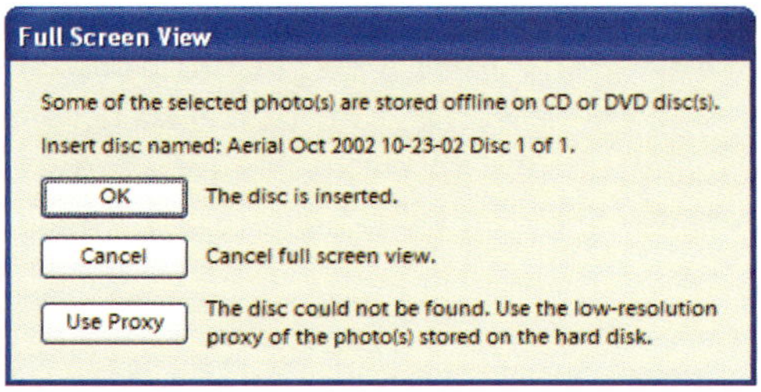

Figure 3.10 When you attempt to use a photo that you have archived and removed from the hard disk, Album will prompt you for the archive disc. You can proceed with the proxy file if you can't find the disc, but you'll lose image quality.

Moving files offline is a way to free up space on your hard disk. If you have enough space, however, you're better off leaving the master on the hard disk and treating the archive disc as a copy. That way, you don't need to insert the disc to do anything with the photo. Big hard disks are cheap, and it is a great convenience to always have everything online.

Tip ***Be sure not to select the Move Files option if you're making a disc to give to someone else!***

If you do select the Move Files option, take good care of the disc you create—it is your only copy of the full-resolution files. To be safe, make a copy of it right away using a disc-copy utility.

If you want to bring offline files online later, you can do so with the File > Move command (see the section "Behind the Scenes: Working with Windows," which follows Chapter 4). Just select (in the photo well) the photos you want to move online, choose File > Move, and pick a location on the hard disk for them.

CD Burning Options

There are lots of choices to make when burning CDs. Table 3.1 summarizes these choices and shows when to use each one.

Table 3.1 **Burn Options and When to Use Each One**		
Copy/Move		
"Move Files" box checked	Use to remove full-resolution files from hard disk to save disk space	
"Move Files" box not checked	Edited File Only:	Use to make disc for sharing or to take to a print service.
	Original and Edited Files:	Use to preserve selected photos (archive)
Backup		
Full	Use for initial backup; repeat periodically	
Incremental	Use frequently to update existing full backup set	

A Plan to Keep Your Photos Safe

The backup and archive functions I discussed above give you the tools to keep your photos safe—but they won't work without your help. It's important to put together a plan to use these functions on a regular basis so that you don't end up losing precious photos.

Making a full system backup on a regular basis—perhaps weekly—is a good idea. But it is also a great deal of trouble unless you invest in a backup device, typically a tape drive, that can store the entire contents of your hard disk, and such devices are expensive. You can reduce the amount of space you need for backup by carefully configuring your backups to skip program files that can be re-created by reinstalling software from the master discs.

The easiest way to keep your photos safe, independent of full system backups, is to use Photoshop Album's Backup function. Once you've made one full backup, you can use incremental backups to update your backup set. After many such additions, you should make a new full backup and put the first set, with its incremental discs, away—just in case something happens to your current backup set.

How frequently should you back up? It depends on how precious your photos are and how much you're willing to tempt fate. A good time to update your backups is immediately after any major picture-taking event. You may also want to back up if you've just done a lot of tagging or making creations. And you should update your backups at regular intervals—of perhaps a week if you're a very active picture taker, or a month if you're more typical—no matter what.

You can also back up photos (but not the catalog) by making an archive disc. This is a quick way to immediately back up new photos. First select the new photos you want to archive; the Import Batch arrangement of the photo well makes this easy. Or, if you've just imported photos from the camera and want to back up only those newest photos, proceed with burning the disk immediately after importing the photos, when only those just imported will be shown in the photo well. Select File > Burn, and choose Move/Copy Files in Step 1 of the Burn/Backup dialog. Make sure that you do *not* enable the Move Files option in Step 2.

Making quick backups is easy with an external hard disk that can be connected via USB (preferably 2.0) or IEEE-1394. If it sits right next to your computer, as it usually will, it won't protect you against fire or theft, but it should generally protect you against accidental file erasure or disk crashes (assuming that your main hard disk has a copy of everything, too).

A hybrid approach, which I prefer, is to copy new photos to the external disk as soon as they've been imported from the camera. While the newly imported photos are displayed in the photo well, choose File > Export, and use the Browse button in the Export Items dialog to select a location on the external disk. This way you have a reasonable degree of protection right away, without taking the time to burn CDs. Then update your CD or DVD backup set within a few weeks, and keep the backup discs in a safe place (I use a small fire safe). This way you're immediately protected against computer problems, and if there is a fire or theft, you have no more than a few weeks of photos at risk.

When Should You Erase Your Memory Card?

Erasing your photos from the camera or memory card brings up another safety issue. The easiest approach is to let Photoshop Album delete the photos automatically after importing them. If you want maximum security, though, do *not* enable this option. After you import photos, make an archive disc, export the photos to an external hard drive, or update the backup set. Then you can delete them from the camera or memory card. This way, you always have at least two copies:

- At first, one copy is in the camera or memory card and one is on the hard disk.
- Then, one copy is on the hard disk and one is on your backup or archive disc, or external hard disk.

4 Organizing Your Photos

Organizing undeniably has an element of drudgery for most of us. But once you discover how much fun it is to be able to quickly find whatever photo you're looking for, or just to browse through photos by topic or date, you'll become addicted. If you've tried to keep your photos organized so that you can find the ones you're looking for using folder and file names, you're in for a pleasant surprise when you see how much easier and more effective it is to organize using Photoshop Album.

Photoshop Album provides several ways to organize your photos:

- By date taken
- Using tags
- Using collections
- With notes and captions
- With filenames

You'll find these tools most effective when you use them in concert, keeping in mind how you want to find photos in the future. You can do as much or as little organizing as you want: it's just a means to an end, which is finding the photos you want to view, share, print, or use for creations.

Album also stores information about everything you've done with each photo, such as sharing or printing. You can find photos using this information (see Chapter 5). Because this information is stored automatically, you can always find photos according to how you've used them in the past, even if you've done no tagging, captioning, or other explicit organizing.

Organizing by Date and Time

The most natural way to organize your photos is by the date and time you took them. Digital cameras store the date and time within the image file itself. (For simplicity, in general I'll refer simply to "date," but in all cases this means "date and time.") The capture date in the file is independent of the file-system date (when the file was last modified), so it's preserved even if the photo is edited.

Make sure the date and time on your camera are set correctly—that's all you have to do for Album to automatically organize all your digital camera photos by date. As long as you can remember approximately when a photo was taken, you'll be able to find it easily without doing any explicit organizing at all.

Correcting Incorrect Camera Dates

Whenever you import new photos from your camera, check the date and time to make sure they are correct. If not—for example, if your camera's battery ran out and the camera reset to its default date—all is not lost. Album makes it very easy to correct the date for one photo, or for an entire set of photos.

There are several ways to adjust the date. If you have details on (click the Details box at the bottom of the photo well), the photo well shows the date and time above each photo. Just click the date or time to bring up the Adjust Date and Time dialog and change the date. If you want to adjust multiple photos at the same time, select them first and then click the date or time of any of them. The adjustment options (**Figure 4.1**) allow you to choose from several different ways of changing the dates. If you don't have details on, you can still access this dialog by selecting one or more photos and choosing Edit > Adjust Date and Time.

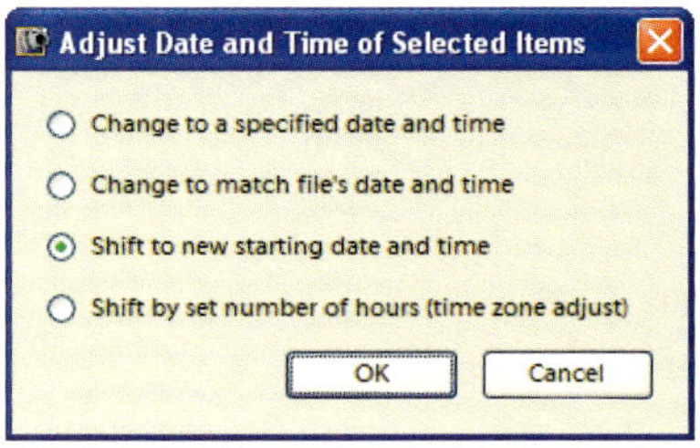

Figure 4.1 If you select multiple photos and click any of their dates or times, you get these choices for adjusting the dates. The third choice is not available if only a single photo is selected.

Camera date that's not set

If you didn't set the camera date, then the date and time will be entirely wrong, but the relative time—the difference in time from one photo to the next—will be accurate, as long as the camera's clock was running. You can take advantage of this fact to correct the entire batch with a single operation:

1. Select all the photos in the batch.
2. In the adjustment options dialog, select "Shift to new starting date and time," and click OK.
3. In the Set Date and Time dialog, enter the date and time of the *earliest* photo in the batch, and click OK (**Figure 4.2**).

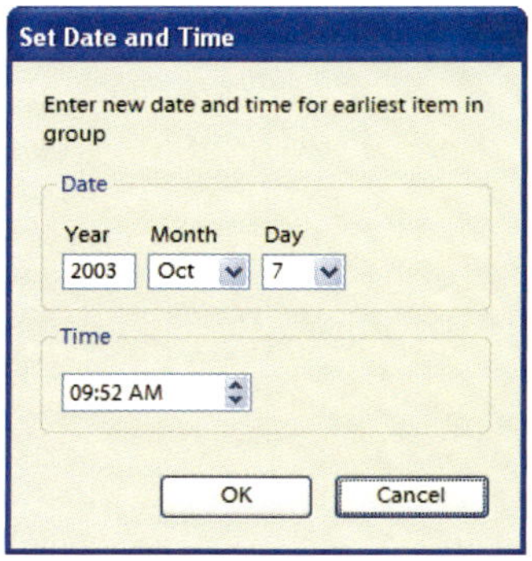

Figure 4.2 If your camera's clock was set incorrectly, use the third option in Figure 4.1 and then enter the date and time of the earliest photo in the group in the Set Date and Time dialog. All the photos will be adjusted to maintain the same relative times.

Album adjusts the date and time of all the photos in the batch, maintaining the time gaps between them.

Pictures in a different time zone

When I travel, I never remember to change the time on my camera to match the time zone that I'm in. Fortunately, Photoshop Album provides an easy way to fix this:

1. Select all the photos you took in a particular time zone.
2. In the adjustment options dialog, select "Shift by set number of hours (time zone adjust)" and click OK.

(continued)

3. In the Time Zone Adjust dialog, enter the number of hours (and direction) between the time zone for which the camera was set and the one where the photos were taken, and click OK (**Figure 4.3**). (For example, if your camera is on California time and you take pictures in New York, adjust the time by 3 hours ahead.)

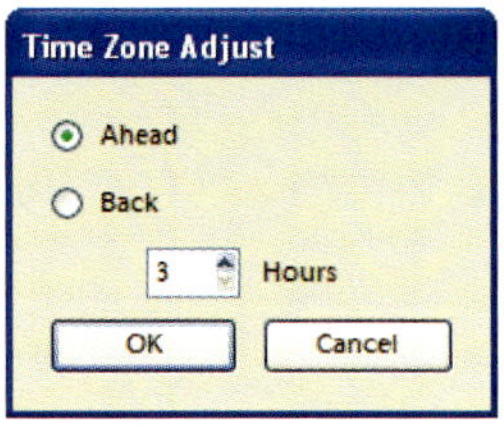

Figure 4.3 The Time Zone Adjust dialog makes it easy to correct a group of photos taken in a time zone other than the one for which the camera's clock is set.

Album will add the time offset to all the photos in the batch, making them match the time zone in which the photos were taken.

Dating Scanned Photos

When you scan a lot of pictures (and have to figure out when each was taken), it really makes you appreciate the luxury of having all your digital camera pictures automatically date-stamped.

If you're scanning photos directly into Photoshop Album, it's often easiest to set the date immediately after scanning each photo, when notes from the back of the photo or other sources are likely to be handy.

You can also scan in a large batch of photos without worrying about dates, and then go back and date them separately or in groups. If the photos are in chronological order when you scan them, they will also be in order when you import them into Album (but without the correct dates, of course, since you're getting the date that you scanned the photo, not when you took it).

To correct a date, just click it in the photo well (if you have details on), or select the photo and choose Edit > Adjust Date and Time. If you have many photos taken at about the same time, you may want to select the entire batch and set them to the same date. You can leave the time—and even the day of the month or the month itself—as "unknown," as the section "Using unknown dates" describes.

Different Dates in Different Programs

Having the correct dates on your photos is crucial to making the most of Photoshop Album. Photos from your digital camera have capture dates, but scanned photos and some others might not. Dates you see in Windows and elsewhere might not be the same as those you see in Album. To understand these differences and how to adjust for them, you need to know a little about how photo dates are stored.

If you look at the date of a photo file using Windows, you'll see the date it was last modified. If you've edited or otherwise modified the photo, that won't be the date the picture was taken. Fortunately, Album still knows the capture date and time, because they're stored in the photo file as metadata (information about the photo, which includes camera settings).

There is a standard format for metadata information called EXIF (Exchangeable Image File format; see Chapter 5). If there is no EXIF data, such as in a scanned photo, Album will normally use the Windows file-system modification date and time (although you can disable that behavior in Album's preferences, if you'd rather that Album identify photos without capture dates as "unknown").

If you change the date or time of a photo in Album, it updates the EXIF metadata so that programs using EXIF dates, such as Photoshop's file browser, will reflect the changes you made in Album. (If Album is unable to write the date to the file—for example, if the file is write-protected or on a CD—you'll still be able to change it, but Album will store the new date only in your catalog. In this case, other programs won't see the modified date.)

If you're capturing video clips, be sure to leave Album's Preferences set to Use Date File Was Last Modified if No EXIF Date Found. Video clips don't have EXIF dates, so if you disable this option, video clip dates will be "unknown."

Photos you scan at home generally have no metadata dates or other EXIF data, so Album uses the file-modification date. If you change the date in Album, EXIF metadata is added to the photo file. From that point forward, that photo has separate capture and file-modification dates.

Scanned photos you get on CDs from film processors may have metadata dates in them, but the date will generally be when the film was processed, not when the photo was taken. For these photos, you can adjust the dates to reflect when the pictures were taken.

Using unknown dates

Sometimes you just won't know when a photo was taken. If it's a recent photo, you might know the month but not the day, or the day but not the time. For older photos, you may know the year but not the month.

By default, scanned photos are dated with the *file-modification date*—either the date they were scanned or the date they were last edited. If this date is close to the date when the picture was taken, you may not want to bother correcting it.

If you want scanned photos in which you have not corrected the date to reflect that fact, you can change Album's Preferences (Edit > Preferences > Files, and deselect Use Date File Was Last Modified if No EXIF Date Found) so that the program will simply mark the date as "unknown" if the file doesn't contain a metadata date (see the sidebar "Different Dates in Different Programs"). Then you can work on replacing the unknown dates with correct ones—or at least good guesses—as you have time.

***Tip** If you change preferences to mark dates as "unknown" if there is no metadata date, then video clips from your camera may be marked as having unknown dates. If so, you can select those clips, choose Edit > Adjust Date and Time, and choose the "Change to match file's date and time" option in the Adjust Date and Time dialog.*

You can also manually set all or any part of the date and time as unknown (**Figure 4.4**). You can set the date and leave the time unknown (such as 11/1/1955); or set the month but not the date (such as November 1955); or the year but not the month (1955). The time must remain unknown if any part of the date is unknown.

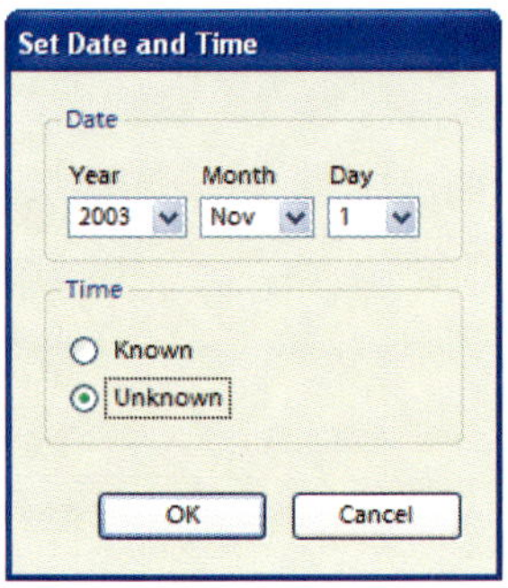

Figure 4.4 You can set the year, month, day, or time as unknown, which is especially useful for scanned photos.

Click the Unknown radio button to make the time unknown. To make the year, month, or day unknown, just select "??" from the pop-up list for that field. You need to set this only for the largest unknown time unit, and the others will follow; for example, if you set the month to unknown, then Album automatically sets the day of the month and the time to unknown.

You cannot, unfortunately, specify a range of months or years; there's no way to set the date as "spring 1999," "March–April 2002," or "1944–1948." You can work around this limitation to some degree by using a date at the start of the desired range and then adding a tag or caption to the photo that provides more information about the date range.

Organizing with Tags: Power and Simplicity

Photoshop Album's visual tags provide an easy, effective tool for organizing all your photos. You can think of each tag as a note written on the back of the photo—with the tremendous added benefit that you can instantly find all photos with any tag, or any combination of tags.

Tags are a lot like keywords, which you may have used in other programs. Tags have a number of advantages, however:

- They're visual, so they're easier to recognize.
- You can apply them to photos simply by dragging and dropping them.
- Tags can carry their own metadata (information about the tag), such as a description of a person, place, or event.

Tagging your photos takes only a few minutes if you do it each time you import a new batch of photos. If you're starting with a large set of photos you've imported from your hard disk, tagging them may take awhile, but this effort will pay off when you want to find photos later. You don't have to do it all at once; you can work on it at your leisure. And it provides a great excuse for browsing through and enjoying all those old photos.

When you've tagged some but not all of your photos, you can view just the untagged ones by choosing Find > Untagged Items.

Tagging Basics

Working with tags is easy, once you get the hang of it. This section guides you through the basic operations so that you're ready to design your tag set to match your needs.

Making tags

Here are the basic operations for making tags:

- To display the Tags pane, click the Organize tab, and then click the Tags tab within the Organize pane, if it is not already selected.
- To make a new tag, category, or subcategory, click the New button at the top left of the Tags pane and select the type of item you want to make (**Figure 4.5**).

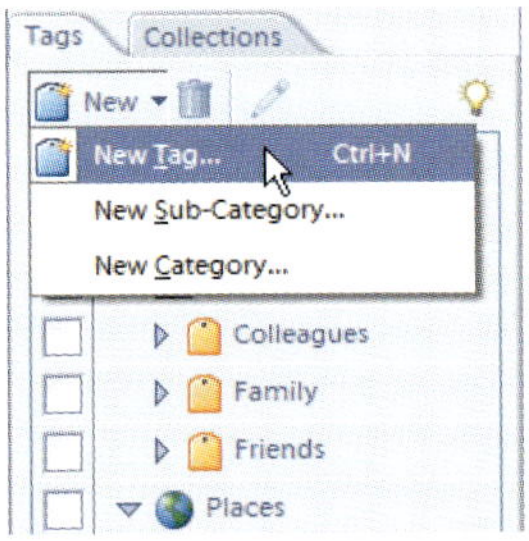

Figure 4.5 To make a new tag, subcategory, or category, click the Organize tab and then the Tags tab (if it's not already selected); in the Tags pane click the New button and choose what you want to make.

- When making a new tag, you can put it in any category or subcategory in the Create Tag dialog (**Figure 4.6**).

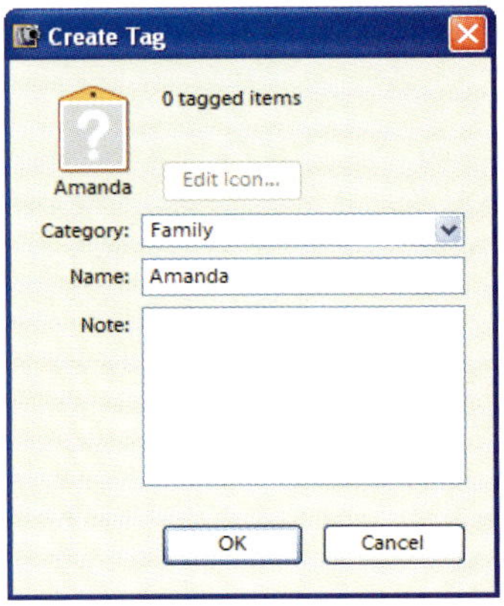

Figure 4.6 To make a new tag, choose the category or subcategory and enter the tag's name in the Create Tag dialog.

- To more quickly create a new tag in an existing category or subcategory, right-click the category or subcategory and choose Create New Tag.
- To modify a tag name or the photo used for its icon, click the tag and then click the pencil (edit) button at the top of the Tags pane, or right-click the tag and choose Edit. (See the following section for details on changing an icon's photo.)
- To delete a tag, subcategory, or category, select it and then click the trash can button at the top of the Tags pane, or right-click it and choose Delete.

Choosing the icons for tags

To make the most of a visual tag, it's important to select a good image to represent it. When you first apply a new tag to a photo, that photo becomes the icon for the tag.

***Tip** If you select multiple photos and tag them as a group, the photo onto which you drag the tag becomes the tag's icon.*

This default behavior rarely yields a good icon, however. You may want to choose another photo, and often (especially for people tags) you might want to zoom in on a specific area of the photo to use for the icon. The icon doesn't have a lot of pixels, and you have to choose the image carefully to get a good visual representation. For people, tightly cropped faces are best. **Figure 4.7** shows some good and poor icons.

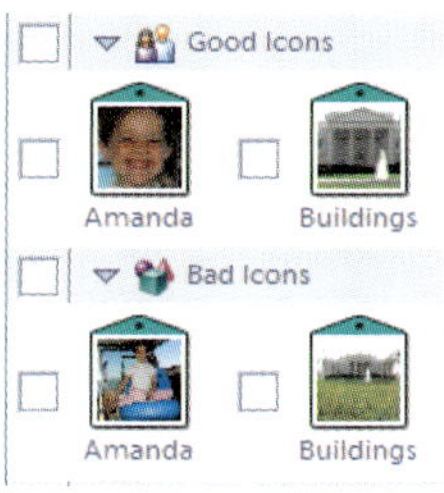

Figure 4.7 The difference between good and bad icons is often just in how tightly you've cropped the photo's most recognizable feature.

You can only use a photo to which the tag has been attached as its icon, so first you need to tag the photo you want to use. To change the icon,

1. Right-click the tag and choose Edit Tag.
2. Click the Edit Icon button in the Edit Tag dialog.
3. To choose a different photo, in the Edit Tag Icon dialog use the left and right arrow buttons next to the Find button to cycle through all the photos with this

(continued)

tag (**Figure 4.8**). If there are lots of them and you want a faster way to scroll through them, click the Find button and you'll get a scrolling window with thumbnails of all the photos with this tag.

4. Once you've chosen the photo, crop it to the smallest clearly recognizable square region.

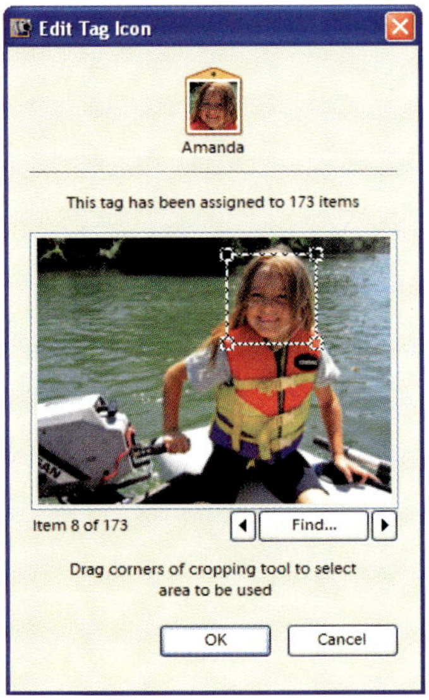

Figure 4.8 When editing the icon photo area, drag the corners to make the cropping box smaller, or drag any point inside the box to move it.

Choosing the icon for a new category

If you make a new category, you can choose from among a selection of graphic symbols to represent that category. You cannot choose a photo or an image of your own. These icons appear in the photo well to show what categories of tags you have applied to each photo.

You'll be presented with a choice of icons in the Create New Category dialog when you make a new category (**Figure 4.9**). If you want to change the icon later, right-click the category and choose Edit.

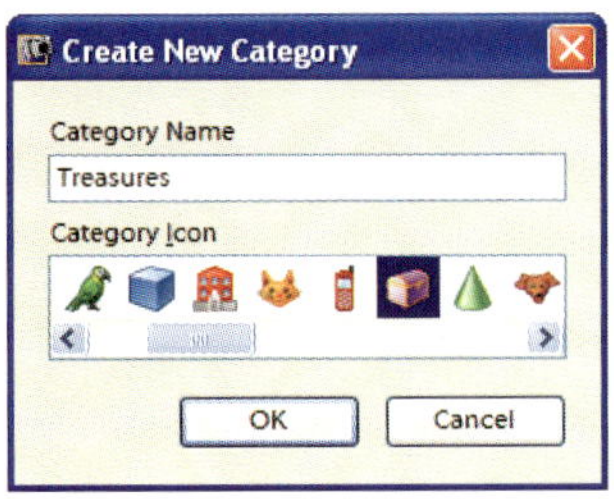

Figure 4.9 When making a new category, you can choose the symbol that will represent it, as well as its name.

Working with the Tags pane

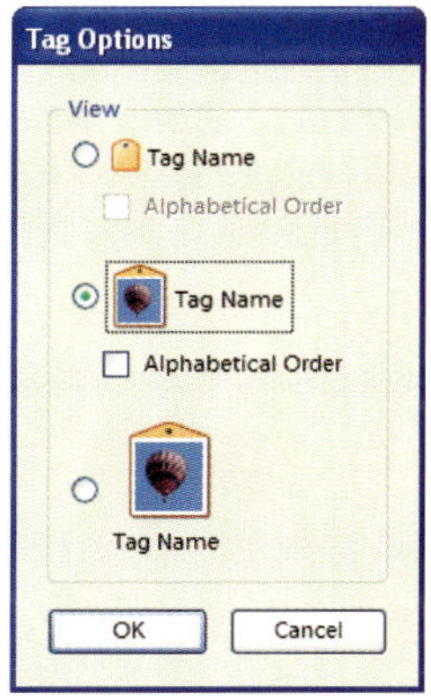

Figure 4.10 **In the Tag Options dialog you can choose how to arrange the Tags pane.**

You can control how the Tags pane is laid out so that it suits your needs. The best configuration depends on how many tags you have, how they are structured, how recognizable your tag icon photos are, and your personal preferences. Try each of the settings until you find the one you like best.

Access the Tags pane options via View > Tag Viewing Options (**Figure 4.10**).

You can choose from three sizes of tags. The smallest does not show any photo icons (**Figure 4.11**). This is the best choice if you identify the tags by their names more than by the photos.

The medium tag view shows a small photo icon but still leaves room for almost as much text (**Figure 4.12**). The Tags pane is less dense, however, because of the size of the icons, so you can't see as many tags at one time.

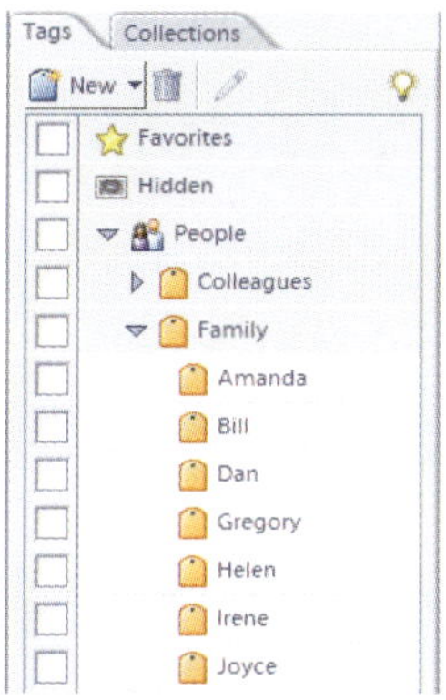

Figure 4.11 **The small tag view gives the most room for names but shows no photo icons.**

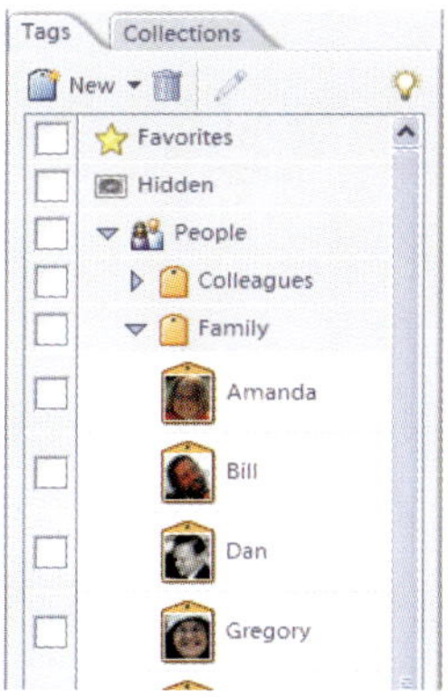

Figure 4.12 **The medium tag view is a good compromise, with lots of room for the names but also a small photo icon.**

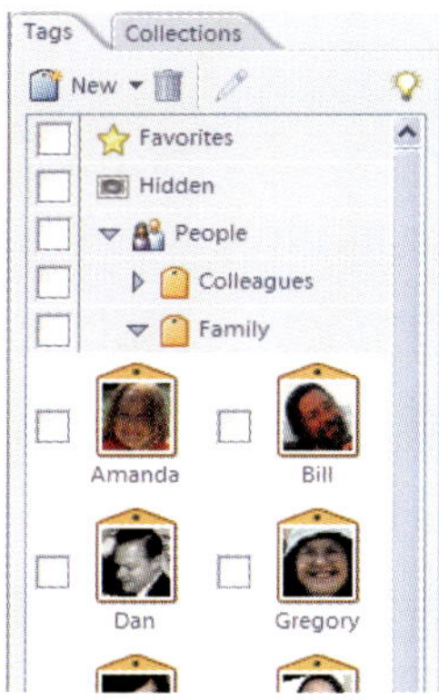

Figure 4.13 **The large tag view emphasizes the photo icons more than the names.**

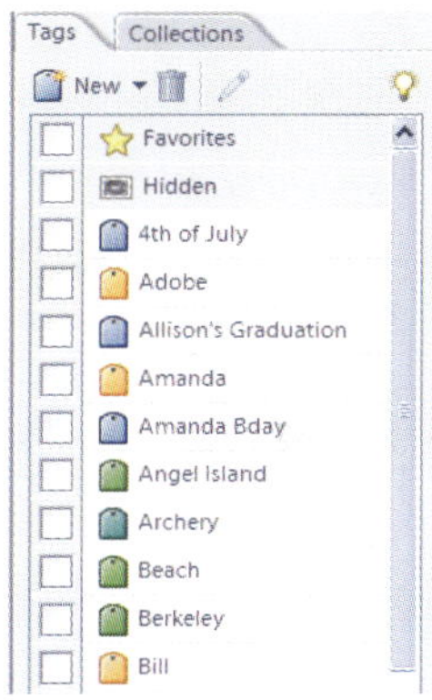

Figure 4.14 **If you select the alphabetical option, all the tags are listed together without categories or subcategories.**

The large-icon view is best if you use the tag icon more than the name to choose a tag (**Figure 4.13**). It puts the icons in two rows, which allows larger icons but leaves less room for text. (You can always see the name of an icon by hovering your pointer over it.)

The triangle to the left of a tag category or subcategory allows you to expand or collapse that group. Just click the triangle to expand, and click again to collapse.

Tip ***You can expand all the categories and subcategories with a single action via View > Expand All Tags (or Alt-Ctrl-X), and collapse them all via View > Collapse All Tags (or Alt-Ctrl-T). This is a quick way to dive into the full list of tags and then retreat back to the broad overview.***

For the small and medium views, you can also enable alphabetical ordering via the check box in the Tag Viewing Options dialog. The Tags pane then dispenses with categories and subcategories altogether, and sorts all tags, regardless of category, into a single alphabetical order (**Figure 4.14**). This is the best choice if you have few tags (probably less than 25) and don't want to bother with categories or subcategories.

Attaching tags to photos

To attach tags to photos, use drag and drop:

- To tag a single photo with a single tag, click and hold the tag, drag it to the photo, and release the mouse button.
- To attach multiple tags to a single photo, select the first tag by clicking it. Then Ctrl-click additional tags to select them. After they're all selected, click any one of them and drag the group to the photo.
- To tag multiple photos at the same time, select all the photos you want to tag in the photo well, using Ctrl-click (to add individual photos to the selection) and Shift-click (to select all photos in a range). Then select one or more tags, and drag to any of the selected photos.

You can also attach categories and subcategories to photos, just like you can with tags. You could, for example, attach the People category to a photo with unknown people in it. The utility of this is limited, however; you can then find all People photos, but you can't find only photos with the category tag but no individual tag.

It is better, in this example, to make an Unknown tag within the People category and use that instead of using the category as a tag. With this approach, you can search on the Unknown tag if you're looking only for unknown people (perhaps to try to identify and tag them). Note that category and subcategory icons are generic and you cannot choose a photo to represent them.

Viewing tags on a photo

To see what tags are on a photo,

- Be sure you have details on. You'll then see icons representing tags in the photo well.
- In small thumbnail views, there is a single tag icon on the bottom-right corner of the photo (**Figure 4.15**). Hover your pointer over this icon for a moment, and the tool tip will show the tag names.

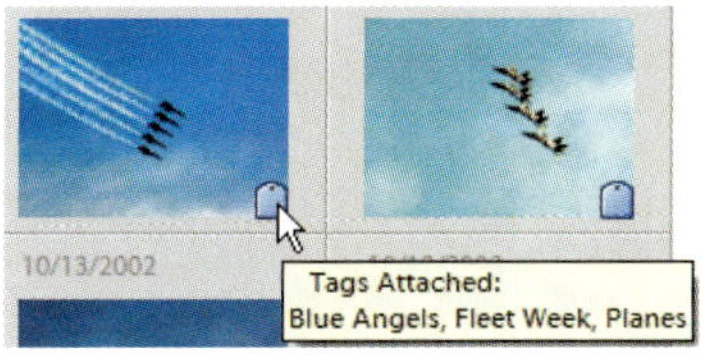

Figure 4.15 In small thumbnail views, you can pause your pointer over the generic tag icon to see the tags attached.

- In larger thumbnail views, tag icons showing which categories of tags have been applied appear below each photo (**Figure 4.16**). Pause your pointer over the category icon to see the tag names.

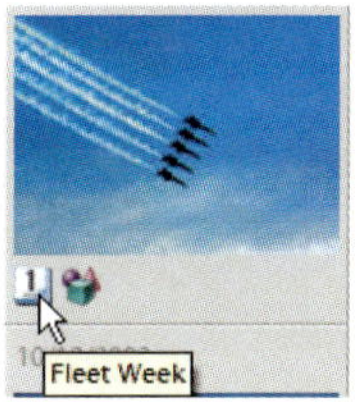

Figure 4.16 In larger thumbnail views, hover over the category icon to see the tags attached.

- In any view, whether details are on or not, you can see the tags by displaying the Properties palette (**Figure 4.17**). Select the photo and then click the Show or Hide Properties button at the bottom of the photo well, or right-click the photo and choose Properties. Then click the Tags button at the top of the Properties palette.

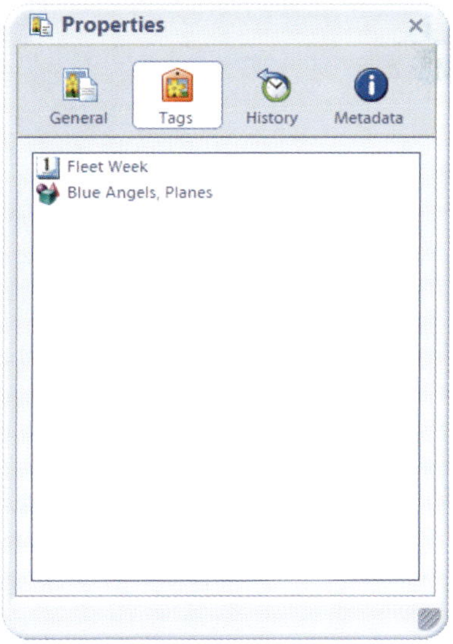

Figure 4.17 You can see all the tags applied to any photo by selecting the Tags view of the Properties palette.

Using tags to find photos

Finding photos with tags is discussed in depth in the next chapter, but the basics are very simple:

- Double-click any tag to perform a new search for all the photos with that tag.
- Click the check box to the left of a tag to add more tags to the search criteria.

Now that you know the basics, you can start playing with tags. But before you do much tagging, it's a good idea to think about what tags you want, and how you want to organize them into categories and subcategories.

Designing Your Tag Set

You have nearly complete freedom to design your tag set. The standard categories of People (with subcategories of Family and Friends), Places, Events, and Other are preinstalled, but you can rename or delete them. You can add as many categories, subcategories, and tags as you'd like.

There is one restriction: you can't put a subcategory within a subcategory, so you can't have a hierarchy deeper than category > subcategory > tag. This can be inconvenient if you want to use a complex organization, but with a little creativity it's easy to work around.

Keep in mind that you can use tags in combination with each other, and with dates. For example, you can have a Zoo tag, a Los Angeles tag, and a San Francisco tag, and use these in combination instead of having Los Angeles Zoo and San Francisco Zoo tags. And you can use a single Greg's Birthday tag for all years, rather than Greg's 10th Birthday, Greg's 11th Birthday, and so on, since you can use the date in combination with the tag to locate photos.

You're likely to find that with experience you'll change your mind about how you want your tags arranged. Don't worry—it's generally easy to rearrange them, as described later in this section. It will save you some time, though, in the long run, to read the tips in this section before you do a lot of tagging.

Using people tags

You'll probably use a lot of people tags, since the people in your photos are probably what you look for the most. The simplest approach is to make a tag for each person in your family in the Family subcategory, and a tag for each friend in the Friends subcategory. If you take pictures of lots of people, though, the lists of tags can get pretty long. There are two approaches to keeping the number of tags in each subcategory down:

- You can use a single tag for a group of people (such as the Smiths). This is especially useful if there are lots of people in that group but you don't take many pictures of any of them.
- You can delete the Family subcategory and create multiple subcategories for different parts of the family (such as Our Family, Grandparents, Grandchildren, In-Laws, and Suzy's Family).

In the Friends subcategory, you may want to have some generic tags to cover friends of your children (such as Amanda's Friends, Gregory's Friends) or friends from a particular part of your life (such as Garden Club, Coworkers). If you want to have individual tags for the people in these groups, don't make tags for the groups in the Friends subcategory; instead, create in the People category a new subcategory for each group, and put tags for each person in those subcategories.

Using place tags

Often, you'll want to find pictures according to where you took them. Place tags make this easy.

There are various ways you can think about place tags, depending on how rigorous you want to be:

- Put a place tag on every photo, so that each is identified with where it was taken. This is usually easy to do, since you can tag lots of photos at a time (unless your place tags are very specific).
- Or you can put place tags only on photos that are actually *of* a particular place. For example, you might put a San Francisco tag on pictures of the San Francisco skyline but not on pictures of a birthday party at a friend's house in San Francisco.

The first approach is simpler, because you don't have to think very much about whether a photo should get a place tag or not. It doesn't, however, give you a way to find just those pictures that are of a place, as distinguished from those that happen to have been taken at that place.

If you don't travel much and take most of your photos of people, you may want to have just a few place tags directly in the Places category. At the other extreme, you may want to have subcategories for each state or each country, with tags for all the places within them.

There's no need to be terribly consistent; for example, I have a subcategory for California, because I take pictures at lots of places there; I have another subcategory for Other U.S., because I haven't taken photos at many locations in the United States outside of California. I have subcategories for Mexico, the Caribbean, Asia, and Europe, because I've gone on trips to several places in each of those regions—but I put photos that I take anywhere else in a Rest of World subcategory.

I also have a Places subcategory called Special Places, which I use for locations that don't have so much to do with geography. In this category, I have tags for places such as Home, Beach, Office, and Zoo. I use the Beach tag for any beach and the Zoo tag for any zoo. If the beach or zoo is not the one I usually go to, I'll also apply a tag for the city or country it is in.

If you travel to a country where you're visiting lots of different cities or regions, it's usually a good idea to make a new subcategory for that place. Then you can make tags for each city or region. Or if you're really detail oriented and want to go a step further, you can move out of the Places category entirely and give the country its own top-level category. Then you can have subcategories for regions of the country and tags for specific places within those regions.

Using event tags

Most people take lots of photos at special events, such as birthday parties, Christmas, and so forth. Creating a tag for each event makes it easy to locate these photos later. Note that you can also find photos using the calendar, so you may not need to tag events such as Christmas. It can be useful, though—you might, for example, want to tag tree-trimming photos from mid-December as Christmas.

Depending on how many event tags you have, you may or may not want to put them in subcategories; if you have just a few, all the tags can go directly in the Events category. I divide my events into four subcategories:

- Holidays, such as Hanukkah and New Year's
- Parties, such as Greg's Birthday and Amanda's Birthday
- Vacations, such as Baja Sailing Trip and Caribbean Cruise
- Other Events, such as Circus and Renaissance Faire

Note that there is often some overlap between places and events. Vacation tags, for example, can be eliminated if you just use the place tags for where the vacation was. I tend to use both place and vacation tags, though, so I can easily find all the photos of a place, regardless of whether I was there on vacation or for some other reason, as well as all the photos from a vacation trip, even if it was in multiple places.

***Tip** Don't put dates in your tag names, such as Delta Trip 2003. When you're finding photos, you can use a date range in addition to the tag, so you can find the photos from a particular trip. This reduces the number of tags you need, and it also makes it easy to find the photos from all the trips, if you did a similar trip in multiple years (though place tags can also fulfill this function).*

"Other" tags and new categories

The Other category is a catchall for subcategories and tags that don't fit into people, place, or event categories. You may want to delete this category and replace it with more specific ones of your own choosing; or you can leave it, and put everything in a subcategory within Other.

I chose to delete the Other category and add several new categories, such as

- Animals, with tags for Cats, Dogs, Horses, Cattle, and so on
- Interests, with tags (or subcategories, if I want to further break it down with tags) such as Boats, Cars, Sunsets, and Landscapes
- Misc., which is my catchall for tags that I can't figure out where else to put, like House Remodeling and Gregory's Projects

There are countless other categories, subcategories, and tags you may want to create, depending on your particular needs and interests. For example,

- If you're a bird-watcher, you may want a Birds category, with subcategories for each family and tags for each species.
- If you're a classic car enthusiast, you could have a Classic Cars category, with subcategories for each car manufacturer and tags for each model.
- You can make a Type category or subcategory, with such tags as Scans, Panoramas, Black-and-White, and Experimental.

Restructuring your tags

After you've been tagging photos for a while, you'll probably have new ideas about how you'd like to organize your tags. Fortunately, it's easy to do. You can simply drag and drop subcategories into different categories, or tags from one subcategory or category to another. You can rename any tag, subcategory, or category by right-clicking it and selecting Edit.

If a tag has too many items and you want to make it more specific, first find all the photos with that tag. Then make new tags and apply them selectively to the appropriate photos.

If a category has too many subcategories in it, create a new category and drag some of the subcategories to it. If a subcategory has too many tags in it, break it into multiple subcategories and drag each tag to the appropriate subcategory.

To promote a subcategory to a category so that you can create subcategories within it, first create the new category. Then drag all the tags from the old subcategory to the new category, and delete the old subcategory. Make new subcategories within the new category, and sort the tags into the new subcategories.

Converting a Folder Organization to Tags

If you've already organized your photos into folders, you can convert this organization into tags to take full advantage of Photoshop Album. If you have a lot of folders, this can take some time, but it's well worth it for the superior searching abilities you'll have when you're done.

The major limitation in converting folder structures to tags is that tags have a three-level hierarchy: category, subcategory, and tag. The hierarchy of folder structures, on the other hand, is essentially unlimited. So if you've created a folder structure like California > Northern California > San Francisco > Waterfront, you'll have to modify things a bit to create a tag structure to represent it.

In this example, you could make a category for California (instead of putting it under Places), skip the Northern California division, and create a subcategory for San Francisco. Within that subcategory, you'd have a Waterfront tag.

To make the conversion, switch the photo well to the Folder Location arrangement (via the pop-up menu at the lower left). The photo well will then show photos grouped by folder, with a banner for each folder (**Figure 4.18**). You'll probably find it best to switch to the smallest thumbnail size.

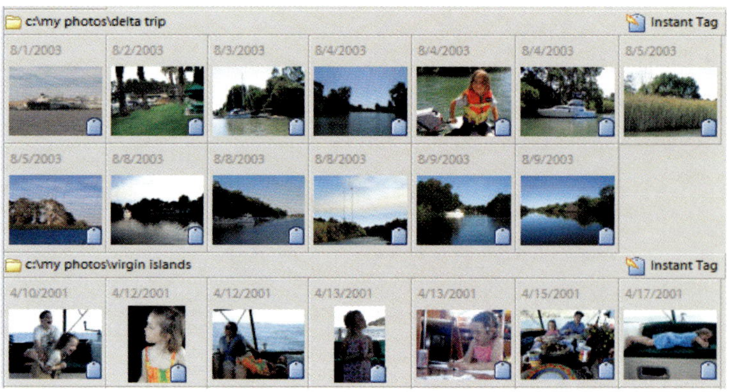

Figure 4.18 **In the Folder Location arrangement, click in the banner to select all the photos in the folder, or on the Instant Tag button to automatically create a tag and apply it.**

If you have an existing tag you want to apply to all the photos in a folder, click anywhere in the banner (except on or to the right of the Instant Tag button). This selects all the photos in that folder, and you can then drag a tag onto any of them to tag them all.

If you want to make a new tag, click the Instant Tag button at the right of the banner. All the photos in the folder are selected automatically, and the Create and Apply New Tag dialog appears (**Figure 4.19**). The name of the tag is set by default to the name of the folder. You may want to edit that, especially if you want to include information from the names of folders higher in the hierarchy.

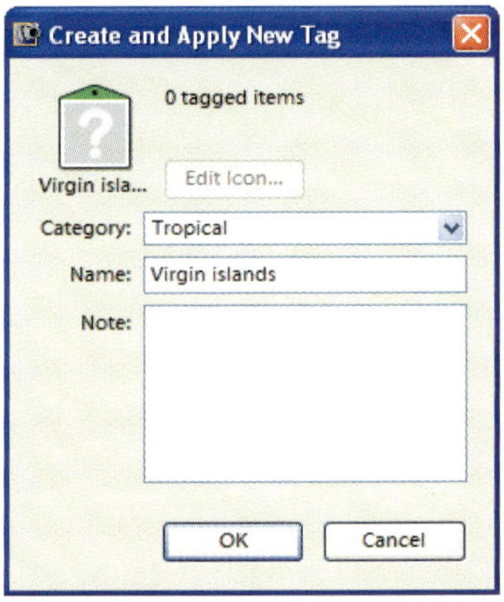

Figure 4.19 The Create and Apply New Tag dialog allows you to specify the name for the tag and select what category and subcategory it should go in.

Repeat this process for each folder, and you will have converted your folder organization to tags. Note that your folder structure remains intact. If you apply the new tags to photos in different folders, the photos will of course remain wherever they are located and will not be moved. Once you've switched to an Album-centric workflow, the folder structure will cease to matter.

If your folders are organized by date only, and the photos are from a digital camera (so they have capture-date metadata in them), then there's no point in converting them to tags; you can simply find the photos by date using the timeline or calendar. If, however, you have scanned photos that you have organized into folders by date, you should convert this folder organization into date metadata. To do so, follow this procedure:

1. Click the banner to select all the photos in the folder.

2. Click the date of any of the photos (assuming you have details turned on).

(continued)

3. Choose the "Change to a specified date and time" option in the resulting dialog and click OK.

4. Enter the date in the Set Date and Time dialog. If the folder is named March 1962, for example, set the year to 1962, the month to March, and the day to "?."

Using the Favorites and Hidden Tags

There are two tags that are always present and perform special tasks: Favorites and Hidden (**Figure 4.20**). These tags make it easier to sort out the best photos from the rest, and to hide photos that don't quite make the grade. You apply these tags just like any other. They exist outside any category, however, and you cannot rename or delete them.

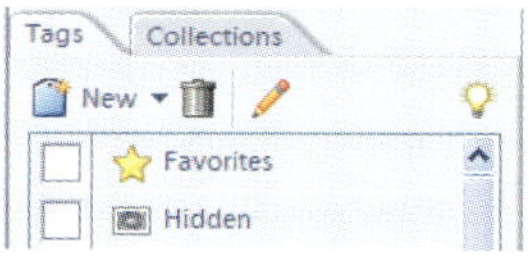

Figure 4.20 The Favorites and Hidden tags always appear at the top of the Tags pane.

Digital cameras enable and encourage us to take lots of pictures, which has a dark side—there are a lot of pictures to sort through! When you're looking at your pictures later, you don't really want to view the lesser versions of a certain shot. You can eliminate the poor shots from the photo well by attaching the Hidden tag to them, or make it easy to find the best ones by applying the Favorites tag to those. There are many different ways to use these tags, depending on your personal preferences.

Photos with the Hidden tag do not appear in the photo well *unless* you use the Hidden tag as part of the search criteria. Photos that have the Hidden tag applied are the only ones that don't appear in the photo well when no search or filter is active (for example, at startup or when you click Show All).

***Note** The Hidden tag is not intended to keep photos confidential. There is no password protection, and the photos remain visible in Windows, just like any other photo. If you're looking for ways to really hide photos, you'll have to find a method outside Album.*

The Favorites tag acts much like any other tag in a search: if you don't include Favorites in the search, you'll see all photos whether they have this tag or not, and if you do include it, you'll see only photos that have it (and any other tags you've included in the search).

I use these tags the most when I'm reviewing photos I've just imported. I look at each photo (generally using the maximum-size view, which fills the window with one photo), and I attach the Favorites tag to the best ones and the Hidden tag to the ones that I can probably delete but don't want to send to oblivion quite yet.

***Tip** Use Alt-F1 (mark as Favorite) and Alt-F2 (mark as Hidden) to quickly tag the selected photo. In the maximum-size view a photo is implicitly selected, so you can just use the shortcut keys.*

When you have multiple photos of the same or a similar scene, you can use either the Favorites tag to mark the best one or the Hidden tag to mark all the others. The latter approach gives you a cleaner photo well, since it keeps all the lesser photos from view.

If you are disciplined about marking all the best photos of a certain subject with the Favorites tag (or hiding all the others with the Hidden tag), then you'll be able to quickly sort out the best ones from the rest when you're looking for photos to print, share, or use in creations.

I like marking photos with the Hidden tag instead of deleting them because I'm always concerned that I might find some reason to use that photo. Disk space is cheap, and I'm a pack rat. If you can let go more easily and prefer to keep things clean, you can of course delete photos instead of hiding them. I hide them instead, unless they are clearly useless photos, and periodically I look at all the hidden photos and delete the ones I'm willing to get rid of. (Somehow it's easier to delete them when it has been some time since I've taken them—sort of like letting the leftovers age in the refrigerator before tossing them out.)

To view photos with the Hidden tag, include that tag in the search (by clicking the check box next to it, as with any other tag). If you search only on the Hidden tag (double-click it), all the hidden photos (and only those) will be shown. If you search on both the Hidden tag and one or more other tags, all photos that have the other tag(s) will be shown, whether they have the Hidden tag as well or not.

Moving Tags Between Catalogs

Tags are stored in your catalog, and they are specific to each catalog. There is no direct way to move tags from one catalog to another, but there is a workaround.

If you want to create a new catalog with the same tag set as an existing catalog's, follow these steps:

1. Choose File > Catalog and click the Save As button in the Catalog dialog.

2. Enter the name for the new catalog in the Save Catalog As dialog and click Save.

3. You are now viewing a copy of your catalog. Press Ctrl-A to select all the photos, and then press Delete.

4. Click OK in the deletion-confirmation dialog, but *do not* click the check box to delete the items from the disk.

5. You now have an empty catalog with the same tag set as the catalog you started with.

There is one other way to move tags between catalogs. When you share photos, the tag names (but not their category or subcategory) are embedded in the photo file's metadata. When you import such photos, you'll have the option to import the tags as well (see Chapter 10).

***Note** Using the E-mail share function (Share > E-mail) is the only way to have the tag names embedded in the photo file.*

Organizing with Collections

Photoshop Album provides another primary organizing tool in addition to tags: collections. When you are in the organize view, you can choose to view collections instead of tags simply by clicking the Collections tab (**Figure 4.21**).

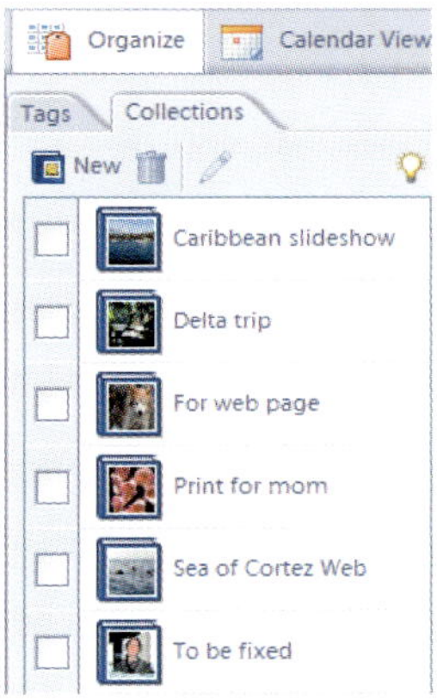

Figure 4.21 If you select the Collections tab, the Organize pane shows collections instead of tags.

Tags are designed to identify features of a photo, such as who is in it and where it was taken; collections are intended to assemble groups of photos for a particular purpose. Collections work a lot like tags, with several important differences:

- You can reorder photos within a collection—this is its key distinguishing feature. (When not in the collection mode, the photo well is always arranged according to the arrangement you've selected, such as Newest First.)
- There is no hierarchy for collections (no categories or subcategories).
- You can view only one collection at a time.

When I return from a party, vacation, or other major picture-taking event, I first tag all the photos. Then I make a collection with a relatively small selection of those photos that I want to share with someone, and rearrange the order if necessary to tell the story best. Later, I can view an instant slide show of the collection, print the photos in it, or use it as the starting point for a creation.

Making Collections

To make a new collection, display the Collections pane (click the Organize tab and the Collections tab) and click New. In the Create Collection dialog, enter the name of the collection, along with a note, if you'd like (**Figure 4.22**).

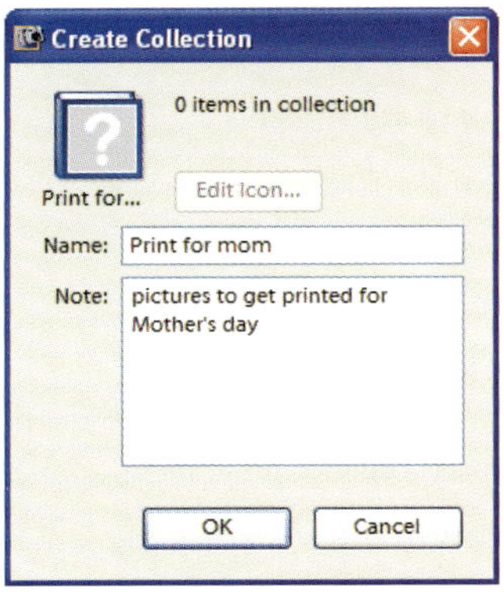

Figure 4.22 **Creating a collection is just like creating a tag.**

To add photos to a collection, drag the collection icon to the photo(s), as you do with tagging, or drag the photos to the collection icon. You can switch to the Tags pane (by clicking the Tags tab), use tags and any other tools to find photos of interest (see Chapter 5 for more on finding photos), and then click back to the Collections pane to add the photos to a collection.

You can also add photos to a collection directly from the photo well, regardless of whether the Tags or Collections pane is displayed. Right-click a photo (or one photo of a multiple selection) and choose Add to Collection. Pick the collection from the submenu, which lists all your collections.

Reordering Photos in Collections

In the collection view, a small number appears in the upper-left corner of each photo to show that the sequence can be changed (**Figure 4.23**). Rearrange the photos by simply dragging and dropping them to get them in the order you want.

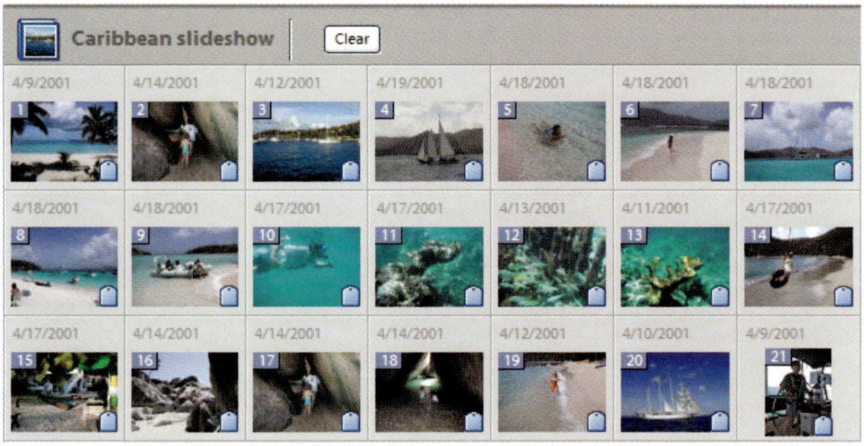

Figure 4.23 When you're viewing a collection, all the photos are numbered and you can drag them around to change their order.

You can drop a photo at a location that doesn't show in the window by dragging the photo to the top or bottom of the window, which will cause the window to scroll. You may find it helpful to use the smallest thumbnail size when rearranging collections so that you can see the maximum number of photos at a time without having to scroll.

Using Captions and Notes

Adding captions and notes helps you remember details about a photo and tell a story with it. When you make a creation (such as an album or slide show), Photoshop Album automatically (if you so choose) shows the captions you've entered next to each photo (see Chapter 8). You can also print captions using the contact sheet layout (see Chapter 9). Captions are limited to 63 characters, so you have to be brief. (This limitation, while admittedly annoying, ensures that all captions fit in the various creation layouts.)

If you want to enter larger amounts of text, use the notes field. The notes field is not printed in creations or contact sheets (in fact, you can't print it at all), but it can hold up to 1,000 characters.

To enter either captions or notes, open the Properties palette by selecting a photo and clicking the Show or Hide Properties button (**Figure 4.24**) at the bottom of the photo well (or select the photo and press Alt-Enter); then select the Properties palette's General pane, if it isn't already selected (**Figure 4.25**).

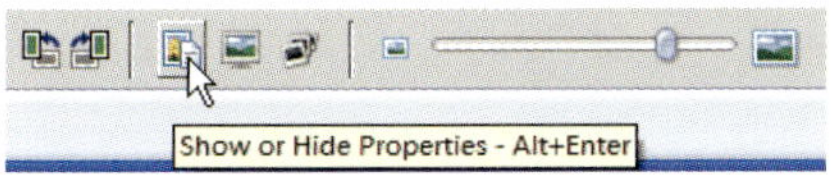

Figure 4.24 To open the Properties palette, select a photo and click the Show or Hide Properties button.

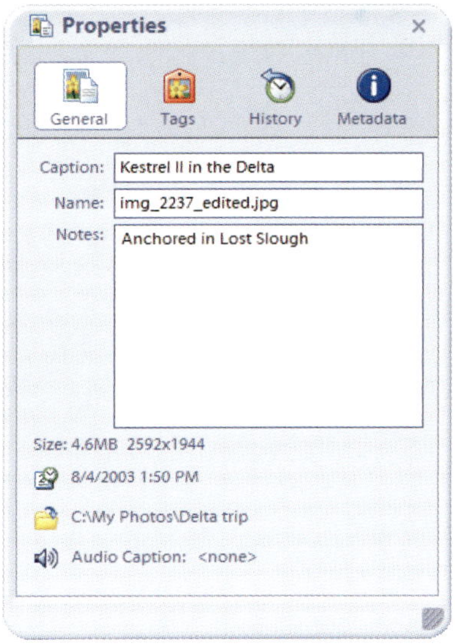

Figure 4.25 You can enter captions and notes in the General pane of the Properties palette.

You can also enter captions in calendar view if you are in the day mode, which you can access by clicking the Day button at the bottom of the window (**Figure 4.26**). Select a photo and enter the caption in the field at the lower-right corner of the window.

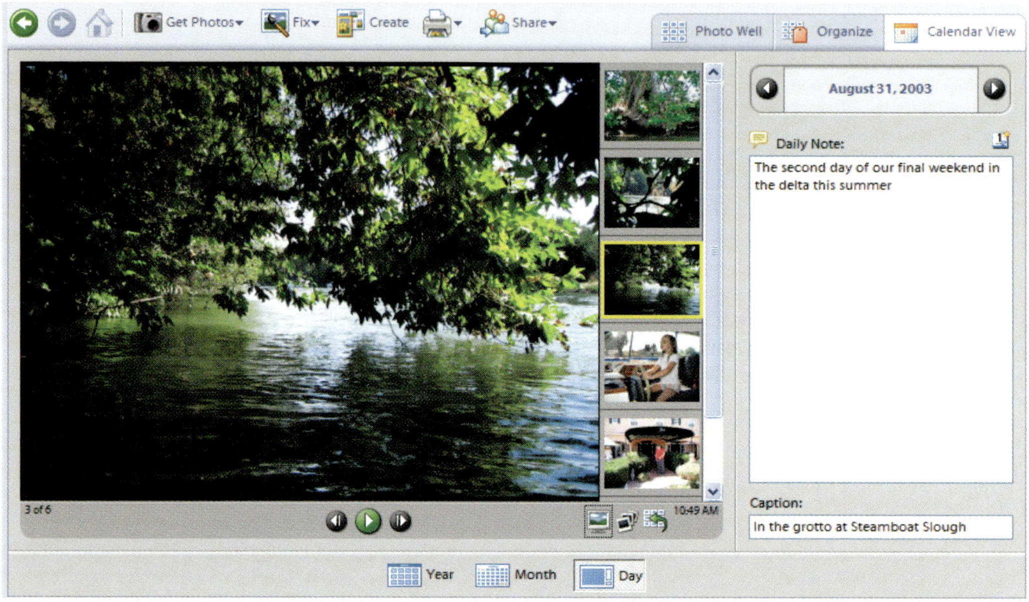

Figure 4.26 **The day mode in the calendar view is the only place where you can enter (or view) daily notes. You can also enter photo captions there.**

Sometimes it's useful to enter the same caption for a group of photos. In the photo well select the photos to which you want to apply the caption, and choose Edit > Add Caption to Selected Items. In the Add Caption to Selected Items dialog you can then enter the caption and choose whether to replace any existing captions (**Figure 4.27**). If you do not select the Replace Existing Captions option, the new caption will apply only to photos that have no caption.

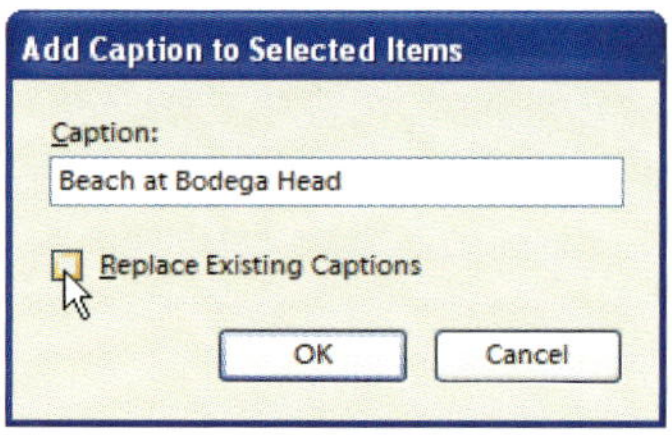

Figure 4.27 **In the Add Caption to Selected Items dialog you can add a caption to several photos at once.**

Strange Text in Your Captions?

Is your camera name or something else unexpectedly showing up in your captions? This is usually a result of using one of the cameras that automatically write information into the caption metadata field in the photo file. They should put this information elsewhere, but they don't, so we have to live with it.

You can fix this in two ways. For photos you have already imported, you can select them, choose Edit > Add Caption to Selected Items, select the Replace Existing Captions option, and leave the caption blank. This will clear out all existing captions on the selected items.

If this repeatedly happens with your camera, choose Edit > Preferences > Files and deselect Import EXIF Caption in the File Options section (**Figure 4.28**). The caption will no longer be read from files that you import. For photos coming from your camera, this is fine. It does mean, however, that if you import photos with legitimate captions in their EXIF caption fields that may have been entered in Photoshop or another program, the captions will not be imported.

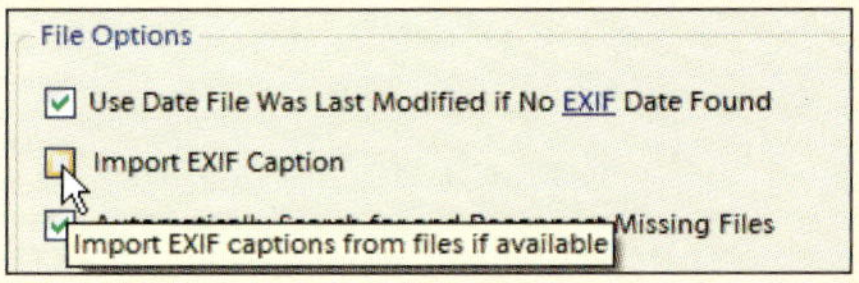

Figure 4.28 If your camera is putting its name into your captions, deselect the Import EXIF Caption option in the Preferences dialog (File pane).

The Daily Note field in the calendar day mode is different from the Notes field in the Properties palette. This note is not associated with any specific photo but with the day itself. Thus, there can be only one such note per day. This is a good place to keep photo diary or travel notes for the day, to which you can refer later when tagging the photos, writing captions, or trying to remember just where you were and why you took those pictures. Unfortunately, you cannot print the day notes or use them in creations.

You can find photos by their captions and notes (but not daily notes) by choosing Find > By Caption or Note (see Chapter 5). You can use this to find photos according to details you may not have represented in your tags. For example, you might use a generic Friends tag for friends who you don't often photograph. If you put their names in the captions or notes, then you can find photos of them by using Find by Caption or Note.

Having made it this far, you've probably realized that one of the goals of Album is to create a photo environment that saves you from having to worry about Windows' file system. You can see all your photos in the photo well, regardless of where they're stored on your disk. After you've found them in the photo well, either by checking their dates or by using tags or other methods (see Chapter 5), you can fix them, print them, share them, and make creations with them without ever having to deal with files or folders.

As soon as you step outside of Album, though, you're in the Windows file system, with folders and files as the only way to navigate. When you need to use photos in other programs, you'll find that Photoshop Album has several methods to help you do this, including drag and drop and exporting. You can also export copies to a temporary folder, as described later in "Organizing folders for exported photos," which makes it easy to find files regardless of where the original photos are located.

To make the most of Album, it's important to reconsider any habits you may have developed about naming photo files and folders. Now that you have Album's tools at your disposal, it isn't worth giving descriptive names to the folders or photos. If you organize your photos into folders or rename them, you'll duplicate a lot of effort that's better spent tagging your photos in Album. In most cases, it really doesn't matter what you name your folders or files; however, Album makes it easy to change filenames or move files, individually or in batches, should you need to.

***Tip** You may want to enter descriptive filenames when sharing photos (see "Renaming Files," below). If you're giving someone a CD slide show or emailing a PDF slide show, the filenames won't generally matter. But if you email individual photo files, it's helpful to name them descriptively so that the recipient will know what they are.*

Photoshop Album works most smoothly if you don't make changes in Windows but instead use the functions built into Photoshop Album. It can adjust itself to cope with most changes in filenames or locations you may make in Windows, but you'll have the fewest surprises if you understand the implications of each kind of change you might make.

Exporting Files

To use photos in another application, such as a Web authoring tool or a page-layout program, the easiest approach is to export them from Photoshop Album first.

You always have the option of using Windows to find your photo files directly, but it's more convenient to use Photoshop Album to find and export the files. Doing so allows you to use Album to select the photos you want, and you have all its finding tools at your disposal. When you export photos, Photoshop Album generates a set of duplicate files in a location you choose, so they're easy to find in Windows, even if the original files are scattered across a number of different folders.

To export photos, first find the ones you want in Photoshop Album. You can search by date, tags, filename, caption, or any of the other criteria described in Chapter 5. When you've selected the photos you want, choose File > Export. The Export Selected Items dialog (**Figure 4.29**) allows you to control how the files are reformatted, if at all, and where they are stored.

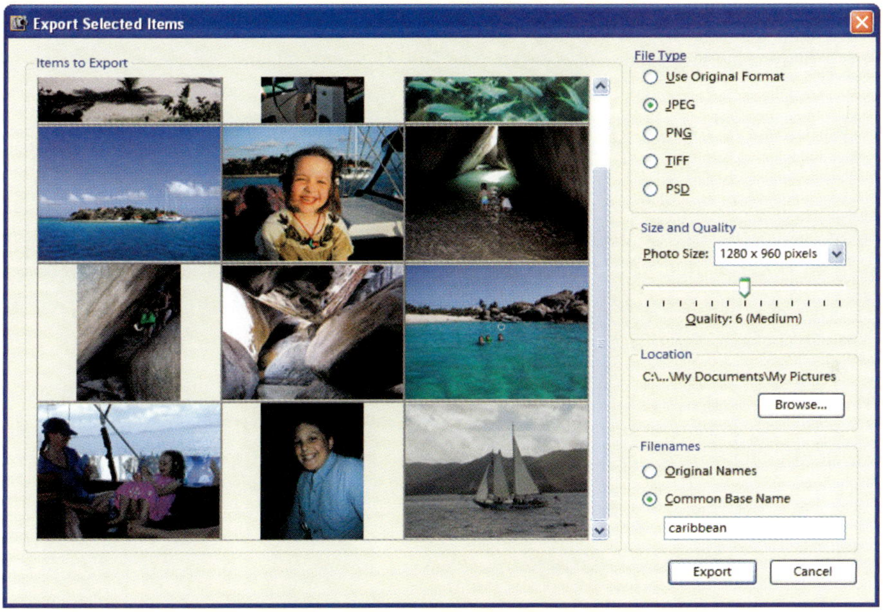

Figure 4.29 When exporting, you can choose the file format and optionally resize and rename photos, as well as control where they are stored, in the Export Selected Items dialog.

If you leave the file type set to Use Original Format, then the files are not modified at all when they are exported—they are simply copied. If you want to reduce the size (in pixels) of the photos while they are exported—which is often desirable, since most applications don't require the full resolution—select one of the file types. For most applications, JPEG is best; if you plan to edit the photos in Photoshop and want maximum quality, use PSD; if you want an uncompressed file with maximum application compatibility, use TIFF.

Then the Photo Size pop-up menu is enabled, and you can select the size you want (**Figure 4.30**). Choose one of the standard sizes, or choose Custom to enter any other size.

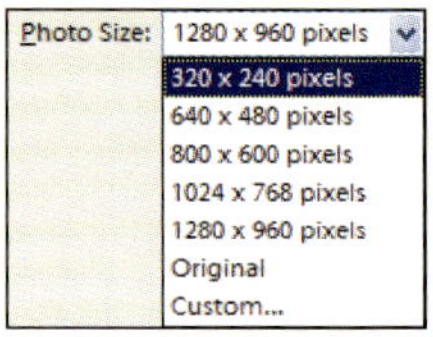

Figure 4.30 In the Photo size menu, you can choose from a standard size or enter your own custom size if you want to resize photos when exporting.

***Note** The resizing function adapts to portrait and landscape photos, and it never distorts a photo. If a photo has a portrait orientation, the export resizing reverses the two dimensions. For example, if you export a portrait photo and have chosen 640 x 480 as the resolution, Photoshop Album will resize the photo to 640 pixels high by 480 pixels wide. A landscape photo, on the other hand, will be resized to 640 pixels wide by 480 pixels high.*

If a photo has a different aspect ratio than that of the chosen export dimensions, it won't be stretched to fill the specified resolution. For example, in the case of a landscape photo with a 3:2 aspect ratio exported with the 640 x 480 setting, Album would export it as 640 pixels wide by 426 pixels high.

If you choose the JPEG file type, you can also control the compression ratio with the Quality slider. A quality of 6 or 7 is fine for most purposes, but you may want to use 9 or 10 for maximum quality if you're not worried about file size (see Chapter 7 for more on JPEG compression quality).

Organizing folders for exported photos

By default, the exported files are stored in My Pictures. It is often useful to make a folder for each export batch. Click the Browse button to choose a destination folder or make a new one in the Browse For Folder dialog (**Figure 4.31**). Click the plus sign (+) next to My Pictures to expand that folder, and then click the Make New Folder button. The folder will initially be named New Folder, but you can type in a new name, such as Exports, before clicking OK.

***Tip** It's best to expand the My Pictures folder before you click Make New Folder. If you don't, the new folder might not be highlighted after it is created; you'll have to right-click it and select Rename to change its name.*

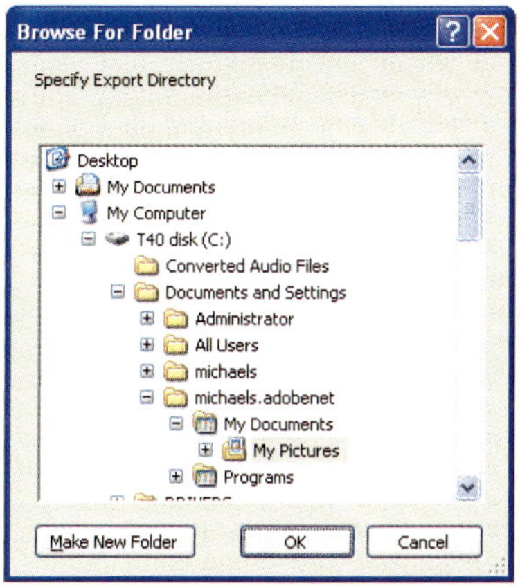

Figure 4.31 **In the Browse For Folder dialog you can select the location where the exported photos will be written.**

When you're done with the exported photos, you can delete the temporary folder, since the copies there are just that—extra copies.

Tip *If you're exporting temporary copies, use the word* **temp** *in the folder name so that you'll know it's a folder you can delete when you clean up your disk.*

Renaming exported photos

You can also have Photoshop Album rename the photos as you export them, which will help you identify the batch of photos easily. Just click the radio button next to Common Base Name in the Export Selected Items dialog and enter the base name, such as `vacation pics`, in the field below it. The photos will be named vacation pics-1, vacation pics-2, and so on.

Note ***If there is already a photo that has the given name, "-1" will be added to make it unique; files are never overwritten. So if you are repeating an export (for example, if you changed your mind about the resolution you want), be sure to delete the first batch you exported before exporting again.***

Using the export approach is a good way to work with Web services that Photoshop Album doesn't support. (You can order prints online directly from Adobe's partners, such as Shutterfly, as Chapter 9 describes, but if you want to use other online photo-finishers, you'll need to use this alternative workflow.) After exporting the photos of interest to a temporary folder, use the service's Web site or its client program, if any, to upload the photos.

Renaming Files

You can also rename photos without exporting them. If you use a Photoshop Album–centric workflow, there's usually no need to do this, with one exception: if you're emailing a photo to someone, you may want to give it a descriptive name. Renaming files can be critical if you want to find photos directly in Windows (though you shouldn't generally need to do so, as the sections above describe).

To rename a single photo, right-click it and select Show Properties. You can then edit the name directly in the Name field of the Properties palette, and the file will be renamed and the catalog updated so that the file remains correctly linked to the catalog.

To rename a batch of files similarly to the way they can be renamed in the export function described above, first select all the photos you want to rename. Then choose File > Rename, and enter the base name in the Rename dialog that is displayed. The renamed files will remain linked to the catalog (which is different from what happens when you rename upon export).

You can also rename photos in Windows, and Album's automatic reconnect function will automatically adjust the catalog to match when you access the photo.

Caution ***Do not rename files managed by Photoshop Album directly in Windows if they have been otherwise modified outside of Photoshop Album. If there are two changes to the file (such as name and date or name and size), Album will not be able to find it automatically—but you can still reconnect it manually, as described below in "Reconnecting Missing Files."***

Moving Files Using Photoshop Album

In an ideal world, before you import your photos into Photoshop Album, they'll all be in a location on the hard disk where you'll be happy to leave them forever. But in the real world, sometimes you want to rearrange things. You might change your user name (if you are using Windows 2000 or XP), which changes the actual location of My Pictures. You may have left photos scattered around your disk and now want to tidy up and move them all to folders within My Pictures. Or you may run out of space on your C drive and add a D drive, and then want to move your photos there.

If you move files using Windows, Photoshop Album will not find them at the location where the catalog indicates they should be. The reconnect function, described in the following section, can generally correct this problem, but it may slow you down. If you want to move a folder to another location, or even to another hard disk, use Photoshop Album's move function, and all the catalog links will be automatically updated.

To move photos, select the ones you want to move in the photo well and choose File > Move. The Move Selected Items dialog shows the photos you have selected and the location to which they will be moved (**Figure 4.32**). Click Browse to navigate to the location where you want to move the selected photos. You'll see a dialog like the one shown in Figure 4.31, and you can make a new folder if you want.

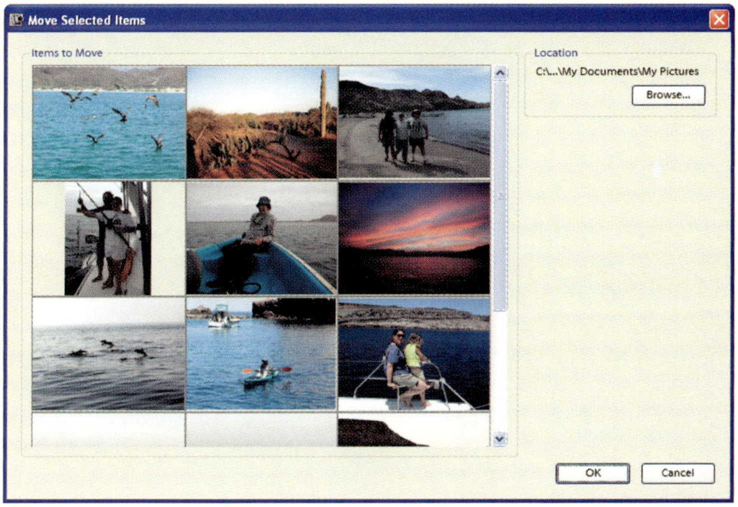

Figure 4.32 Using File > Move to relocate files keeps the catalog links intact. Click Browse to select the destination location.

When you click OK in the Move Selected Items dialog, Photoshop Album moves the selected photos to the destination folder. The filenames won't change unless you're moving two or more photos with the same filename. In that case, the first one will keep its name and the second one will have a "-1" suffix.

If you want to move an entire folder of photos, use the Folder Location arrangement in the photo well to select all the photos in the folder (click the folder title bar to select everything in the folder), and then use File > Move to move them all to the desired folder. Note that the files selected in one move operation are all written to the same destination folder, so you can't move more than one folder at a time.

***Note** The folder itself is not moved; the File > Move command only moves individual files. Therefore, you'll have to create the folder to which you want to move the files (which you can do in Windows or in the Browse dialog, accessed with File > Move > Browse), and after you've moved them, use Windows to delete the old folder.*

Reconnecting Missing Files

Moving files using Windows is more convenient than using Photoshop Album's move function if you want to rearrange lots of folders. You might also sometimes move or rename photo files without thinking about the fact that they are cataloged in Photoshop Album. Album adjusts itself to most changes—often so quickly that you'll barely notice.

When you do anything other than viewing thumbnails for a photo whose file you have moved or renamed using Windows, Photoshop Album notices that it is missing and attempts to reconnect it (**Figure 4.33**), displaying a "Searching for missing file" dialog. If you know the location and Album doesn't find it quickly, you can speed up the process by clicking Browse in the dialog.

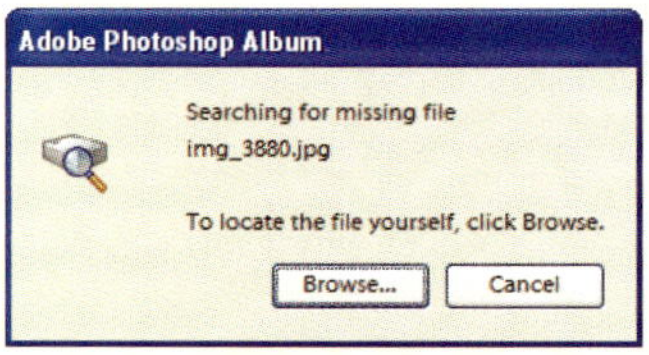

Figure 4.33 When Photoshop Album doesn't find a file where the catalog indicates it should be, it searches for the file.

As long as you make only one type of change to a file, Photoshop Album is able to locate it automatically. You can rename it, move it, or modify it. But if you do any two of these things, Photoshop Album will not be able to tell that it is the correct file, and you'll have to locate it manually.

Depending on where you have moved the file, the reconnection may occur quickly or it may take some time. Photoshop Album first looks in folders where it has found files recently and gradually broadens the search to include other folders and other disks.

***Tip** In some cases you can significantly speed up the process by intervening manually. Suppose, for example, you move a folder of photos from the C drive to the D drive. Instead of waiting while Photoshop Album searches the entire C drive before looking at D, you can stop the search process right away and navigate manually to the D drive by clicking Browse in the auto-reconnect dialog.*

If Photoshop Album cannot locate the file automatically, or if you don't want to wait for its search to complete, you will have to manually locate the file. If the auto-reconnect fails or you click Browse, the Reconnect Missing Files dialog (**Figure 4.34**) allows you to locate the matching file and reconnect it. Initially, the file list on the right shows the folder where the catalog indicates the photo was last located. If you have edited the file and renamed it, just select it in the list on the right and click Reconnect. Use the thumbnail display to verify that it is the correct file.

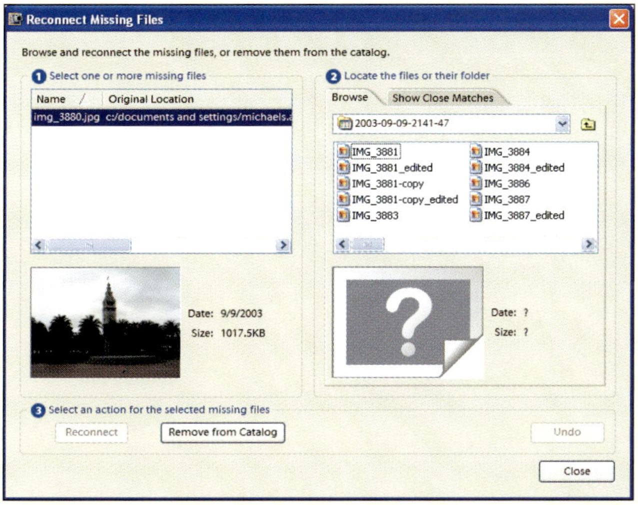

Figure 4.34 The Reconnect Missing Files dialog shows what file Photoshop Album is looking for on the left and the location where Album expects to find it on the right.

If you have moved the file, use the pop-up folder list to navigate to the disk drive and folder where the file is now located. If you have only moved the file and not modified it, you can select a higher-level folder that contains the file and click Find, and it will be automatically reconnected (**Figure 4.35**). You are essentially focusing the automatic reconnect on a specific location, which is a good way to speed up the search when you've moved photos to a different disk drive.

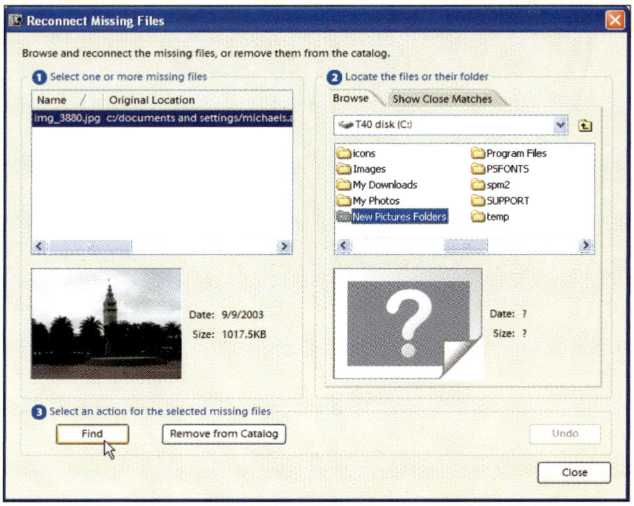

Figure 4.35 If you identify the folder (or any higher-level folder) where the photo is located and click Find, the reconnection will be done automatically if possible.

If you have made two changes to the file—such as moving it and editing it outside of Photoshop Album—you'll have to locate it manually. Navigate to the folder that includes the photo and select the file (**Figure 4.36**).

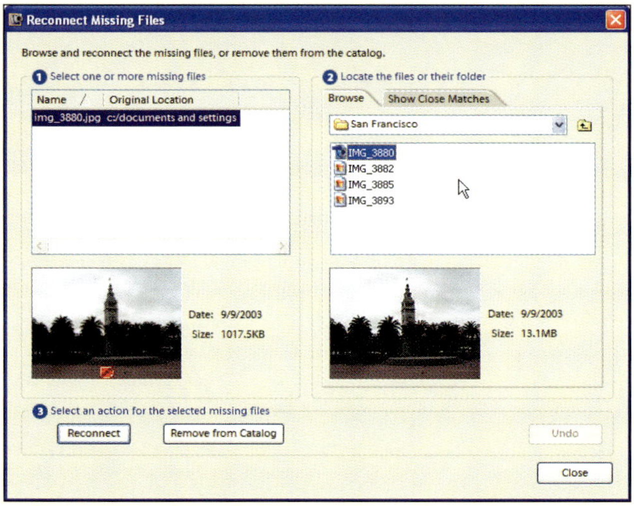

Figure 4.36 If you've changed the file type (in this example the photo was edited in Photoshop and saved in PSD format), you'll have to select the photo manually and then click Reconnect.

Tip *If you have moved lots of files and want to force Photoshop Album to reconnect them all at once, choose File > Reconnect All Missing Files—and go take a coffee break. This way you get all the pain over with at once, instead of sitting through a delay each time you do something that requires access to a missing file.*

If one or more files cannot be reconnected automatically, or you click Browse during the search, the Reconnect Missing Files dialog will be displayed with all the missing files shown in the left-hand list. You can select multiple files using Shift-click and Ctrl-click, and then locate the correct folder in the list on the right; when you click Find, they will all be reconnected.

5 Viewing and Finding Photos

Being able to easily and quickly find the photos you're looking for—or just browse them by subject or time—is the payoff for investing in organization, as Chapter 4 describes. You can view your photos in a grid of thumbnails, one at a time, or full-screen as an instant slideshow.

If you've tagged your photos, you can instantly find them according to one or more tags. For example, when I'm looking for a photo of my family to send for a holiday card, all I have to do is search on the Michael, Irene, Amanda, and Gregory tags to see photos with all of us.

When I'm collecting a set of photos for a holiday letter, I perform a series of searches on various tags, such as the one for a vacation we took during the summer, or the kids' school performances. After each search, I add my favorites to a collection, remove some photos if I chose too many, and I have a nice set of photos to share.

There's a lot you can do even if you haven't done any organizing with tags or collections. Just scrolling through the photo well by date is often enough to find photos quickly. You can also find photos according to their history. For example, if you haven't been diligent in using the Favorites tag, you can find all the photos you've ever printed, which probably include many of your favorites.

In this chapter, you'll learn about each of these approaches and more for finding and viewing photos—the most powerful, and often the most fun, aspect of Photoshop Album.

Viewing Photos and Video Clips

The photo well is the primary place where you'll view your photos. You have a lot of control over how the photos appear there, so you can optimize it according to your preference and your current task. You can also view photos full screen and as instant slide shows. (For the basics about the photo well, refer to Chapter 1.)

Using the Photo Well

The photo well normally shows your photos sorted by time and date (**Figure 5.1**). You can choose how to arrange the photos via the pop-up menu in the lower-left corner of the window (or by choosing View > Arrangement).

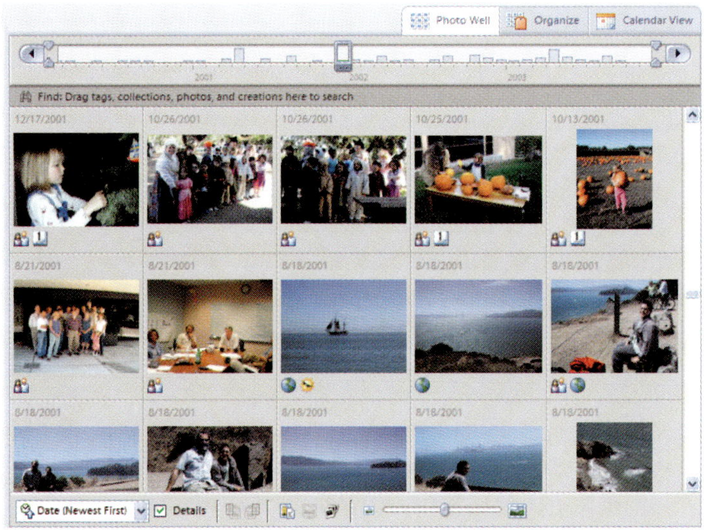

Figure 5.1 **In the photo well you can change the size of the thumbnails, the sorting arrangement, and whether or not details (such as the date and time) are displayed.**

The three tabs at the upper right determine the mode of the main Photoshop Album window. If you click the Photo Well tab, the entire window is devoted to your photos. Clicking the Organize tab adds the Organize pane to the photo well; clicking the Calendar tab brings up the calendar view, described in the section "Finding by Date," later in this chapter.

The default order for items in the photo well is Date (Newest First), which is not quite reverse chronological order. This arrangement puts the most recent day first, so you'll see your newest photos at the top of the photo well. Within a day, however, photos remain in forward chronological order, since you generally don't want to reverse the natural time sequence of the pictures.

If you're looking at several days' worth of photos, the Newest First ordering can be annoying, since you see each day in forward time order but the days themselves in reverse order. In this case, you can switch to the Date (Oldest First) arrangement, which is a simple chronological order. You'll always see your oldest photos at the top of the photo well, and you'll have to scroll to the bottom to see the newest photos.

If you have details enabled, the date (or date and time, if there is room) will be shown above each photo. The text is in bold for the first photo of each day. So you can find photos by date just by scrolling through the photo well, in either date order. If you drag the scroll bar slider, a tool tip shows the month and year of the photo at the top left of the photo well.

Using Thumbnail Views

You can choose the size of the photos (thumbnails) in the photo well by moving the thumbnail slider at the bottom of the window. The size range varies from quite small to large enough to fill the window. To move the slider, you can either click and drag it to a new position, or just click the position you want to move it to. You can instantly move the slider all the way to the left or right by clicking the icons at either end.

***Tip** To make a small adjustment in the thumbnail size, use the shortcut keys, Ctrl-– (minus) and Ctrl-+ (plus), to decrease or increase the size.*

You'll find the smallest size useful when you're tagging large groups of images or scanning through lots of images for one that is easily recognized. The medium sizes are most useful for general tagging and browsing, while the largest sizes are great when you want to see a photo close up.

You can also choose whether the photo well shows any information about each photo, or just the photos themselves. Click the Details box to show the date and tag information. In general, you'll want to leave details on. The details that are shown vary with the space available. With the smallest thumbnails, the date doesn't include the month or day, and the time is not shown. As the thumbnail size increases, these details are filled in.

The information shown below the photo also varies with size. For the smallest thumbnails, tags are represented by a single generic tag icon overlaid on the photo. If you pause your pointer over this tag, the tool tip shows all the tag names. As the thumbnail size increases, tag category icons appear below the photo, giving you hints about which tags have been applied. Pause your pointer over these icons to see tag names.

You can also choose to display the filename below the thumbnail. To enable this, choose Edit > Preferences > General and click the box for the Show File Names in Details option. Usually, filenames aren't important and there is no need to clutter up your photo well with them. But if you are looking for a file with a particular name, this option can be helpful.

Selecting Photos

When you want to print, share, export, or perform any other action with one or more photos, the first step is to select them. Then choose the action you want to perform.

To select a single photo in the photo well, just click it. (Click the photo itself, not the date or time, or you'll trigger the date-editing dialog.) To extend the selection to multiple photos, use Shift-click and Ctrl-click, which operate the way they do in Windows and most other applications:

- Ctrl-click adds a photo to the selection. The photos do not need to be contiguous.
- Shift-click extends the selection contiguously. This selects the range of photos from the photo you Shift-click through any other selected photo.

You can also remove photos from a selection by Ctrl-clicking them after they are selected.

Using Single-Image View

To make each photo as large as possible, while staying within the Photoshop Album window, click the button at the right end of the slider or double-click the thumbnail of the photo you want to view. This puts the photo well into single-image view (**Figure 5.2**). Navigation and selection also work slightly differently in this view.

In single-image view, the image is scaled to fill the screen. (If you want to zoom in and see part of the photo enlarged, select Fix Photo to get to a view with zoom controls, as described in Chapter 6.) When you click the scroll bar, the photo well scrolls by exactly one photo. You can also use the left and right arrow keys to move from one photo to the next.

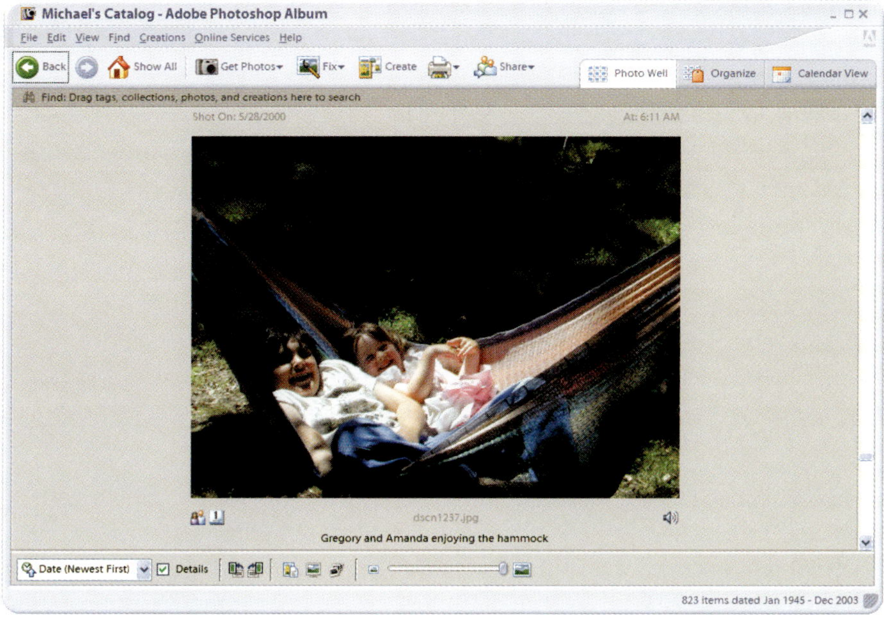

Figure 5.2 In single-image view, you get a good view of a single photo and can enter a caption.

In single-image view, the caption is shown if details are enabled, and you can enter a new caption or edit an existing one. The audio-caption icon also appears, allowing you to play the audio caption if there is one. (To learn how to record an audio caption, see Chapter 8.)

Selection also works differently in single-image view. You don't have to select the image, since there is only one photo in view, and that is presumably the one you want to act upon. The photo currently being viewed is automatically selected, so you can tag it, print it, export it, or whatever, without having to first click it to select it.

If you have multiple photos selected in a thumbnail view and go to single-image view and then back to a thumbnail view, without having performed any action on the photo, the multiple selection is maintained. But if you do anything in single-image view, the photo you last acted upon will be selected when you return to a thumbnail view.

Smooth Scrolling

A critical under-the-hood part of Photoshop Album's photo well is the *thumbnail cache*, a special file that stores small copies of all your photos. In general, you shouldn't have to be aware of the thumbnail cache, but it helps to know about it in a few circumstances, such as when you have out-of-date thumbnails or when scrolling is sluggish in the photo well.

When you import new photos, Photoshop Album must generate the thumbnails and store them in the cache. While this is going on, you'll see a rotating hourglass icon in the lower-right corner of the screen. Scrolling performance will not be as good as usual while this is happening. You can avoid some of the resulting jerkiness by waiting for the thumbnail generation to complete (the rotating hourglass icon will go away) before doing further work in the photo well.

The thumbnail cache stores three different sizes of thumbnails, and only one is generated automatically upon import. So you may notice some jerkiness in the photo well when you scroll through photos for the first time at a given size. You can avoid this by scrolling through new photos and then waiting for the rotating hourglass to go away.

If you edit a photo outside of Photoshop Album, the copy in the thumbnail cache will not match the current version of the full-resolution file. To remedy this, right-click the thumbnail and choose Update Thumbnail. You can also do this on a multiple selection.

The thumbnail cache file can get quite large, and since it can be entirely regenerated from the photo files themselves, it is not saved as part of the backup process. Therefore, when you restore a backup to a new system, the thumbnail cache will initially be empty. Thumbnails are generated and stored in the cache as they are needed—that is, as you scroll through the photo well. The photo well may be sluggish until you have viewed every photo in a range of sizes.

Using the Properties Palette

You can view all the information (such as the file size and location in Windows' file system) associated with a photo by opening the Properties palette. There are several ways to do this:

- Right-click a photo or thumbnail and choose Show Properties.
- Select a photo and press Ctrl-Enter.
- Select a photo and click the Show or Hide Properties button at the bottom of the photo well (**Figure 5.3**).

- Select a photo and choose View > Properties.

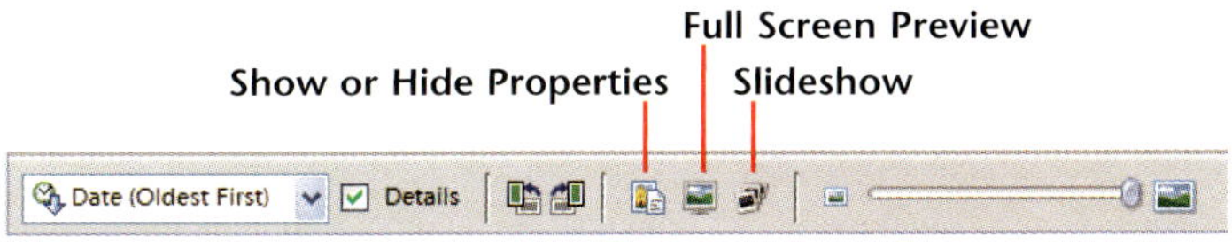

Figure 5.3 **Shortcut buttons at the bottom of the photo well provide quick access to the Properties palette, full-screen view, and instant slide shows.**

You can view properties for only one photo at a time; the Properties palette is dimmed if you select multiple photos before you open it. However, you can leave the Properties palette open and see the properties of each photo by clicking the photos in the photo well to change the selection from one photo to another.

The Properties palette is divided into four panes: General, Tags, History, and Metadata. When you open Properties, the pane you last used is displayed.

The General pane shows a photo's caption, filename, and notes (**Figure 5.4**). You can edit all these items in this pane. If you edit the filename, the name of the file on the disk changes, and the link in the catalog is updated to match. This is the best way to rename individual files, if you're going to bother with file renaming at all.

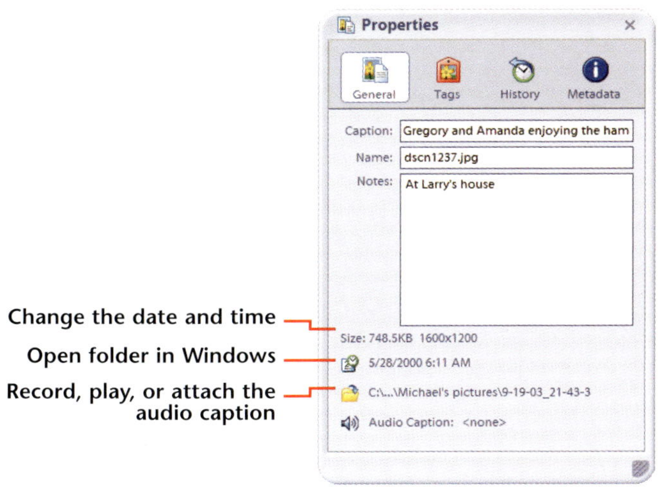

Figure 5.4 **The Properties palette has four panes; the General pane is the most commonly used.**

You can also see the photo's file size, pixel dimensions, folder location, and capture date. If there is an audio caption, you can play it by clicking the Audio Caption button in this pane. You can also record an audio caption (Chapter 8).

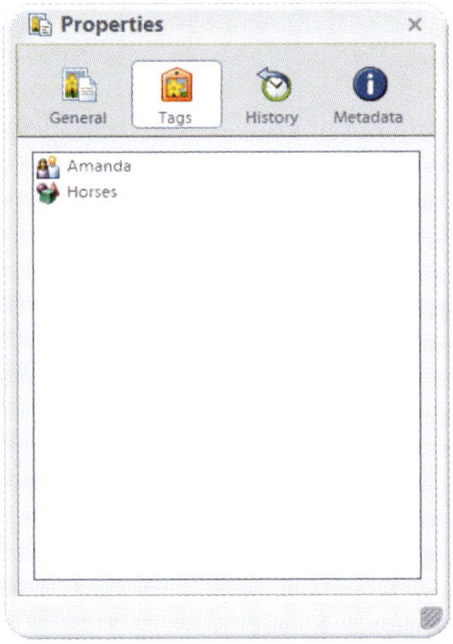

Figure 5.5 The Tags pane of the Properties palette shows all the tags you've attached to a photo.

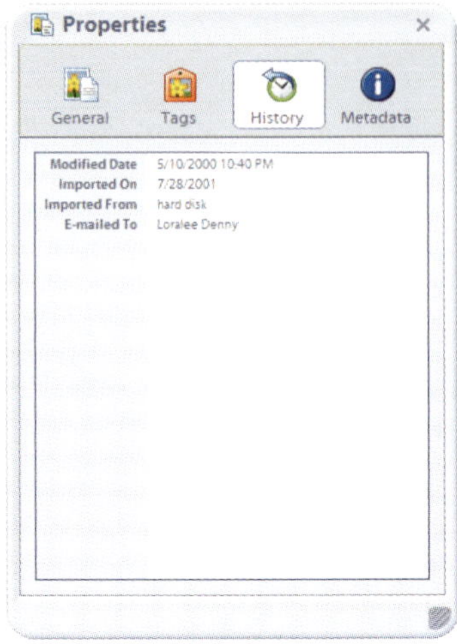

Figure 5.6 The History pane of the Properties palette shows what you have done with a photo in the past.

The Tags pane shows all the tags that have been assigned to a photo (**Figure 5.5**).

The History pane shows the history that Photoshop Album has tracked for this photo (**Figure 5.6**). It shows the date when the file was last modified, the date it was imported, and the location from which it was imported. It also lists other actions you have taken with the photo, including

- Whether the photo has been edited
- To whom the photo has been emailed
- When the photo has been printed
- When the photo has been sent for online photofinishing
- What creations include the photo
- When the photo has been exported

You can search for photos using this history information; see "Finding by History," later in this chapter.

The Metadata pane shows information that is embedded in the photo file. In general, this information comes from your digital camera, though some scanners and other software may provide information here as well. In Brief mode the Metadata pane shows the items you're most likely to be interested in: the basic camera settings (**Figure 5.7**). This information varies to some degree depending on the camera you are using, and it may be absent entirely if the image did not come from a digital

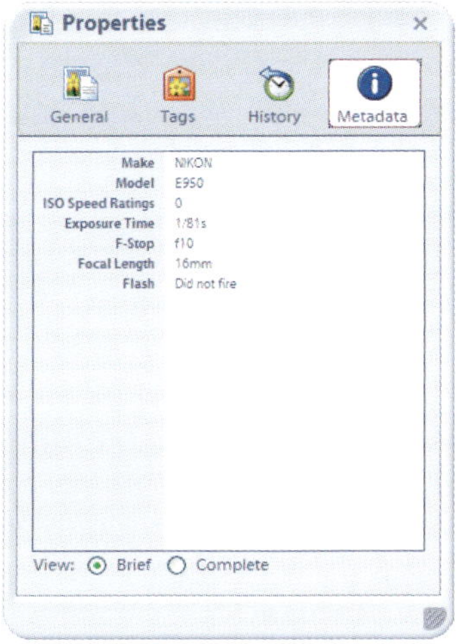

Figure 5.7 The Metadata pane of the Properties palette in Brief mode shows the most important information from the photo file.

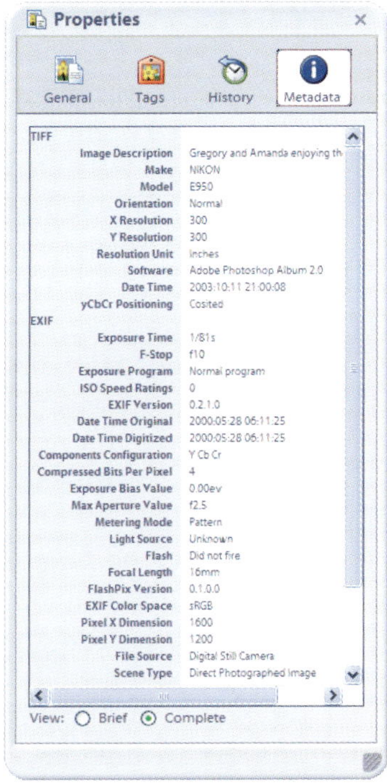

Figure 5.8 The Metadata pane in Complete mode shows all the metadata in the file.

camera. It may also be absent if you have edited the photo in certain programs; most older programs, such as Photoshop 5.0 and earlier, and even a few newer ones strip out the metadata when you edit a photo.

For all the gory details, you can choose to view the complete metadata by clicking the Complete radio button at the bottom of the pane (**Figure 5.8**). You may want to enlarge the window by dragging the lower-right corner so that you can see all the data at once. This pane shows every bit of metadata in the photo file. You won't generally need any of this information, however. Some camera-specific metadata, called *maker notes,* is stored by the camera's vendor in proprietary formats, and Photoshop Album displays it as numeric information that you'd need specialized knowledge to interpret.

Using Full-Screen Mode

The quickest way to get a close look at a photo is to select it and press F11 or click the Full Screen Preview button at the bottom of the photo well (Figure 5.3). (You can also right-click the photo and choose Show Full Screen.) This fills the entire screen with the photo. You can't do anything other than look at it in this mode, but it provides a great look. To return to normal operation, press Esc or click the mouse.

You can use this mode for manually advanced slide shows. Use the left and right arrow buttons to move between photos. These are limited slide shows, though: only the first frame is shown for video clips (as in the photo well), captions are not shown, and audio captions are not played.

I like to use the full-screen view to review my photos after I've imported them. If I want to mark one as a favorite or to be hidden, or want to delete, tag, or fix it, I just press Esc to return to the photo well, perform the actions I want, and press F11 to go back to full-screen view. You can avoid the back and forth if you just do all this in single-image view, but I like seeing the photo entirely filling the screen, without any surrounding user-interface components. And as long as you view each photo for a few seconds, you can move nearly instantly to the next photo, because Photoshop Album "looks ahead" and prepares the next one.

If you have no photos selected and are viewing thumbnails, full-screen view is disabled because Album doesn't know which photo you want to show. If you are in single-image view or have one photo selected, it will start with that photo, and you can then use the left and right arrow keys to move among photos. Only photos that are present in the photo well, with whatever search or filter is active, will be shown, and they will be shown in the same order as in the photo well (which depends on the arrangement you have selected).

To include only certain photos in the full-screen view, select them all before switching to full-screen view. This is useful for comparing multiple photos of a scene to decide which you like best; just select the ones you want to compare, go to full-screen view, and use the right arrow button to switch from one to the next.

If you select multiple photos when you enter full-screen mode, the first one (according to the layout in the photo well) appears, and you can use the left and right arrow buttons to move among the selected photos. Only the selected photos are shown. After the last photo, Album cycles back to the first one.

Using Instant Slide Shows

For a more full-featured slide show than the full-screen mode provides, use the instant slide show feature. To start an instant slide show, just select the photos you want to include and click the Slideshow button (Figure 5.3), choose View > Slideshow, or press Ctrl-spacebar.

Note *Instant slide shows always show one photo at a time, full screen. If you want a slide show with a more complicated layout, use the Creations feature (Chapter 8). Slide show creations can also be emailed, written to CD, or saved to your hard disk as PDF files.*

If nothing is selected in the photo well (such as when you've just done a search or are viewing a batch of photos you just imported), the slide show will include everything in the photo well. If any photos are selected, only the selected photos are used.

***Note** Instant slide shows (and creations) are limited to a maximum of 999 photos. If you select more than that, Album shows only the first 999.*

The instant slide show provides a number of features that full-screen view does not:

- All photos are shown in chronological order, regardless of the current arrangement of the photo well.
- You can have an automatic, timed advance from one photo to the next, with transitions.
- You can have captions shown.
- Video clips can be played.
- You can have background music, and audio captions can be played.

You choose these options in the slide show Preferences dialog (Edit > Preferences > Slideshow) (**Figure 5.9**). These preference settings affect all instant slide shows; you cannot change them other than via the Preferences dialog. (If you make a slide show creation, you can choose the settings separately for each slide show.)

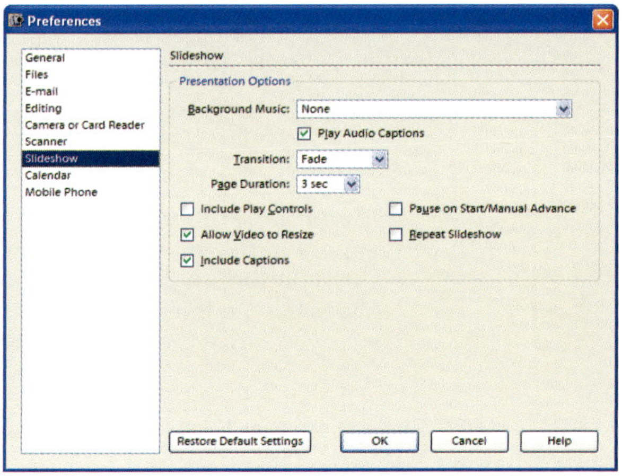

Figure 5.9 The Slideshow Preferences dialog lets you control how Album presents instant slide shows.

To play background music during your slide show, just select the music you want in the Background Music pop-up menu. This menu shows only music files that are in your catalog. If you haven't added any music files to your catalog, it will show only the standard music clips provided with Photoshop Album. To use your own music, first import the files into your catalog (see Chapter 2).

If you have audio captions on any of the photos, you can choose whether they are played during an instant slide show. You can record audio captions in your camera if it has that capability, or you can record them using Photoshop Album.

The Transition selection determines how the screen changes from one photo to the next. If you select None, there will be a sharp change. Fade does simply that: one photo fades into the next. Experiment with the other choices to see if you like them better. (Personally, I prefer to keep the focus on the photos and use no transitions or just a simple fade.)

The Page Duration pop-up menu gives you a choice of 2, 4, or 10 seconds per photo, but you aren't limited to those choices. While it may not be apparent, you can click this field and then type in any number you want, from 1 second to 3600 seconds (1 hour).

The options with check boxes control various aspects of how the slide shows are displayed:

- Include Play Controls—If this is selected, play controls are shown in the upper-right corner of the slide show (**Figure 5.10**). The play controls are displayed regardless of this setting if you move the mouse while the slide show is playing, so I prefer to keep this option off. That way, I get the play controls when I want them by moving the mouse, but they aren't always there cluttering up the slide show.

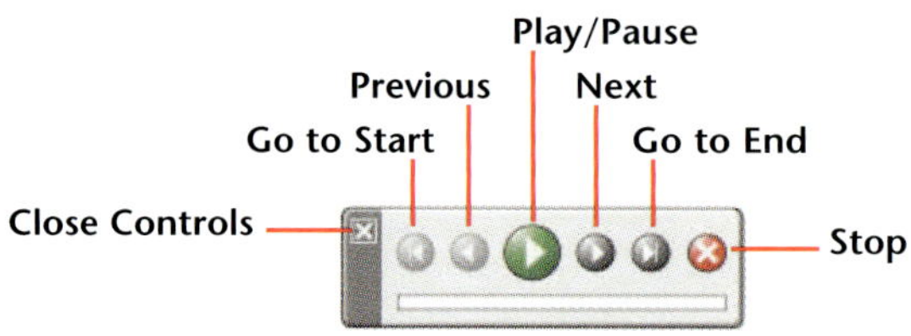

Figure 5.10 The play controls appear in the upper-right corner of the slide show if you enable them in Slideshow Preferences, and whenever you move the mouse if not.

- Allow Video to Resize—Video clips are generally of much lower resolution than your screen. If you check this box, they will be stretched to fill the screen and will therefore look grainy and fuzzy. If you're viewing the slide show from a distance, this may still be preferable, but if you're looking at it up close, leave this box unchecked and the video will be shown in a small window at the center of the screen and will have its maximum sharpness.
- Include Captions—Determines whether text captions are displayed.

- Pause on Start/Manual Advance—If this box is checked, the slide show will start in the paused state. You can then use the play controls to manually advance from one photo to the next or to start the slide show playing automatically. To have your slide shows play automatically, keep this box unselected.
- Repeat Slideshow—If this box is checked, the slide show will start over automatically when it is over. If the box is left unselected, the slide show will fade out and return to the normal Photoshop Album window after the last slide.

Viewing Video Clips

With video clips, only the first frame is shown in the photo well. A small icon appears in the upper-right corner of the video's thumbnail to indicate that it is a video (**Figure 5.11**).

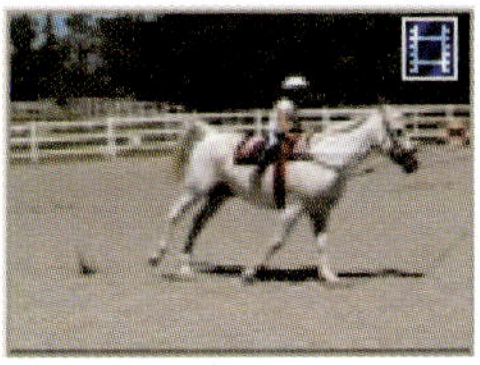

Figure 5.11 The filmstrip icon in the upper-right corner indicates that this thumbnail represents a video clip. The image is the first frame in the clip.

To view the video, double-click the thumbnail, which opens the video-player window (**Figure 5.12**). You can play the video or move to a particular spot in it by dragging the large slider.

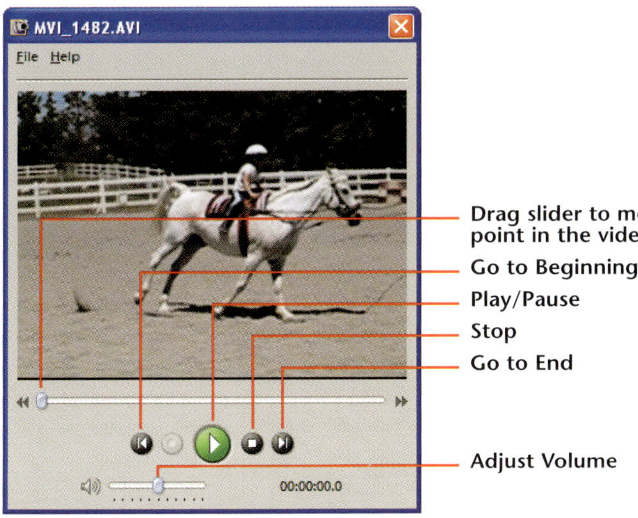

Figure 5.12 Double-clicking a video clip displays the video player.

This window automatically opens at a size that shows the video at its optimum resolution—that is, each pixel of the video is represented by one pixel on the screen. You can enlarge the window by dragging any corner or side (just as with any Windows window). You'll lose some crispness, since the video doesn't have many pixels, but if you're viewing the screen from any distance (especially if multiple people are watching), it will give you a better view. Unfortunately, the window reverts to the minimum size each time, so you have to resize every time you play a video if you want it larger than the minimum.

Finding Photos and Video Clips

One of the greatest benefits of Photoshop Album is the ease with which you can find photos. It offers several tools and methods:

- Finding by date, either by scrolling in the photo well or using the calendar view. With this method you aren't limiting the photos shown in the photo well; you're just navigating to a particular one.
- Searching by tags, collections, history, caption, note, filename, or media type. With this approach, you're narrowing the range of items displayed in the photo well.
- You can also apply filters to the photo well to do things like narrowing the time range shown or eliminating certain media types, such as videos or creations. Filters are not reset when you clear a search, but they are reset when you click the Show All button in the shortcuts bar.

The following sections describe each method of finding photos in Photoshop Album. Once you become familiar with these methods, you'll realize just how quickly and easily you can find the photos you want.

Feedback About Searches

Whichever searching method you use, certain areas in the main Photoshop Album window give you feedback about your searches. Any time you do a search, the find bar at the top of the photo well shows what the search is based upon (**Figure 5.13**). To return to viewing all photos, click the Clear button at the right.

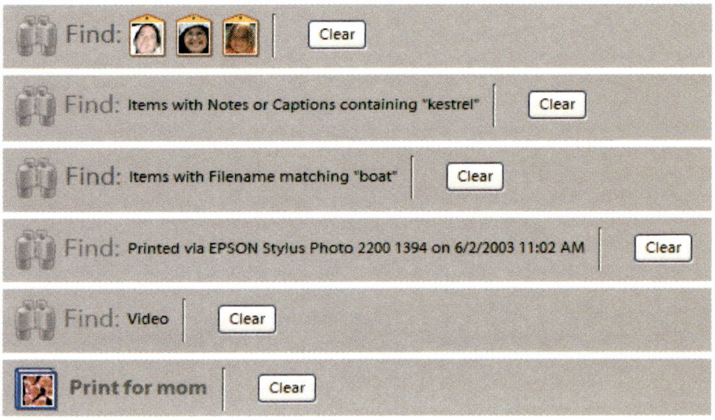

Figure 5.13 **The find bar indicates what searches you have performed so that you'll know how the contents of the photo well have been constrained.**

At the right of the find bar are check boxes that you can select to show up to three sets of results—best matches (Best), close matches (Close), and nonmatches (Not). It also shows the number of photos in each set (**Figure 5.14**). By default, only the best-match set is shown; you can display the others by clicking their check boxes (see "Finding with Tags").

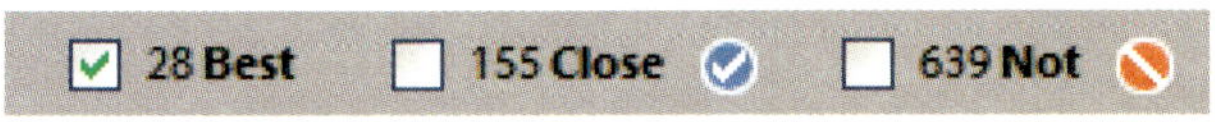

Figure 5.14 **At the right of the find bar are check boxes to enable or disable the display of the best-, close-, and nonmatching sets; also shown is the number of photos in each set.**

The bottom-right corner of the window shows additional status information: the total number of photos (or other items) currently displayed in the photo well, the range of dates represented, and the number of items not shown (**Figure 5.15**). Those not shown include photos that don't meet the search criteria and ones that have the Hidden tag applied.

Note *The date range shown in the status line reflects the range of photos searched; the range of dates in the results is likely to be narrower.*

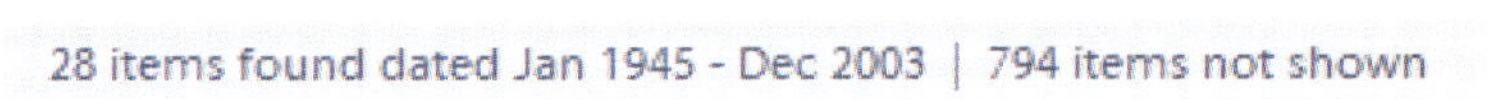

Figure 5.15 **The status text at the bottom right of the window shows the total number of photos found, the date range that was searched, and the number of photos not shown.**

Finding by Date

In many cases you may only need to find photos by date—and as long as your photos come from a digital camera, this organization is automatic. Photoshop Album provides several tools that make it easy to find photos by date.

Scrolling with the Timeline

The timeline at the top of the photo well makes it easy to see the months in which you took a lot of photos and to quickly scroll to any month. The height of each bar indicates the number of photos in that month. If you have done a search, the bars are colored according to the search results. The bar's outline represents all the photos in the catalog, while its dark portion reflects the search results.

To scroll immediately to the desired month and year, just click the bar for that month in the timeline. If the month or year you're looking for is not visible on the timeline, click the arrow button at either end of the timeline to make it scroll. When you select a month on the timeline, a green rectangle appears briefly surrounding the first photo for that month, and its date flashes.

Setting the date range

You can also use the timeline to restrict the range of photos shown in the photo well by dragging the end points (**Figure 5.16**). This applies a time filter to the photo well; items outside the selected time range won't be shown, regardless of any tag, caption, or history search you've done. The timeline filter won't be cleared just by clearing a tag search, but it is cleared if you click the Show All button.

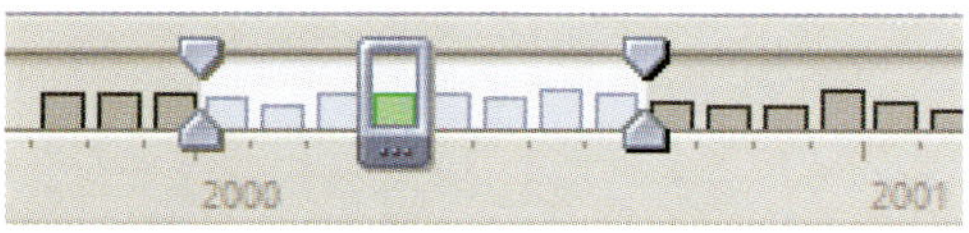

Figure 5.16 You can narrow the time range considered in any search by dragging the end points from either end of the timeline.

Dragging the timeline end points allows you to select as little as one month, but only on month boundaries. You can set these end points to specific days in the Set Date Range dialog (Find > Set Date Range) (**Figure 5.17**). To clear the end points, choose Find > Clear Date Range or click the Show All button.

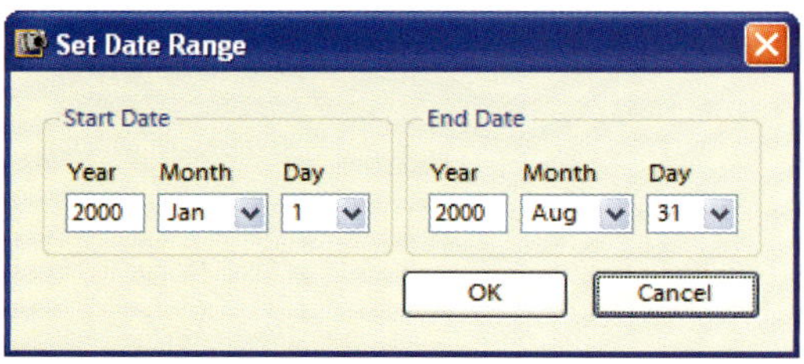

Figure 5.17 To set the start and end points to specific days, choose Find > Set Date Range.

Using the calendar view

The calendar view gives you an entirely different way to find and browse your photos. When you click the Calendar View tab, Photoshop Album switches into a different mode of operation. In this mode all photos are always shown, regardless of any timeline constraints you may have set or tag searches you may have done in the photo well.

Using the year view. Click one of the Year, Month, and Day buttons at the bottom center of the window to choose among those views. The year view shows an entire year at a glance (**Figure 5.18**). All days for which you have photos are highlighted with a color. If you pause your pointer over one of the dates, a tool tip shows how many photos (or other items, such as video clips) are associated with it.

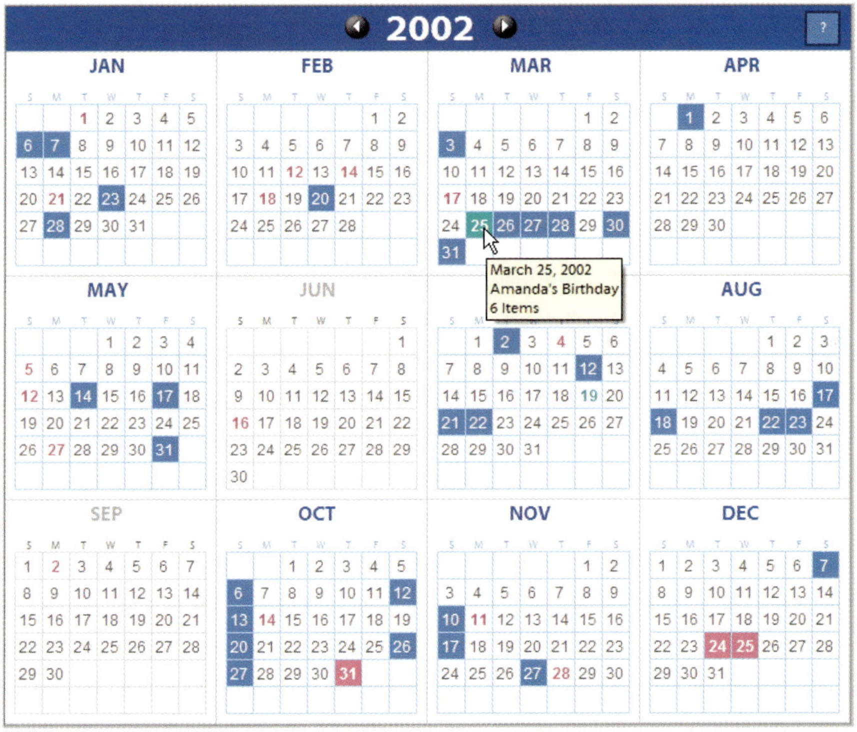

Figure 5.18 In the calendar window's year view, each date that has photos associated with it is highlighted with color. Different colors indicate holidays and user-defined events.

To move one year forward or back, use the arrow buttons to either side of the year at the top of the window. To jump to a specific year, click the year and a menu listing all years for which you have photos will pop up.

To view the photos from a particular date, click the date and the first photo from that day will appear at the top right of the calendar window (**Figure 5.19**). Click the green arrow button under the photo (the Start Sequencing button) to see a mini–slide show, or use the left and right arrow buttons to move one photo at a time.

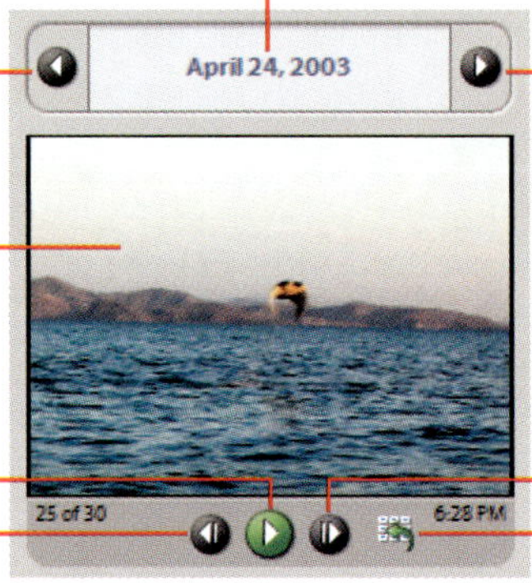

Figure 5.19 The photo viewer at the right of the year and month views allows you to view individual photos.

Acting on photos in the calendar view. After you've found a photo using the calendar view, you can fix, print, edit, export, and do most other things with that photo without leaving the calendar view; just right-click the photo and select the function you want. You can't select multiple photos in the calendar view, however, so you can't perform any multiple-photo actions (like making a creation).

To use the calendar view to find photos and assemble a collection, first make the collection in the collections view (Organize > Collections). You can then add photos to it from the calendar view by right-clicking the photo and choosing Add to Collection. You'll see a list of all your collections; pick the one to which you want to add this photo.

You can alternatively use the calendar view to find the photo of interest and then automatically return to the photo well with that photo selected, by clicking the Show in Photo Well button below the photo.

You can view a photo full screen without leaving the calendar view by using the F11 shortcut or right-clicking the photo and choosing Show Full Screen. To see a full-screen instant slide show (conforming to the settings in Edit > Preferences > Slideshow) for all the photos on one date, click the day once to select it and then press Ctrl-spacebar.

Holidays and events. You'll notice that certain dates in the year view are highlighted in maroon instead of blue. These are standard holidays. You can change which holidays appear; choose the Calendar pane of the Preferences dialog (**Figure 5.20**). Uncheck the boxes next to any holidays you don't want to be specially marked in the calendar view.

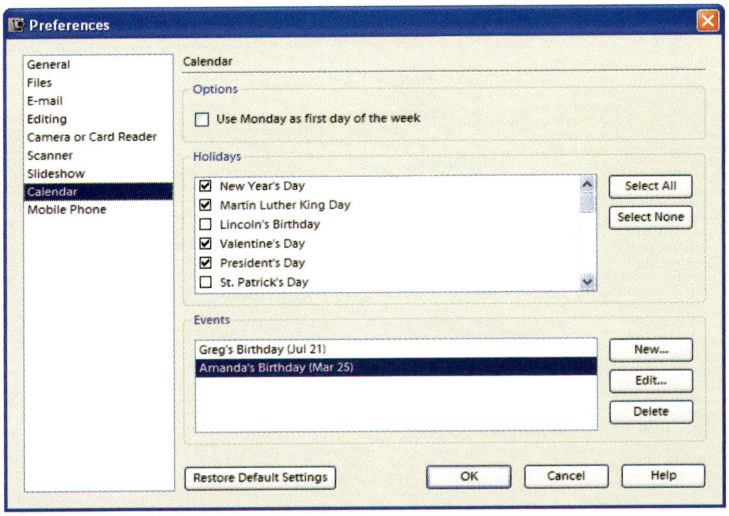

Figure 5.20 In the Calendar pane of the Preferences dialog you can choose which holidays are highlighted and add your own special events.

You can also add your own special dates, which will be highlighted in green in the calendar view. This is useful for birthdays and other dates when you're likely to take pictures. You can make a day event by clicking the New button in the Calendar pane of the Preferences dialog, or by clicking the Create New Event button above the Daily Note field in the calendar view.

When making a new event, you specify the name of the event and its date in the Create New Event dialog (**Figure 5.21**). Day events are associated with a single date and cannot span multiple dates. You can choose whether the event repeats every year, is only in one year, or spans a certain number of years.

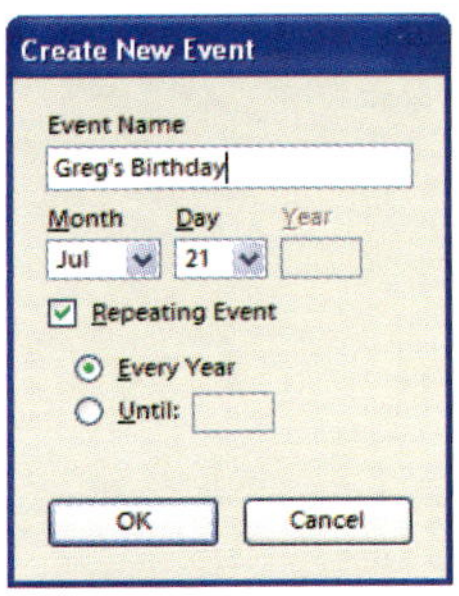

Figure 5.21 In the Create New Event dialog you can make your own day events for birthdays and other occasions on which you regularly take photos.

Note ***Don't confuse day events with event tags; they're entirely different. A day event is just a name associated with a particular date, which is specially colored on the calendar.***

Using the month view. I find the month view generally to be the most useful (**Figure 5.22**). This view shows the first photo for each date right on the calendar. It also shows the names of holidays and day events on the calendar.

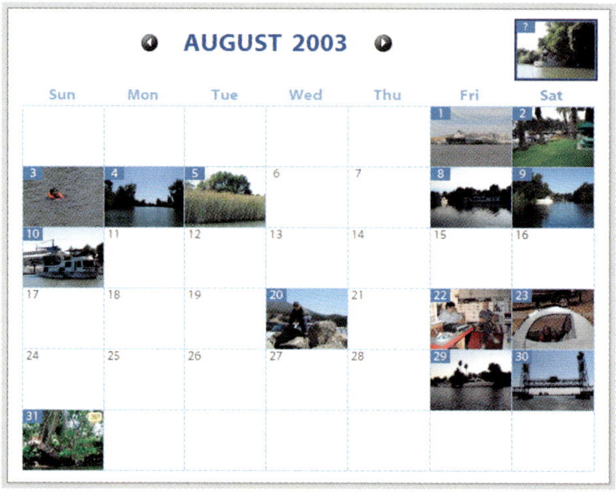

Figure 5.22 **The month view is similar to the year view but shows only one month, with the first photo from each date displayed in that date's square.**

If you pause your pointer over a date on the calendar, a tool tip shows how many photos you have for that day. To see the photos for a day in the viewer on the right, click the date. The Viewing and Daily Notes panes on the right work just as they do for the month view.

You can move forward or backward a month at a time using the arrow buttons at the top of the calendar, or you can jump to a month or a year by clicking the month or year at the top of the calendar view and choosing from the pop-up list that appears. The small photo icon in the list shows months and years for which there are photos in the catalog.

Using the day view. You can get to the day view by either clicking the Day button at the bottom of the calendar view or double-clicking a day in either the month or year view. The day view divides the screen between a scrolling list of all the photos from that day and a large image of one photo (**Figure 5.23**).

To choose a different photo for the large display, just click its thumbnail in the strip to the right. Use the scroll bar slider to access more thumbnails. You can also use the Next Item and Previous Item (left and right arrow) buttons below the large image, or start a self-running slide show by clicking the green play button in the middle.

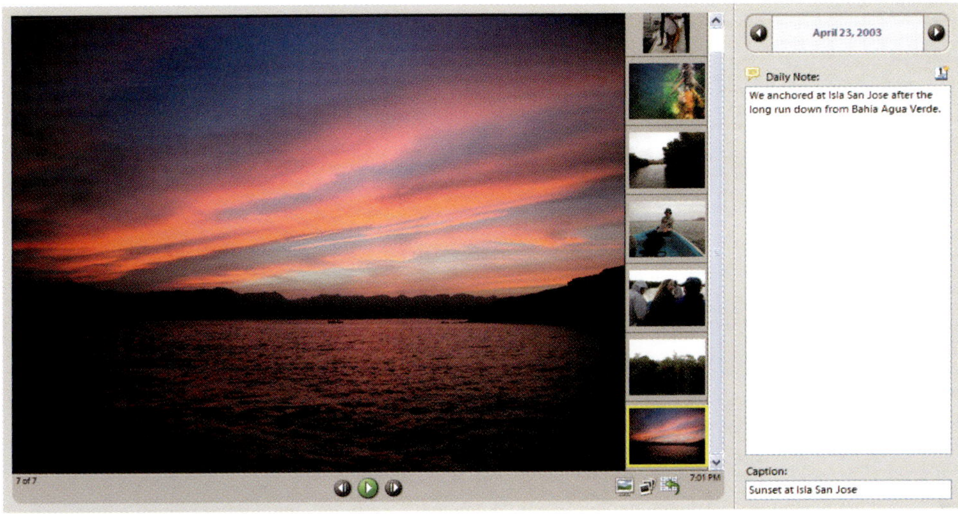

Figure 5.23 **The day view gives you quick access to all the photos from one day and allows you enter both a day note and captions.**

In the day view, you can also enter captions for individual photos, in addition to the day note. You can move to another day using the controls at the upper-right corner of the window.

Working with unknown dates

If you have scanned photos, you may want to use the unknown-dates feature (see Chapter 4). You can set a date to entirely unknown or partially unknown (for instance, you might know the year but not the month).

Photos with unknown dates are sorted in the photo well as being earlier in time than photos with known dates. If the date is entirely unknown, the photos appear at the top of the photo well if arranged by oldest first, or at the bottom of the photo well if arranged by newest first.

Photos for which only the year is known appear before (in the time sequence) any other photos in that year. Similarly, photos for which the year and month are known appear before any others in that month, and photos for which only the time is unknown appear before any others on that day.

You can find all photos with unknown dates or times by choosing Find > Items with Unknown Date or Time. The best-match set shows photos with entirely unknown dates; the close-match set shows items with partially unknown dates or times (see the following section for more about best- and close-match sets).

In the calendar view, photos with entirely unknown dates are not shown. A box in the upper-right corner of the year view indicates photos for which only the year is known (Figure 5.18). Photos for which the month but not the day is known are shown in the upper-right corner of that month in either the month (Figure 5.22) or year view.

Finding with Tags

If you have invested the time to tag your photos, the payoff comes when you want to find them. You can instantly find photos using any number of tags as search criteria.

To find with tags, first display the Tags pane by clicking the Organize tab and then (if it is not already selected) the Tags tab in the organizing pane. Expand categories and subcategories as needed so that you can see the tags you want to use for searches. To search on a single tag, just double-click that tag. The photo well will show only photos with that tag.

To find photos with more than one tag, click the box to the left of each additional tag you want to include (**Figure 5.24**). (Don't double-click tags to add them to the search; double-clicking a tag is a shortcut for clearing any existing search and then clicking the box for that tag.) Alternatively, you can drag tags to the find bar. You can include as many tags as you want. You can also use categories or subcategories.

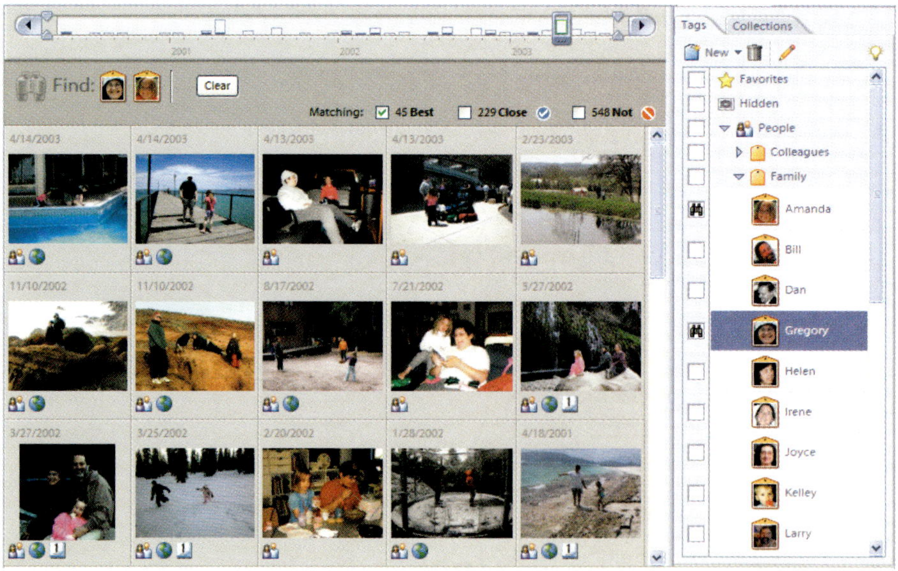

Figure 5.24 You can search using multiple tags by clicking the box next to each tag. Note that the timeline shows small dark bars for the search results.

Best-match and close-match results

Photoshop Album divides the results of the search into two categories: best match and close match. The best-match results are those that have *all* the specified tags. The close-match results are those with *any* of those tags. (Best-match and close-match sets are defined differently for other kinds of searches, but they are conceptually similar. For example, if you search for multiple words in a caption, the best-match set includes photos with all the words in the caption, and the close-match set includes photos with any of the words.)

Normally, Photoshop Album displays only the best-match results. To display the close-match results, click the Close box at the right of the find bar (**Figure 5.25**). The photo well then shows results that are either close or best matches, intermixed in a single sequence. (If there are no best-match results, the close-match set is displayed automatically.)

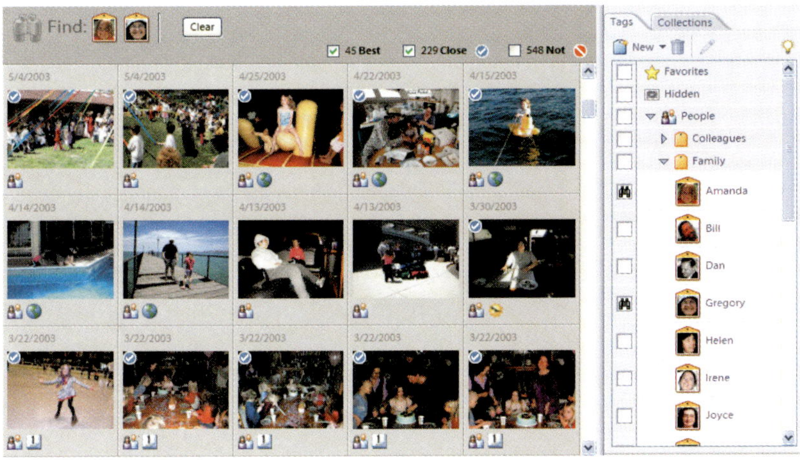

Figure 5.25 With the Close box checked, photos with all or any of the specified tags are shown. Photos that don't have at least some tags are indicated with a check mark in the upper-left corner.

The close-match results are identified by a check mark in the upper-left corner of the thumbnail. In other words, the photo well shows photos with any of the tags chosen; photos that have some but not all of the tags are indicated with a check mark.

Tip *If you find that you generally want the close-match results displayed, you can change the default behavior by choosing Edit > Preferences > General and checking the box for Show Closely Matching Sets for Searches. Now the close-match box in the Find Bar will be automatically checked for every search. You can still uncheck it when you want to see only the best-match results.*

Boolean Searching

If you're comfortable with Boolean search concepts, you may wish you could specify searches directly using the AND and OR of selected search components. Unfortunately, you can't—but it may help to understand how the searches performed by Photoshop Album translate to Boolean searches.

Suppose you search on three tags, TagA, TagB, and TagC. The search results are

- Best match = TagA AND TagB AND TagC
- Close match = (TagA OR TagB OR TagC) AND NOT (best match)

If you search on categories, the logic is a little more complex. If you search on CategoryA and CategoryB, each of which has two tags (for example, CatA-TagA, CatA-TagB), the search performed is

- Best match = (CategoryA OR CatA-TagA OR CatA-TagB) AND (CategoryB OR CatB-TagA OR CatB-TagB)
- Close match = ((CategoryA OR CatA-TagA OR CatA-TagB) OR (CategoryB OR CatB-TagA OR CatB-TagB)) AND NOT (best match)

If you select a category or subcategory as part of the search criteria (by checking the box to its left), Album searches for any photos to which you have applied that category or subcategory, plus any photos that have any of the tags in that category or subcategory. For example, if you search on the Family subcategory, the results will include any photos to which the Family subcategory has been applied, as well as all photos with any of the Family tags.

Photoshop Album's search capabilities are very easy to use and meet most needs. There are some advanced searches you cannot perform directly: for example, you cannot search for photos with Amanda and Gregory only (no other people tags), or for photos with Amanda but not Gregory. Usually, it's not too hard to do the more general search and then scan visually for what you're looking for.

There are some workarounds, if you're really determined. If you want to be able to find pictures that have people by themselves, for example, you can make a tag called Only in the People category. When you're tagging people photos, apply this tag to any photo with only one person in it. Then you can use this tag in your searches to find photos that contain only one particular person (for example, search on Gregory and Only to find pictures that have only Gregory in them).

Finding by Collection or Creation

Finding by collection is, in some ways, just like finding by tags. Click the Organize tab to display the organizing pane, and then the Collections tab to display the list of collections. Double-click any collection to display it in the photo well (see Chapter 4 for more on collections).

Collections are mutually exclusive, so you can search based on only one collection at a time, and you cannot combine a collection with any other type of search.

If you have made a creation (see Chapter 8), it will be represented in the photo well by a thumbnail with the creation icon in the upper-right corner (**Figure 5.26**). You can find all the photos in the creation by right-clicking the creation's thumbnail and choosing Show Creation Items in Photo Well, or by dragging the creation's thumbnail to the find bar at the top of the photo well.

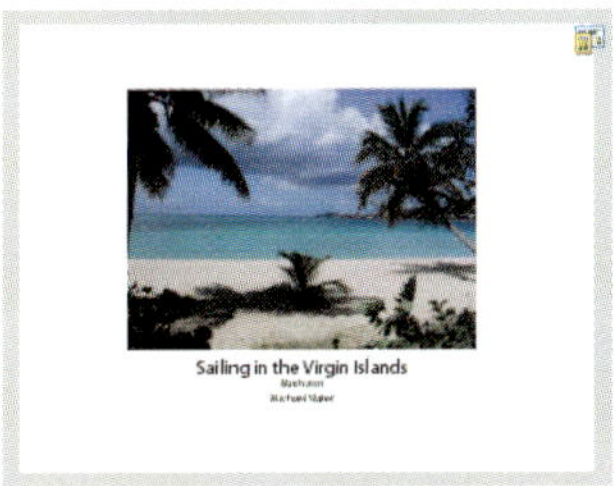

Figure 5.26 **Creations are represented in the photo well by a thumbnail of the creation's first page, with a creation icon in the upper-right corner.**

Finding by Caption or Note

You may sometimes have information in a caption or note that is not reflected in your tags. For example, if you take a trip to Paris, you might tag all the pictures you took there with a Paris place tag. For the pictures of the Eiffel Tower, you might put the name Eiffel Tower in the caption.

In such cases, searching the captions and notes is a quick way to find specific photos. Choose Find > By Caption or Note, and enter the text for which you want to search in the Find by Caption or Note dialog (**Figure 5.27**).

Note *Caption, note, and filename searches are not case sensitive.*

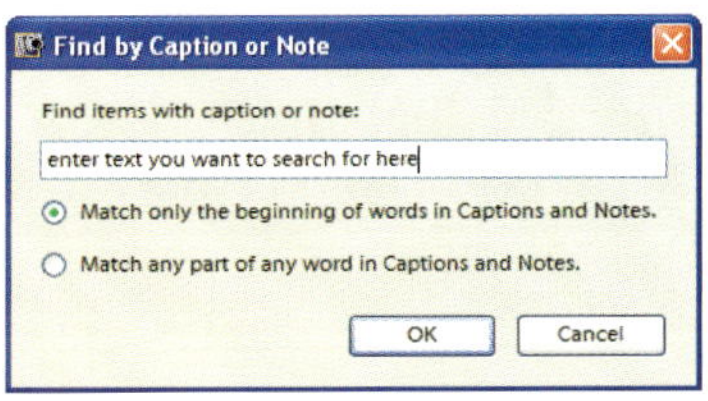

Figure 5.27 **Choose Find > By Caption or Note to search on text in those fields.**

This search always clears any existing search. So if you have previously searched based on tags and then do a search on captions or notes, Album will find all photos that match the search, even if they did not match the tag search. (You might sometimes wish you could constrain the caption search to photos that match a tag search, but unfortunately you can't.)

If you enter more than one word, Photoshop Album does not search for the phrase. Instead, it provides in the best-match set all photos that have all the words you entered, regardless of the order in which they appear and what other words may be present. The close-match set, if you choose to display it, includes all photos with *any* of the words you entered.

For example, suppose you search for *beach Bermuda.* The best-match set would include photos with captions like "On the beach in Bermuda" and "On our trip to Bermuda, we spent lots of time at the beach." The close-match set would include any photo with a caption that has either of these words, such as "Our hotel in Bermuda" or "My favorite beach."

Photoshop Album will match any word that contains the text you enter. For example, if your search word is *beach,* it will find captions that include not just *beach* but also *beaches, beached,* and *beachhead.*

By default, Album will match only words in which the text you entered is at the start of the word, like *playing, played,* and *playground.* You can change this behavior, however, by clicking the radio button for the "Match any part of any word in Captions and Notes" option. You'll get all the matches as described above, but you'll potentially get additional—and sometimes surprising—matches as well. For example, if you choose this option and search for *play,* Album will also find captions with the words *display* or *replay.*

Finding by Filename

If you have renamed some of your files with meaningful filenames, you may want to take advantage of them in searches. Just choose Find > By Filename and enter part or all of the filename you're looking for in the Find by Filename dialog.

Unlike finding by captions or notes, finding by filename searches for the exact text you enter, including any spaces. It matches that text if it appears anywhere in the filename. For example, if you search for *Bob,* it will find "Bob and Mary," "My brother Bob," and "Bobbing for apples." But if you search for *Bob and Mary,* it will find only the first of these examples.

Tip ***You can also use finding by filename to find files of a particular type. Search for* .jpg *to find all JPEG files with this extension, for example (but note that some JPEG files may have extensions of ".jpeg," so you may want to just search for* .jp*, which will find either). Search for* .psd *to find Photoshop files.***

Finding by History

Photoshop Album automatically tracks information about what you have done with each photo. (You can view this information in the History pane of the Properties palette.) Finding using this information can be especially useful if you didn't tag the photos you're looking for.

Suppose, for example, that you regularly email your mother the best pictures of your kids, and now you want to make some prints. You could search for photos you emailed to your mother.

Tip ***This would be a good time to go ahead and tag those photos as Favorites for future use.***

Conversely, you could find all photos you've printed if you're looking for good ones to share via email or to put in an album. To find photos by their history, choose Find > By History, and then select one of the choices in the submenu (**Figure 5.28**).

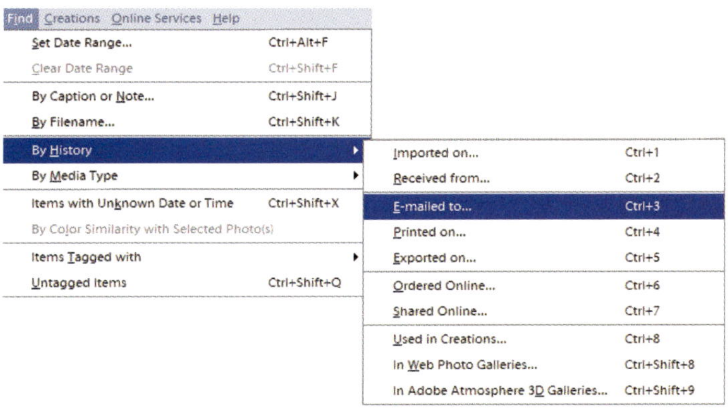

Figure 5.28 **Find > By History enables you to find photos according to what you have done with them in the past.**

Most of these options work similarly. Searching by import batch (Find > By History > Imported on), for example, brings up the "Select one or more groups you Imported" dialog, which displays a list of all the import batches, including the source of the import, the date, and the number of photos (**Figure 5.29**). Initially the list is sorted by date, with the most recent first. You can change the order to oldest first by clicking the Date/Time heading, or sort by another category (such as "Imported from," in this example) by clicking the header for that category. Click the Imported from header to sort photos by the camera from which you imported them.

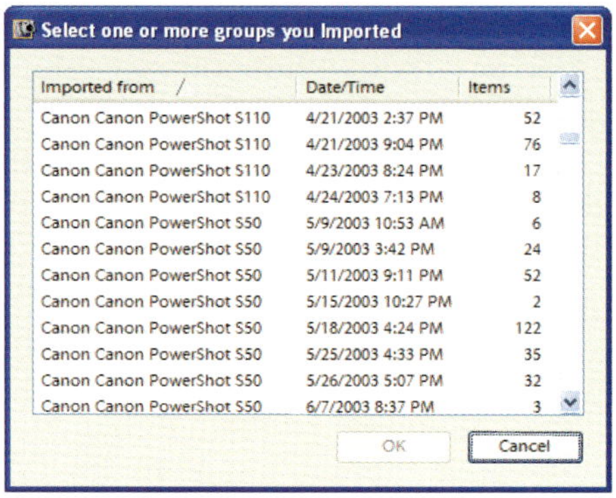

Figure 5.29 **Click the desired import batch to select it, and then click OK to find all the photos from that batch. Click the column headers to change the sort order.**

To see the photos in a particular batch, just click the batch in the list of import batches and then click OK. You can use Shift-click and Ctrl-click to select multiple batches.

To find photos that you've emailed, choose Find > By History > E-mailed to. To sort by the recipient, click the "E-mailed to" column header (**Figure 5.30**). To find all the photos you've emailed to someone, click the first batch you sent to them, Shift-click the last one, and click OK. (If the recipient is shown as "unknown," that means you addressed the email in your email program instead of in Album, so Album has no way of knowing who they were sent to. You can still find them by date emailed, however.)

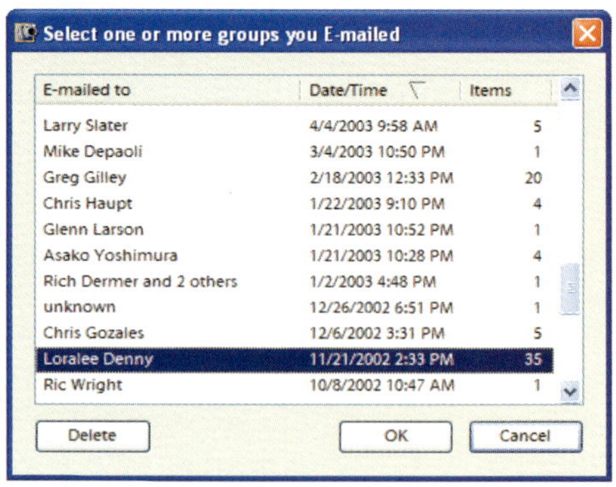

Figure 5.30 **Finding photos by the person to whom you've emailed them can be especially handy if you can't search by tags.**

To find photos you printed, choose Find > By History > Printed on. You can sort photos by date printed or by printer used in the dialog in **Figure 5.31**.

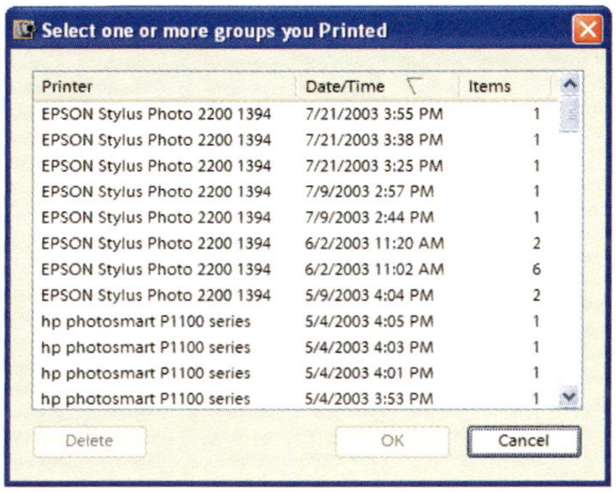

Figure 5.31 You can also find photos by the date you printed them and by the printer used.

Tip *To find all the photos you've ever printed, click the first item in the list, scroll to the bottom, Shift-click the last item, and click OK. You can use the same approach to find all the photos you've exported, used in creations, or shared. You can also select all the print batches in a certain date range to find, for example, all the photos you printed in a given year.*

Finding by Media Type

There are two different ways to find all the items of a particular type, such as photos, video clips, audio files, and creations:

- You can control which types of items are shown in the photo well by choosing View > Media Types (**Figure 5.32**). In the Items Shown dialog the default setting is to show everything except audio files. This is a filter, which persists from one search to the next.
- You can search for all the items of a single type by choosing Find > By Media Type and choosing the desired type from the submenu. You can view items of any type this way, even if you've disabled the display of the selected type in the View > Media Types options.

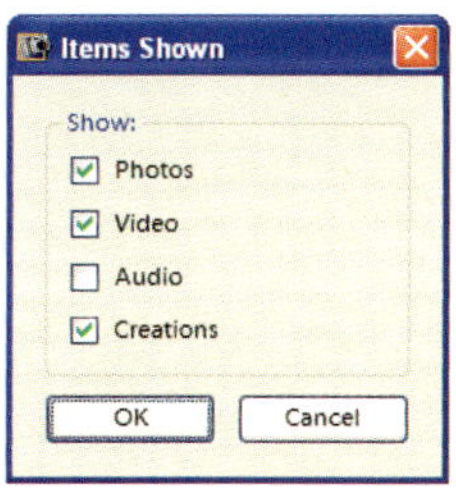

Figure 5.32 Choose View > Media Types to control what types of items appear in the photo well.

You probably won't ever need to use the first approach, unless you specifically want to disable display of video or creations in the photo well. If you do so, avoid using the Show All button, as this will re-enable the display of photos, video, and creations.

Finding by media type is most useful when you're looking for video clips. If you do this often, remember the shortcut: Alt-2. Or if you want to see only photos, eliminating the clutter of video clips and creations, use Alt-1 as the shortcut for finding photos. These finds clear out any existing tag search, however.

Finding creations

Photoshop Album normally displays creations in the photo well just as it does photos. They are dated according to when you made them, which may or may not put them in a spot in the photo well where you can easily find them. To show only creations in the photo well, use Find > By Media Type > Creations (or Alt-4). Or use Creation > Open to see a list of all creations by name. For this to be effective, you must enter names for all your creations. (See Chapter 8 for more on creations.)

You may find it helpful to change the dates of your creations to put them next to the relevant photos. Click the date above the creation, just as for a photo (assuming that you have details turned on), and you'll be given the option to enter a specific date or to use the date of the first photo in the creation.

Working with audio files

You can have Photoshop Album display audio files in the photo well, but in general there is no need to do this; audio files are supported in Album primarily as background music for slide shows. Audio files must be imported into the catalog in order to be usable as background music, but generally there is little value in their being visible, as their thumbnail is only a generic audio icon and you choose background music from other dialogs. Because of this, the default media-types filter is set to not display audio in the photo well.

Viewing the audio files temporarily is useful, however, if you want to play them to decide which you want to use for background music. Choose Find > By Media Type > Audio, and the audio files will be displayed even if the media-types filter is set to not display them. To play an audio file, double-click the icon and then click the green play button in the player window.

If you want to always display audio files in the photo well, choose View > Media Types and check the box for Audio.

To learn about selecting audio files for background music for instant slide shows, see the section "Using Instant Slide Shows," earlier in this chapter. To learn about using background music in creations, see Chapter 8.

Finding by Color Similarity

All the methods for finding photos depend on the metadata associated with the photo, such as its date, tags, or history, except one—color similarity. When finding by color similarity, you can find photos that look similar to another.

To initiate a color-similarity search, just drag one or more photos to the find bar at the top of the photo well (or select the photo and choose Find > By Color Similarity). If you select more than one photo, Album searches for photos that have colors in common with all the selected photos.

The color-similarity search compares the amount of each color present in each photo and displays the results in order of similarity. It doesn't consider shapes or the colors' positions, so while the results are often useful, they can sometimes be surprising (**Figure 5.33**).

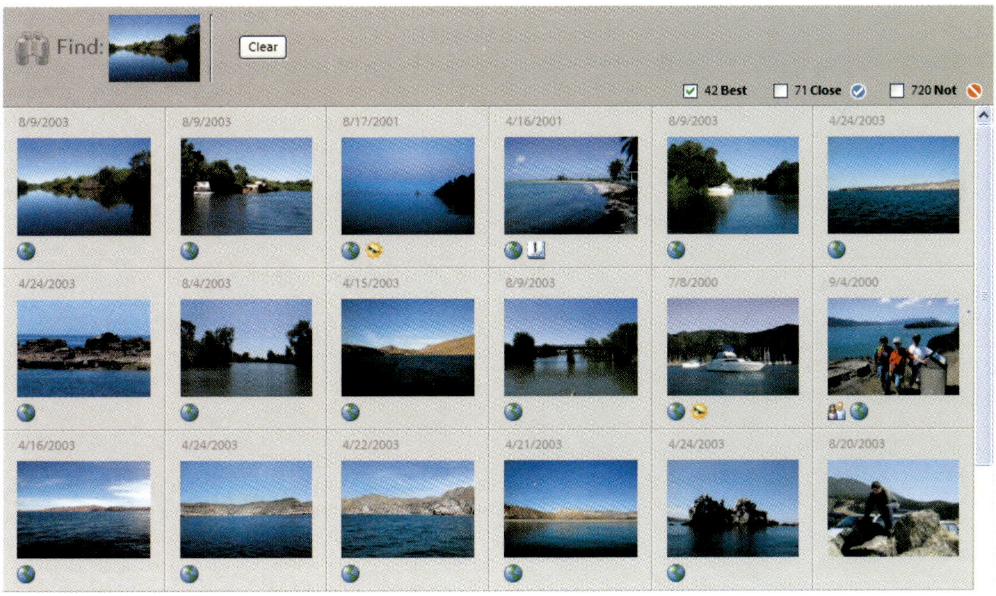

Figure 5.33 **Drag one or more photos to the find bar to find photos with similar colors.**

When you've performed a color similarity-search, the arrangement of the photo well changes to color-similarity order; that is, photos that rank highest in similarity are displayed first. All those above a certain threshold are put in the best-match set, while lower-ranking photos are in the close-match set, and very-low-ranking photos are in the nonmatching set.

Depending on the size and contents of your catalog and the photo(s) you are using as the search criteria, you may find that only some of the best-match set photos are useful. You may also find that there are interesting matches further down in the set, after photos that don't seem like such good matches.

You can narrow the range of photos included in the color-similarity results either by time or by tags. To narrow it by time, see the section "Setting the Date Range," earlier in this chapter. To restrict the color-similarity search to photos with certain tags, drag those tags to the find bar or click the boxes next to them. You can do this before or after initiating the color-similarity search.

The color-similarity search is perhaps most useful when your catalog contains multiple copies of a photo, perhaps at different resolutions or in different file formats. Searching on one of them will generally turn up all the copies at the top of the photo well.

6 Fixing Your Photos

One of the joys of digital photography is how easy it is to correct many common photo problems. Photoshop Album includes some of the most effective automatic enhancements available—including fixes for lighting, color, and red-eye—as well as easy cropping. In this chapter you'll learn everything you need to know about Photoshop Album's photo-fixing capabilities.

If you want to go further into photo editing, either to make enhancements beyond what Photoshop Album can do or to change the content of the photo, Photoshop Elements and Photoshop CS are great tools (see Chapter 7).

Preserving Your Originals

If you've edited digital photos, you've had to keep track of the connection between the original file and the edited version. Both are representations of the same photo, but the Windows file system provides no way to link them, other than naming conventions you may create. Photoshop Album takes care of this for you, showing only the most recent version in the photo well but retaining the link to the original file as well.

Your original photo files, as they came from your camera or scanner, are your "negatives"—the master copies of your photos. If you open a photo in any editing program, make any change, and click Save, you have forever lost the original information. Depending on the file format and what changes you made, the loss may be insignificant or it may be drastic.

Photoshop Album automatically protects your photos when you edit them by making a copy. The original file is never modified; when you edit a photo, the resulting photo is written to a new file. The new file is stored in the same folder as the original file, and it has the same name but with "_edited" appended to it.

Editing Photos from CDs and Read-Only Files and Folders

If you edit a photo that is stored offline (typically on a CD or DVD), Photoshop Album cannot write the edited file back to the same folder where the original is located. If the photo is offline and you attempt to edit it, the original is copied to the hard disk (in a folder within My Pictures/Adobe/Other Photos), and the edited copy is written there as well. If the photo is stored on your hard disk but is read-only, then the original is left in place but the edited copy is written to a folder in Other Photos.

If you edit a photo multiple times, the edited copy will be overwritten; Album maintains only two versions, the original and the most recent edited copy. If you want to save multiple edited versions, duplicate the photo first (right-click it and choose Duplicate Item from the contextual menu).

Using Photoshop Album, you'll never overwrite your original files by accident. With hard disks as large as they are today, it's generally well worth keeping the original file, just in case you later find that you want to edit the file differently.

If you really want to get rid of the original, however, you can right-click the photo and choose Replace Original with Edited.

Caution *I don't recommend doing this—by Murphy's Law, right after you do so, you'll discover that your edits horribly messed up a valuable photo. Don't worry about the extra copies of the files. If necessary, buy a bigger hard disk. Disks are cheap and photos are precious.*

You can perform this action on multiple selected items at once, so if you want to get rid of all the originals in a batch of photos, just select them all, right-click any one, and choose Replace Original with Edited. (And then pray that you never want any of those originals.)

Assuming you don't overwrite the originals, if at any time you decide that you don't like the edits you made, just right-click the photo (or any photo in a selected group) and choose Revert to Original (**Figure 6.1**). This is a much less dangerous operation, since you are losing only your modifications, not your original photos.

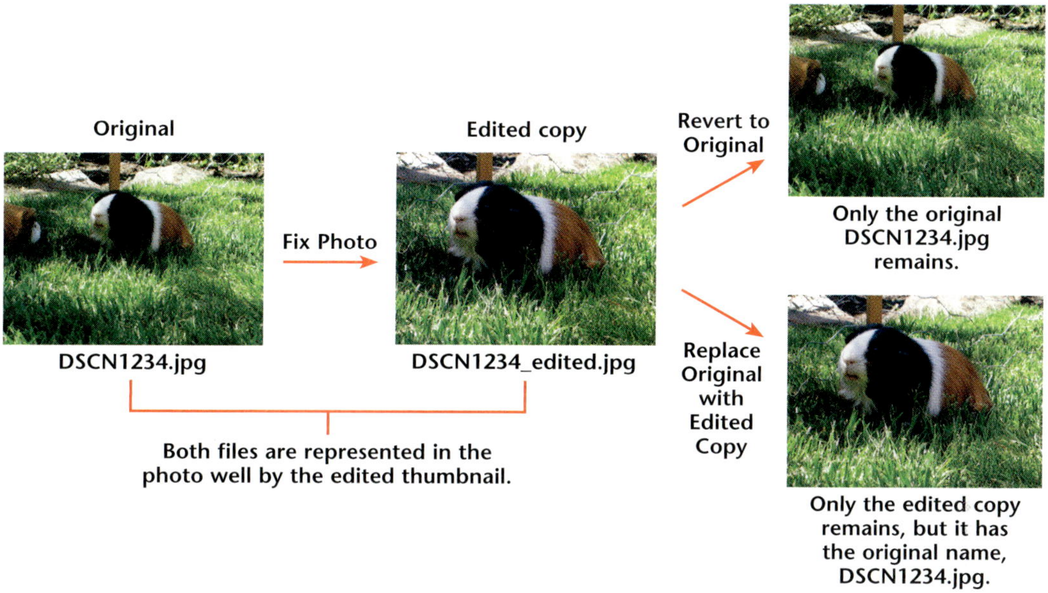

Figure 6.1 **Photoshop Album always preserves the original file when you edit a photo, unless you explicitly choose to overwrite it by choosing Replace Original with Edited.**

Once you edit a photo, the thumbnail in the photo well shows the edited copy, and any action (such as printing or viewing) you take on that photo uses only the edited copy. Album treats the original and the edited copy as a single picture that exists in two versions, and it assumes that the edited version is the one you want to use. You can see the original version in the Fix Photo window by selecting the Before & After view, as described later in this chapter.

Note *The only time the original file can be used (other than by reverting to it) is when burning CDs (see Chapter 3). When making a backup set, Album saves both original and edited files. When you create an archive CD, you have the choice of putting both versions on the disc, or only the edited version.*

Tip *If you want to keep both the original and the edited copy visible in the photo well, duplicate the photo by right-clicking it and choosing Duplicate Item. Then right-click the duplicate copy and choose Revert to Original to get rid of its edited copy. If you want, you can also right-click the other copy and choose Replace Original with Edited. If you do this, however, there will be no connection between the original and the edited copy.*

Rotating Portrait Photos

If your camera doesn't sense rotation automatically, your portrait-oriented photos will be sideways when you import them into Album and you'll have to rotate them manually. You can rotate any number of photos at a time with a single action: select the photo(s) in the photo well and click the appropriate rotate icon (for clockwise or counterclockwise rotation, depending on which way you turned the camera) at the bottom of the photo well (**Figure 6.2**). Alternatively, you can right-click a photo and choose Rotate Left or Rotate Right.

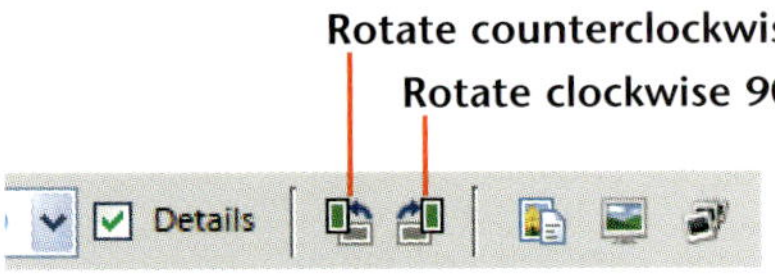

Figure 6.2 Select one or more photos that need to be rotated and click the appropriate rotate button at the bottom of the photo well.

If you have a new digital camera, you may wonder why you'd ever need to rotate a photo manually—and you might never need to. Many cameras now have position sensors built in, so the camera knows when you've rotated the camera and includes this information in the image file. Album reads this information and rotates the photo automatically for display.

Rotate Without Losing Quality

Photoshop Album never overwrites the original image data when you edit a photo—with one exception. When you rotate a photo in Photoshop Album, it usually rotates the photo in a special way that does not require the JPEG file to be decompressed. This *lossless* rotation does not degrade the image in any way, unlike opening a photo in a photo-editing program (such as Photoshop Elements), rotating it, and saving it. (Lossless rotation is possible when the image size is an exact multiple of 16 pixels in both dimensions.)

When Album performs a lossless rotation, it writes the rotated image data back to the original file, rather than creating an edited copy. Photoshop Album does this because there is no information lost, unlike what happens with other kinds of edits, so there is no need to create a new file (**Figure 6.3**).

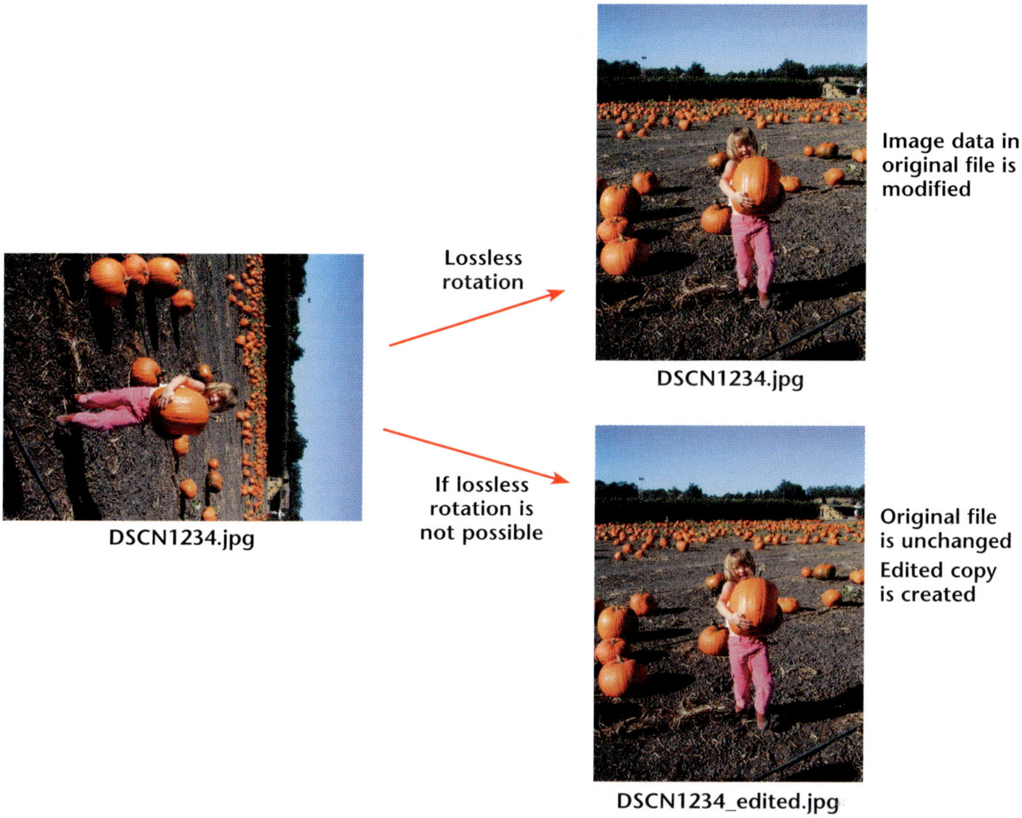

Figure 6.3 Most digital camera photos can be losslessly rotated, in which case Album does not make an edited copy.

If Photoshop Album cannot perform a lossless rotation, which is the case for most scanned images and for images that have been cropped, it creates an edited copy, just as with any other kind of edit.

If you rotate a photo in the Fix Photo window instead of in the photo well, the rotate is not lossless. Any operation in the Fix Photo window generates an edited copy, so if all you are doing is rotation, it is better (and easier) to do it in the photo well.

Beyond Photoshop Album

If you want to rotate a photo in other than 90-degree increments, such as to straighten a horizon or to flip it left or right, you'll need to use an external editor such as Photoshop Elements (see "Straightening and Flipping Photos" in Chapter 7).

How Automatic Rotation Works

If you have a camera that senses rotation, you may find that Album shows the photo differently than some other programs do. This is because the camera doesn't actually rotate the image data when it senses that you have rotated it to a portrait position. Instead, it just adds some orientation information to the image file's *metadata* (data about the image rather than data that represents the actual image), indicating that the image should be rotated before it is displayed.

When you import a photo that has orientation metadata that indicates it should be rotated, Photoshop Album does not initially modify the image data; instead, it rotates the photo automatically whenever the photo is displayed, printed, or used for any other function (**Figure 6.4**). Some other programs, however, ignore the orientation metadata, so they may show such photos in a different orientation than Photoshop Album does.

If you encounter this problem and you want to make sure that all programs see the photo with the same orientation, use Photoshop Album to rotate the image in one direction and then the other. The result will be an identical-looking image, but when Photoshop Album does the rotation, it clears the orientation bits, so the result will be an image that has its data actually rotated, rather than just having the orientation metadata set.

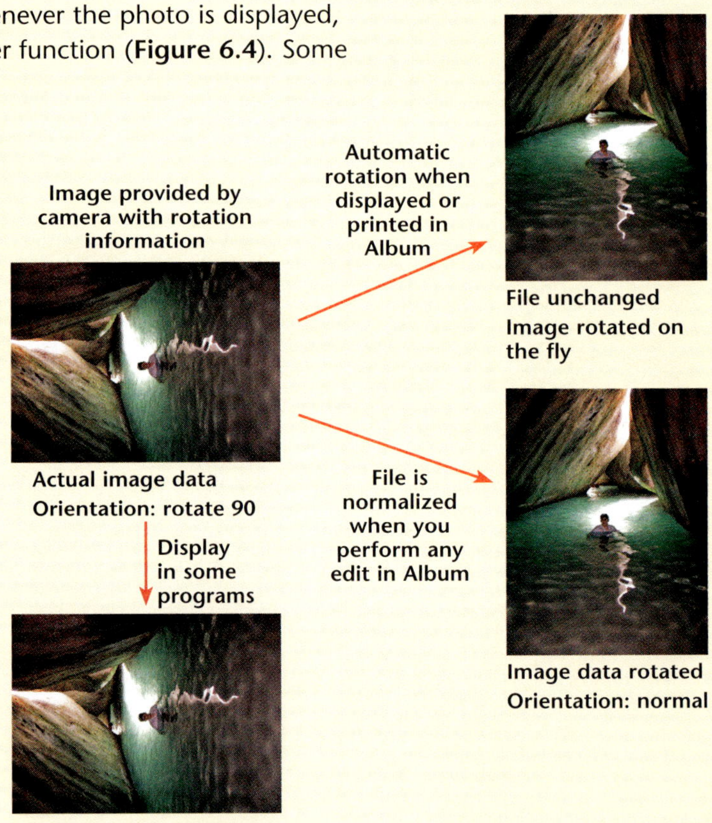

Figure 6.4 If your camera provides orientation (rotation) metadata, Photoshop Album rotates the photo on screen. If you make any type of edit, Album rotates the image data itself and deletes the orientation metadata.

Fixing Photos in Photoshop Album

You can correct many common photo problems using two features built in to Photoshop Album:

- Auto Fix, a completely automated fix you can perform from the photo well and can apply to multiple photos at once
- The Fix Photo window, which gives you more control than Auto Fix does and provides more capabilities

Auto Fix: as Easy as It Gets

The quickest way to improve a photo is to use Auto Fix. Just right-click the photo, select Auto Fix, and you're done! Alternatively, select one or more photos, click the Fix button in the shortcuts bar, and choose Auto Fix from the drop-down menu (**Figure 6.5**); or select one or more photos and press Ctrl-Shift-I.

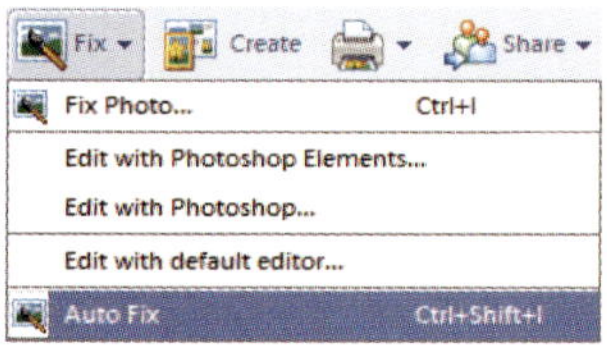

Figure 6.5 Auto Fix is the quickest way to improve your photos; choose it from the Fix menu in the shortcuts bar.

Photoshop Album's Auto Fix is among the most sophisticated automatic photo-enhancement tools in any consumer product today, combining the lighting and color fixes described later in this chapter. It corrects for bad exposures (**Figure 6.6**), brings out detail in shadow areas (**Figure 6.7**), increases color saturation (**Figure 6.8**), and eliminates most color casts (**Figure 6.9**).

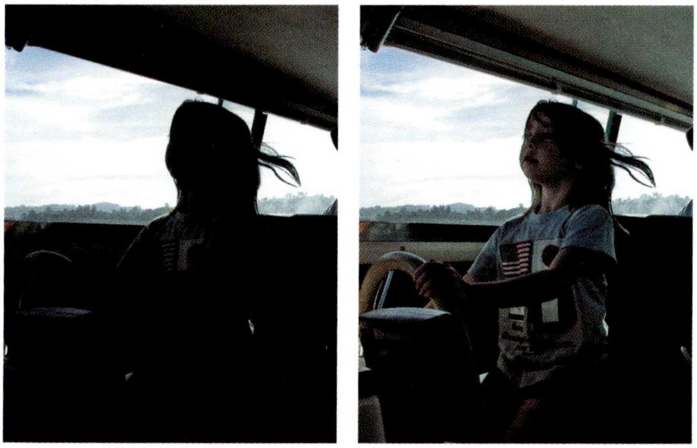

Figure 6.6 Auto Fix can work miracles on photos that are poorly exposed due to back-lighting or other problems.

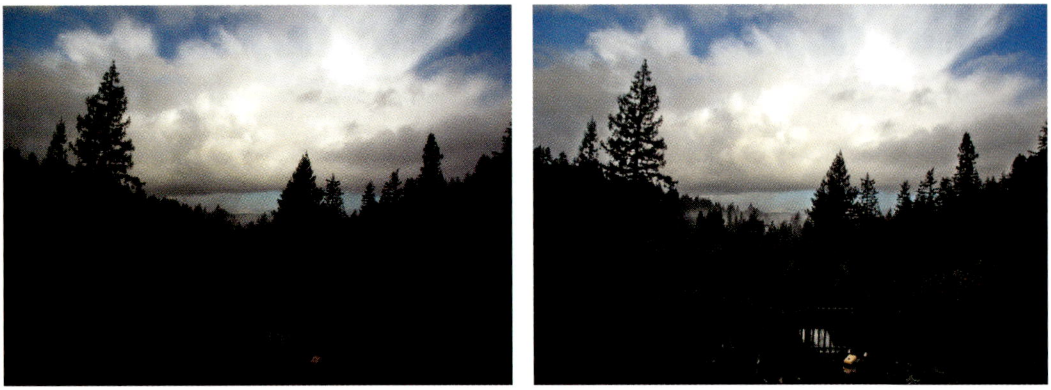

Figure 6.7 Auto Fix brings out detail in shadow areas, creating an image that is much more like what your eye perceived when you took the photo.

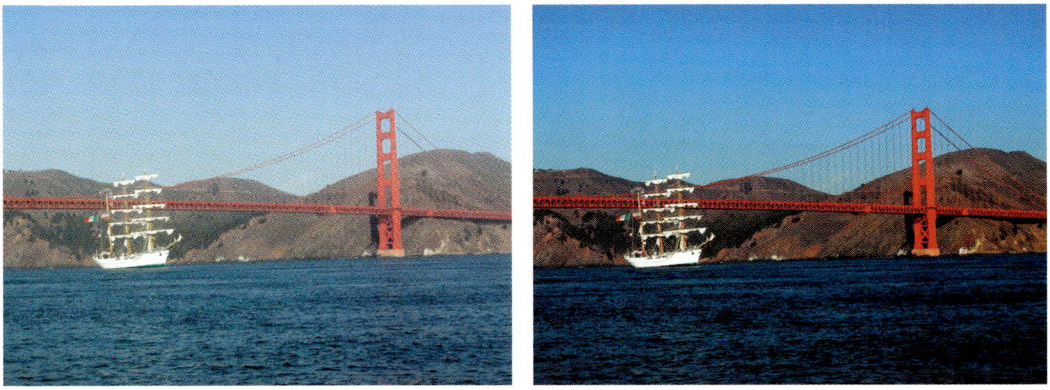

Figure 6.8 Washed-out photos get a nice boost from Auto Fix. If the boost is too much, you can adjust it in the Fix Photo window.

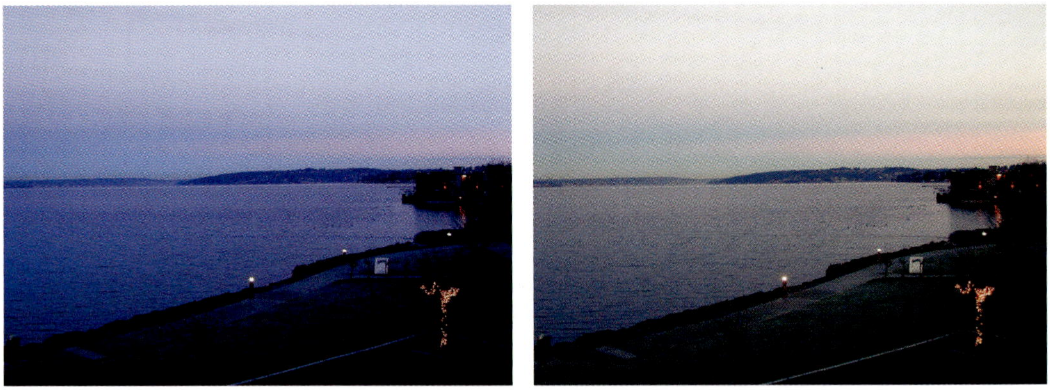

Figure 6.9 Auto Fix corrects modest color casts instantly. You can increase the degree of correction and adjust the color temperature in the Fix Photo window.

You may want to apply Auto Fix routinely to any photo you're going to print or share. Keep in mind, however, that you're roughly doubling the disk space required for each fixed photo, since the original is kept as well. And if you want to have more fine-tuning control, use the Fix Photo window instead of Auto Fix.

As advanced as Auto Fix is, there are cases where the result is less pleasing than the original picture. There is no way for the software to know what the original scene looked like, so unusual photos may be "corrected" in undesirable ways. If, for example, you take a picture at night and want it to look like a night shot, Auto Fix may brighten it more than you want (**Figure 6.10**). If you take a picture in colored light, or in a scene with one overwhelming color, then you probably want to keep the resulting coloration—which Auto Fix will unfortunately reduce (**Figure 6.11**).

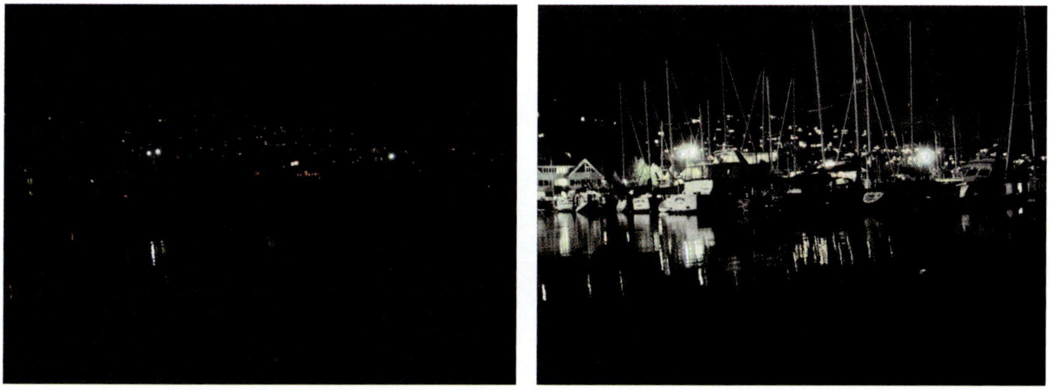

Figure 6.10 Night shots may get brightened more than you want by Auto Fix. (Note that although this is a color photo, there just isn't much color information in the original image.)

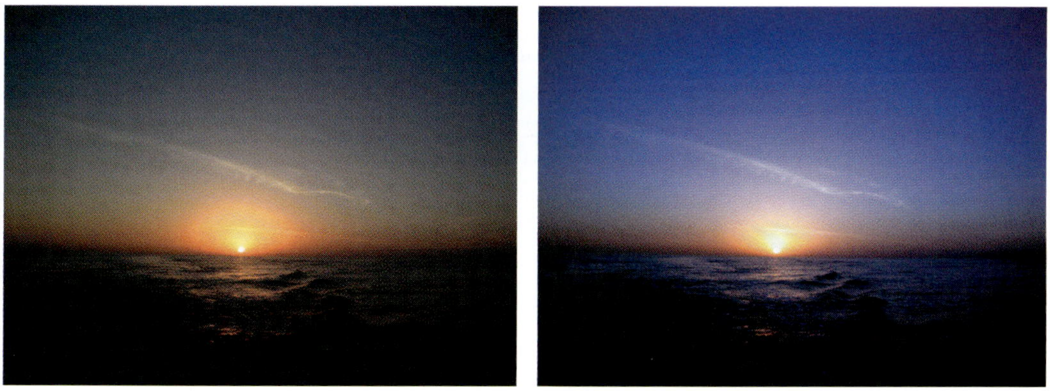

Figure 6.11 Auto Fix doesn't know what the scene really looked like, so if it had a real and desirable color cast, you may prefer not to "correct" it.

Tip ***If you don't like the results of an Auto Fix, you can always use Revert to Original (right-click the photo and choose from the contextual menu) to go back to the way the photo was. You can also use the Fix Photo window to adjust the settings for the fix.***

Using the Fix Photo Window

To have more control than Auto Fix provides, or to sharpen, crop, or fix red-eye, use the Fix Photo window (**Figure 6.12**). You can open the Fix Photo window in several ways:

- Right-click a photo and select Fix Photo
- Select one or more photos, click the Fix Photo button in the shortcuts bar, and choose Fix Photo
- Select one or more photos and press Ctrl-I

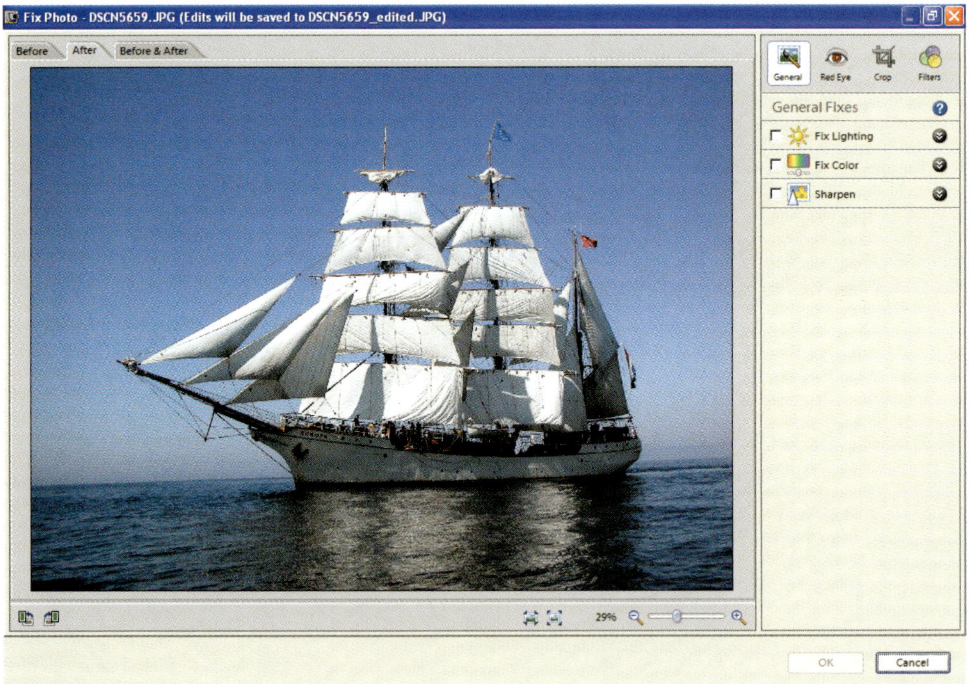

Figure 6.12 **The Fix Photo window gives you more control over enhancing a photo.**

You can resize the Fix Photo window independently of the main application window. Click the maximize button, the middle button at the upper-right corner, to have the window fill the screen. I always keep this window maximized so that the photo is as large as possible.

If you select more than one photo before opening the Fix Photo window, arrow buttons appear at the bottom of the window that allow you to move to the next or previous photo (**Figure 6.13**). Thumbnail images next to each button show the adjacent photos. This is very handy when you're fixing a batch of photos; you don't have to go back and forth to the photo well.

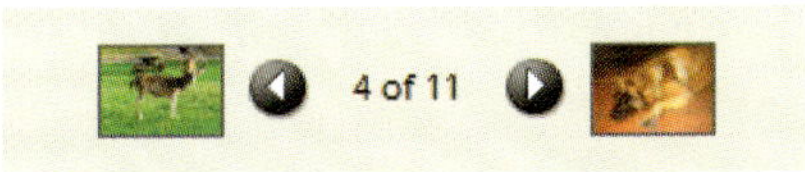

Figure 6.13 **If you select multiple photos before opening the Fix Photo window, you can switch between them without having to return to the photo well by using the arrow buttons at the bottom of the window.**

Fix Photo window modes

The photo display in the Fix Photo window has three modes, which you select by clicking the tabs—Before, After, and Before & After—at the top left. Normally, it's best to select the After tab so that the results of your latest edits are displayed as large as possible. If you're not sure whether you've improved the photo or made it worse, switch to the Before & After tab (**Figure 6.14**) to compare the result with what you started with. To get a large view of the original photo, use the Before tab.

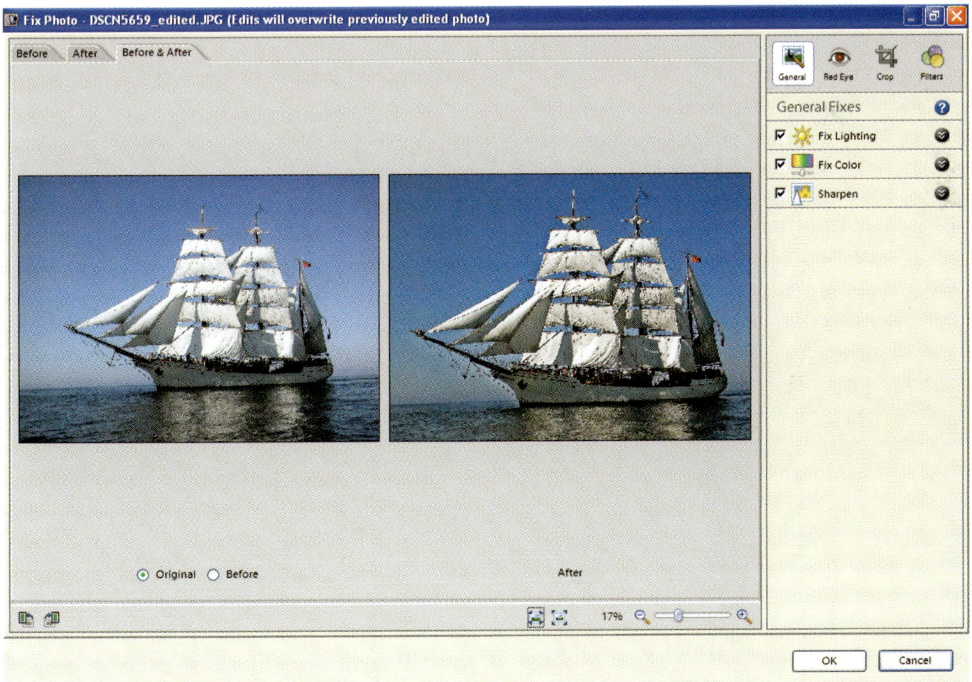

Figure 6.14 **Using the Before & After view, you can see how your fixes have changed the photo.**

The Before and Before & After tabs may have Original and Before radio buttons at the lower left that let you choose whether the "before" version is the original or the most recent saved version of a photo. If this is the first time you've fixed this photo (as is generally the case), there is no difference, and the radio buttons won't appear. But if you fix a photo, close the window, and then open the Fix Photo window again with the same photo, this distinction can be useful.

Note ***Using the Before & After view is the only way to view the original photo once you have made an edited copy, unless you use Revert to Original.***

Zooming for close looks

The zoom slider at the lower-right corner allows you to zoom in to see details more closely (**Figure 6.15**). Shortcuts buttons to the left of the slider let you jump directly to the two most useful zoom levels:

- The left button sizes the photo to fit the window. This is done automatically when you open the window, so you use this button when you've zoomed in and want to return to the initial view.

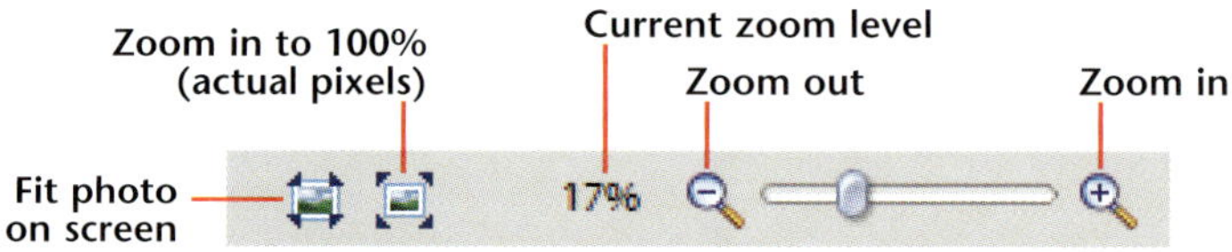

Figure 6.15 You can quickly zoom in to see each individual pixel or zoom out to see the whole photo.

- The right button jumps to the Actual Pixels zoom level. This means that each pixel on the screen displays one pixel of the photo. Since your photos will generally have more pixels than your screen is capable of displaying, the screen shows only part of the photo at this zoom level. At any zoom level less than this, you're not seeing all the detail that is in your image. In the Fit to Window zoom level, for example, you see the entire photo, but each pixel on the screen represents several pixels in the image.

Tip ***To best evaluate the results of any change, and especially when sharpening, look at the photo at the Actual Pixels zoom level.***

Zooming in any closer than the Actual Pixels view doesn't display any additional detail; it just makes the details bigger, assigning each pixel of the image to more than one pixel on the screen. This is sometimes useful if you want to look very closely at details in the image, but it is rarely needed.

When you are zoomed in, scroll bars appear so that you can move around the image. You can also zoom in on a particular area of the image by clicking it. Each time you click, the zoom level increases, and the point you clicked is centered in the window. You can also zoom out by pressing Alt while you click. To return to seeing the entire image, click the Fit to Window button.

Tip ***If you use zoom frequently, remember the shortcut keys: Ctrl-0 (zero) to fit to the window, and Ctrl-Alt-0 to show actual pixels.***

In the Before & After view, zooming and scrolling work on both the before and after images at the same time, so you can easily compare details of both versions.

Avoiding Progressive Loss of Quality

If you've edited photos in the past, you may have been taught that repeated editing of photos can cause loss of quality. This is because each time you open a JPEG file, it is decompressed, and then when you save it, it is recompressed. If you do this multiple times, each cycle further erodes the image.

Photoshop Album uses a clever technique to avoid progressive loss from multiple edits, so you don't have to worry about saving your photos in a lossless format like TIFF or PSD.

When you edit a JPEG photo in Album, it stores the edited copy in JPEG format. If you edit that photo a second time, however, Photoshop Album does *not* start from the edited file, unlike virtually all other programs. Instead, it opens the original file, reapplies the edits you did in the past, and then applies any new edits you make.

Album must compress the file when saving the edited copy, but since it starts each time from the original file, it decompresses and compresses only once, no matter how many times you edit the same photo.

This special treatment applies only to edits you make with Photoshop Album's Auto Fix feature or its Fix Photo window; it does not apply to edits you make in any external editor, including Photoshop or Photoshop Elements.

Special note to users upgrading from Photoshop Album 1.0: Photoshop Album 2.0 cannot regenerate edits that you performed in the earlier version. So if you edit a photo that was previously edited in version 1.0, Album must start from the edited copy, not from the original. To avoid the additional compress/decompress cycle, select Revert to Original and then redo all your edits using Photoshop Album 2.0. Be aware, however, that the enhancement functions in Album 2.0 are different from those in Album 1.0, so you may not be able to exactly re-create your previous edited version.

Changing your mind

Don't worry about getting your photo fixes exactly right the first time. You can always go back to the Fix Photo window and enable or disable certain fixes, or change the settings for any of them. Because Photoshop Album stores this information in the catalog, not just in the photo file, successive edits don't cause any loss of quality (see the sidebar "Avoiding Progressive Loss of Quality"), unlike what occurs with other programs. You can also see exactly what fixes you have applied when you return to the Fix Photo window, and you can adjust them individually; you don't have to start over, as you do with most photo editors.

If you decide you want to get rid of your changes entirely, you can always right-click a photo (in the photo well, not in the Fix Photo window) and choose Revert to Original. You can also go back to the Fix Photo window and change individual fixes.

If you want to make multiple edited versions of the same photo, right-click the photo in the photo well and choose Duplicate Item (multiple times if you want more than two versions). Then you can perform different fixes on each copy.

Fixing Lighting Problems

Probably the most common photo problem is poor lighting. Our eyes do amazing things when we look at a real-world scene, adjusting as we gaze from a dark region to a bright one so that we can perceive a very wide range of light levels. The sensor in a digital camera does not have nearly as wide a range. As a result, the images you capture often don't look the same as your eye and brain perceived them.

Photoshop Album's Fix Lighting function analyzes the photo and adjusts the brightness and hue of every pixel to provide a more pleasing image. Just click the box next to Fix Lighting in the General Fixes pane of the Fix Photo window, and Photoshop Album will automatically fix the photo. In most cases the automatic settings should be fine.

If you want to adjust the settings, click the double-arrow button to the right of the Fix Lighting label (**Figure 6.16**). You can use the two sliders to control the degree of adjustment:

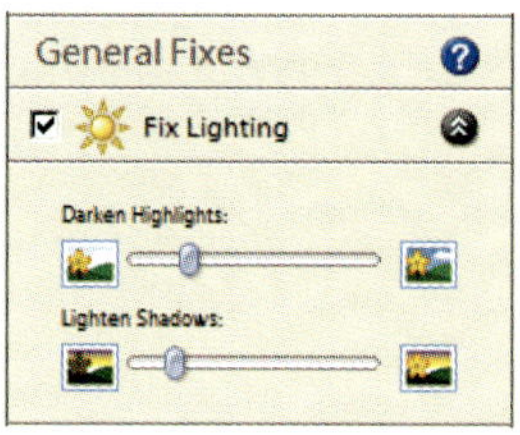

Figure 6.16 If you don't like the automatic setting for Fix Lighting, click the double-arrow button to make the two adjustment sliders appear.

- If the bright areas of the photo are too bright, drag the Darken Highlights slider to the right (**Figure 6.17**). If you want them to be brighter, drag the slider to the left.

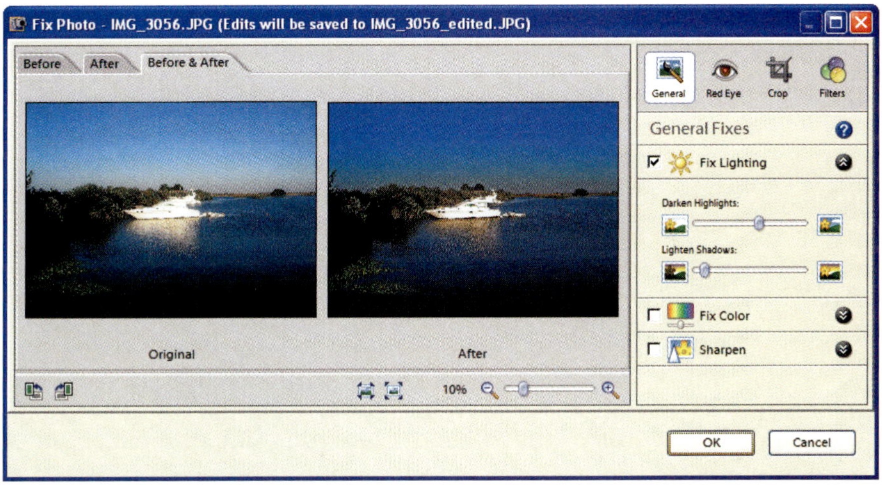

Figure 6.17 **Photos with brightly lit white subjects benefit from increasing the Darken Highlights setting.**

- To bring out more detail in the dark areas, drag the Lighten Shadows slider to the right (**Figure 6.18**). If the dark areas seem too pale, drag the slider to the left.

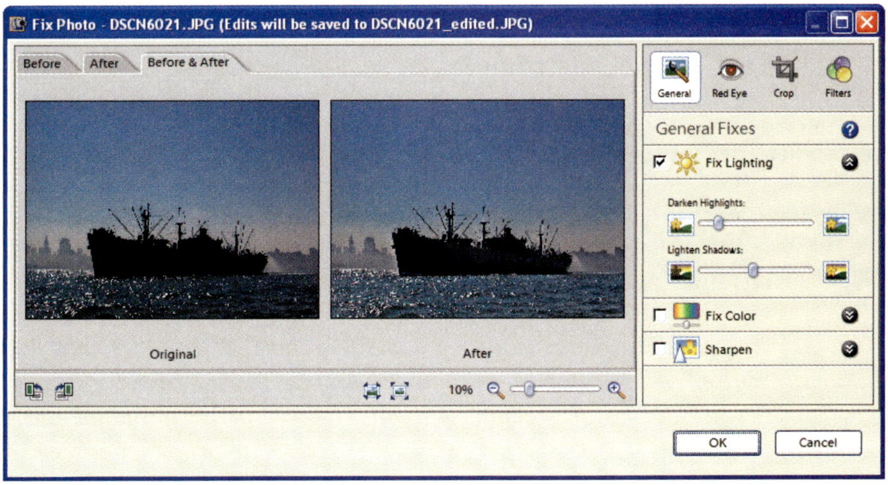

Figure 6.18 **Photos with heavily shadowed subjects look better if you increase the Lighten Shadows setting.**

***Tip** Photoshop Album automatically chooses the initial settings for these sliders based on its analysis of the photo, so the settings will be different for different photos. If you have moved the sliders and want to return to the automatic settings, you must turn off the Fix Lighting function by unchecking the box; close the Fix Photo window by clicking OK; and re-open the Fix Photo window and click the Fix Lighting box again.*

Fix Lighting does an exceptional job of brightening backlit subjects and bringing out detail from shadow areas. These are enhancements that are generally hard to do by other means, and Fix Lighting works far better than the usual contrast and brightness adjustments.

***Note** Contrast and brightness controls are not included in Photoshop Album because Fix Lighting generally does a better job. Simple contrast and brightness adjustments almost always degrade image quality.*

Fix Lighting also makes colors more saturated by ensuring that each color spans the full intensity range from light to dark. There are some photos for which you may want to maintain more subtle coloration, in which case you should not use this fix. In addition, very dark photos may be brightened in an unpleasing way, even with very low settings of the sliders.

Beyond Photoshop Album

If you want more control over lighting enhancements, you'll need to use an external photo editor, such as Photoshop Elements. See "Correcting Color, Contrast, and Brightness" in Chapter 7. Photoshop gives you even more controls over lighting enhancement. (Only the most recent version of Photoshop, called Photoshop CS, has lighting fixes like those in Album.)

Fixing Color Problems

If the colors in your photos don't seem quite right, you can often correct them using Photoshop Album simply by clicking the Fix Color box in the General Fixes pane of the Fix Photo window.

***Caution** Before you adjust colors in your photos, read the sidebar "Getting Accurate Colors on Your Monitor." If the colors are fine when printed but incorrect on the monitor, the problem is with your monitor. If so, changes you make to the photo might only make it worse when you print it. If, on the other hand, the colors look right on your monitor but don't look good when the photo is printed, you may need to adjust your printer settings or use different paper (see Chapter 9).*

Some cameras tend to produce photos with a blue or yellow color cast in certain lighting situations. The Fix Color function can be truly magical for such photos. On the other hand, if you have a photo that is supposed to have a yellow cast (such as from late afternoon sunlight), then "fixing" the color may in fact make the photo worse.

Tip *In general, you should be more judicious in applying Fix Color than Fix Lighting. I find that most photos benefit from Fix Lighting, but I only use Fix Color if there is an obvious color problem.*

As with Fix Lighting, you can change the automatic settings that Fix Color selects by clicking the double-arrow button to the right of the label (**Figure 6.19**) and then making adjustments using the two sliders:

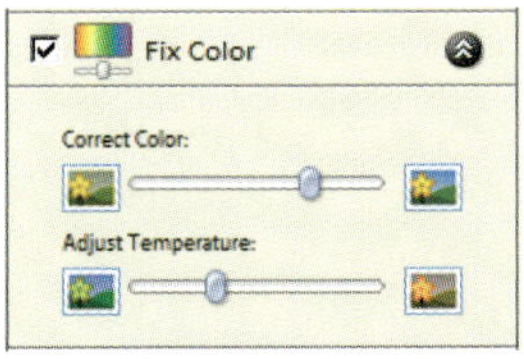

Figure 6.19 To override the automatic settings, click the double-arrow button, which exposes the color-adjustment settings.

- Move the Correct Color slider to the right to increase the amount of color correction (**Figure 6.20**). If you want a more subtle adjustment, move the slider to the left.
- If the photo is too red, move the Adjust Temperature slider to the left. If it too blue, move it to the right.

There is some interaction between these two sliders, so you may want to try changing one and then the other to see what effect you like best.

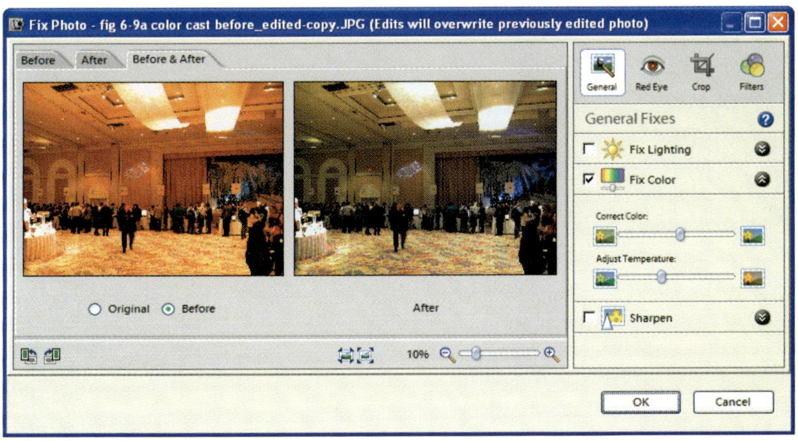

Figure 6.20 This photo required a high setting for Correct Color and a nudge of the Adjust Temperature slider toward blue to get accurate colors.

Getting Accurate Colors on Your Monitor

If your display isn't showing colors accurately, your prints won't look like what you see on the display. Furthermore, if you adjust color or lighting so that it looks good on your display, but your display isn't accurate, then you have actually misadjusted your photo to compensate for the display. So it is important that your display be at least reasonably accurate.

If you have a CRT display, be sure to adjust its brightness and contrast properly. The Adobe Gamma utility, which is included on the Photoshop Album CD but which you must install separately, will help you do this.

For accurate color, you need something called an ICC (International Color Consortium) profile for your monitor. You can get an ICC profile in several ways:

- Many displays come with a default profile. This "factory" profile cannot take into account individual variations, but it's a lot better than nothing.
- For CRTs, the Adobe Gamma utility can create a profile. It does this based on your responses to a series of visual questions. This is an acceptable approach for CRT displays but does not work well for LCDs, for which there is so much color variation with viewing angle that "by eye" judgments are very hard to make reliably.
- If you're willing to accept the additional cost and complexity, consider a hardware calibrator. It creates the most accurate profiles by measuring the light coming from the display. One inexpensive device is ColorVision's Spyder, which is available for under $150 and works with both LCD and CRT displays (www.colorvision.com). You place it on the front of your display and then run software that comes with it.

To install a display profile, right-click on the desktop and choose Properties. In the Display Properties dialog click the Settings tab, then the Advanced button, and finally the Color Management tab. This will show any profiles that have been loaded. If you have another profile, click the Add button and select that profile. If you have multiple profiles, click the one you want to use and then the Set As Default button.

Once you have installed a profile, you can create a very accurate image with software that uses this profile. All Adobe imaging products use a profile if one is present. Many other products, however, including Windows itself, ignore profiles (even though the profile is set in the Windows Displays control panel!). As a result, you may see different colors in different applications. (If your photos look wrong in Adobe applications but correct in others, you may have a bad profile.)

There are lots of subtleties in getting accurate color. If you want the best results, refer to the references listed in Appendix A to explore this in more depth.

Beyond Photoshop Album

If you want to make fine adjustments in color correction, you'll need to use an external editor. Photoshop Elements provides powerful and easy-to-use tools for color correction, as described in the section "Correcting Color, Contrast, and Brightness" in Chapter 7. Photoshop provides several additional tools, including one that allows you to directly adjust the curves that control how each color is rendered; this is usually the professional's method of choice, but it requires considerable experience to master.

Sharpening Photos

Most digital photos can be improved with sharpening. Scanned photos benefit to an even greater extent than digital camera images. You may want some images to look soft, but in most cases a little sharpening is beneficial.

You can perform a modest degree of sharpening by clicking the Sharpen box in the General Fixes pane of the Fix Photo window. For routine use, the default sharpening setting should be fine for most photos.

To adjust the amount of sharpening, click the double-arrow button to the right of the Sharpen label and then move the slider to increase or decrease the degree of sharpening (**Figure 6.21**).

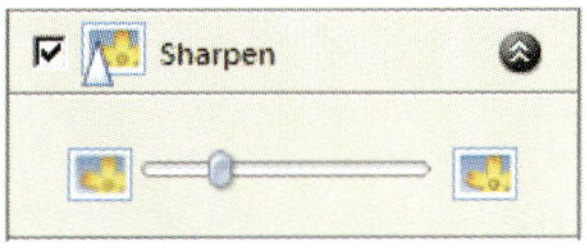

Figure 6.21 You can adjust the degree of automatic sharpening by clicking the double-arrow button to reveal the slider.

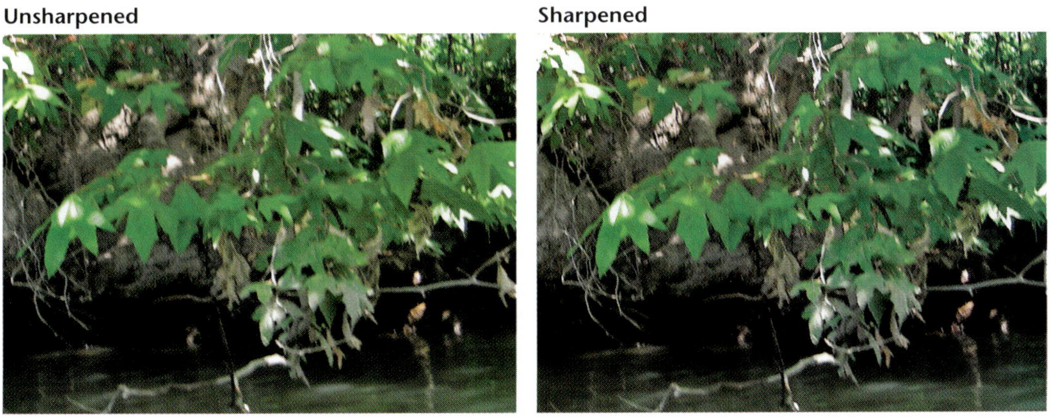

Figure 6.22 If a photo is out of focus, sharpening won't do much. (More extreme sharpening using Photoshop Elements would help a bit.)

Don't expect sharpening to work miracles with fuzzy pictures (**Figure 6.22**). This is sharpening, not refocusing. Sharpening increases contrast at edges—that's all. It can make pictures that are in pretty good focus quite a bit crisper. Small details tend to pop out much more (**Figure 6.23**).

Unsharpened | **Default sharpening level** | **Maximum sharpening level**

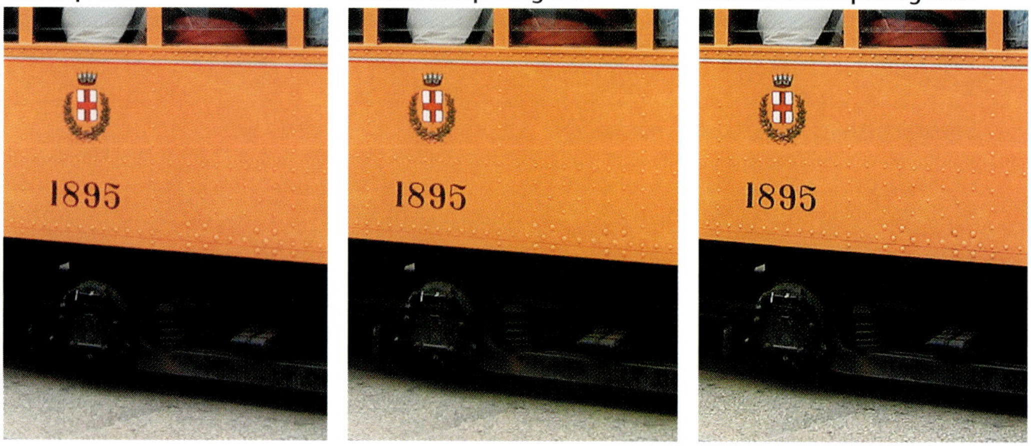

Figure 6.23 **The default level of sharpening gives this photo a nice crispness, but taken to its limit, the sharpening makes the photo look unnatural.**

One downside of sharpening is that it can make noise, or grain, more obvious, since the edges of those elements get sharpened, too. Excessive sharpening can also cause a halolike effect at high-contrast edges. Watch for these artifacts, and reduce the level of sharpening if you see them.

Tip *An image that is optimally sharpened for printing may look oversharpened onscreen. You may find that the best sharpening for printing is when the image just starts to look oversharpened on the screen.*

Beyond Photoshop Album

If you want more control over sharpening, you can use Photoshop Elements' Unsharp Mask, which provides several dimensions for adjustment (see "Sharpening with Finesse" in Chapter 7). By using an editing program to sharpen, you can also select certain areas to sharpen, which typically yields a better result than sharpening the entire image. It is a matter of how much time you want to invest in this level of refinement.

If you want to experiment with taking blur out of images, there are a few third-party products that extend Photoshop and Photoshop Elements to provide that capability using techniques other than Unsharp Mask. Two examples are Acclaim Software's Focus Magic ($45; www.focusmagic.com) and FixerLabs' FocusFixer ($49; www.fixerlabs.com).

Correcting Red-Eye

One of the most commonly occurring problems when people are photographed with flash is red-eye—light reflects from the back of the eye to create those devilish-looking eyes in the photo. Fortunately, red-eye is usually easy to correct with Photoshop Album (**Figure 6.24**).

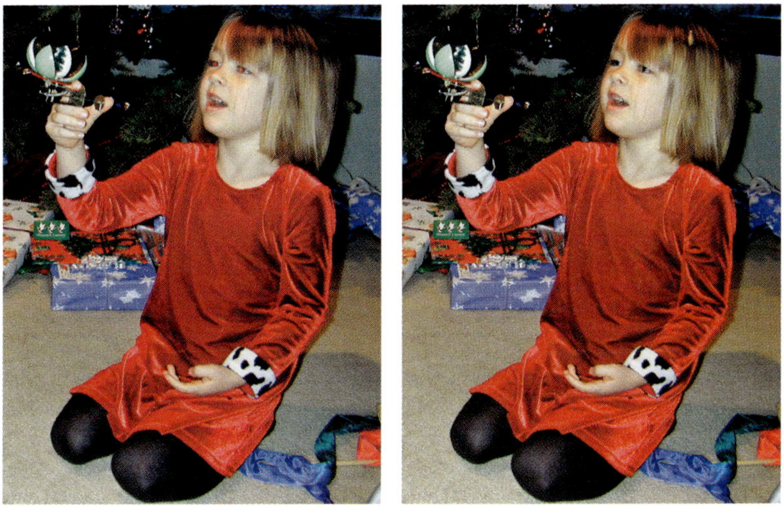

Figure 6.24 **Photoshop Album can instantly fix most red-eye problems.**

To fix red-eye, click the Red Eye button at the top-right corner of the Fix Photo window (**Figure 6.25**).

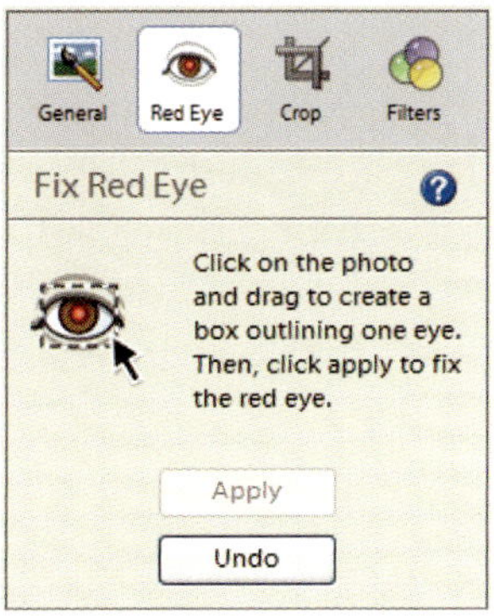

Figure 6.25 **Click the Red Eye button to prepare to fix red-eye problems.**

Select the eye you want to correct by clicking one corner of the area that includes it (such as the top-left corner) and then dragging to the diagonally opposite corner (**Figure 6.26**). It may help to zoom in on the photo first if the face is small. If the area you've selected does not include the entire eye, the correction may not work properly. If you select an area that is too large, you may get undesirable changes (such as gray spots on the face). So make this selection carefully; with a little practice it's easy to do.

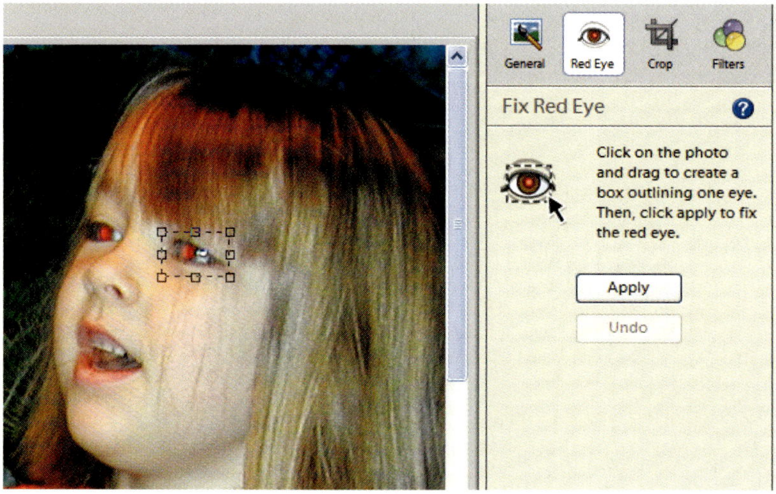

Figure 6.26 To fix red-eye, click and drag to outline one eye, and then click the Apply button. Repeat for the other eye.

***Tip** Don't draw a selection around both eyes together; for good results, you must correct one eye at a time.*

After you have selected the area, you can adjust it by dragging any of the small boxes at the sides or corners. With most photos, you don't have to be very precise.

To make the correction, click the Apply button in the Fix Red Eye pane after you've finished selecting the area. If you don't like the result, click the Undo button and try again, making sure you've selected the area properly. Assuming that your photo has two red eyes, as most do, repeat the process for the second eye. If there is more than one person in the photo with red-eye, just repeat for each eye. Occasionally, the red-eye fix removes some but not all of the red. In this case, draw the selection rectangle again and reapply the fix a second, or even a third, time.

Beyond Photoshop Album

Some photos have unusual red-eye problems that Photoshop Album can't correct. In such cases, the Red-eye Brush in Photoshop Elements and Photoshop can be very useful. It requires more effort, but with practice you can fix virtually any red-eye problem.

In some cases, however, it's difficult to restore a fully natural-looking eye, because too much visual information has been lost to the reflected flash. In such cases, full "correction" is really a matter of painting in a natural-looking eye, or copying one from another photo and pasting it in. These kinds of changes require considerable editing skill.

The eyes of dogs, cats, and other animals display a similar effect when photographed with a flash, often appearing yellow or green. Photoshop Album cannot correct these problems, however, so you'll have to use Photoshop Elements or Photoshop.

Avoiding Red-Eye

Red-eye occurs when the light source—the camera's flash—is close to the camera's lens, so light bouncing off the back of the eye comes right back to the lens. The best way to avoid red-eye—assuming that you cannot photograph with natural light—is to use a separate flash unit rather than one built into the camera. This allows the flash to be further from the lens and eliminates most red-eye problems. With a compact digital camera, however, this is often not practical, and with many models it's not even possible.

Many cameras offer a red-eye-reduction mode, which attempts to reduce red-eye by triggering several short flashes before the final flash that captures the photo. These pre-flashes cause the eye's iris to close down, reducing the amount of light that can reflect back. This technique is sometimes effective, but I don't use it because it increases the delay between the instant when I press the shutter and the instant when the photo is captured—a delay that is frustrating enough in digital photography without this addition. Fortunately, the red-eye fix in Photoshop Album can correct most photos easily.

Cropping for Maximum Impact

Ideally, you always frame your pictures just right when you take them. Often, however, you can increase the impact of your photos by cropping them. Cropping allows you to eliminate distracting elements and make the composition more interesting.

To crop a photo, select it, choose Fix Photo, and click the Crop button (**Figure 6.27**). A dotted rectangle shows the outline of the crop area, and parts of the photo that fall outside the crop area are darkened. To change the crop area, click and drag any of the small squares around the edge of the dotted rectangle. You can also move the crop area without changing its size by clicking anywhere within the crop area and dragging it.

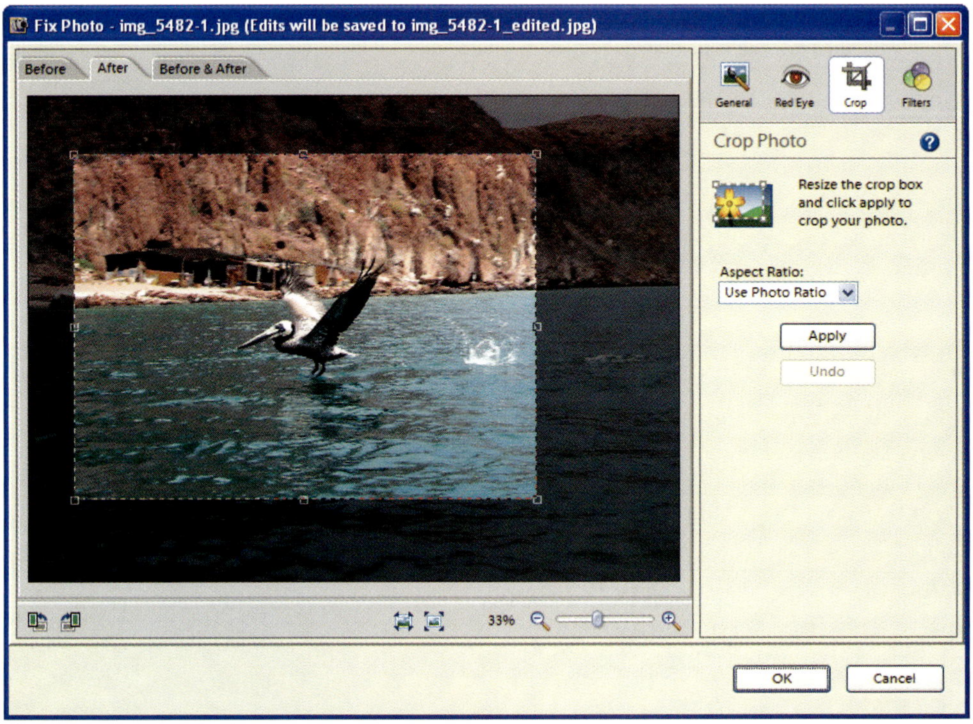

Figure 6.27 To use only part of a photo, click the Crop button and adjust the dotted box to show where you want the photo cropped.

It is easy to crop your photos to any shape you want, but if you choose an arbitrary shape, the photo probably won't fit any standard frame, fill any standard size paper, or fill your screen.

Most consumer digital cameras capture images with a 4:3 *aspect ratio* (the proportion of width to height), which is another way of saying that the width is 1.33 times the height (**Figure 6.28**). Most professional-grade digital cameras, as well as some consumer models, however, use a wider, 3:2 aspect ratio (the width is 1.5 times the height), like that of 35 mm film. Each common print size has a different aspect ratio, as do some display resolutions.

Aspect ratios:	5:4	4:3	3:2	16:9
Prints: (inches)	8 by 10 16 by 20	9 by 12	4 by 6	—
Displays: (pixels)	1280 by 1024	1024 by 768 1600 by 1200	—	1280 by 720 1920 by 1080
Devices:	Some PC monitors	Most PC monitors; most consumer digital cameras	35 mm and most pro digital cameras	HDTV

Figure 6.28 **Unless you can live entirely in a 4:3 world, you'll have to keep aspect ratios in mind to avoid having parts of your photos unintentionally cropped out.**

Photoshop Album provides many options for controlling the aspect ratio when cropping (**Figure 6.29**). If you want complete freedom in choosing the crop shape, select No Restriction from the Aspect Ratio pop-up list (in the Fix Photo window's Crop Photo pane)—but be aware that if you print at a standard size (Chapter 9) or use creation templates (Chapter 8), you may not be able to use all of your cropped photo without leaving some blank space either above and below or to the sides (depending on the shape of your cropped photo).

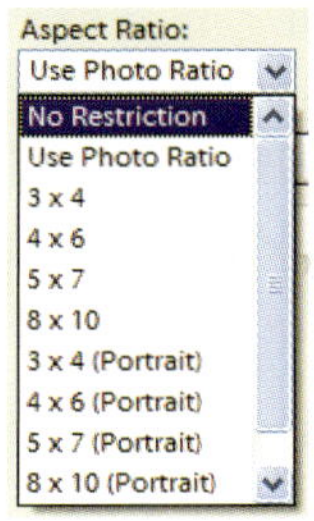

Figure 6.29 **Select the aspect ratio you want before cropping to stick to standard shapes.**

To constrain the shape, pick an aspect ratio from the Aspect Ratio pop-up list. Choose Use Photo Ratio to keep the shape of the original photo, or pick one of the standard aspect ratios.

Note ***These selections do not control the physical size of the image, just its shape. Selecting 4 x 6, for example, does not mean that you must print at 4 by 6 inches; you could also print at 2 by 3 inches or 6 by 9 inches, or any other size with the same proportions.***

Most of the creation templates are designed for a 4:3 aspect ratio, which is what most digital cameras produce, so 3 x 4 is the best choice if you are planning to make creations. There is a tradeoff, however: none of the standard print sizes match this aspect ratio. Thus, if you know that you will be making a 4-by-6 or 5-by-7 or 8-by-10 print, choose that aspect ratio so that your cropping can be precisely reflected in the final print.

Tip *For special photos that you want to print in multiple sizes, you may want to have several versions with different cropping. To do so, duplicate the photo in the photo well one or more times before going to the Fix Photo window, and then crop each copy separately.*

If you view most of your photos onscreen rather than in print, and you want them to fill the screen, the 3 x 4 aspect ratio is the best choice. Most common screen resolutions (including 800 by 600, 1024 by 768, and 1600 by 1200) use this ratio. Unfortunately, the common 1280 x 1024 size does not; if you can set the display to 1280 by 960 instead, the ratio will match. If you display your photos full screen on a 1280-by-1024 monitor, the left and right edges will be trimmed slightly so that the photo can fill the screen in both dimensions.

Note *Although it is sometimes tempting to crop to a small part of a photo—such as selecting just one person from a group photo—keep in mind that when you do, you are dramatically reducing the number of pixels in the photo. This is the same as so-called digital zoom in the camera. If you print such photos at large sizes, they may look poor.*

To see the actual pixel dimensions (the number of pixels in each dimension, horizontal and vertical), view the photo's properties after completing the crop. (To view photo properties, select the photo and press Alt-Enter or click the Properties button at the bottom of the photo window.) You need at least 150 pixels per inch for good-quality printing, so if you crop to a 450-by-600-pixel region, the largest size at which you can print with good quality is 3 by 4 inches.

As with all edits performed in the Fix Photo window, you can undo the crop later—even after exiting the window—if you change your mind. Just select the photo, open the Fix Photo window again, and select the crop mode. Click the Undo button to eliminate the crop, or adjust the crop by dragging the edges of the crop rectangle or changing the aspect-ratio constraint.

Beyond Photoshop Album

Photoshop Album crops only to a rectangular area that is aligned with the edges of the original photo. You may want to use Photoshop Elements to crop to an angled rectangular area, such as to straighten a horizon (see "Straightening and Flipping Photos" in Chapter 7). You can also use Photoshop Elements to make a vignette (cropping to an oval area with fuzzy edges).

Changing to Black and White or Sepia

If you want to give an old-fashioned look to a photo, convert it to black and white or sepia. In the Fix Photo window, click the Filters button (**Figure 6.30**) and select the effect you want. Sepia is the same as black and white but with a brown tone (**Figure 6.31**).

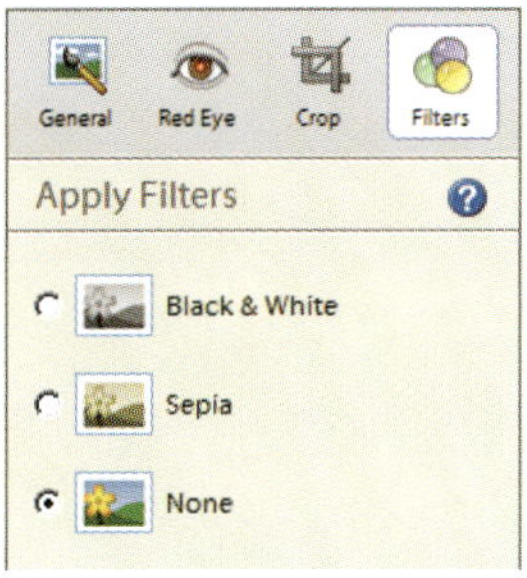

Figure 6.30 **The filters allow you to make a photo black and white or sepia toned.**

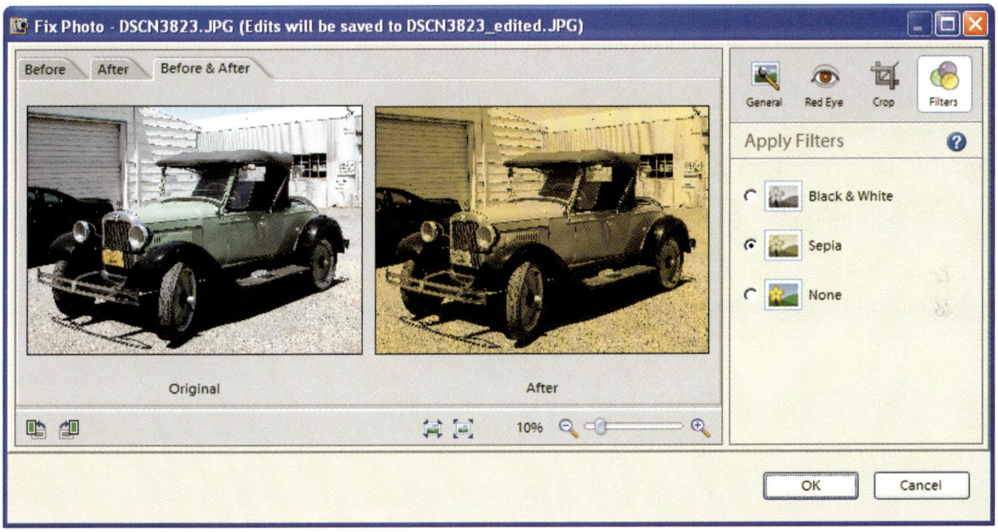

Figure 6.31 **Sepia is a nice effect for photos that you want to look old-fashioned.**

Tip *Try applying Fix Lighting on photos you convert to black and white or sepia; it can often improve them considerably. Even the Fix Color adjustment will have some effect, because the color adjustments are made before the image is converted to black and white.*

There are many more filters available in Photoshop Elements; see "Adding Special Effects with Filters" in Chapter 7.

In most regards, digital photography involves the same skills and techniques used in film photography. But if you take into account some unique aspects of digital photography, you'll be more likely to get the most from your camera. Teaching how to take better pictures is beyond the scope of this book, but there are some basic tips you can apply right away to improve your results.

Tips 1, 2, and 3: Take Lots of Pictures!

The most fundamental difference between film and digital photography is that the cost of each additional photo is essentially zero for a digital camera. You might fill up your memory card, but if you have another card, or you can empty the card into your computer, or you review the photos on the camera and delete the bad ones, you can keep shooting. Batteries can be a limiting factor if you haven't brought along enough spares. But to a much greater degree than when shooting on film, with a digital camera you can shoot and shoot and shoot without going broke.

This is a tremendous benefit, because you can follow the key principle of taking good pictures, which is to take lots of them, essentially for free. I almost never take only a single photo of anything. If there's any movement in the subject, or if you are moving, take several photos so that you can choose the sharpest one. If there are people in the photo, take a series of shots so that you can choose the one with the best expressions. Take shots with different framing. Zoom in and out, move around, take photos from different heights. Shooting digitally, you're not going to have to throw out double prints of all the bad shots—you can just delete them, or even leave them on your hard disk but ignore them.

Bracketing and Bursts

The exposure can be critical for digital cameras, even more so than with most film. If the scene has extremes of darkness and light, it can be very difficult—if not impossible—to capture detail in the shadows without "blowing out" the highlights (that is, having bright areas turn pure white, with no detail). The more advanced digital cameras allow you to select an automatic exposure-bracketing option, which causes the camera to take a series of shots at slightly different exposures. This allows you to select the one with the best exposure once you're back at your computer. And if you want to delve into more advanced Photoshop techniques, you can even combine multiple images shot at different exposures to use shadow detail from one image and highlight detail from another, allowing you to create a digital image with more detail than the camera is capable of capturing with any single exposure.

Many digital cameras offer a burst mode, which takes a series of photos in quick succession. More expensive cameras can take faster and longer bursts. When shooting moving objects, this can be a great aid, since you don't have to capture the exact right moment; you capture a series of moments, and you can choose the best one later.

Dealing with Shutter Lag

Speaking of capturing the moment, the delay between the time when you press the button and when the photo is actually captured can be one of the more exasperating aspects of digital photography, especially when taking pictures of people or action scenes. The more expensive cameras generally have a much shorter delay, and as technology progresses, the delay is being reduced in even the less expensive cameras. With most cameras, you can greatly reduce the delay by depressing the shutter button halfway. The camera then focuses and sets the exposure, which is the cause for most of the delay. When you press the button fully, the delay before the image is captured is then much shorter.

You may find that with fast-moving subjects, getting the right moment is difficult even with the half-press trick. The only solution then is to take lots of pictures, anticipating the timing as best you can and trusting that eventually you'll get the timing just right. If you're shooting an event where you have to capture the perfect instant and it only comes once, this may be the time to drag out your old film camera—or splurge on a digital SLR with super-short shutter lag.

Adjusting ISO Speed

With a film camera, you can choose a higher-speed film, which allows you to shoot in lower light but results in a grainier image. Digital cameras involve a similar tradeoff, except all you need to change is a setting—if your camera provides this option (fully automatic cameras typically do not).

Sensors in most digital cameras are not as sensitive as high-speed film; they are typically the equivalent of 50 to 100 ISO. You can increase this speed setting, up to 400 in many midrange cameras and as high as 1600 in some prosumer models. Just as faster film has more grain, images captured at higher speeds have more digital noise (random colored dots that can make an image look grainy). This noise can be even more bothersome than film grain, so don't increase the ISO setting unless you must.

If you do shoot at higher ISO speeds, you may be able to significantly improve the quality of your images by using Photoshop or Photoshop Elements along with a plug-in filter that reduces noise, as described in Chapter 7.

Creating Panoramas

Finally, keep in mind the potential of panoramas. With Photoshop Elements, you can stitch together multiple photos into a single, seamless photo (see Chapter 8). This works both horizontally and vertically, so you can make wide landscapes or capture tall buildings. There are three keys to shooting good panoramas:

1. Figure out how to use the exposure lock on your camera: you'll get the best results if all the shots in the panorama are taken with the same exposure. Aim the camera at a part of the scene that is neither the brightest nor the dimmest, and lock in the exposure. Keep it locked while you shoot the series of photos.

2. Overlap the photos by about half of the frame so that the software will have plenty of information with which to align them accurately.

3. Move the camera as little as possible. Try to rotate it around its axis; don't hold it at arm's length and rotate your body. Use a tripod if you can.

7 Working with External Editors

Photoshop Album's Fix Photo window provides simple, powerful fixes that will probably meet most of your needs. If you want to go further with photo editing, you can use Album in concert with any photo editor. The integration works most smoothly with the latest versions of Adobe's editors, Photoshop Elements 2.0 and Photoshop CS.

This chapter will teach you how to fix some of the most common photo problems, such as crooked horizons and scratches, using Photoshop Elements. You'll also see how to use some of the same photo-fixing features that you can use in Album but take more control of them in Elements. You can even see how to tap into the strength of Photoshop with a powerful tool for retouching photos.

Accessing Photo Editors from Photoshop Album

If you have either Photoshop Elements 2.0 or Photoshop 7.0 or CS installed, menu items in Photoshop Album allow you to launch an edit session using either editor. Right-click a photo in the photo well, choose Edit With from the pop-up menu, and then select the editor, or select the photo and choose Edit With from the Edit menu.

When you first edit a file using any external editor, Album makes a copy of the file, with "_edited" appended to the filename; this is the file the editor opens. Thus your original is always preserved, and if you want to get rid of your changes, you can use the Revert to Original option. If you edit the photo a second time, however, with either Album's Fix Photo window or an external editor, Album must start from the edited copy because it doesn't have access to a list of all the edits you made. Therefore, you'll lose some quality each time you edit the photo, if you save it in JPEG format. (See the sidebar "Avoiding Progressive Loss of Quality" in Chapter 6 to learn why this doesn't occur if you make your edits with Album's Fix Photo window.)

Using Non-Adobe Editors

If you're using a non-Adobe editor (or an earlier version of one of the Adobe editors), you can still launch it in the same way. Your Windows settings determine what program is the default editor for each file type, and Photoshop Album will use those default settings unless you tell it to do otherwise. If you want Album to use a specific program that is not the default, choose Edit > Preferences > Editing to go to the Editing pane of the Preferences window. Click Choose Application and click the Browse button. Finally, in the Choose Editing Application window, locate the .exe file for the program you want to use.

If you use a non-Adobe editor, Album doesn't have as much control over the interaction, so you need to exercise some additional care. Always use Save, rather than Save As, in the editor, or Album won't know how to find the edited file, and the file won't be linked to the original or imported into your catalog—you'll have to import it just as you would any other new photo. Using Save won't overwrite your original, as Album makes a copy before launching the external editor. (If, however, you edit for the second time a photo that you edited previously, Album retains only the most recent version.)

Tip *If you expect to edit multiple photos using an external editor during the same work session, don't close the editing program when you're done editing each photo; just close the document window. That way, you won't have to wait for the editor to start up each time you choose to edit a photo. Also, you can initiate editing sessions on multiple photos at the same time by selecting them all and then choosing Edit > Edit With.*

Note *While an edit session using an external editor is in process, the photo is locked in Album and cannot be modified. When you close the external editor or the document window in the editor, Album will unlock the photo. If you want to continue the editing session but abandon the link to Album, right-click the photo in the photo well and choose Cancel External Edit. The photo will remain open in the editor, but Album will not track any new version you create there.*

Editing with Photoshop Elements

Photoshop Elements is an excellent companion to Album for more advanced editing. You can use Photoshop Elements to do such tasks as the following fairly easy ones:

- Rotate a photo by a small amount to straighten a crooked horizon
- Do color correction, lighting adjustments, and sharpening with more control
- Apply filters for artistic effects
- Add text or graphics
- Combine multiple photos into a panorama

You can also perform more challenging tasks, such as erasing scratches or distracting background objects and combining parts of multiple photos into one. This section will get you started with some of these tasks; for full details, refer to Photoshop Elements' integrated help system and the references in Appendix A.

Photoshop Elements provides *recipes* (sets of instructions) to guide you through many common tasks. The Recipes palette is normally displayed at the right edge of the window; if it's not, choose Window > How To. Then select what kind of task you want to perform from the pop-up menu at the top of the palette and follow the instructions (**Figure 7.1**).

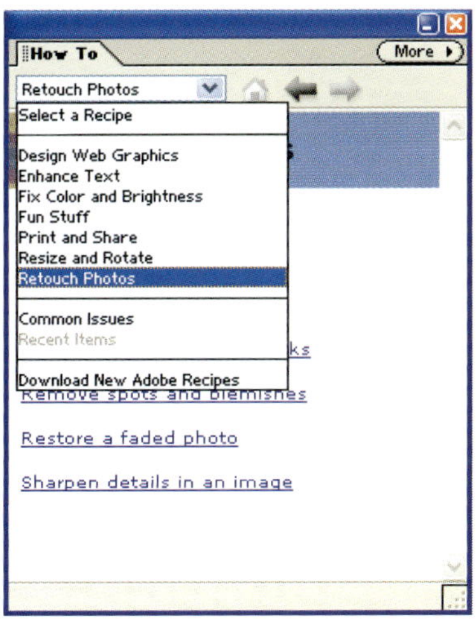

Figure 7.1 **Photoshop Elements' How To (recipes) palette provides helpful guidance for performing common tasks.**

Straightening and Flipping Photos

Perhaps the most common problem you won't be able to fix in Album alone is a crooked horizon. This is easy to do in Photoshop Elements. You can use any of three different approaches:

- If the horizon is distinct, Photoshop Elements may be able to straighten it automatically. Choose Image > Rotate > Straighten and Crop Image. Photoshop Elements will analyze the photo to find the closest thing to a horizontal line, rotate the image to make this line exactly horizontal, and then crop the photo to eliminate the slanted edges that result from the rotation.
- If the automatic approach doesn't deliver the result you want, you can undo it by pressing Ctrl-Z (or click the Step Backward button, represented by a counterclockwise arrow, in the shortcuts bar). Enlarge the image window so that you have some gray space surrounding the photo. Then choose Image > Rotate > Free Rotate Layer, and click OK in the dialog that asks if you want to make this a background layer, and again in the dialog that asks you to name the layer (don't worry about what all this means for now.) Move your pointer past any edge of the photo until it turns into a curved, double-headed arrow (**Figure 7.2**). Click and drag to rotate the photo. When you're done, click the check mark in the Options bar to complete the operation (**Figure 7.3**). You'll probably then want to crop the photo to make it rectangular; if you don't, you'll have empty triangular areas on all sides.

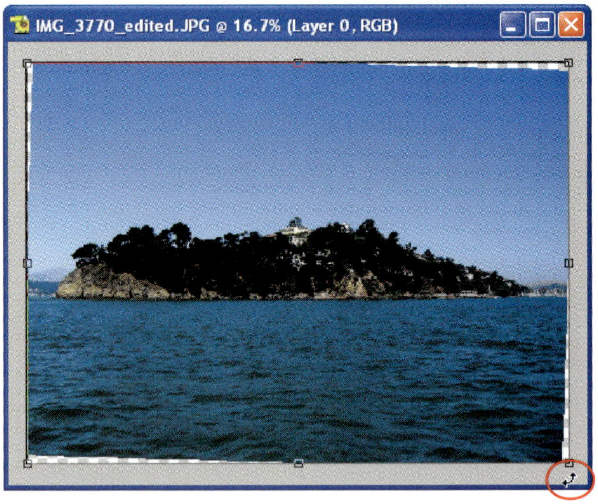

Figure 7.2 The free-rotate option allows you to precisely rotate a photo to straighten the image or achieve a special effect.

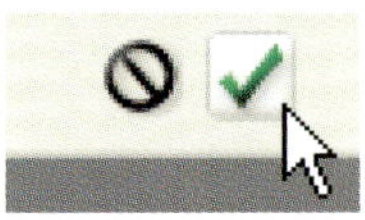

Figure 7.3 To complete each operation in Photoshop Elements, click the check mark in the Options bar at the top of the window.

- You can rotate a photo by a certain number of degrees by choosing Image > Rotate > Custom and entering the desired number. If the result isn't quite right, click Ctrl-Z to undo and try again.

Sometimes you may want a photo to be flipped—that is, a mirror image of itself, swapping left for right. For example, you may prefer that a photo show a person running from left to right instead of right to left. Just choose Image > Rotate > Flip Horizontal. Be sure there is no text in the picture, however, or it will be reversed, too.

Correcting Color, Contrast, and Brightness

You can correct most color and lighting problems using the Fix Color and Fix Lighting features in Photoshop Album, adjusting the sliders if needed. But if you want to manually modify the color, brightness, or contrast, or want to have more control over the changes, you can do so with Photoshop Elements.

After opening the photo in Photoshop Elements, choose Enhance > Quick Fix (**Figure 7.4**). If you choose the Brightness adjustment category in the Quick fix dialog, you can select from a variety of adjustment methods. Choose Brightness/Contrast in part 2 to access manual adjustment sliders. To get manual sliders for hue, saturation, and lightness, choose Color Correction in part 1 and Hue/Saturation in part 2. Use caution, however; it's far easier to damage your photos with these adjustments than it is to enhance them.

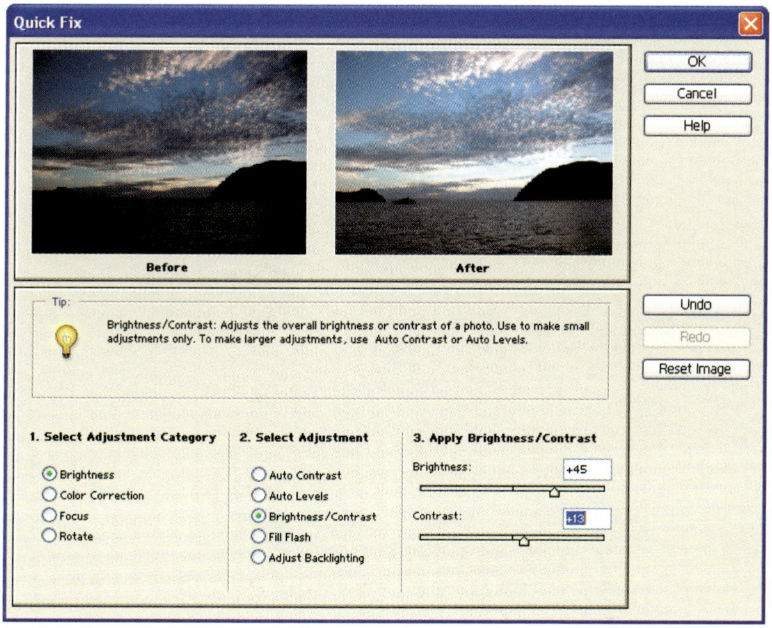

Figure 7.4
Photoshop Elements' Quick Fix dialog provides easy access to common adjustments and shows before and after views of the photo.

You may find that some photos are improved more by Auto Levels (Enhance > Auto Levels) than by the fixes in Album. Auto Color (Enhance > Auto Color) will generate a somewhat different result than Album's Fix Color, but in general you're likely to find Album's result to be at least as good. (Photoshop Elements 2.0 was released before Photoshop Album 2.0, so the advanced auto-fix algorithms in Album are not present in Photoshop Elements.) There's no harm in trying them, though; just press Ctrl-Z to undo if you don't like the result. (For more sophisticated controls, use the Levels adjustment, as described later in this section.)

Caution ***If you're changing brightness, contrast, or color by any method, be sure your monitor is calibrated, as discussed in the sidebar "Getting Accurate Colors on Your Monitor" in Chapter 6. If it isn't, your adjustments may yield a photo that looks good on your monitor but poor on other monitors or when printed.***

Other methods to adjust colors may be more effective in some situations. One way to get rid of a color cast is to specify a spot on the photo that should not have any color other than a shade of black or white. Choose Enhance > Adjust Color > Color Cast. You can then click any area of the photo that should have a neutral tone—anything that should be pure white, black, or gray—and the photo's colors will be shifted to make that color neutral (**Figure 7.5**). You can keep clicking different areas until you get to the color balance you want.

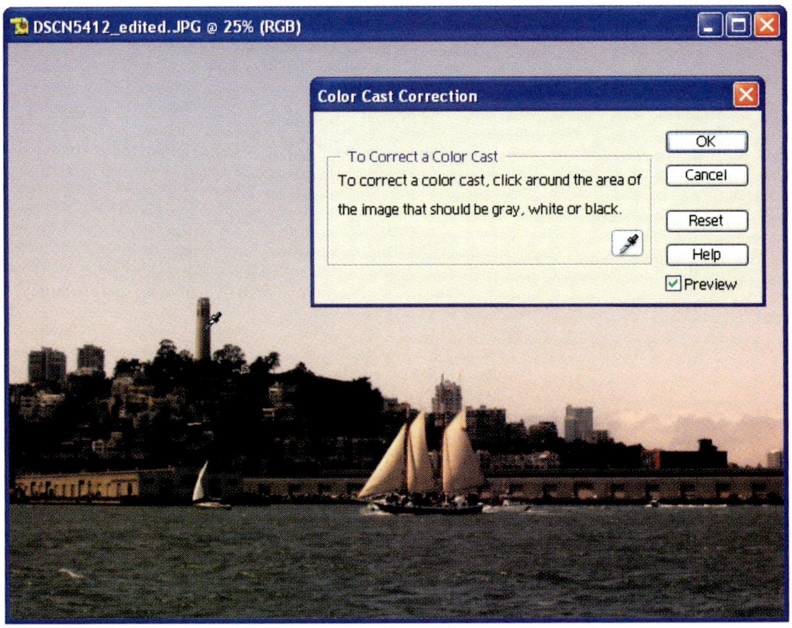

Figure 7.5
The Color Cast Correction tool lets you specify what should be white, gray, or black by clicking it with the eyedropper. Try different spots until you get the effect you want.

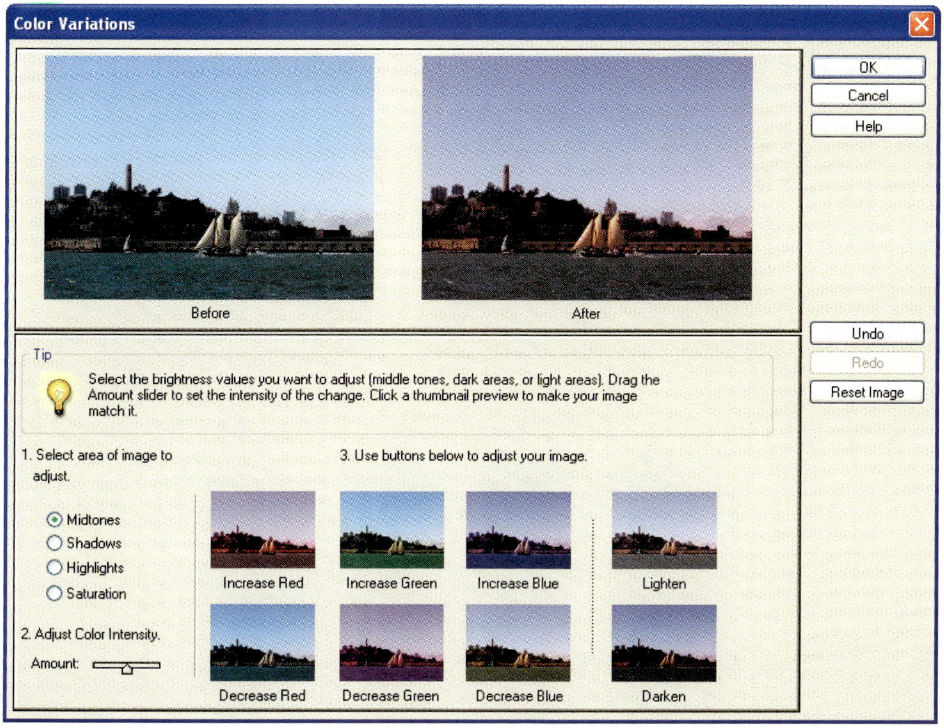

Figure 7.6 Choosing from color variations is an easy way to manually color-balance a photo.

Another way to manually adjust the color balance is to use the Color Variations window. Choose Enhance > Adjust Color > Color Variations (**Figure 7.6**). You can make separate adjustments for the shadows, midtones, highlights, and overall saturation in part 1. If you want more difference (or less) between the choices, move the slider in part 2. Then click the small image that is closest to what you're seeking.

***Tip** You'll have the most control if you drag the Amount slider in part 2 to the left, so that the change at each step is subtle, and make repeated changes until you get the result you want. Each time you click one of the small images, you get another set of choices centered around the choice you just made. You can then choose another of the small images to make an additional adjustment.*

Click the Undo button to go back one step at a time, or the Reset Image button to go back to the original.

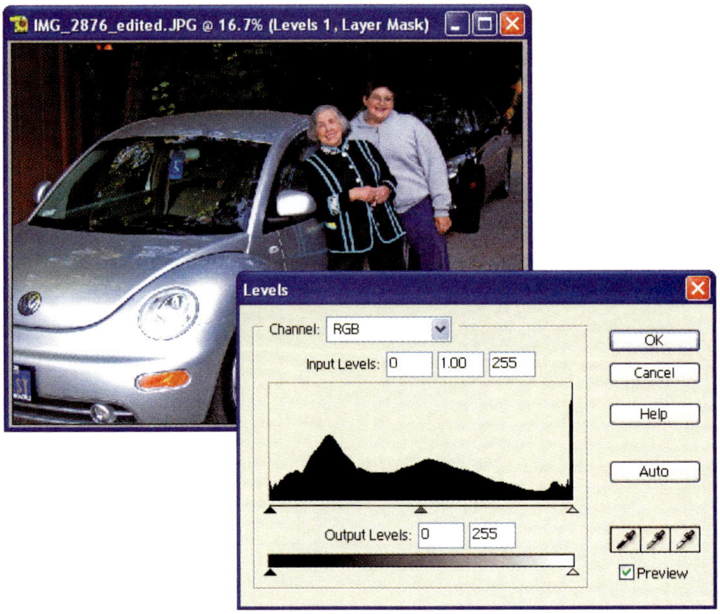

Figure 7.7 **This image has a good range of tones, as the histogram shows, reaching both ends of the range. The high peaks at the right are because of the bright reflective areas on the car.**

If you want to experiment with more-sophisticated adjustments, choose Layer > New Adjustment Layer > Levels and accept the defaults in the dialog that appears by clicking OK. The histogram shows the distribution of brightness levels within the image (**Figure 7.7**). If the image lacks any really black blacks, for example, the histogram levels will be very low at the left; if the image has no bright whites, the levels will be very low at the right (**Figure 7.8**).

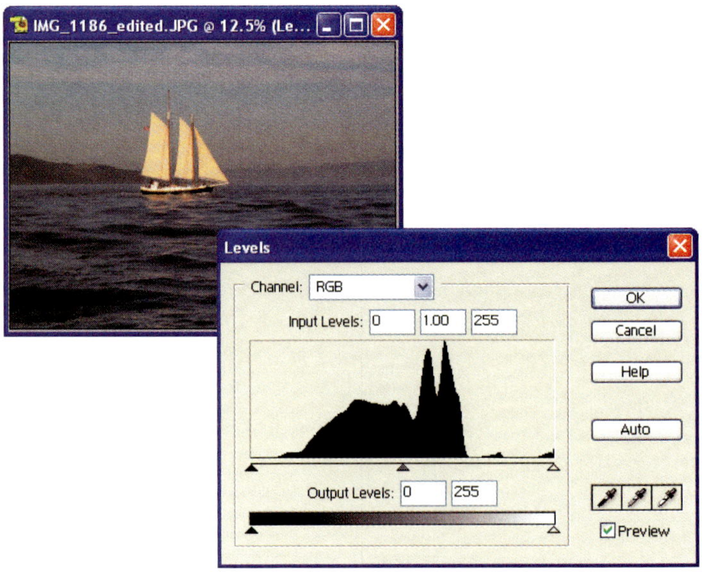

Figure 7.8 **This photo lacks both black blacks and bright whites.**

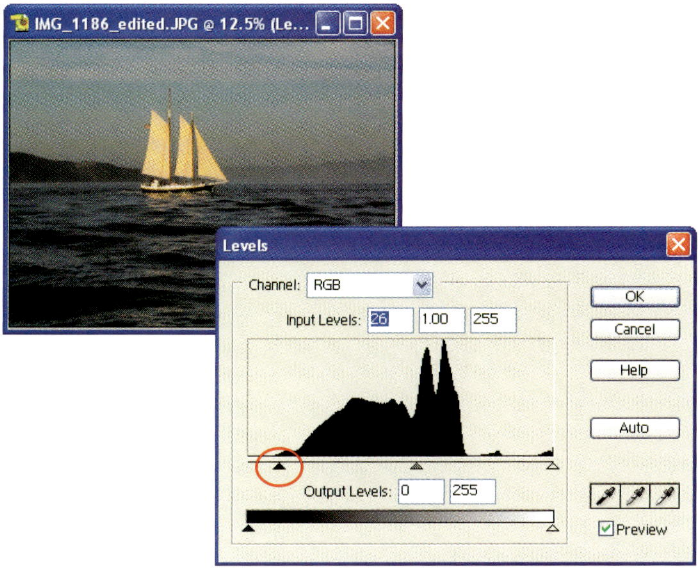

Figure 7.9 Moving the left triangle under the histogram to the right increases the amount of black in the photo.

In this dialog, you can make many adjustments in how each level in the original image is translated to a new level in the edited image. If you drag the black triangle at the bottom-left corner of the histogram (not the triangle at the very bottom, below Output Levels) to the right, some of the dark grays in the original photo will be converted to black (**Figure 7.9**). If you drag the triangle at the bottom-right corner to the left, some of the brightest areas will be converted to pure white (**Figure 7.10**). Moving the middle slider adjusts the mid-tones.

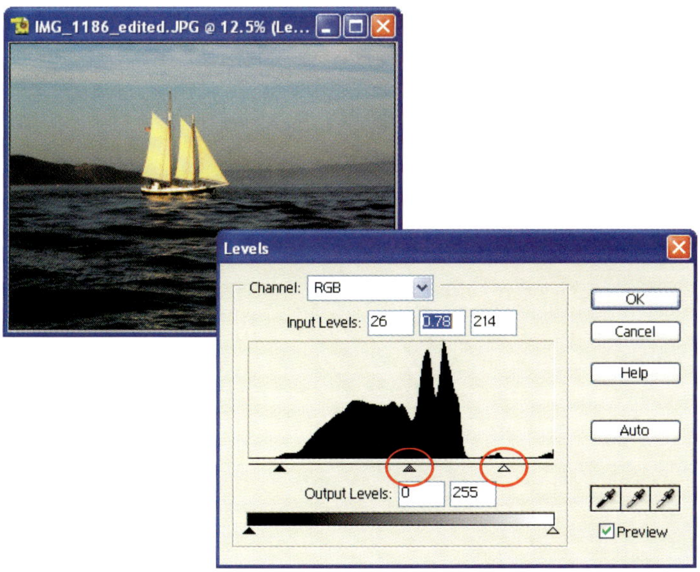

Figure 7.10 Sliding the right triangle to the left brightens the image, and moving the center triangle balances the mid-tones.

One of the more powerful—and potentially confusing—aspects of Photoshop Elements is the concept of *layers*. If you stick to very simple edits, you can avoid them, but coming to grips with them will enable you to do much more. With layers, you can store changes to your photos separately from the photos themselves, which allows you to go back later and adjust or remove the changes.

Layers can contain parts of a photo, text or graphics you've added to it, or information about how the photo is to be modified (such as the Levels adjustment in an adjustment layer, as described in the previous section).

JPEG files cannot store multiple layers. To save a photo with layers as a JPEG, choose Layer > Flatten Image when you're done editing. You will then lose the ability to go back to the layers and make further changes, but you'll be able to save the photo in JPEG format.

If you choose to save the file in Photoshop (.psd) format, the layers are preserved and no compression is used. This gives you maximum quality and flexibility, but the file size is much larger. In addition, some other programs will not be able to read the file.

Caution ***If you edit a .psd file with layers using the Fix Photo window in Album, the layers will be flattened automatically. So if you want to preserve the layers, always use Photoshop Elements or Photoshop for editing.***

If you've added layers to a photo, perhaps by using the Levels adjustment or adding text, it is helpful to show the Layers palette (Window > Layers) (**Figure 7.11**). This shows which elements are on each layer, and it allows you to choose which layer you are working on. Any edits you make are applied only to the selected layer, so if you're finding that the changes you're trying to make are mysteriously ignored, make sure the correct layer is selected. To select a layer, just click the thumbnail for that layer in the Layers palette.

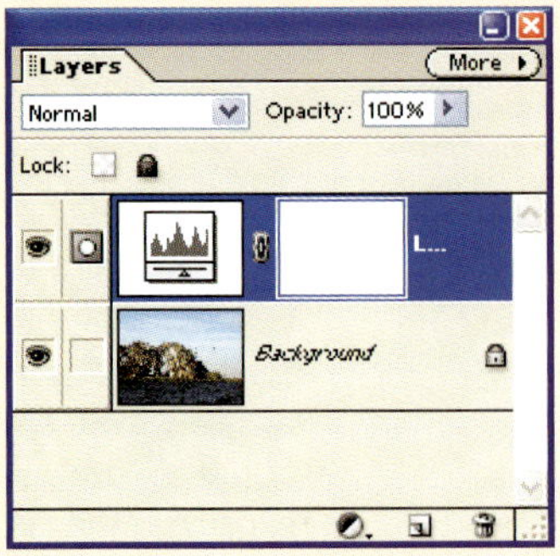

Figure 7.11 **When you have multiple layers, show the Layers palette so that you can control which one is active.**

The information about the change is stored separately from the image in an *adjustment layer;* see the sidebar "Understanding Layers" for the essentials of layers, which are a powerful aspect of Photoshop Elements.

This window contains many other options, which require experience to use most effectively. For more details refer to the Photoshop Elements help file or manual, or to the references listed in Appendix A.

Sharpening with Finesse

One of the most widely used sharpening tools, which is available in Elements and is also used by Album's Sharpen function in the Fix Photo window, is called *Unsharp Mask*. Despite its confusing name, it increases the sharpness of edges. You can gain more control over how a photo is sharpened by using Unsharp Mask in Elements instead of the Sharpen feature in Album.

To sharpen a photo in Photoshop Elements, open the photo in Elements and choose Filter > Sharpen > Unsharp Mask (**Figure 7.12**). The Unsharp Mask dialog preview shows actual pixels by default; you can zoom in or out by clicking the plus and minus buttons, and you can pan by clicking and dragging in the preview window.

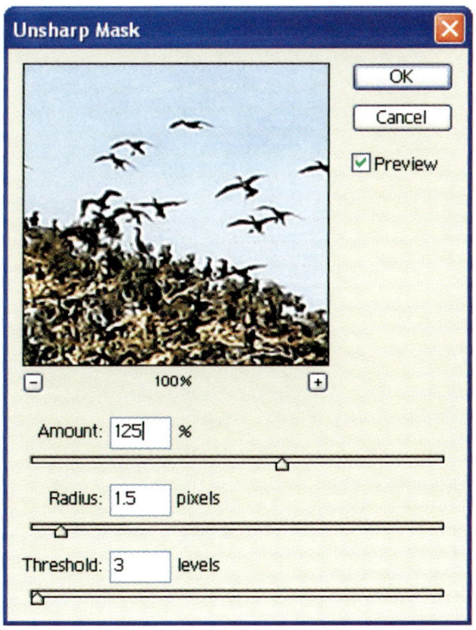

Figure 7.12 With Photoshop Elements' Unsharp Mask, you can control each of the parameters that affect the sharpening algorithm.

There are three adjustments for unsharp mask: Amount, Radius, and Threshold. Album chooses the settings automatically and provides a slider so that you can adjust the amount (you can't adjust the radius or threshold in Album). Elements lets you adjust all three.

Choosing JPEG Quality Level

If you open a JPEG file in Photoshop Elements, when you save it, Elements will use the same quality level as in the original. If the file is a new one, as when you have flattened a layered document, Photoshop Elements will prompt you to choose the quality level and other options (**Figure 7.13**). The Baseline Optimized option is the best for most uses. A quality setting of 10 will minimize any compression artifacts but the file size will be large. This is a good choice for critical photos. (Settings of 11 or 12 produce much larger files with little or no visible improvement, so they have little use.) A setting of 6 or 7 will produce a much smaller file with modest artifacts, which is fine if you don't plan to print the photo at large sizes, and it will save disk space (**Figure 7.14**). A setting of 8 is a good compromise.

If you think you might want to edit the photo again, it's best to save it in .psd format, which does not use any compression and also saves layers (if any). You can then edit again at a later time and have access to the layers, and your photo won't suffer from any JPEG compression artifacts. When sharing photos, use a smaller JPEG; Album will automatically convert .psd files to JPEGs for you when you share.

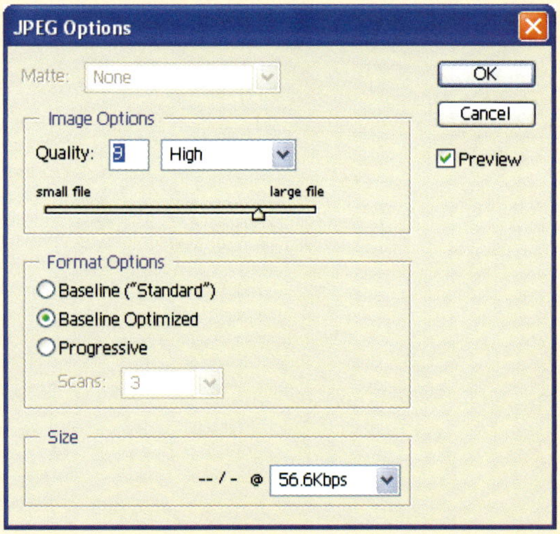

Figure 7.13 Baseline Optimized is generally the best format to use. Use high-quality settings for important photos and lower settings when file size is paramount.

Figure 7.14 (Opposite) If you're printing or viewing at a small size, you may not see any difference with varying levels of JPEG compression. But if you look closely at an enlargement, the loss of detail in the lower-quality files is apparent.

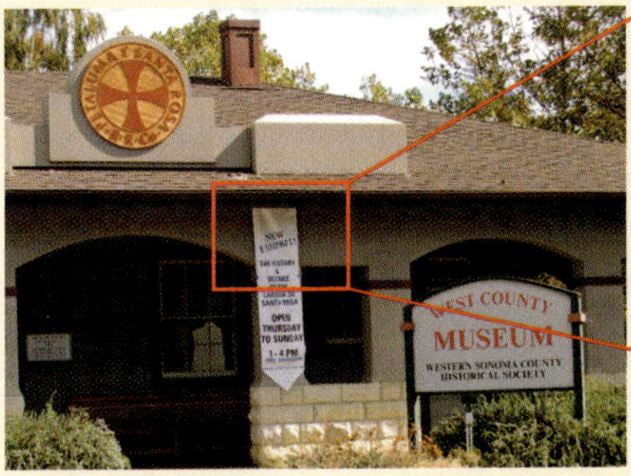

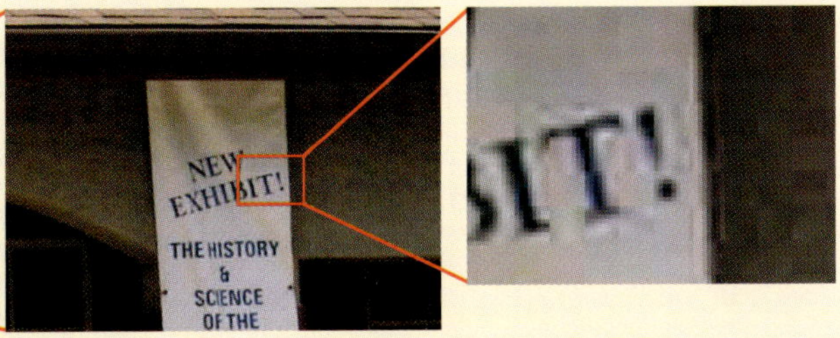

Quality 2: Note extensive noise around letters, loss of detail in stucco (file size: 186 KB)

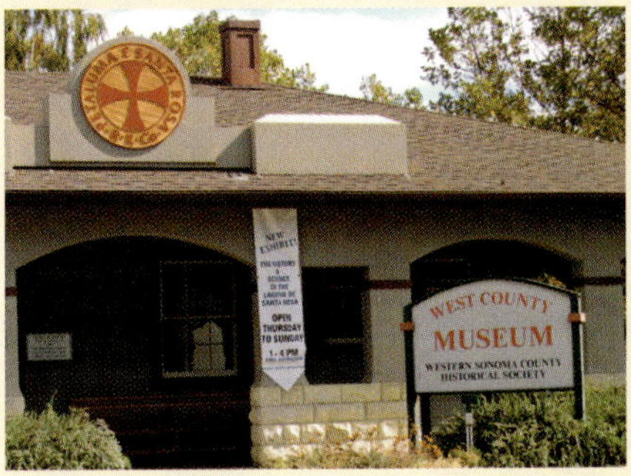

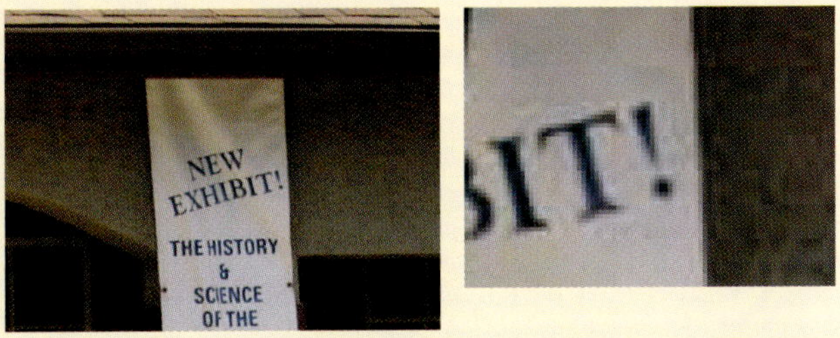

Quality 6: Most artifacts are gone, but close-up inspection shows blockiness in stucco pattern and noise surrounding letters (file size: 372 KB)

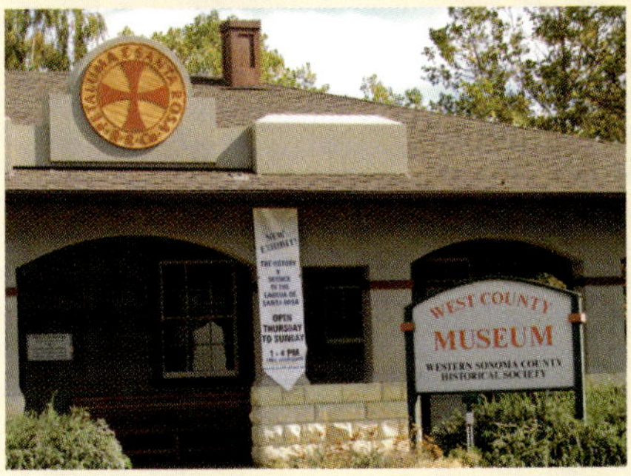

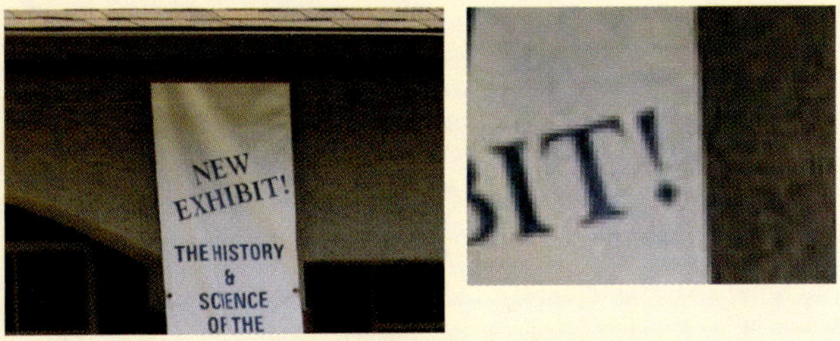

Quality 10: Virtually all artifacts are gone, but very close inspection shows some noise around letters (file size: 968 KB)

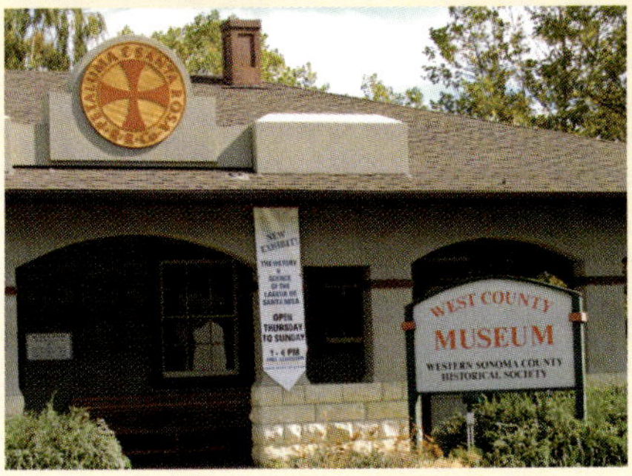

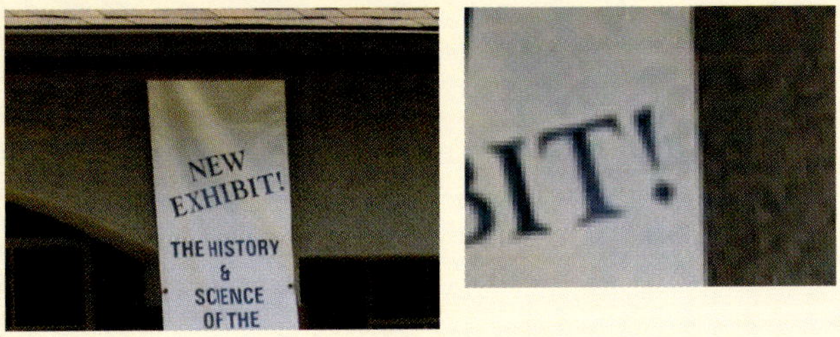

Uncompressed original TIFF file (file size: 10 MB)

Adjusting the three settings is tricky, since they interact with each other. Increasing either the Amount or Radius values will increase the degree of sharpening, but the two have different effects. The Radius setting controls how many pixels are affected in the vicinity of each edge. In general, use lower Radius settings for images with a lot of fine detail, and larger settings for images with expanses of similar color (like skin or sky).

Typical settings for the Amount are 50% to 250%; Radius settings are generally between 0.5 and 5 pixels (usually at the lower end of that range). For images of at least 2 megapixels, a Radius of 1.0 and an Amount of 100% is a good starting point; use a lower Radius setting for low-resolution photos. Only experimentation and experience will teach you what settings to use for which photos.

The Threshold setting determines how much difference there must be between adjacent pixels for sharpening to be applied. For most photos, a threshold of 3 to 5 levels should be fine; you may want to increase this to around 10 in photos with lots of skin or other smooth surfaces whose imperfections you don't want to intensify. Use a threshold between 0 and 2 if you want to sharpen every detail.

When evaluating sharpening results onscreen, always view at 100% (actual pixels) so that you see all the detail. For critical photos you plan to print, you'll have to make a test print to fully evaluate your sharpening results.

There are many advanced sharpening techniques you can use to selectively sharpen certain areas while minimizing artifacts; refer to the references in Appendix A.

Tip ***Sharpening is most effective when you do it at the final resolution you'll be using. If you're planning to use a photo at reduced resolution on the Web or in email, for example, you'll get the best results by first resizing the image to the final resolution and then applying sharpening. In doing so, however, you're throwing away image detail, so make a duplicate of the image in Album before taking this step.***

Adding Special Effects with Filters

Photoshop Elements provides a wide array of filters you can apply to your photos (**Figure 7.15**). Trial and error is the only way to become familiar with them—remember, you can always undo a change in Photoshop Elements or revert to the original in Album. If used with restraint and skill, certain filters can improve your photos—but they are often more useful for making creative derivatives, not necessarily enhancements, of your pictures.

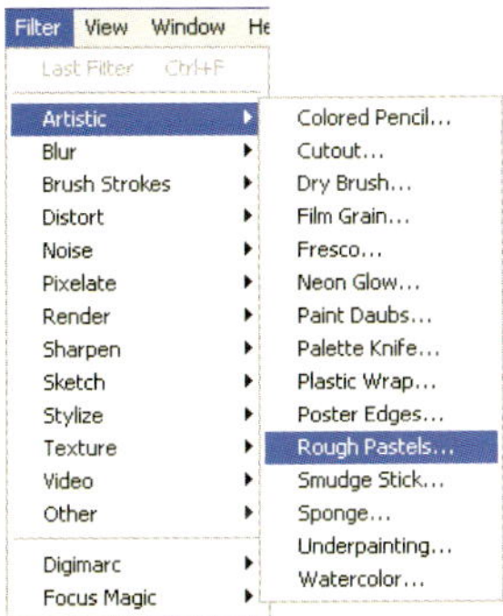

Figure 7.15 Photoshop Elements has a huge assortment of filters; this shows just the Artistic ones.

Filters can make your photo look like a painting or drawing. Try Filter > Artistic > Watercolor (**Figure 7.16**), Filter > Brush Strokes > Spatter (**Figure 7.17**), Filter > Distort > Ocean Ripple (**Figure 7.18**), or Filter > Distort > Spherize (**Figure 7.19**). You can spend days doing strange things to your photos.

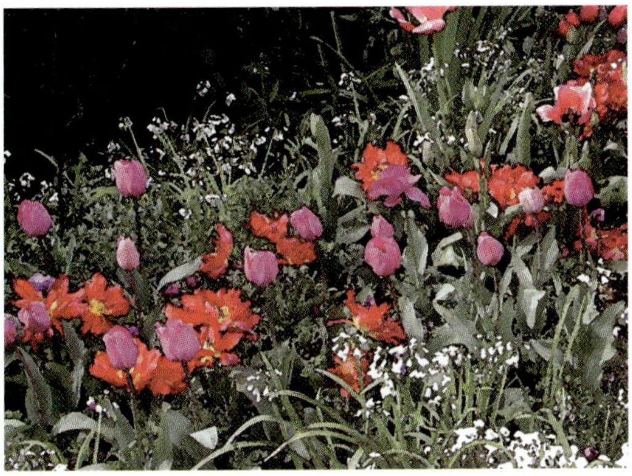

Figure 7.16 The Watercolor filter.

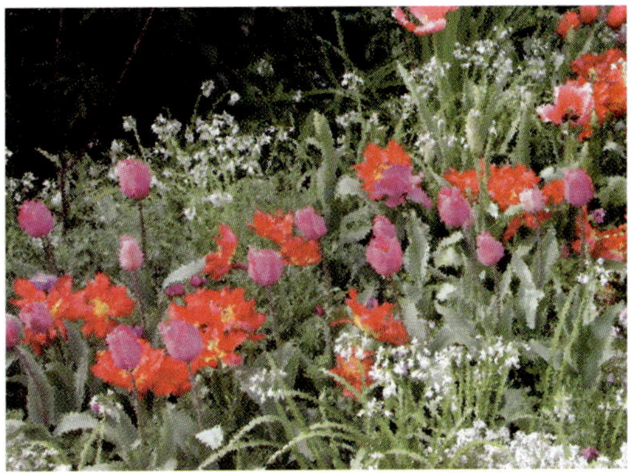

Figure 7.17 The Spatter filter.

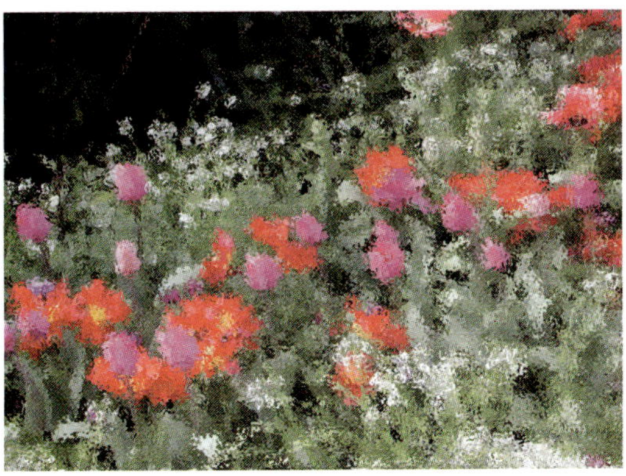

Figure 7.18 The Ocean Ripple filter.

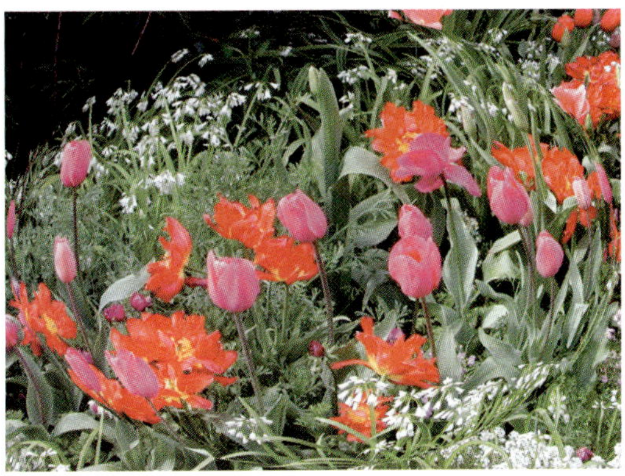

Figure 7.19 The Spherize filter.

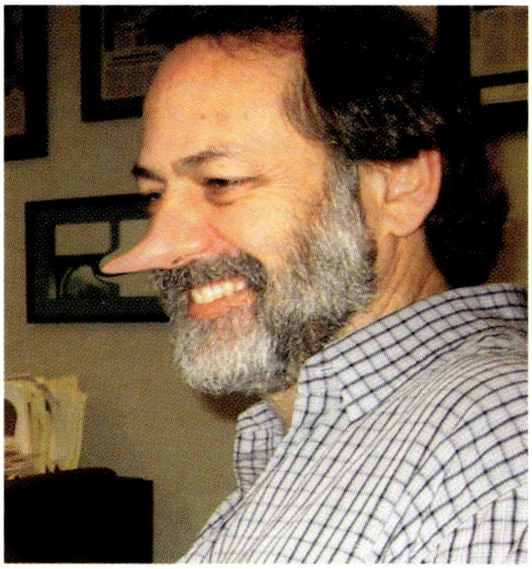

Figure 7.20 **Be careful who you allow to use the Liquify filter.**

Kids especially like Filter > Distort > Liquify, which lets you manually mess up the photo (**Figure 7.20**). If you're really careful, you can use Liquify to turn frowns into smiles, but it is more likely to be used to turn Dad into Pinocchio.

If you've explored all the filters in Photoshop Elements and are hungry for more, there are lots more available from third parties; check the Web sites listed in Appendix A.

Photoshop Elements has a few filters that are useful for improving your photos. If you have a scanned photo with lots of dust and scratches, try Filter > Noise > Dust and Scratches. This filter inevitably eliminates detail while it is eliminating the dust, however, so you'll want to select a small area that has dust and scratches but not any important detail (see the sidebar "Selecting Part of a Photo," later in this chapter). You can also try Filter > Noise > Despeckle if the photo has annoying film grain or digital noise (which looks like random colored dots).

Adding Text

Putting text on top of a photo is easy in Photoshop Elements:

1. Click the Text tool (**Figure 7.21**).
2. Choose the type style, size, and color in the options bar above the photo. (Click the colored square near the right side of the bar to set the color.) Do this *before* you type any text.

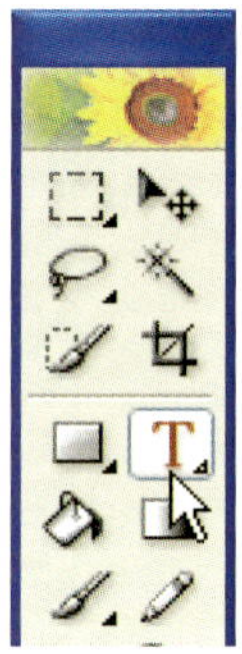

Figure 7.21 **Select the Text tool to enter text.**

3. Click the spot in the photo where you want the text to begin.

4. Type the text.

5. Click the arrow button in the options bar to "commit" the text. (Until you do this, you will not be able to make any other changes to the photo.)

If you want to change the style, size, or color of text you have entered, you have to select it first. Make sure the text tool is selected, and then click and drag over the text you want to change. Now you can change its characteristics.

Choosing the size can be confusing. Photoshop Elements assumes that you're going to print the photo at the resolution indicated by the photo's metadata, which will yield a size that may not be anything like the size you want to print.

To make the text size come out as you expect, first choose Image > Resize > Image Size (**Figure 7.22**). Make sure the box labeled Resample Image in the Image Size dialog is *not* checked; you don't want to change the pixels of the image, just Photoshop Elements' idea of the size at which the photo will be printed. Enter the width you intend for the final printed output in the Width field in the Document Size section. The height will be automatically set to maintain the proper proportions. Double-check that the Resample Image box is *not* checked and click OK. Now the text sizes shown in the pop-up list in the options bar will match the size at which the text will appear in your printed output.

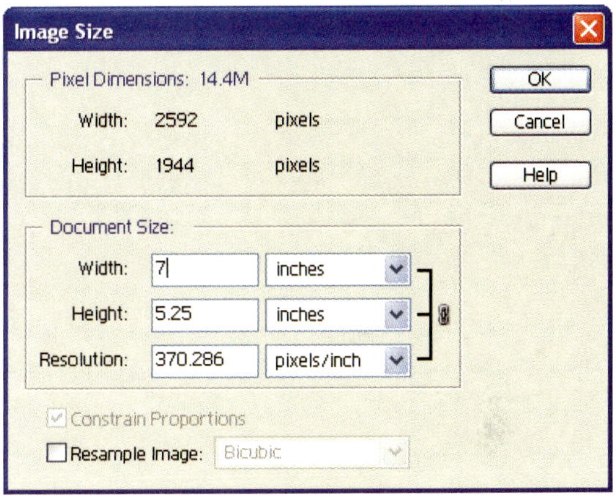

Figure 7.22 If you want the type size to come out as expected on your print, you must tell Elements at what size you plan to print. Make sure the Resample Image box is not checked.

Text is stored on a separate layer, so you'll have to either save the photo in .psd format, which creates a large file but preserves the ability to edit the text, or choose Layer > Flatten Image to combine the text with the photo's pixels so that it can be saved as a JPEG file.

Selecting Part of a Photo

If you want to change the color, brightness, contrast, or sharpness of only part of a photo, you need to first select that part. Using this technique you can limit virtually any of the things you do in Photoshop Elements to part of the photo.

Selecting a rectangular or oval area is easy. To make a rectangular selection, click the rectangular Marquee tool (**Figure 7.23**). Then click and hold on one corner of the area you want to select, drag to the diagonally opposite corner, and release the mouse button. Now any color corrections, sharpening, filter effects, and so forth that you apply will affect only that area. Pressing Ctrl-D or clicking anywhere else on the image will clear that selection.

To select an oval area, click and hold the rectangular marquee tool, select the elliptical marquee tool in the pop-up menu, and release. Then make the selection just as with the rectangular marquee tool.

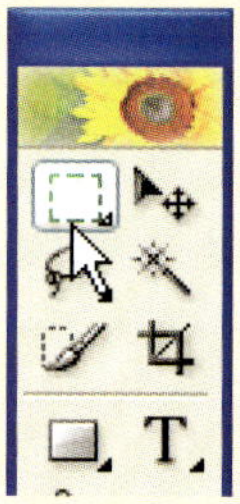

Figure 7.23
To select a rectangular area, use the rectangular Marquee tool.

Selecting an odd-shaped area is more challenging, but it is essential to making sophisticated photo edits. A full exploration of how to do this is beyond the scope of this book, but here are a few pointers:

- To draw the outline of the section freehand, select the *Lasso* tool (**Figure 7.24**) and then click and drag on the photo to outline the desired area.

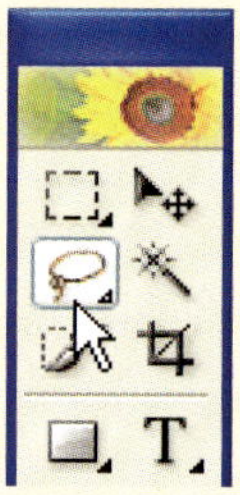

Figure 7.24
With the Lasso tool, you can outline a selection freehand. Zoom in close, and be sure you have a steady hand!

- Click the Magic Wand tool (**Figure 7.25**), and then click in the area you want to select. If it is of a consistent and distinct color, it will be automatically selected (**Figure 7.26**). If you want to add to this selection, hold down the Shift key and click another area. You can widen the range of colors that the tool will include in the selection by increasing the Tolerance value in the options bar.

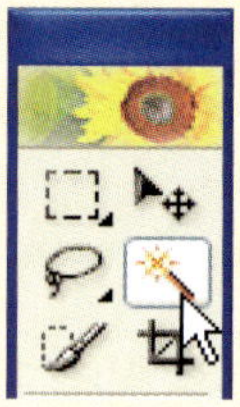

Figure 7.25
Choose the Magic Wand tool to make selections based on color.

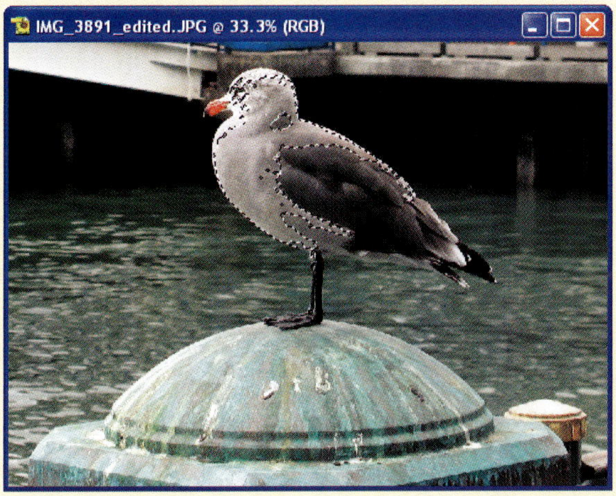

Figure 7.26 Click the Magic Wand on any spot, and every place of similar color will be included in the selection.

- For some more magic, try the *Magnetic Lasso* tool; click and hold the Lasso tool and choose Magnetic Lasso from the pop-up menu (**Figure 7.27**). Now, when you click and drag on the photo, the line will jump to the nearest edge instead of falling exactly where the cursor is (**Figure 7.28**). If at some point the line strays from where you want it, click Backspace as many times as necessary to erase a bit of it, or hold down Alt to turn off the "magnetic" effect and position part of the line manually. When you're done creating the selection, double-click or press Enter.

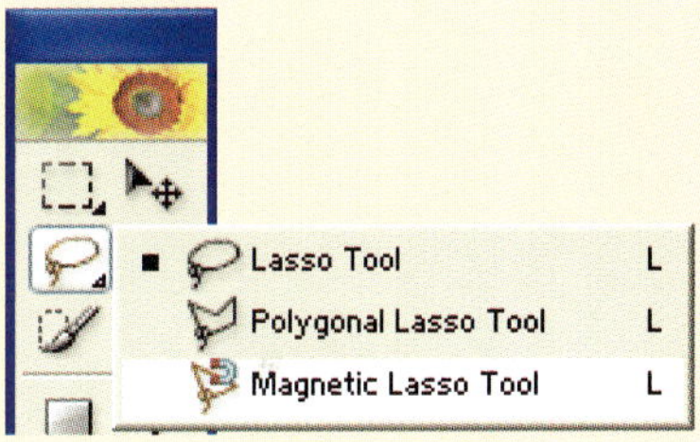

Figure 7.27 Choose the Magnetic Lasso tool to make it easier to draw a selection outline around an object with distinct edges.

- Experiment with the options in the Select menu or in the options bar to modify the selection you've made. For example, Select > Similar will extend the selection to areas of similar color.

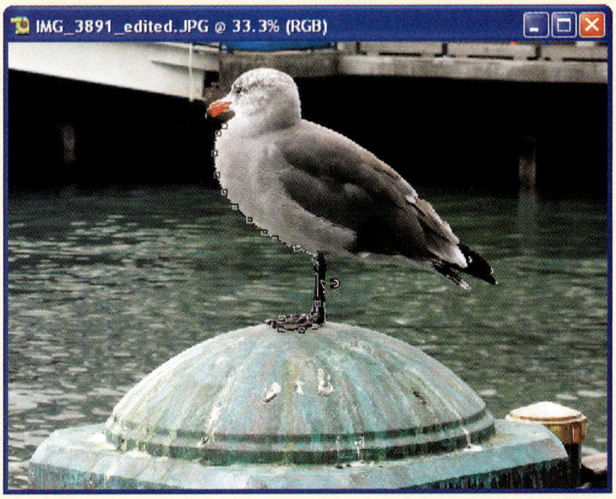

Figure 7.28 As you drag the Magnetic Lasso tool, the selection outline jumps to the nearest edge.

Caution ***Once you flatten the file, you cannot edit or delete the text. Also, if you're saving in JPEG format, compression artifacts will appear at the edges of the text unless you select a high quality level.***

Erasing Objects and Blemishes

With enough skill and experience, you can change almost anything in a photo. (As a result, photos have ceased to be documentary evidence.) Here's one technique to get you started: the clone stamp. You can use the clone stamp to erase distracting objects, hide blemishes, repair scratches, or remove your ex-husband from the photo.

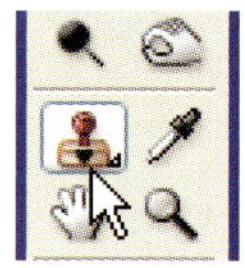

Figure 7.29 Choose the Clone Stamp tool to paint with a pattern chosen from the photo.

Choose the Clone Stamp tool (**Figure 7.29**) and adjust the brush size in the options bar if you like (you may want to start with a fairly large brush to get the hang of what this tool does, and then use a smaller brush to do finer work). Then hold down the Alt key and click an area whose color and texture you'd like to use to paint over the object or blemish. Typically this would be whatever is in the background adjacent to an object. This determines what color and texture the clone stamp will paint with.

Now release the Alt key and click the object you want to paint over. You can click and drag if you want to paint over a larger area. For best results, you may need to frequently reset the cloned area by holding down Alt and clicking a new source portion of the image.

If you want to always start copying from the same spot each time you paint with the clone stamp tool, uncheck the Aligned box in the options bar. This allows you to fill an area with the color and texture from one spot. If, on the other hand, the Aligned box is checked, the clone stamp tool will use the spot at which you Alt-clicked as the starting point but will change the source point as you change the destination to keep the same relative position. This is useful if you're copying an area of the photo from one place to another.

Figure 7.30 shows a photo from which I wanted to remove the distracting stick that looks as if it comes out of the squirrel's paw. I picked a brush size slightly larger than the stick's width and Alt-clicked at a point just above the stick. Then I painted carefully over the stick. In this case, I left the Aligned box checked, so each spot where the stick had been was replaced with the pattern of the rock immediately above it.

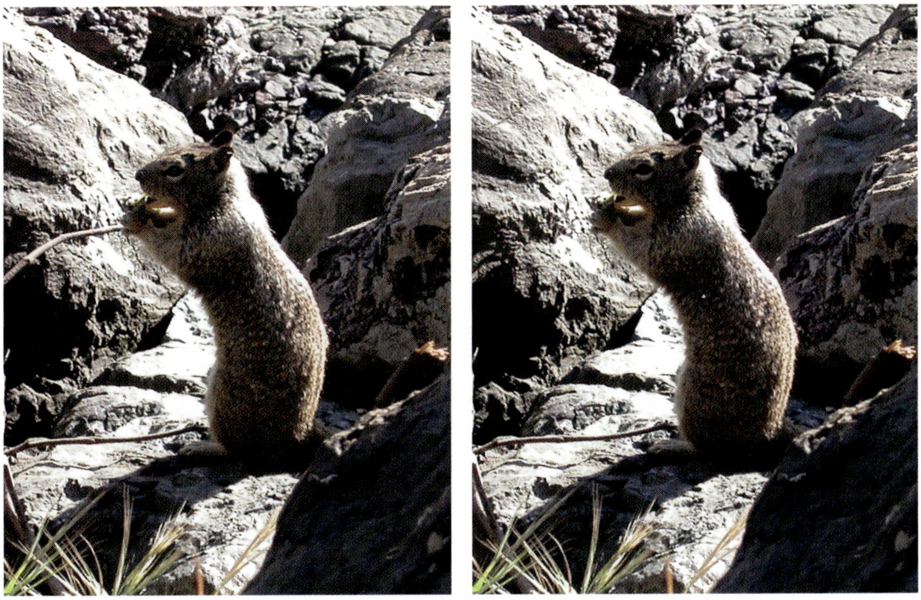

Figure 7.30 **Painting over the stick (left) with the clone stamp makes it disappear (right).**

There's a lot more to making effective use of the clone stamp tool, but this should give you a hint of what is possible.

Taking the Next Step

I've only scratched the surface of what you can do with Photoshop Elements. If you want to combine elements of multiple photos, retouch problem areas in scanned photos, add graphics, brighten teeth, and make nearly any other change you can imagine, Photoshop Elements can do it, but it will take some learning and some practice. Get one of the books listed in Appendix A or, better yet, find a class—there's nothing like watching an experienced user to bring you up to speed quickly.

The Ultimate Editor: Photoshop CS

Photoshop Elements can probably meet all your photo-editing needs, but if you want the best there is, Photoshop CS is it. It's designed for creative professionals, but it does have some great features for the serious hobbyist. For the most part, Photoshop CS is beyond the scope of this book—but to give you a glimpse, I'll describe one of its wonderful tools.

Retouching with the Healing Brush

The healing brush tool in Photoshop CS makes it easy to eliminate wrinkles and blemishes, get rid of dust and scratches, and remove objects from a photo. You can, with enough skill and time, achieve similar results using the clone stamp and other tools in Photoshop Elements, but the healing brush makes it much easier and the results are more seamless.

Open a photo in Photoshop CS by right-clicking the photo in Album and choosing Edit With > Photoshop. To use the healing brush, follow these steps:

1. In Photoshop CS, click the healing brush tool (**Figure 7.31**).

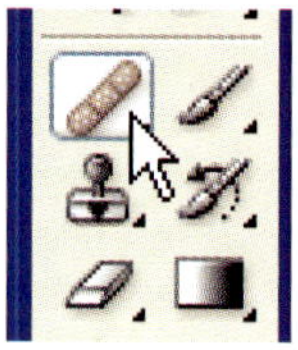

Figure 7.31 The healing brush is one of the truly magical tools in Photoshop CS. (It is not available in Photoshop Elements.)

2. In the options bar, click the black circle with a number under it to display the Brush Picker (**Figure 7.32**).

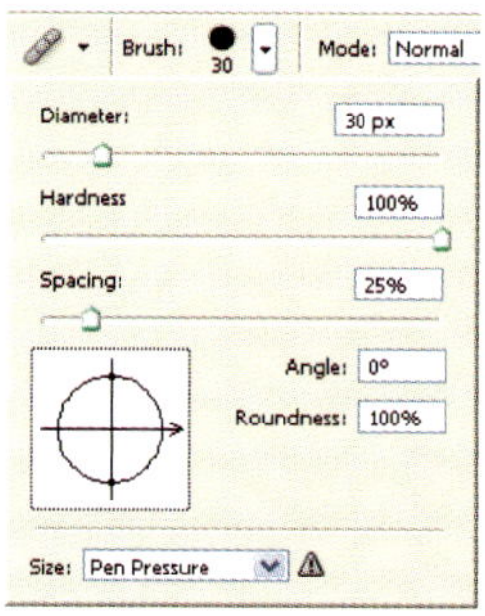

Figure 7.32 After selecting the healing brush, click the brush in the options bar to choose its size, shape, and other characteristics.

3. Drag the Diameter slider until the brush size is about the diameter of the spot or object you want to retouch. (You can see the brush size by moving the cursor out of this pop-up window and onto the photo.) Leave the other settings at their default values.

4. Hold down Alt and click a spot on the photo that has a texture similar to what you would like to fill the spot, blemish, or object with (**Figure 7.33**). Unlike the clone stamp, the healing brush does not require that the source area have the same color as the destination.

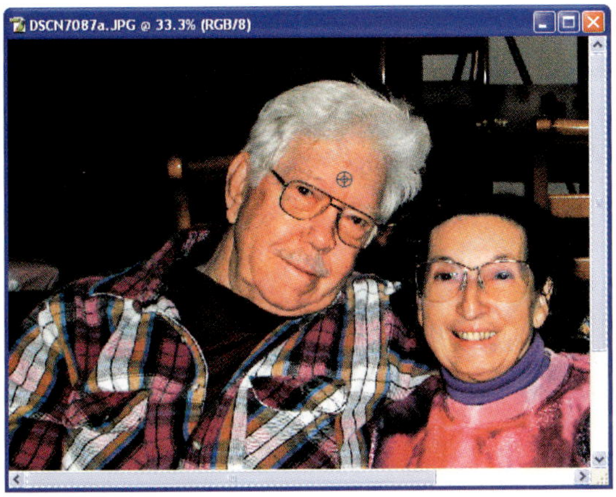

Figure 7.33 Hold the Alt key and click on a spot that has the desired texture.

5. Click and drag to paint over the object you want to eliminate (**Figure 7.34**). The edges will be obvious while you are doing this, but don't worry, because…

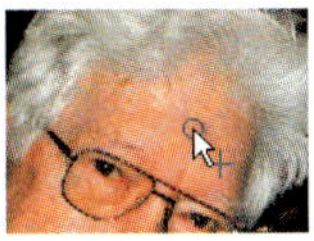

Figure 7.34 Now drag across the area you want to fill. Note that the painted strip is visible if you look closely.

6. When you release the mouse button, Photoshop CS will perform its healing magic, seamlessly blending the edges of the retouched area (**Figure 7.35**).

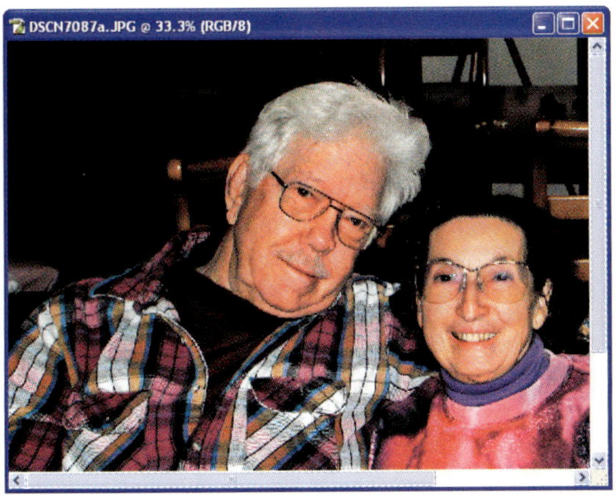

Figure 7.35 When you release the mouse button, the brush completes its healing magic, making the edges of the painted area virtually undetectable.

When retouching portraits, be careful not to go too far—you can make people look years younger, but the result can be unnatural (and unsettling).

If you don't like a result, just press Ctrl-Z to undo it and try again. Try choosing a different spot for the sample or use a smaller brush.

8 Making Creations

Now that you have your photos organized so that you can find them easily, and you've fixed the ones with problems, it's time to do stuff with them! With Photoshop Album it's easy to make *creations*, which is Album's name for slide shows, albums, cards, calendars, or any other formatted collection of photos designed for viewing, printing, or sharing.

In the film-photography world, making albums is such a pain that most people rarely get to it. Making a calendar or a greeting card is tough enough that you might never have even considered it. And creating slide shows that your friends can view on the PC or TV is out of the question.

With digital photography, though, all this is easy. Get ready to have some fun with your photos.

This chapter explains how to prepare for making creations, how to use Album's Creations Wizard, and how to deal with specific issues of various kinds of creations. At the end of the chapter, you'll get a few pointers for going beyond Album to make more advanced creations.

Choosing and Arranging Photos

The first step in making any kind of creation is to find the photos you want to use. There are two different approaches to choosing photos and arranging them in the sequence you want:

- Make a collection with the photos you want to use in the creation, reorder them, and then make a creation from the collection.
- Select photos directly from the photo well and use the Creations Wizard to do all the ordering. You can add photos from within the Creations Wizard.

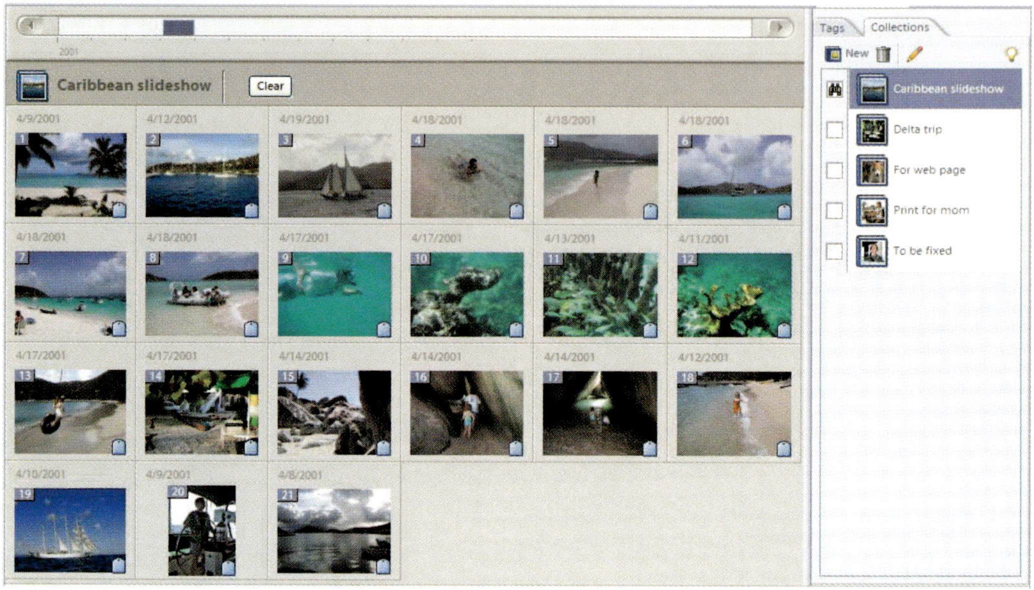

Figure 8.1 **You'll have the most flexibility in making creations if you make a collection first.**

Although the first approach may seem more indirect, I recommend using it for all but the simplest creations. Starting with a collection allows you to assemble the photos and put them in order independently of any creation (**Figure 8.1**). It gives you more flexibility if you later want to add photos to the creation or to make other creations from the same set of photos. For example, you can add to a collection, but not to a creation, from the photo well. Starting with a collection also makes it easier to print or email the same set of photos.

Tip *If you find the terms* **collections** *and* **creations** *confusing, keep these definitions in mind. A* **collection** *is a group of photos you've collected together for any purpose. A* **creation** *is something you've created with them.*

To make a new collection, click the Organize tab and then the Collections tab. In the Collections pane click the New button. (See Chapter 4 for more on collections.) Once you've created a collection, you can add photos to it from the photo well, even if the Collections pane is not displayed, by right-clicking the photo, choosing Add to Collection, and then choosing the collection name.

To view all the photos in a collection, display the Collections pane and double-click the collection's icon. The photos initially will be in the order in which you added them to the collection. If you want to put them in chronological order, right-click the collection's icon and choose Reorder Collection by Date from the pop-up menu. Then put the photos in the order you want by simply dragging and dropping them in the photo well.

If you plan to use captions in your creation, you can browse the collection and add captions as needed. If you're using the Creations Wizard, you must enter the captions before starting the wizard—another reason why it's convenient to make a creation from a collection.

You can also arrange photos within the Creations Wizard, whether or not you've started from a collection, as the following section describes.

Using the Creations Wizard

The Creations Wizard is the path to all Photoshop Album creations except Web photo galleries and 3D galleries. I'll deal with those separately in later sections. The process described here applies to all other creations, including albums, photo books, slide shows, Video CDs, print and electronic greeting cards, and calendars.

The Creations Wizard is designed around an automated, easy-to-use approach. It will guide you through the choices you have in making a creation. You can skip straight to the last step, using the default settings in all the steps, and make a creation in less than a minute. Or you can make quite a few adjustments.

Note ***The Creations Wizard does not give you complete flexibility in layout. Certain templates, as described in the following sections, give you somewhat more flexibility. If you want complete control and are prepared for the additional work it requires, you'll need to export the photos and use another program to make the creation, as described at the end of this chapter.***

Once you have chosen the photos you want, whether or not you have made a collection first, select them all (Ctrl-A) and click the Create button in the shortcuts bar (**Figure 8.2**). If you've done a tag or collection search and no photos are selected, then all the photos in the photo well will be used, up to the limit of 999 photos per creation.

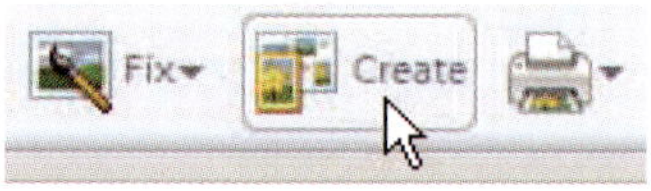

Figure 8.2 Select the photos you want to use in the creation and click the Create button.

The Creations Wizard guides you through the creation process in six steps:

1. Choose the kind of creation you want to make.

2. Pick a template that will determine the creation's overall design. You'll see different template choices depending on the selection you make in step 1.

3. Choose options, depending on the type of creation, such as whether you want a title page for an album or background music for a slide show.

4. Rearrange the photos if necessary and optionally add more. (If you've made a collection first, you'll already have done this and can skip this step.)

5. Preview the creation and optionally make adjustments in the number of photos per page or in the way each photo fits in its frame.

6. Give the creation a name and optionally save a PDF version to the hard disk, print it, email it, write it to a CD, or order a printed copy from an online provider.

Because the Creations Wizard remembers all its settings, you can skip right to step 6 if you want to make another creation with exactly the same settings.

***Tip** Normally you'll use the Next button in the Creations Wizard to move from one step to the next. But if you know where you're headed and want to skip directly to a particular step, just click its number at the top of the Creations Wizard dialog.*

Let's walk through each of these steps.

1. Choose the Creation Type

In the first step you decide what kind of creation you want to make (**Figure 8.3**).

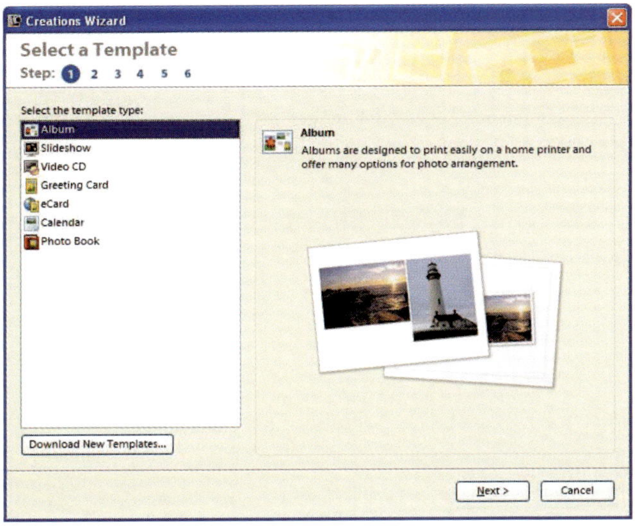

Figure 8.3 **Step 1 of the Creations Wizard.**

The *Album* and *Photo Book* options (the first and last items on the list) are conceptually very similar. The difference is that albums are designed primarily to be printed on your home printer, while photo books are intended to be printed by Adobe's online services partner, My Publisher. Both can be printed in either way, however; see "Creating Albums and Photo Books," later in this chapter.

The *Slideshow* option differs from the *Album* option in that the slide shows are designed for screen viewing rather than printing—although you can print slide shows, and you can also view albums onscreen. The difference is in how the designs are optimized and what options are available. For example, you can choose headers and footers for albums, and background music for slide shows, but not vice versa.

The *Video CD* option produces a special form of slide show, designed for playback on a DVD player. Because of the special needs of TVs and DVD players, the templates and options are different than for regular slide shows.

The *Greeting Card* option, which includes a single photo and some text, is designed to be printed on one sheet of paper that is folded in half twice to make a card.

eCard creations are like two-page slide shows, with one page having your photo and one page having your text. They are designed primarily for emailing.

The *Calendar* option produces—well, you know what calendars are. Each month shows one photo, and you can select any range of months. These calendars are designed for home printing or printing online through My Publisher.

2. Pick a Template

After you've chosen what type of creation to make, step 2 shows templates you can choose from (**Figure 8.4**). The templates are different for each type of creation. They determine the page's layout, any graphics that appear, and the position, style, size, and color of any text. You can always go back to this step and change the template, so don't hesitate to experiment.

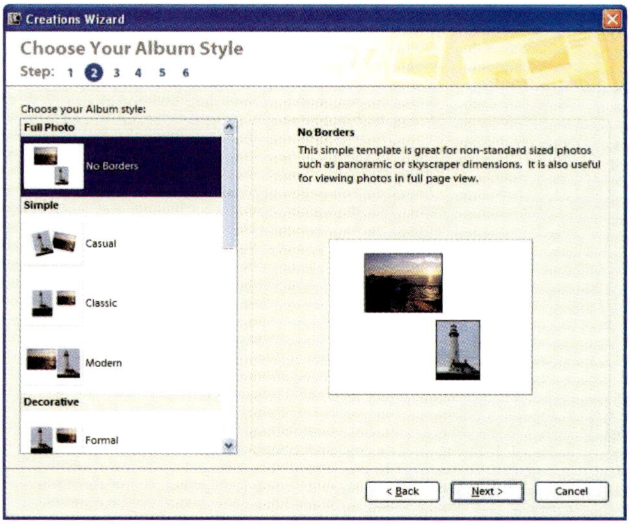

Figure 8.4 Templates, which you choose in step 2, determine layout, type style, and other features, and are different for each creation type.

Each template has several page layouts, for different numbers of photos per page. You can choose the default layout for all pages in step 2, and you can change the layout of any individual page in step 5.

The frames where photos are placed are fixed and cannot be modified, with one important exception: for albums, slide shows, and Video CDs, there is a Full Photo template that does not have any decorative artwork but will adapt the shape of the frame to fit the photo. All other templates have frames with a fixed 4:3 aspect ratio. The full-frame templates also give you more control over photo placement and sizing.

If a photo doesn't have a 4:3 aspect ratio, it will be cropped to fit the frame unless you use a full-frame template. If all your photos have a 3:2 aspect ratio (as some cameras produce), or if you have panoramas or photos cropped to aspect ratios other than 4:3, using the full-frame template is the only way to include the photos in an uncropped form.

You cannot, unfortunately, make your own templates or modify the ones that are provided. Adobe and its partners may provide additional templates for downloading, however; you can check for these by clicking the Download New Templates button in step 1.

3: Choose Options

After you've chosen the template, select options for that template (**Figure 8.5**). Since the options vary depending upon the type of creation, I'll describe them later in this chapter when I describe each type of creation in detail.

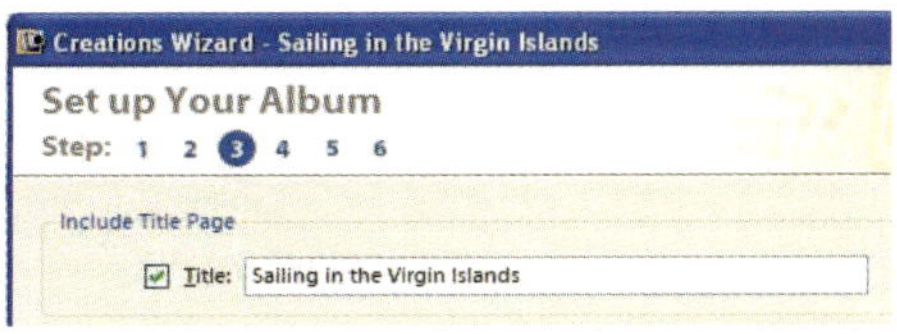

Figure 8.5 **If you choose in step 3 to have a title page, the first photo will be used there.**

One option that's common to all templates except Greeting Card and eCard is the title page. If you check the box next to the Title field, the first photo will be used for the title page, not for the first body page of the creation. You can enter text in this field that will appear with the photo on the title page.

***Tip** If you want the same photo on the title page and the first body page of the creation, then duplicate the first photo in step 4, as described in the following section.*

The title must be short—30 characters maximum—so it may take some creativity to come up with something that will fit. (Album imposes this limit to ensure that all titles fit in all templates—sort of a heavy-handed way to keep you out of trouble.)

4: Rearrange and Add Photos

In step 4 you can rearrange the photos you selected to include in your creation (**Figure 8.6**). Just drag any photo to the place where you want to put it in the step 4 pane.

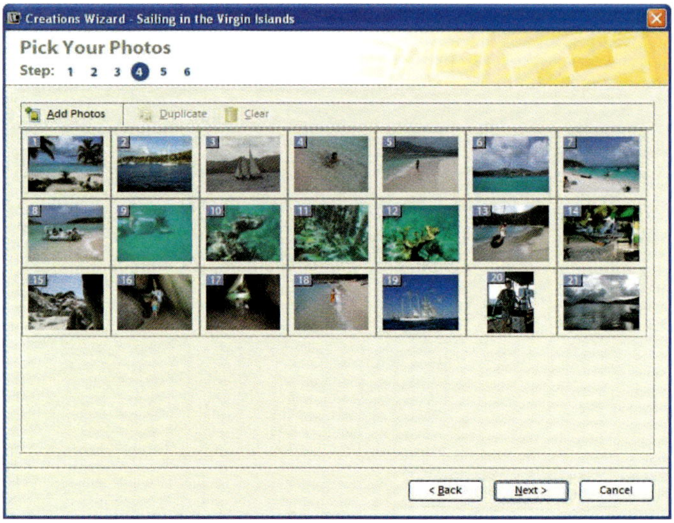

Figure 8.6 **In step 4 you can rearrange photos, add photos, add a copy (duplicate), or remove (clear) photos.**

The process is smoothest if you select all the photos you want to use in a creation before entering the Creations Wizard. If you decide to add photos, however, you can do so by clicking the Add Photos button above the photos in the step 4 pane.

Note ***If you have made a collection to assemble the photos for your creation, you should skip this step, because changes you make here won't be reflected in the collection. Instead, exit the Creations Wizard (go to step 6 and click Done), open the collection, make your changes there, and then reopen the creation by double-clicking its thumbnail in the photo well.***

The Add Photos to Creation dialog provides several ways to find the photos you want to add (**Figure 8.7**). By default, this dialog shows whatever photos were in the photo well when you entered the Creations Wizard. If the photo well reflected the results of a search, and you want to see the entire catalog instead, click the Entire Catalog radio button. In either mode, the order of the photos in this dialog is always oldest first, regardless of the arrangement you have chosen for the photo well. You can also choose to view only the photos from a specific collection, or those with a certain tag.

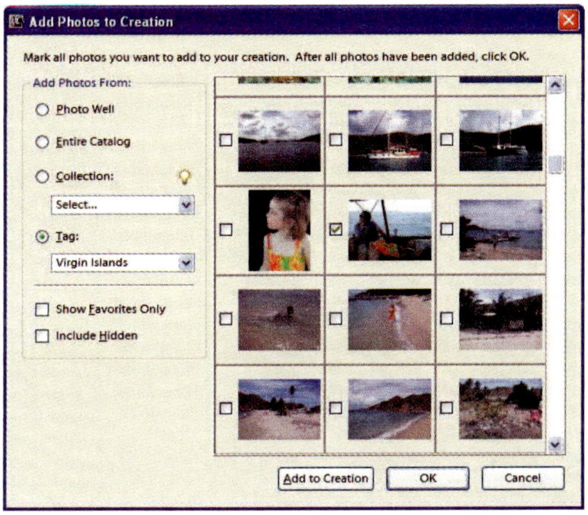

Figure 8.7 In the Add Photos to Creation dialog you can choose from several methods for finding photos to add.

You can also choose whether to limit the photos shown in this dialog to those with the Favorites tag as well, and whether to include photos with the Hidden tag.

To add photos to your creation, just click the check boxes next to them. When you've selected all the ones you want, click OK. Or if you want to add these photos and then switch to a different set and keep adding, click the Add to Creation button instead, and then click OK when you're all done.

Once you're back in step 4, make sure that the order of photos is what you want; any photos you added using the Add Photos to Creation dialog will be placed at the end of the sequence.

If you want any photo to appear more than once in the creation, select it and click the Duplicate button. If you are using a title page, you may want to duplicate one of the photos and put it at the beginning of the sequence for use on the title page. And sometimes it is nice to end a creation with the same photo you started with.

***Tip** In a slide show all photos appear for the same length of time, unless you know this trick: double or triple the duration of a particular photo by adding one or two duplicates of it. The duplicated photos blend seamlessly when the slide show plays so that the first of these photos appears to remain on screen longer.*

To remove photos from the creation, select them and click the Clear button.

5. Customize and Preview

In step 5 you get to see what your creation looks like and make adjustments to the page layouts (**Figure 8.8**). The central window shows one page of the creation; the controls below it allow you to move among pages. You can jump to any page using the pop-up list of pages in the center.

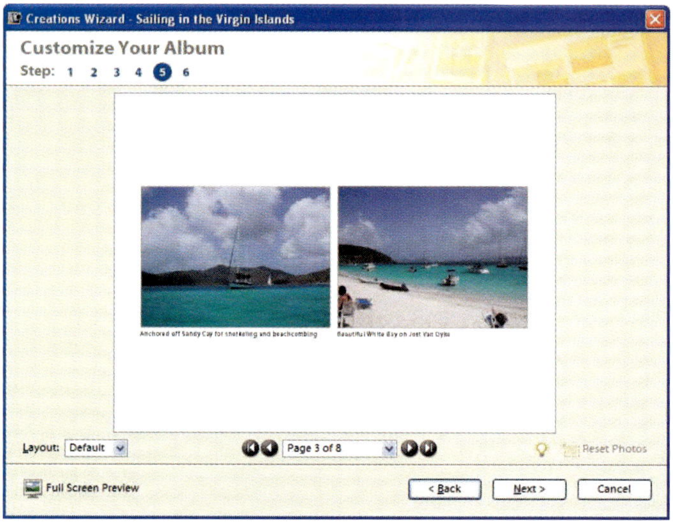

Figure 8.8 **In step 5 you can preview the creation and change the layouts of individual pages.**

If you're making a slide show, album, or Video CD, you can change the number of photos that appear per page for each page individually. Click the right arrow button in the step 5 pane until the page you want to change is displayed, and then click the Layout pop-up menu at the lower left of the pane to choose a different number of photos per page (**Figure 8.9**). (To change the number of photos per page for all pages, go back to step 3.) You cannot change the title page, if you have one, because it has a fixed layout.

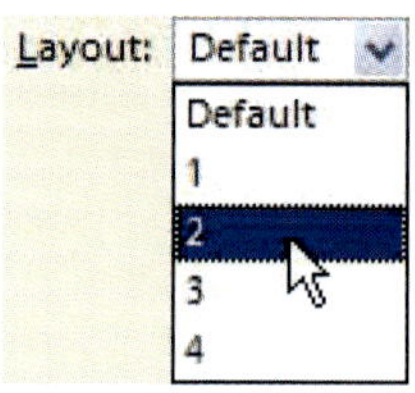

Figure 8.9 **Using the Layout pop-up menu in step 5 you can override the default number of photos per page.**

Adjusting cropping and positioning

You can also make adjustments to how each photo fits in its frame. Click a photo, and a blue outline appears with square handles at the corners (**Figure 8.10**). You can drag any corner to resize the photo, or click and drag anywhere inside the photo to move it without resizing.

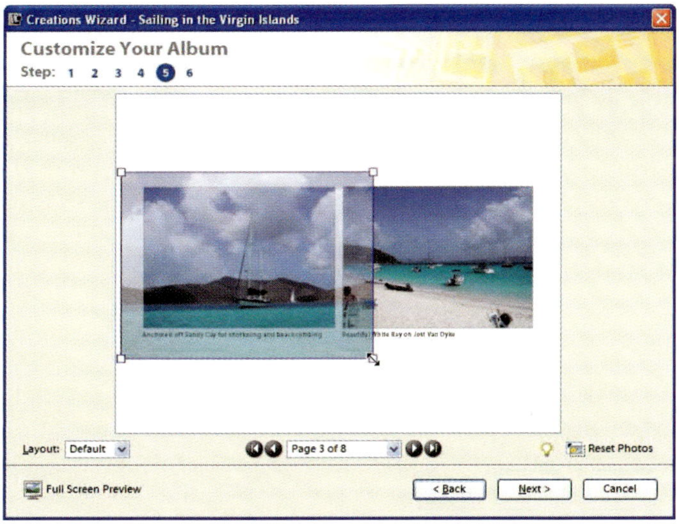

Figure 8.10 In step 5 you can zoom in on part of a photo and change how it is cropped for the creation.

Tip *If you've made changes to the position or size of one or more photos and want to restore the defaults, click the Reset Photos button in the lower right of the pane.*

Note *If you move or resize the photo such that it does not entirely fill the frame, the unfilled parts will be left blank; the frame size cannot be changed, and the frame cannot be moved.*

If you want more flexibility in the layouts of your creations, you have two choices:

- Use the Full-Photo template, which has no frames or other artwork but gives you much greater flexibility.
- Export the photos and use Adobe PageMaker or some other program to create the pages.

If you use the full-frame template, your photos will not be cropped, regardless of their aspect ratio. With this template, because there are no frames, you can drag each photo to nearly any position on the page, you can resize each photo however you want, and none of the photo is cropped regardless of its shape. You may want to give up the graphic frills surrounding the photos to gain this flexibility and control. (Unfortunately, however, you cannot move the caption text.)

If you use any other template, all photos will be automatically cropped to a 4:3 aspect ratio before they are placed in the creation. (Your photos themselves are not affected—just the way they appear in the creation.) Unfortunately, you don't have access in the Creations Wizard to the parts of the photo that have been cropped off.

To gain full control over cropping, do it in the photo well so that the Creations Wizard won't have to do it. Exit the Creations Wizard (go to step 6 and click Done), find the photo in the photo well, click the photo, choose Fix Photo, and select the Crop tool. Set the aspect ratio to 3 x 4 (or 3 x 4 Portrait, if you want to crop to a portrait orientation), and crop the photo the way you want it to appear in the creation. If you want this cropping to apply only in the creation, and not in other uses, duplicate the photo first and make the crop on the duplicate.

Previewing your creation

You can see what the creation will look like, in miniature, by stepping through the pages using the right arrow button. This won't show timing for slide shows, however, nor will you hear the background music or audio captions or see video clips.

To see the creation in its full glory, click the Full Screen Preview button in the lower-left corner of the step 5 window. Your creation will fill the entire screen, and controls will appear in the upper-right corner (**Figure 8.11**). It will play with the timing you have selected (if it's a slide show or an eCard), and you can move manually between pages with these controls. Background music and audio captions, as well as video clips, will play.

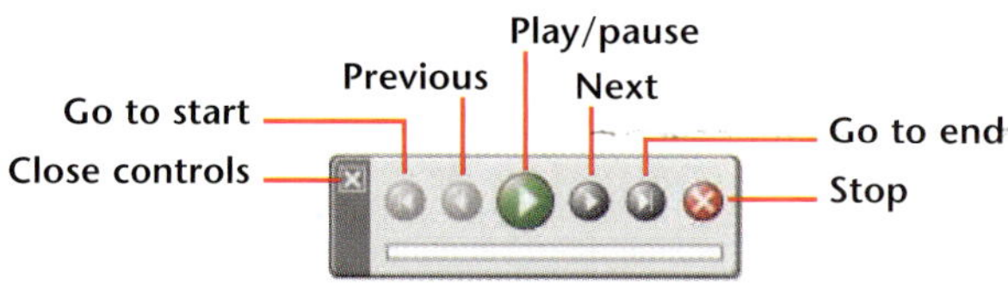

Figure 8.11 When the preview is playing, you can pause it or move back and forth.

Note *Album does not support precise timing synchronization between background music and photos. If you create a PDF slide show or a Video CD or a CD for computer playback, the exact duration of each photo may be different than it is in the Creations Wizard's preview. It can be very frustrating to try to get photo transitions to line up with points in the music. I recommend not making slide shows that rely on such synchronization.*

When the preview reaches the end of the creation, the display will return to the program window. If you want to return before it's done, click the Stop button in the controls in the preview display.

Click Next when you're done to move on to the final phase.

6: Finishing Up

You've finally made it to step 6! Your creation is now complete, and you just need to name it and create whatever output you want (**Figure 8.12**). If you entered a title back in step 3, that title will be the name of the creation by default. If you want to use a different name, uncheck the box next to Use Title for Name and enter the name in the Name field. If you didn't use a title in step 3, enter a name now.

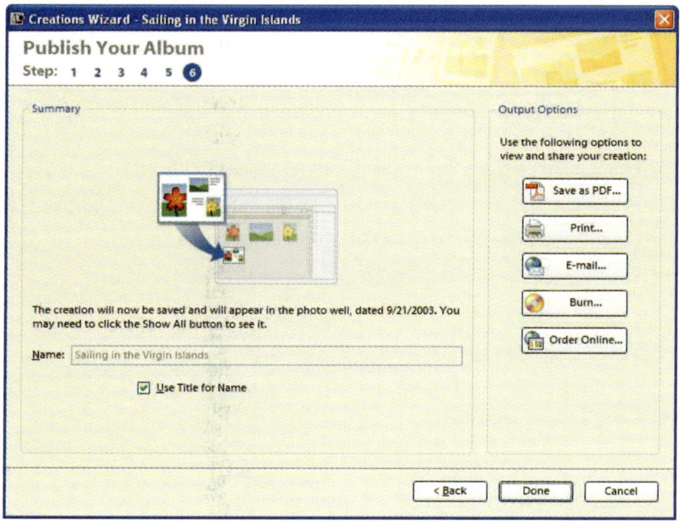

Figure 8.12 In step 6 you can name the creation and publish it in a variety of ways.

You don't have to give your creations names, and if you do, the names don't have to be unique. If you do, however, it's easier to find them in the future (see "Finding Creations," later in this chapter).

If you don't want to do anything further with your creation at this point, you can click Done in the step 6 pane. All creations are stored in the catalog as descriptions with links to the photos they include. Because of this, creations don't consume a lot of disk space, and if you edit the photos after putting them in a creation, the creation will reflect the latest version. (This can be either a good feature or a drawback, depending on your perspective—if a photo is used in a creation, keep in mind that any changes you make to the photo will automatically be reflected in the creation.)

You probably made this creation so that you could share it, and this step is where you can do that by publishing it. There are several approaches you can take:

- Click Save as PDF to produce a PDF file of your creation. This file will have all the photos embedded in it, so you can send this single file to anyone and they will be able to view it as long as they have a recent version of Adobe Reader.
- Click Print to print on your home printer. (See Chapter 9 for tips on getting the best results from your printer.)
- Click E-mail to automatically generate a PDF file and attach it to an email message. (See Chapter 10 for more about emailing creations.)
- Click Burn to create a CD. This option is available only for slide show and Video CD creations. Video CDs are discs intended for playback on a DVD player. Slide shows create discs intended for playback on a PC.
- Click Order Online to order a printed copy from an online service provider. As of this writing, My Publisher is the only such partner, and the only creation types they can print are albums, photo books, and calendars.

When you output your creation, you may see a warning dialog that lists issues with some photos (**Figure 8.13**). If any of the photos have missing files, this is a chance to reconnect them. You'll also be warned if any of the photos are below the optimal resolution for the size at which you are using them.

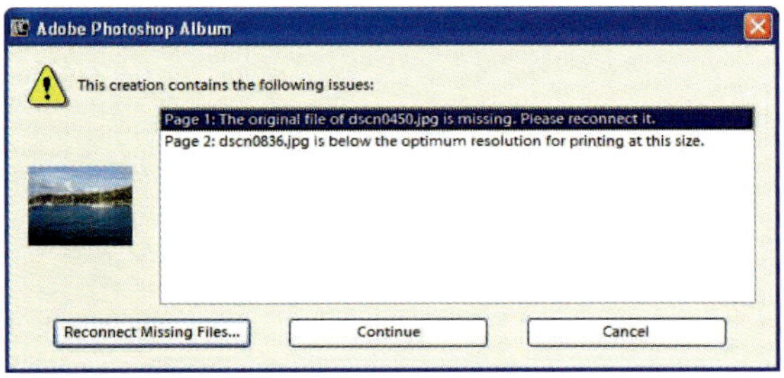

Figure 8.13 **If photos are missing or are of low resolution, the issues dialog will warn you.**

Tip *You can usually ignore warnings about inadequate resolution, especially when creating slide shows or Video CDs. Unless you have another, higher-resolution version of the photo, there's not much you can do about it, anyway. If you're sending a creation to be printed, however, you may want to look at these warnings carefully so that you don't have any surprises after you've bought a costly photo book or other type of output.*

Making PDF files

You can share your creations by saving them as PDF files, which anyone with a computer and a recent version of Adobe Reader will be able to view. (Slide shows can also be viewed on Macintosh computers with Reader, but not all features are available.) Unless you save the creation as a PDF file, it exists in the catalog but not in the file system.

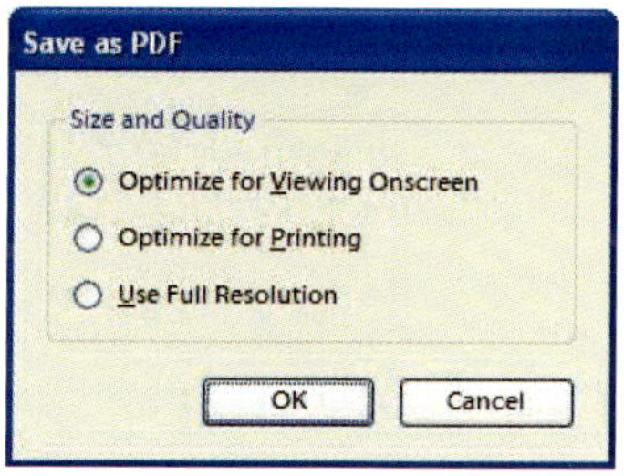

Figure 8.14 In the Save as PDF dialog choose the first option unless you intend for them to be printed.

When you choose Save as PDF, you'll have the choice of three quality levels (**Figure 8.14**). Here's when you should use each level and what each level does:

- Optimize for Viewing Onscreen: Choose this option for minimum file size, when you expect to view the creation onscreen only. Album resizes the photos so that the slide show pages will fill a 1280-by-1024 screen. If you use a full-photo, one-per-page template, that is the size of each photo; if you use a template that has white space around the photo or multiple photos per page, the photos will be resized proportionally smaller.
- Optimize for Printing: Use this option if you want to be able to print the PDF with high quality. Album resizes the photos so that they will be 150 dpi when the creation is printed at the page size specified by the template (typically 8.5 inches by 11 inches). The file size will be considerably larger than with the first option.
- Use Full Resolution: Use this option only if you want to be able to extract full-resolution files from the PDF and can accept a potentially very large file size. This is useful if file size is not an issue and you want to use the PDF to encapsulate your full-quality files so that you or someone else can extract them later.

Working with Creations

When you make a creation, Album saves its description in your catalog and represents the creation in the photo well with a thumbnail image of the first page. An icon in the upper-right corner near the thumbnail (**Figure 8.15**) identifies it as a creation.

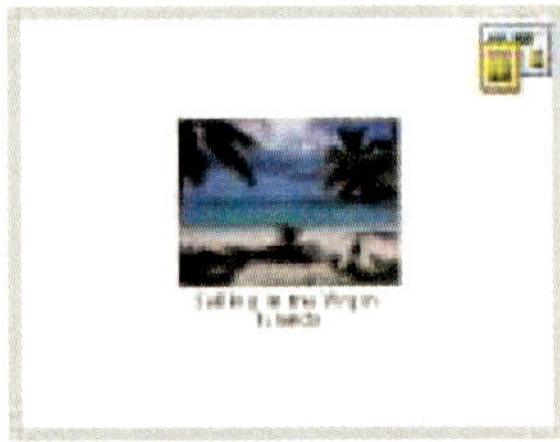

Figure 8.15 **Creations appear in the photo well as a thumbnail of the first page, with a special icon in the upper-right corner.**

Finding Creations

You can find creations in two ways: visually, by locating their thumbnail in the photo well; or by name, using the Creations menu.

To be able to find creations in the photo well more easily, make sure that the tags and date are appropriate. When you make a creation, it inherits all the tags on all of the photos in it. You may want to remove some of these tags if they are incidental to the creation.

Creations are dated by when they are made. You can change this, if it would help you find the creation in the future, by clicking the creation's date (assuming you have details on). You can choose to set the creation's date either to that of the first photo it contains or to any arbitrary date.

You can filter out everything except creations from the photo well by choosing Find > By Media Type > Creations (or press Alt-4). This helps greatly in locating creations scattered among thousands of photos in the photo well.

You can also find creations by name, assuming that you entered one in the Creations Wizard. Choose Creations > Open, pick the one you want from the list displayed, and click OK (**Figure 8.16**).

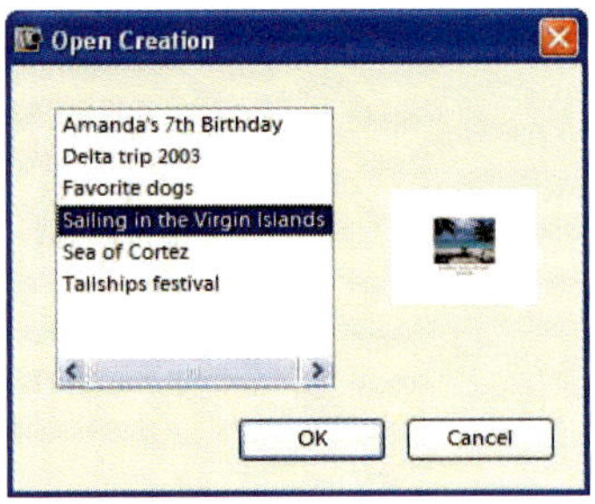

Figure 8.16 **You can also find creations in the Open Creation dialog (Creations > Open).**

Modifying Creations

You can re-enter the Creations Wizard to revise creations or to publish additional output from ones you have made in the past. There are several ways to do this, all of which are essentially equivalent but start at different steps of the Creations Wizard:

- Right-click the creation's thumbnail to show the contextual menu (**Figure 8.17**) and choose Edit to open the wizard at step 3 (choosing options).
- Choose Show Photos instead to open the wizard at step 4 (arrange and add photos). If you want to change the creation type, click the number 1 at the top of the dialog to go to step 1; to change the template, go to step 2 (or just click the Back and Next buttons at the bottom of the dialog until you get to the step you need).
- Double-click the creation's thumbnail, or right-click it and choose Preview, to re-enter the Creations Wizard at step 5 (preview and customize).

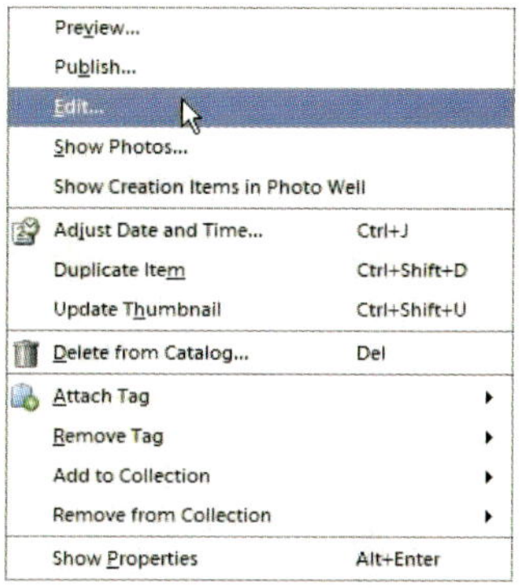

Figure 8.17 **Right-click the creation's thumbnail for quick access to various functions.**

Viewing, Sharing, and Publishing Creations

To generate new output from an existing creation, right-click its thumbnail and choose Publish. This opens the Creations Wizard at step 6, where all the publishing (output) options are available.

You can also print a creation directly from the photo well by selecting its thumbnail and then choosing File > Print, pressing Ctrl-P, or using the print button in the shortcuts bar. For creations for which online printing is available, you can access the online service from the photo well by selecting the creation and choosing Online Services > Order Creations.

You can email a creation from the photo well by selecting its thumbnail, clicking the Share button in the shortcuts bar, and choosing E-mail from the drop-down menu (or choose File > Attach to E-mail).

To burn a CD from a creation, however, you must go to the Creations Wizard. Right-click the creation and choose Publish, and then click the Burn button.

Making Multiple Versions of Creations

You can create a duplicate copy of a creation by right-clicking its thumbnail in the photo well and choosing Duplicate Item. This is entirely different from generating output from the creation; instead, it simply generates a new catalog entry that has a copy of the description of the creation.

This is very convenient if you want to make two or more versions of a creation. Make one version, then exit the Creations Wizard and duplicate the creation in the photo well. Now you can edit the duplicate copy, even changing its creation type if you want. You may, for example, make a slide show first and then duplicate the slide show and change the duplicate to an album for printing.

Caution ***Duplicates have no connection to each other once you have made them. If you rearrange photos or add photos to one copy, it won't affect the other. So don't make duplicates until you're pretty sure you're done choosing and arranging photos.***

Working with the Photos in a Creation

Once you've assembled photos for a creation, you may find that you want to work with those photos. For example, you may want to perform an Auto Fix on all of them, or use the Fix Photo window to enhance some or all of them, or add captions.

You can find all the photos in a creation by right-clicking its thumbnail in the photo well and choosing Show Creation Items in Photo Well. Alternatively, drag the thumbnail into the find bar at the top of the photo well.

Note ***If you've made your creation from a collection, you can always access the photos in the creation by viewing the collection. Keep in mind, though, that photos you add or rearrange in the Creations Wizard won't affect the collection.***

Because the creation exists as a conceptual construct in your catalog and just links to the photos it contains, changes you make to the photos or their captions will be immediately reflected in the creation. Any output you have created, including PDF files, on the other hand, includes its own copies of the photos and is static; it represents the state of the photos at the time you published the creation.

Tip ***If you want to use a photo that is in a creation for another purpose, such as making a print in a particular size and aspect ratio, and you want to crop or otherwise edit the photo for that purpose, be sure to duplicate the photo first and make your changes to the duplicate. This way, those changes won't be reflected in the creation.***

Creating Slide Shows

Remember slide projectors? Slide shows are a great way to share your photos, and it's a lot easier to make and share them with a PC than with slides and a projector. You can also include background music, audio captions, and video clips—and you can show them on your computer or make a disc that friends and family members can view on their computers.

***Note** If you want to make a slide show for viewing on a DVD player, see the section "Creating Video CDs," later in this chapter.*

For general information about the Creations Wizard, refer to the preceding section, "Using the Creations Wizard." In this section I'll deal only with issues specific to slide shows.

Choosing Layout and Timing Options

You have a number of options to choose from in step 3 of the Creations Wizard after you've selected the template (**Figure 8.18**). You set the title just as you do for any other creation, but many of the other options are specific to slide shows.

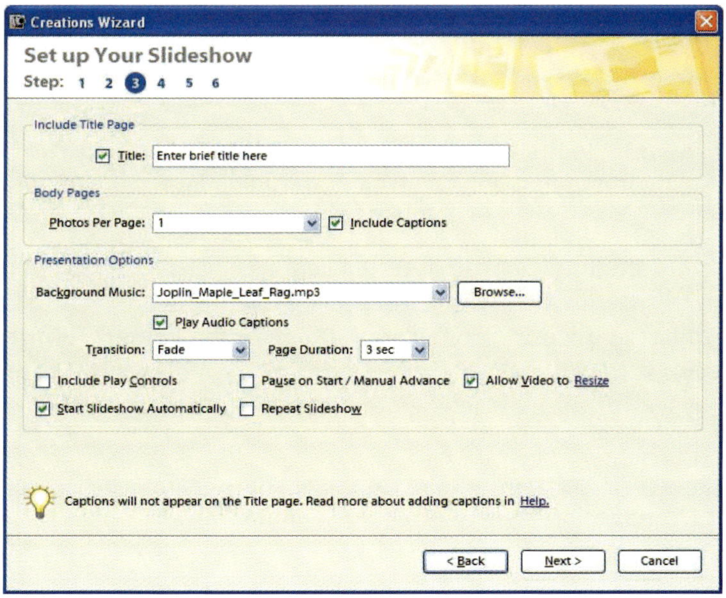

Figure 8.18 When making a slide show, you can choose background music and transitions in step 3 of the Creations Wizard.

Most slide shows use only one photo per page, to maximize the size of the photo. Unlike printing an album, creating a slide show with lots of "pages" doesn't run up costs. If you choose, however, you can have two or even three photos per page.

You can also have a rotating sequence, such as one per page, two per page, one per page, two per page.

If you're making a slide show to send to someone else, including captions is a nice option. You can't enter the captions as part of making the slide show, however; you need to enter them first in the photo well, either in single-image view or via the Properties pane, or in the Calendar day view. If I'm planning to present the slide show personally, I prefer to give my own commentary and not have the caption cluttering the screen.

You can choose from a variety of transitions between pages by selecting one from the Transition pop-up menu in step 3 (**Figure 8.19**). I prefer the simple Fade transition. The smoothness of the fade depends, to some degree, on the processor speed and graphics card of the system playing the slide show; if the fade is jerky, I revert to None. I find the fancier transitions distracting and like to keep the focus on the photos. But if you like the interest they add, try the various transition options. If you want maximum transition fun, choose Random.

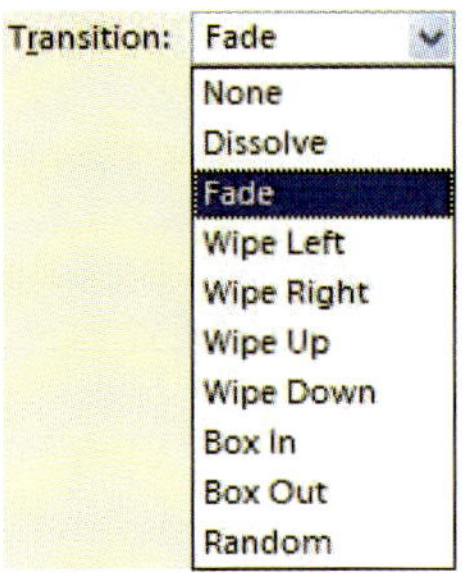

Figure 8.19 **In the Transition pop-up menu you can choose to have no transitions, any one type of transition, or a random mix.**

The Page Duration pop-up menu gives you standard choices of 2, 4, or 10 seconds per page—but you don't have to use any of these. Just click in the Page Duration field and enter any number you want , from 1 to 3600 seconds (1 hour) (**Figure 8.20**). I like to use 3 seconds for fast-paced shows with lots of photos, or 8 seconds if there are few pictures or I want to say a few words about each photo.

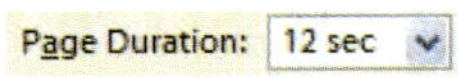

Figure 8.20 **Click in the Page Duration field and enter the number of seconds to override the standard durations.**

Note *If your slide show includes video clips or audio captions, the duration for the affected pages will automatically be extended to ensure that the video and audio are played in their entirety.*

Configuring the Playback Options

You can control various aspects of how your slide show plays. Some of these options aren't obvious and require some explanation.

If you check the Include Play Controls box in step 3, then the play controls (see Figure 8.11) are always displayed. I prefer to leave this box unchecked, because I find the controls distracting. They are displayed anyway whenever you move the mouse, so the controls are always available if needed. The only reason to display them all the time, as checking this box will do, is if you want them to be obvious to a viewer who might not think to move the mouse.

The Start Slideshow Automatically option controls how slide shows saved as PDFs behave when they are opened in Adobe Reader. If this box is checked, then the slide show switches automatically into full-screen playback mode when the PDF is opened. If not, a dialog with a Play button is displayed in Reader (**Figure 8.21**), and the viewer has to click this button to enter full-screen playback mode. Leave this checked unless for some reason you want viewers to be confronted with the full Reader user interface when they double-click your slide show's PDF.

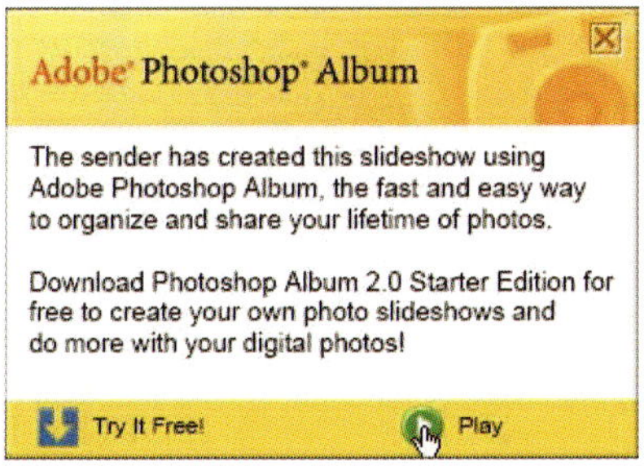

Figure 8.21 **If you don't enable Start Slideshow Automatically, Adobe Reader shows this dialog instead of going right into full-screen mode.**

The somewhat confusingly named Pause on Start/Manual Advance option makes the slide show act as if you have clicked the Pause button as soon as the first slide was displayed. Select this option if you know you're going to want to manually advance through the slides rather than letting the slide show run by itself. (Note that this may sound the same as Start Slideshow Automatically, but its effect is different. Start Slideshow Automatically determines whether Reader goes automatically into full-screen mode, whereas Pause on Start/Manual Advance controls whether the full-screen mode begins with the slide show paused or playing.)

Click the Repeat Slideshow box if you want the slide show to loop at the end and repeat indefinitely. This is a great option if you want to leave the slide show running as people come and go, such as during a party, but usually it's better to leave this option off.

Finally, the Allow Video to Resize option determines whether video is displayed as actual pixels or if it is enlarged to fill the screen. Most still cameras capture relatively low resolution video, so if you select this option, the playback may look very grainy. But if you don't select it, the video will play in a small window. I check this box if I expect the viewers to be in a group, relatively far from the screen, but uncheck it if I expect one person sitting at the computer to view it.

Using Background Music

The Background Music pop-up menu in step 3 lists all the music in your catalog. By default, it includes only the free music that comes with Photoshop Album.

Tip ***The only way to listen to the music within the Creations Wizard is to pick a music file, go to step 5, and click the Full Screen Preview button. To more easily listen to all the different music files, exit the Creations Wizard and choose Find > By Media Type > Audio to show all the music files in the photo well. To play one, double-click its icon and click the Play button in the Media Player window.***

If you want to use your own music files, click the Browse button and choose the file you want to use from the Import Audio dialog. The file is automatically imported into your catalog, so in the future it will appear in the pop-up list.

If the music clip is shorter than the slide show—as it often will be unless you have a short slide show or a very long piece of music—the music will repeat when it is over. If instead you want to play a series of different music clips, you have to stitch them together outside of Album (see sidebar "Using Multiple MP3 Files"), which allows only one music file per slide show.

Keep in mind that Album slide shows do not support precise synchronization of music with photos. The player in Adobe Reader unfortunately uses a different timing algorithm than the previewer in Album, so don't expect the timing to match.

Using Audio Captions

Using audio captions is a great way to provide a narrative for your slide shows. In addition to narration, they give you two capabilities you don't otherwise have in Album: variable duration for each page, and synchronization of photos and audio. You can also use audio captions captured by your camera, if your camera has this capability. Such captions are good for capturing ambient sounds, like rushing water or birds singing, as well as voices.

Using Multiple MP3 Files

You can join MP3 files together using Windows with the following trick, if you're willing to deal with old-fashioned DOS commands:

1. From the Windows Start menu select Run.
2. Enter `cmd` in the Open field of the Run dialog, and click OK to open a DOS window.
3. In the DOS window, use the `cd` (change directory) command to access the folder that includes the music files (for example, `cd c:\music`).
4. Use the copy command to make the new file:

   ```
   copy /b file1.mp3+file2.mp3+file3.mp3 mergedfile.mp3
   ```

5. Type `exit` and press Enter to close the DOS window.

If you'd rather have a Windows-style user interface for this task, and more flexibility, there are many free and inexpensive music-editor programs available that can do this and much more. (Go to a search engine, such as Google, or Download.com [http://download.com.com] and search for "audio editors" or "merge mp3 files.") Or if you want to go all out, consider Adobe's top-of-the-line audio editor, Audition.

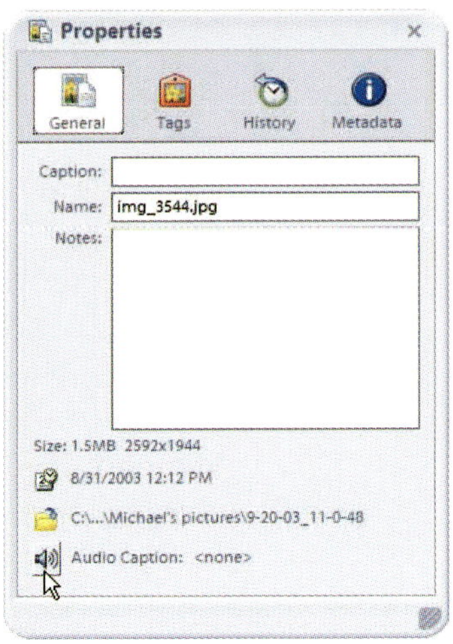

Figure 8.22 Click the Audio Caption button to record an audio caption.

To add audio captions using Album, you must record them in the photo well before making the creation. To do so, select a photo, open the Properties palette, and in the General pane click the Audio Caption button (**Figure 8.22**). (Alternatively, view the photo in single-image view, with details displayed, and click the Record Audio Caption button, which looks like a speaker, at the bottom right.) Then click the Record button in the Select Audio File dialog to start recording (**Figure 8.23**).

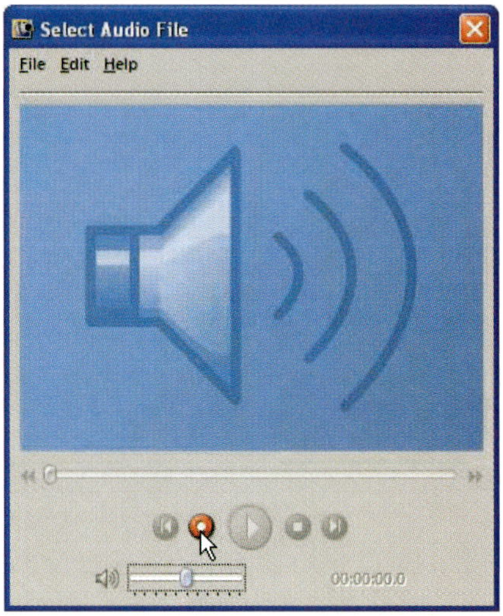

Figure 8.23 **Click the red button in the Select Audio File dialog to start and stop recording. You can also use the grey button with a white square to stop.**

Speak the audio caption into your PC's microphone. When you're done recording, click the Stop button (the gray button with the white square on it). Click the green Play button to listen to what you've recorded; if you want to discard it and record again, just click the Record button and record a new audio caption. When you're all done, close the dialog and click Yes in the confirmation dialog that asks whether you want to save the audio file.

In the step 3 pane of the Creations Wizard, make sure the Play Audio Captions box is checked. You can use both background music and audio captions; the music will fade to about half its usual volume while the audio captions are playing. If you choose this option, make sure you have the volume high enough when you record your audio captions.

Sharing Slide Shows

You can share a slide show in several ways:

- Play it from within Album. Select the thumbnail for the slide show in the photo well and start the slide show by pressing Ctrl-Spacebar, choosing View > Slideshow, or clicking the View Slideshow button at the bottom of the screen.
- Save it as a PDF file, which you can email or post on a personal Web site.

(continues)

Recording Good-Quality Audio Captions

If you're going to record audio captions, it's worth taking a few minutes to get everything set correctly so that the audio quality will be good. First, make sure you have a decent microphone hooked up; the built-in microphones on most notebook PCs aren't great, and they tend to pick up disk-drive and fan noise.

You'll get much better quality if you set the recording level carefully. Open the Windows control panel Sounds and Audio Devices, click the Audio tab, and click the Volume button in the "Sound recording" section (**Figure 8.24**). Turn it up relatively high, and go back to Album and make a test recording. If there is no distortion, try increasing it a bit more. If there is distortion, turn it down. Repeat until you get the optimal setting, and then try to keep your distance from the microphone and the loudness of your voice constant.

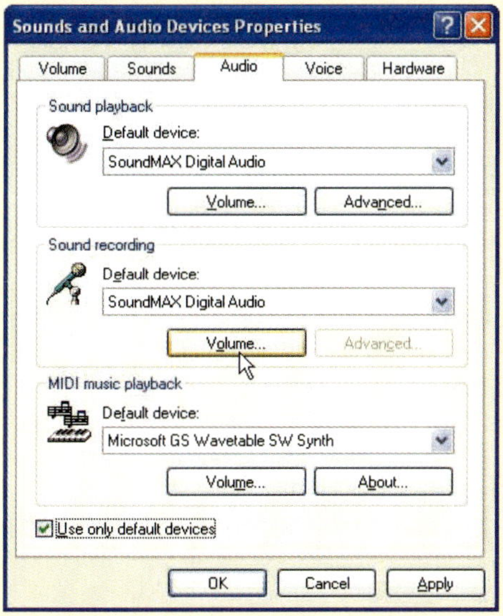

Figure 8.24 Set the microphone volume via Windows' Sounds and Audio Devices Properties control panel for maximum sound quality.

Tip *Photoshop Album uses a modest audio quality setting (a 11 kHz sample rate) to keep the file size reasonable. If you want high-quality audio, record the audio captions using Windows' Sound Recorder (Start > Accessories > Entertainment > Sound Recorder) or an audio utility program. Then link the caption to the photo by choosing File > Browse in the Select Audio File dialog (displayed when you click the speaker button in either the Properties palette or the single-image view; Figure 8.23). This approach is especially useful if you want to use music as an audio caption. Keep in mind, however, that high-quality audio captions will yield large file sizes when you include them in slide shows.*

- Email it. Clicking the E-mail button in step 6 of the Creations Wizard is a quick way of making a PDF and then attaching it to an email message.
- Make a CD for computer viewing. This is more than just a CD with the slide show PDF on it, as the following section describes.
- Make a Video CD for playback on a DVD player. To do this, you need to use different templates, and your options are different; see "Creating Video CDs," later in this chapter.

Making CDs for computer slide shows

Photoshop Album can make special, auto-playing CDs that enable you to easily share your slide shows with other PC users. Just click the Burn button in step 6 of the Creations Wizard, insert a blank CD, and follow the prompts. By using a CD instead of email, you get around almost all concerns about file size (many slide shows are too big to comfortably email).

Making the Most of Slide Show Discs

Recipients of your slide show CDs can do more with them than just play the slide show. They can import the photos into their Album collections, or they can copy a PDF from the disc that will enable them to print or view the photos easily. But they'll need to know a little about how the CD content is arranged.

The CDs that Album creates when you click Burn in step 6 of a slide show creation have a special slide show player program on them. This slide show player uses the photos from the folder \files\media. Album resizes the photos to 1600 by 1200 pixels when it creates the disc, so the photos provide excellent resolution for any PC display, yet they are small enough to allow quick slide show playback even on slow PCs.

The slide show is also written to the disc as a PDF file. This PDF file is not used by the auto-play slide show, but it can be very useful if recipients want to make other uses of the slide show. For example, they can copy this PDF file to their hard disk if they want to keep a copy of the slide show there.

To access the PDF, open My Computer in Windows, right-click the CD icon, and choose Explore. Then double-click the "files" folder and look for the file "slides."

This PDF file has full-resolution copies of the photos, so it is relatively large, but the recipient can access all the photos in their full quality. If recipients are Album users, they can import the PDF into Album, and all the photos in it will be added to their catalogs, in full resolution. Recipients who don't have Album but have Adobe Reader (6.0 or later) can print or extract the photos using the Picture Tasks feature of that program.

The CD you've just created should auto-play when inserted into any PC. Users will have to accept a license agreement, but they don't need to have Album, or even Adobe Reader, installed on their systems; the disc has everything they need.

Tip *Macintosh users can't use the auto-play slide show viewer. They can still view the slide show if they have Adobe Reader, but they'll have to open the folder on the disc called Files and then open the PDF file called Slides using Adobe Reader. Mac OS X users need to be sure to open the file in Adobe's Reader, not the PDF reader built into the operating system, or many of the audio and video features, as well as automatic slide transitions, will not be available.*

If you're making a disc specifically for someone using a Mac, life will be simpler for the user if you use Save as PDF to write the slide show PDF to your hard disk and then use your CD-burning utility to write the PDF to a CD. This creates a smaller PDF and eliminates a lot of PC-specific auto-play files that can only cause confusion on the Mac.

Tip *Album is not able to put multiple slide shows on one CD. If you're willing to give up the auto-play feature, however, you can do this yourself. Instead of using the Burn button in the Creations Wizard, use Save as PDF to create PDF files for the slide shows on your hard disk. Then use your CD-burning utility to write as many PDFs as you can on a CD.*

Creating Video CDs

Computers are great, in some ways, for displaying slide shows—most notably, they have high-resolution displays, allowing your photos to appear crisp and detailed. They suffer from several shortcomings, however:

- The display is small, compared to that of a typical TV.
- The computer is generally not in a place where lots of people can comfortably gather.
- Grandpa might not have a computer.

Televisions, on the other hand, are nearly ubiquitous, and they typically have large screens and are located where lots of people can watch—and where people gather socially. DVD players, which are quickly becoming pervasive, provide a nice bridge from the computer to the TV. (But not the only one—see the section on sharing to TiVo in Chapter 10.)

You may not be aware that there are actually several different kinds of discs that most DVD players can play. True DVD discs are the ones used for movies, and Album cannot create those. Album does make Video CDs, however, which use CD media (and thus require only a CD burner, not a DVD burner). The vast majority of DVD players can play Video CDs, but some cannot; if you're unable to play Video CDs produced by Album, check the specs for your DVD player.

To make a Video CD, follow the usual creation routine, choosing Video CD for the type in step 1 of the Creations Wizard. After choosing a template (I prefer the simple Full-Photo template because it fills the entire screen with photos), you have some important choices to make in step 3 that are unique to the Video CD format (**Figure 8.25**).

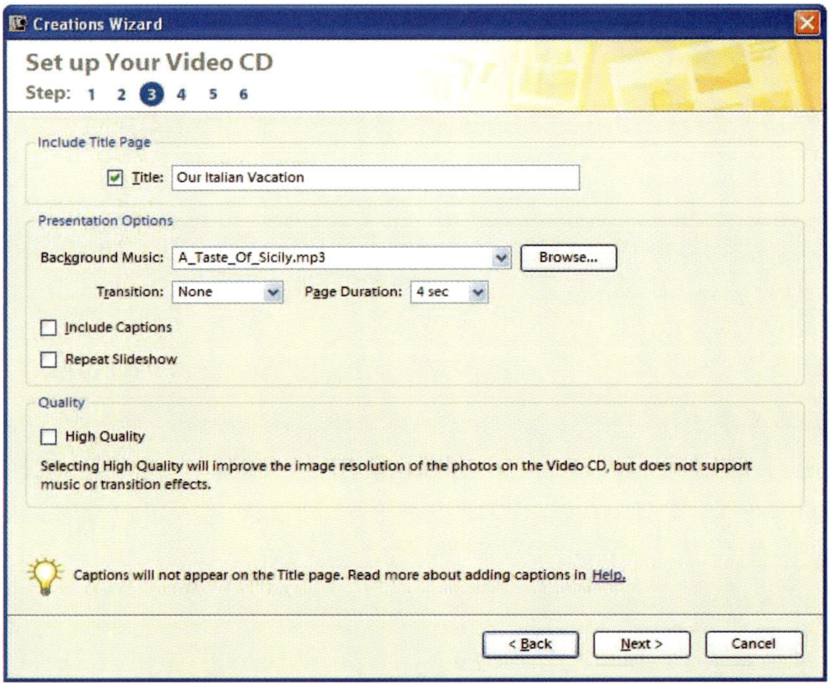

Figure 8.25 Standard Video CDs allow background music, audio captions, video, and transitions, which you set in step 3 of the Creations Wizard.

If you make a standard Video CD, you can use background music and audio captions, as well as video clips. These Video CDs are limited to a resolution of 352 by 240 pixels (assuming NTSC; slightly higher for PAL—see the sidebar "Sending Video CDs to Other Countries," below). On a computer this would seem like an awful resolution, but on a TV it looks surprisingly decent; VHS tapes aren't much better.

There is an alternative Video CD format, exclusively for still images, which provides twice the resolution in each dimension (four times the total pixels): 704 by 480. You can choose this format by checking the High Quality box in step 3 (**Figure 8.26**). Photos with a lot of detail look noticeably crisper at this resolution, although the difference on typical TVs is not as dramatic as you might expect. The downside of this format is that only still photos can be used—no video clips, no background music, and no audio captions. And because transitions are encoded as video, it means no transitions, either—just a quick change from one photo to the next.

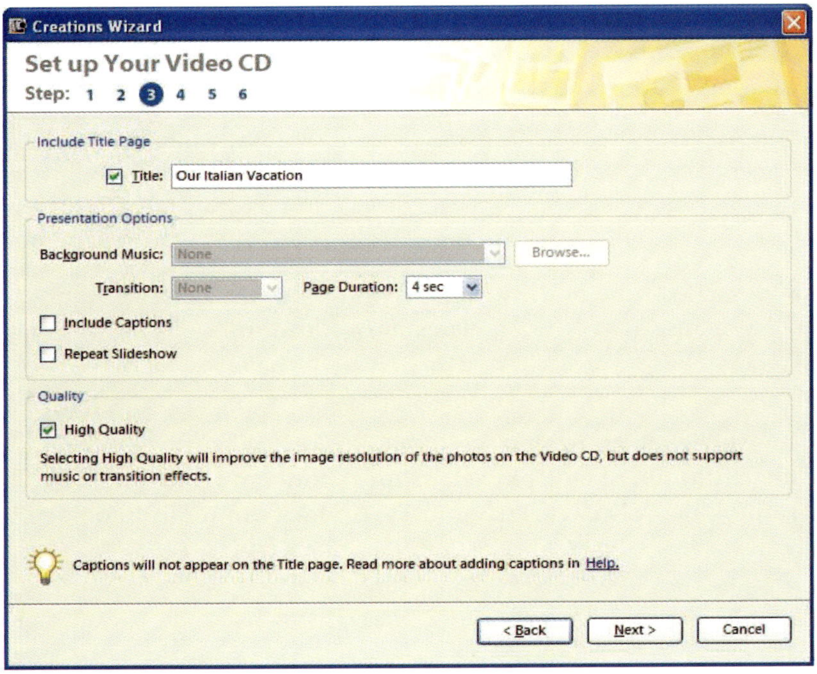

Figure 8.26 Choose the High Quality option in step 3 for more detailed photos.

Just how good each of these formats looks depends, to some degree, on the particular photos, DVD player, and TV. I recommend that you put together a test Video CD and make one copy in each format so that you can see for yourself. The standard Video CDs provide a richer experience if you have video clips and audio captions or you like to use background music, but the high-quality version delivers sharper-looking photos.

If you decide to take the high-quality path, any video clips included in your slide show will be represented by the first frame of the video.

Sending Video CDs to Other Countries

If you want to send Video CDs to friends and relatives in other countries, you need to know what TV standard their countries use. Album can make Video CDs using either the NTSC or PAL format.

NTSC (National Television Standards Committee, sometimes jokingly called Never Twice the Same Color) is used in the United States, Canada, Mexico, Japan, and much of Central and South America.

PAL (Phase Alternating Line, also called Perfection At Last or Pay A Lot) is used in most of Western Europe (except France and Greece), Australia, and parts of the Middle East and Africa.

SECAM (*Séquentiel Couleur Avec Mémoire,* also known by some American engineers as Something Essentially Contrary to American Method), which is *not* supported by Album, is used in France, Greece, Eastern Europe, and parts of the Middle East and Africa.

For other countries, check one of the many lists on the Web, such as TenLab's International TV Systems Chart (www.tenlab.com/worldtv.htm).

To burn the disc, just click Burn in step 6 of the Creations Wizard. Skip through any resolution warnings that may be displayed, as any shortcomings are unlikely to be significant when the Video CD is viewed on a TV, and Album tends to go overboard with warnings.

Creating Albums and Photo Books

If you've always wished you had your photos in albums but rarely have been willing to go to the trouble to put them together, now's your chance—making albums in the digital world is much easier than in the analog world, now that you have the right software. Even better, once you've created an album, you can get as many copies as you want with just a few clicks.

Photoshop Album distinguishes between two types of albums: regular albums and photo books. The differences arise from the fact that albums are designed primarily to be printed on your home printer, while photo books are designed primarily to be printed by online partner My Publisher.

Standard Albums

As when used with slide shows and Video CDs, the Full-Photo template is the only one that allows aspect ratios other than 4:3 and allows you to move and resize the photos arbitrarily. So if you like plain layouts that keep the emphasis on your photos and give you maximum flexibility in arranging the photos, use this template.

If, on the other hand, you want some decoration around the photos—and you're willing to live with a 4:3 aspect ratio and the layouts provided in the templates—you can choose from a variety of templates (**Figure 8.27**).

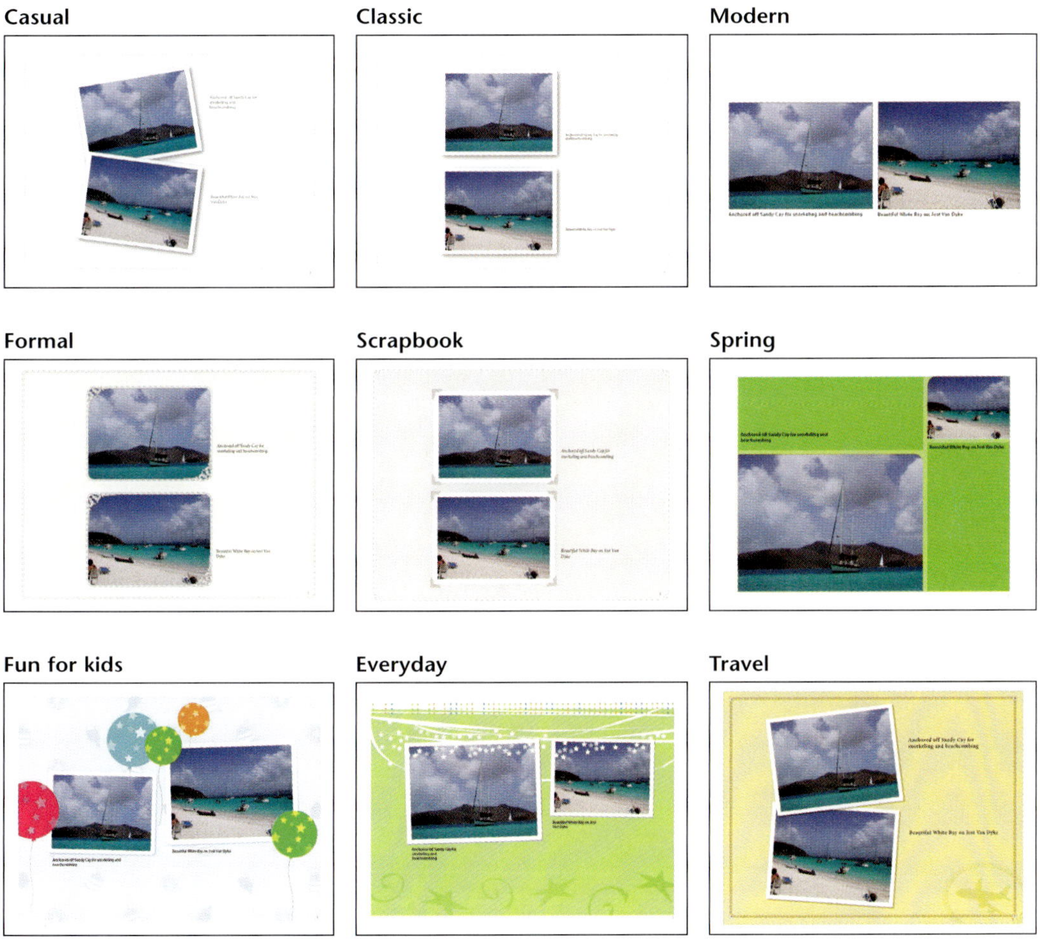

Figure 8.27 The plain Full-Photo template gives you the most control, but you can also choose from any of these decorative designs.

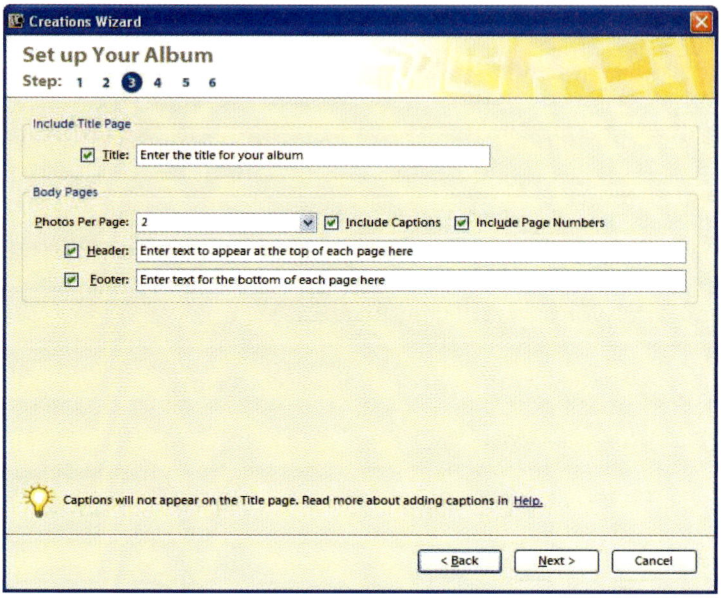

Figure 8.28 You can set up an album to have headers and footers, as well as page numbers, in step 3 of the Creations Wizard.

The options for albums are straightforward (**Figure 8.28**). As with most creations, your album can have a title page. If you enable the Title Page option, the first photo will be used there. You can enable headers and/or footers if you want text at the top or bottom of each page.

You can choose 1, 2, 3, or 4 photos per page, or any of three different alternating sequences (**Figure 8.29**). You can override this selection for each page in step 5 if you want to customize it further. Note that in some of the layouts there is a mix of different photo sizes on each page, so you may want to go back and forth between selecting the number of photos per page and previewing the results in step 5. You may also want to rearrange photos in step 4 to put the photos you want in the larger spots.

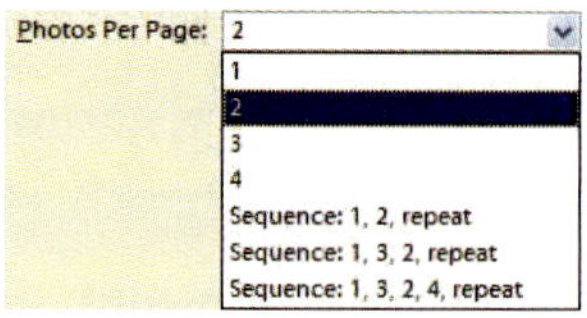

Figure 8.29 In the Photos Per Page pop-up menu of step 3 you can select fixed numbers of photos per page or rotating sequences.

You can save albums as PDF files, with the same resolution options as for slide shows. They can be viewed onscreen in Adobe Reader, of course, but they differ from slide shows in that the pages do not advance automatically, you cannot have background music or audio captions, and only the first frame of a video clip will appear.

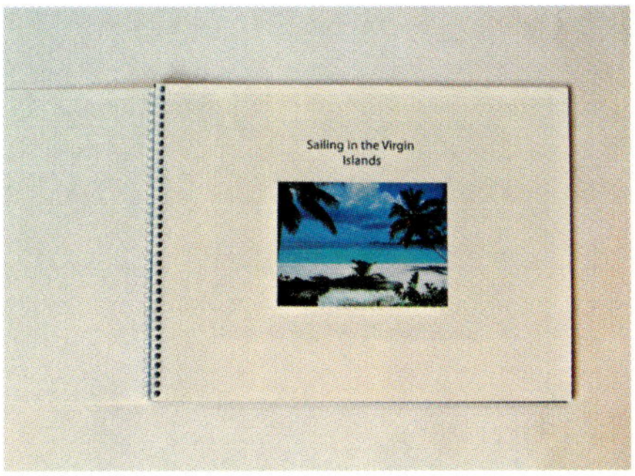

Figure 8.30 **You can order Albums from My Publisher, and they will be spiral-bound.**

You can order albums online from My Publisher by clicking the Order Online button in step 6. Albums are spiral-bound and have a clear plastic cover (**Figure 8.30**); photo books, described in the next section, get a different treatment. If you have a good photo printer you can get similar results by printing the pages and taking them to a local copy shop to be bound.

Photo Books

Photo books are a special type of album designed for printing by My Publisher (though you can also print them at home). The templates (**Figure 8.31**) are quite different from those for standard albums, and there are fewer options (**Figure 8.32**).

Just Photos **Modern** **Traditional**

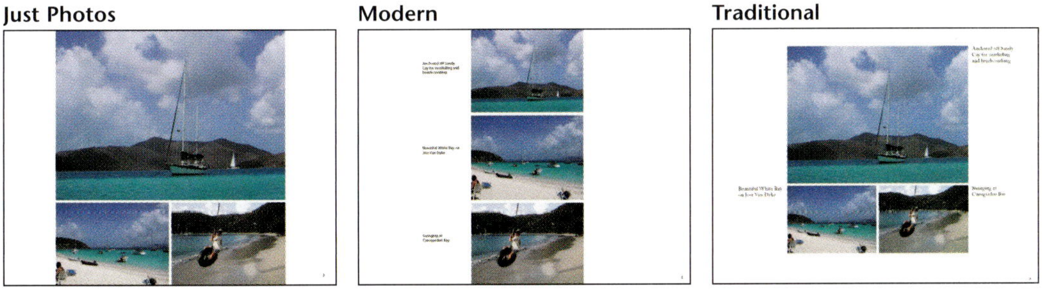

Figure 8.31 **Photo books are similar to albums but use different templates.**

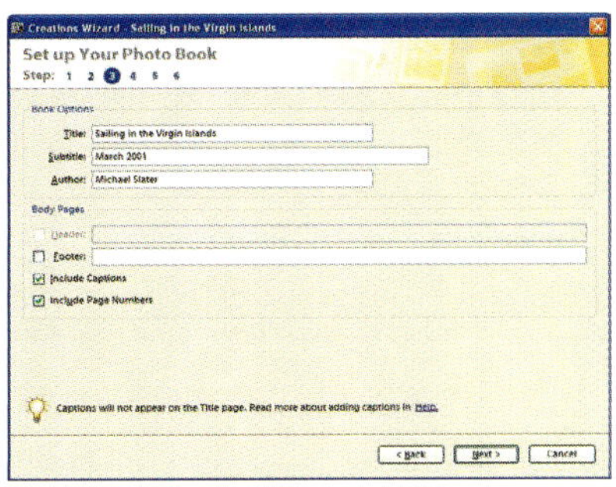

Figure 8.32 **Photo books require a title page, and the template fixes the number of photos per page.**

The Just Photos template is just that—no captions, no headers, and no footers (though you can have page numbers). Both the Just Photos and the Modern templates are full-bleed designs, which means that the photos go all the way to the edge of the paper. Many home printers cannot print all the way to the edge, but some can (and, of course, My Publisher can).

The Modern templates allow captions and footers, and the Traditional templates allow captions but neither headers nor footers. None of the templates allows headers.

Tip ***New templates may be available from My Publisher in the future; click the Download New Templates button in step 1 of the Creations Wizard to check.***

Photo books are different from standard albums in several ways:

- The number of photos per page is specified by the template, so there are no choices for this in step 3 and you cannot change the page layouts in step 5.
- All photo books have both a cover and a title page. The first photo appears on the cover, and the second on the title page. The title appears in both places. The captions for the first two photos are not used, even if you have enabled captions.
- You can have a subtitle and an author name in addition to the title. These two lines of information appear below the title on both the cover and the title page.
- All photo books must have a minimum of ten pages, including the title page (but not the cover). Blank pages will be printed, if needed, to reach this minimum.
- Photo books have a maximum of 50 pages, including the title page.

When My Publisher prints photo books, they are hardbound in your choice of a linen or leather cover in a variety of colors (**Figure 8.33**). They make an excellent keepsake and a way of remembering special occasions. And, unlike photo albums in the film world or even home-printed digital albums, you can order additional copies of photo books with just a few clicks, delivered wherever you want.

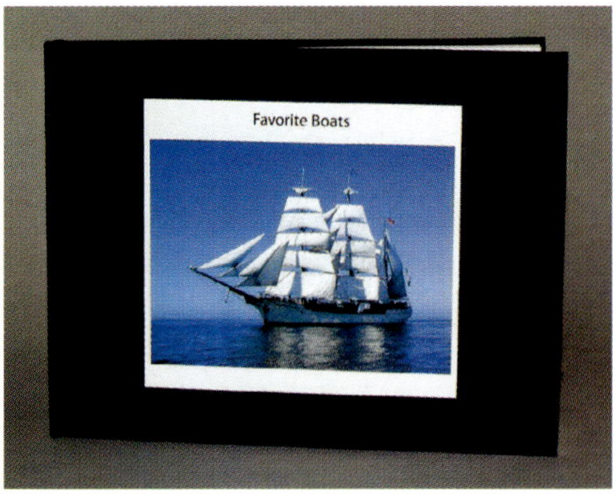

Figure 8.33 My Publisher can print your Photo Book and bind it in hardcover.

As of late 2003, photo books from My Publisher started at about $30 each (for ten-page books with a linen cover, containing up to 40 photos) plus shipping and handling. Additional pages were about $3 each.

Creating Your Own Greeting Cards

Instead of buying greeting cards, you can use Photoshop Album to make them, featuring your own photos. These personalized cards are especially fun when you can use a photo related to the occasion—like an old picture of a friend for his or her birthday card.

Making Printed Cards

Album's greeting cards are printed on one sheet of paper, designed to be folded in half twice to make a card that typically has the photo and title on the front and text on the inside (**Figure 8.34**). The one exception is the Snowglobe template, which puts your photo on the inside. (If you want to make greeting cards that use a single sheet of paper, printed on both sides and folded once, you'll have to do that outside of Album.)

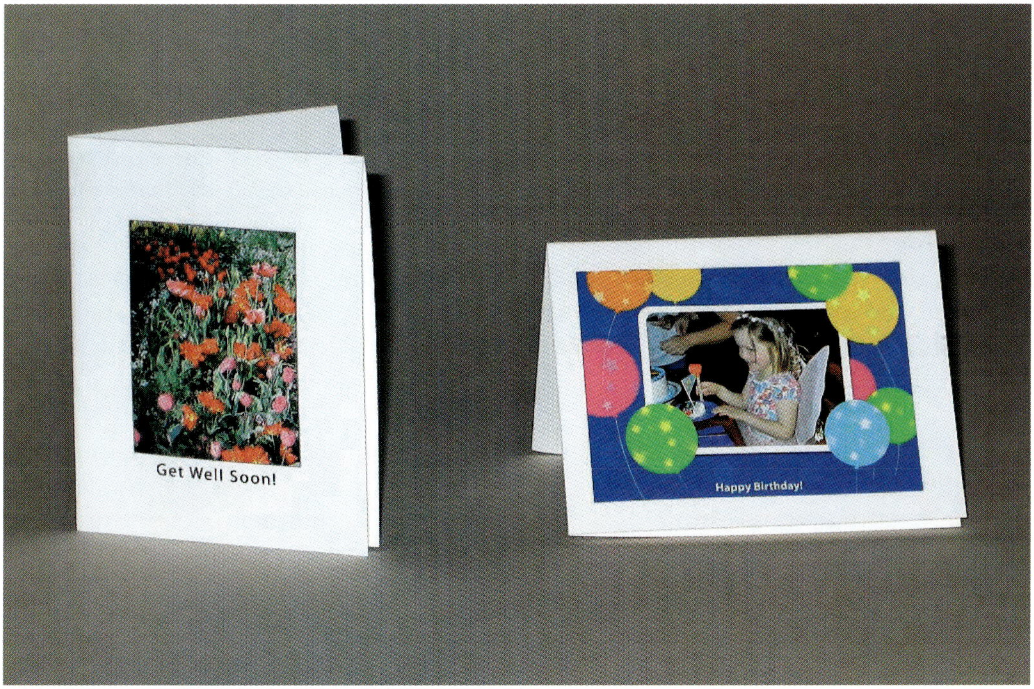

Figure 8.34 **Greeting cards are printed on a single sheet of paper and folded twice.**

Greeting cards use only a single photo. If you select more than one, only the first will be used.

In step 3 you can enter three lines of text for greeting cards: the title, greeting, and message (**Figure 8.35**). The title appears on the cover of the card. The greeting appears inside, with the message below it. If you don't plan to sign your name by hand, the message is a good place to put it.

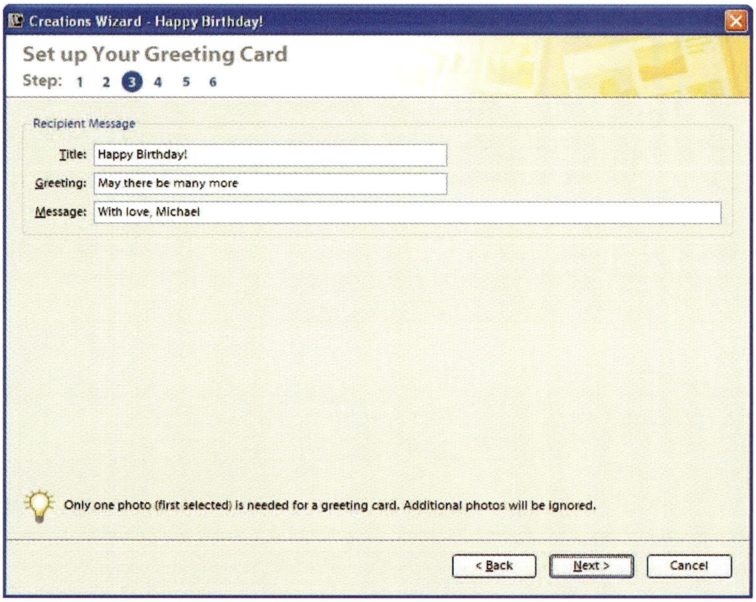

Figure 8.35 **In step 3, enter text for the front of the greeting card in the Title field.**

You can also order printed greeting cards from Shutterfly, Adobe's current online service partner for prints in the United States. These cards look much more professional because they are printed on a single sheet of card stock, folded in half, like a commercial greeting card.

Creating and ordering Shutterfly-produced greeting cards is not supported from within Album. You can, however, upload the photo to Shutterfly as a photo to share, and then use Shutterfly's Web site to create and order greeting cards (see "Ordering Snapbooks and Greeting Cards from Shutterfly," below, and "Using Online Services for Sharing," in Chapter 10).

Sending Electronic Cards

When it's too late to send a physical card—or you don't want to take the time to print one—electronic greeting cards are the perfect solution. They can also do things physical cards can't, such as including a video clip, background music, or an audio annotation.

eCards are essentially two-page slide shows that use templates similar to those for greeting cards (**Figure 8.36**). You can print them or save them as PDFs, but they are intended primarily to be e-mailed.

Page 1 **Page 2**

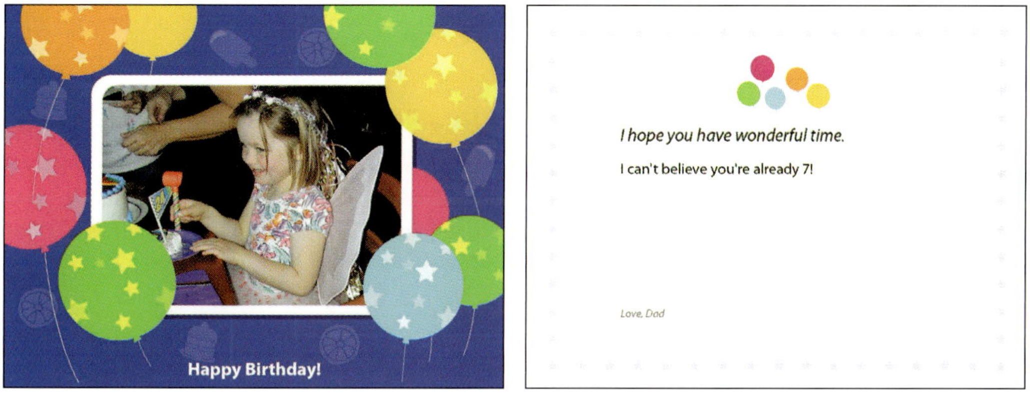

Figure 8.36 eCards are two-page slide shows with a greeting card design.

Since you don't have the option to sign the card physically, there is an additional text field, Signature, for your name in step 3 (**Figure 8.37**). As when creating a slide show, you can also specify background music, whether to use audio captions, and other slide show controls.

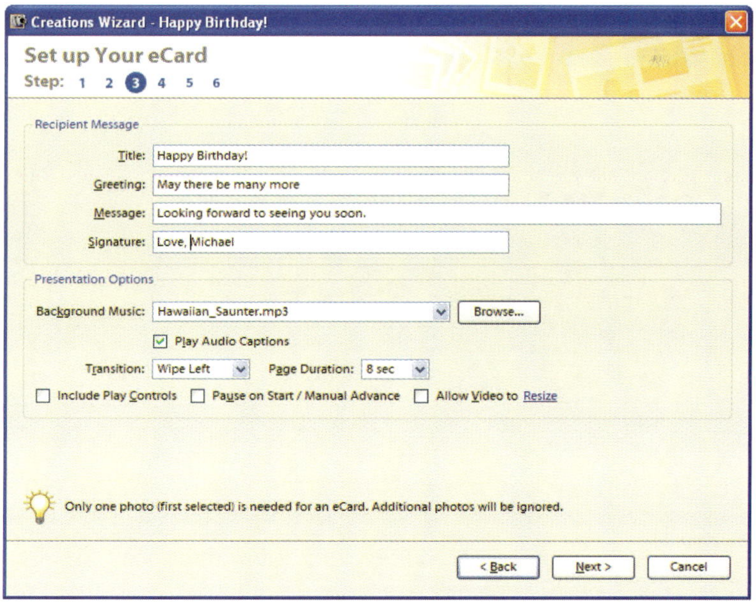

Figure 8.37 eCards add the usual slide show options to the greeting card options.

You'll probably want a relatively long time for the Page Duration, since that determines how long the viewer will have to read the title and enjoy your photo on the first page, as well as how long he or she will have to read the inside. Alternatively, you can select both the Include Play Controls and Pause on Start/Manual Advance options, and the first page will be displayed until the user clicks the Play button in the controls. The controls seem like overkill for a two-slide presentation, however.

Using a video clip instead of a photo makes an eCard a lot more interesting. But remember that doing so will make the file much bigger—possibly bigger than the recipient's email service will accept, if he or she has a limited account (such as a free Hotmail or Yahoo account). If you do use a video, make it a short one. And if size is critical, skip the background music.

When you've finished making the card, click the E-mail button in step 6 of the Creations Wizard to automatically create a PDF file and attach it to an email message. You can alternatively use Save as PDF to create a PDF file so that you can attach it to an email message or burn it to a CD later. Burning it to a CD is a good option if you've included a video clip that is too large for email, but you'll have to do that using a CD-burning utility outside of Album.

Creating Calendars

Calendars are one of the most useful creations you can make, because almost everyone hangs a calendar on their wall. This gives you (or whomever you give the calendar to) a great way to enjoy a different photo each month without having to think about it.

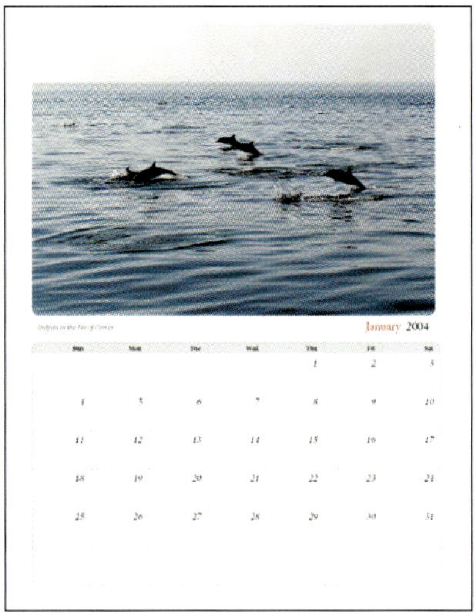

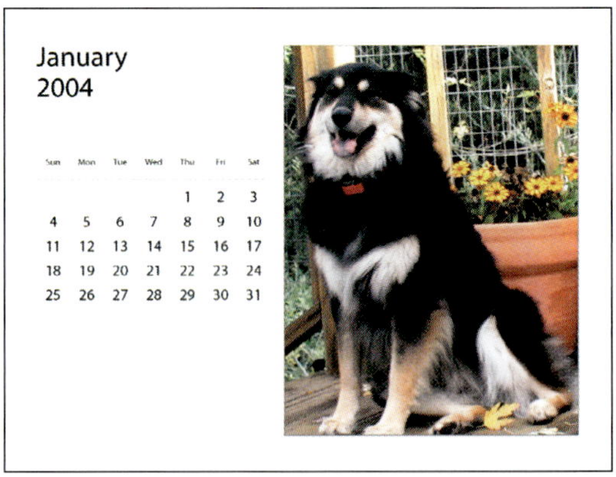

Figure 8.38 You can print calendars in horizontal or vertical designs.

Calendar templates are available in both traditional vertical (portrait) and horizontal orientations (**Figure 8.38**). You can make a calendar with any number of months, for any period of time; it doesn't have to conform to year boundaries. So you can make school-year calendars, 18-month calendars, and so forth—or even just a single calendar page for the current month.

You set the range of months and years in step 3 of the Creations Wizard (**Figure 8.39**). If you select the Title option, the calendar will use the first photo on the title page. The title page has no calendar information; it has only a photo and the title text.

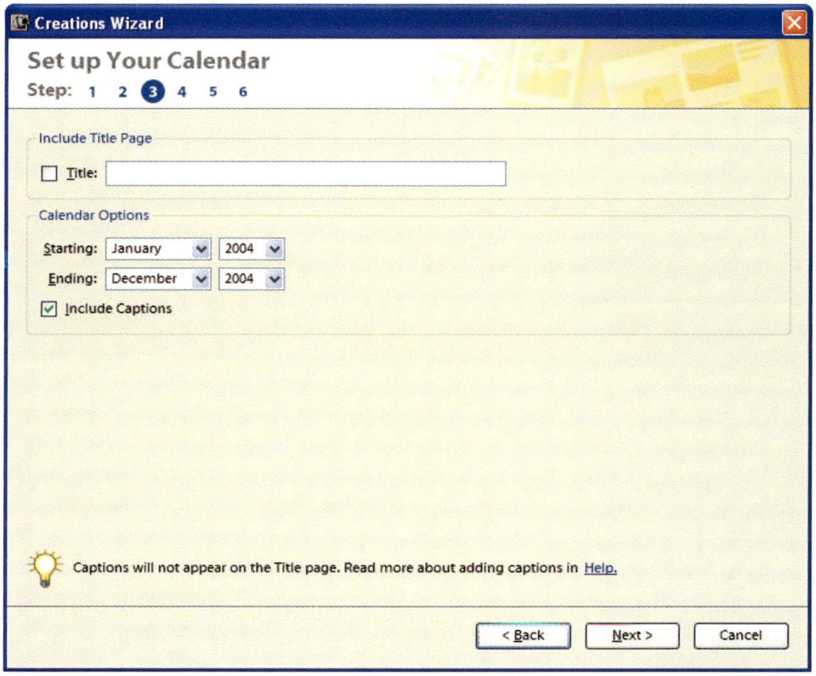

Figure 8.39 In step 3 of the Creations Wizard you set the calendar's range of months, which is not limited to a year.

If you select more photos than months in the date range you chose (plus a photo for the title page, if you have one), photos after those required will be ignored. If you don't select enough photos, the remaining calendar pages will have a blank area where the photo would go. If you want to use the same photo in multiple months, duplicate the photo in step 4 of the wizard.

***Tip** If you want your calendar to start on Monday each week instead of Sunday, choose Edit > Preferences > Calendar and check the box next to "Use Monday as first day of the week."*

You can print calendars on your home printer, or you can order them online from My Publisher by clicking the Order Online button in step 6 of the wizard. Calendars printed online are spiral-bound and are therefore more professional-looking than those you print at home. Or you can print the pages at home and take them to a local copy shop to be bound.

Making Web Pages and 3D Galleries

There are two more special creations—Web pages and 3D galleries—that you can make with Album. They work quite a bit differently from the other creations in a number of respects, and there is one limiting factor that makes them of interest to far fewer people: you must have your own Web site and know how to upload pages to it for these creations to be useful.

If you have a Web site, these creations enable you to make pages with your photos easily. Album creates the pages in a folder on your hard drive; you then need to use your own FTP (File Transfer Protocol) tool to upload the pages to your site. (If none of this makes any sense to you, skip ahead to the next section.)

These Web creations don't use the Creations Wizard, and they don't yield creations that appear in your photo well. In some ways, the Web and 3D gallery makers are better thought of as elaborate export functions; you select photos, and they produce a set of files that includes those photos. Once they're created, you can't modify them in Album. If you want to make any change, you must start over with a new creation (but your settings are saved, so this isn't as painful as it sounds).

Because of this, it is especially important when making this type of creation that you start with a collection. This gives you a place to gather and arrange your photos. If you make a Web photo gallery or a 3D gallery directly from the photo well, you'll have no way to control the order of the photos (they'll always be in chronological order) and no way to easily re-create it or add photos.

Sharing on the Web

A Web photo gallery is a set of Web pages that allows you to post your photos on your Web site. Unlike other creations, a Web photo gallery consists of a series of linked HTML pages and cannot be saved in any other form, such as PDF.

Note *If you want to post photos on the Web but don't have your own Web site, use the Share Online option (see Chapter 10).*

If you want complete control over your Web pages, you'll have to export the photos from Album and use a Web authoring tool to create the pages. But if you can live with the options the Web photo gallery offers, it will make creating Web pages extremely easy.

To make a Web photo gallery, first make a collection with the photos you want to use, and put them in order in the collection. Then select all of them and choose Creations > Web Photo Gallery.

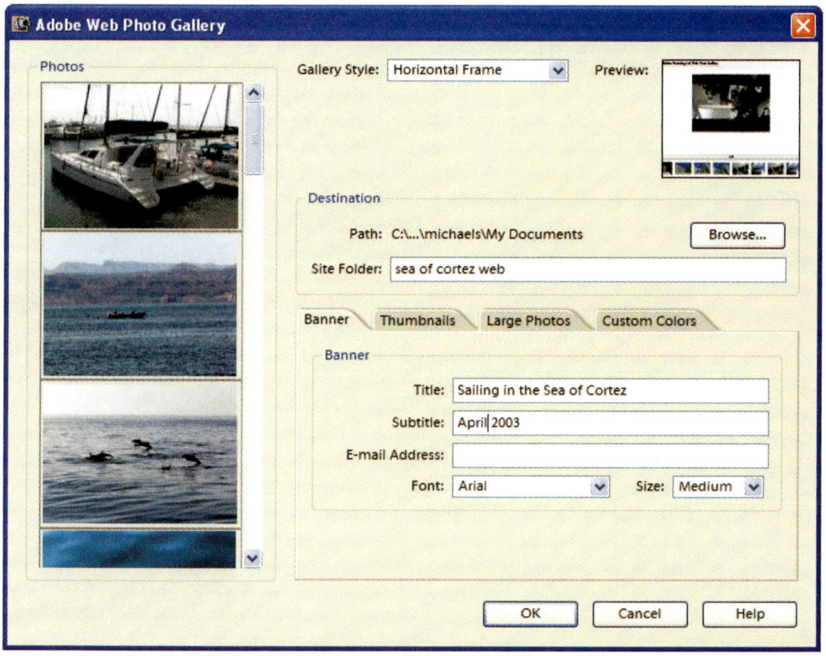

Figure 8.40 When making a Web photo gallery, first choose the style in the Gallery Style pop-up menu and enter a folder name for the HTML files in the Site folder field. You can also enter a title and subtitle on the Banner tab.

The Adobe Web Photo Gallery dialog allows you to choose from a range of styles for your gallery and to customize the text it includes and other aspects of its layout (**Figure 8.40**). Plan to make several variations to find the one you like. Fortunately, it is easy to make and view them. As soon as the Web photo gallery is completed, Album launches a browser window to view it. (The gallery is displayed directly from the HTML files on your hard disk, so you don't need to have a Web site or do any uploading to see the preview.)

These Web galleries use two different design approaches:

- Simple, Classic, Scrapbook, and Dance create index pages with thumbnail photos and single-image pages you jump to by clicking one of the index photos (**Figure 8.41**). There are navigation arrows so that you can also move from one single-image page to the next or previous one.

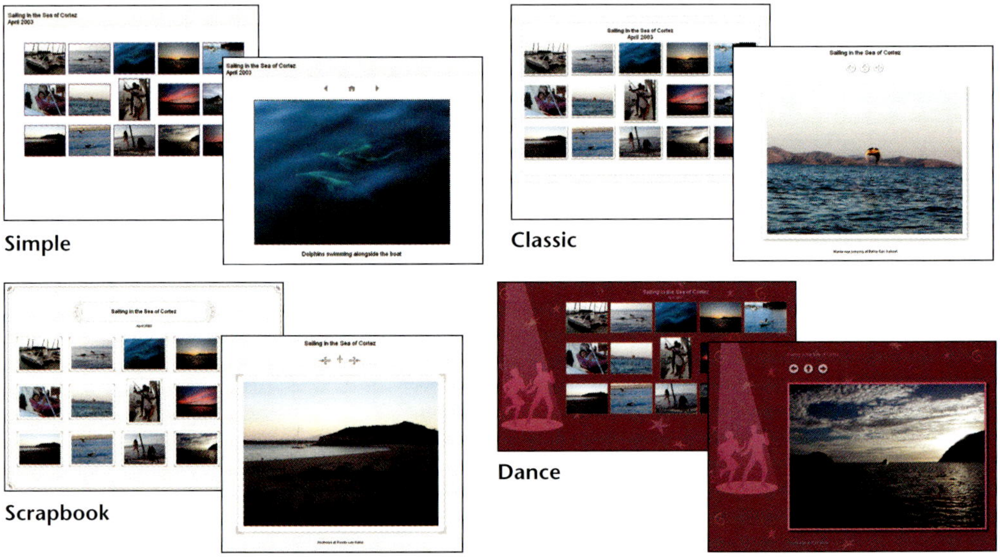

Figure 8.41 These Web photo gallery layouts include index pages (left) and single-photo pages (right).

- The other styles, such as Horizontal Frame (**Figure 8.42**), use frames to create a page with a filmstrip-like row of thumbnails and an area for a larger image. The viewer can scroll the filmstrip if there are more thumbnails than will fit on the screen. To view any photo in the large image area, click the thumbnail.

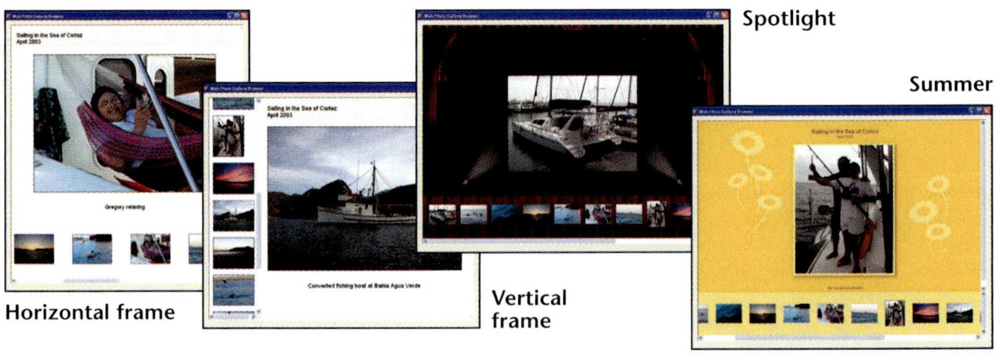

Figure 8.42 The other Web photo gallery templates use a two-frame design with a scrolling thumbnail strip.

There are lots of settings to choose when making a Web photo gallery. In the upper half of the Adobe Web Photo Gallery dialog, choose a style in the Gallery Style pop-up menu, and enter a name for the folder where you want to store the HTML files in the Site Folder field. The lower half of the dialog has four tabs, where you choose various options.

Note *Some gallery styles do not support all options. Unsupported options are grayed out.*

The Banner tab (Figure 8.40) controls information that appears on each page. You can enter a title, subtitle, and email address, or leave any of these blank. Exactly where this text appears varies from one template to another. You can also choose the type font and size.

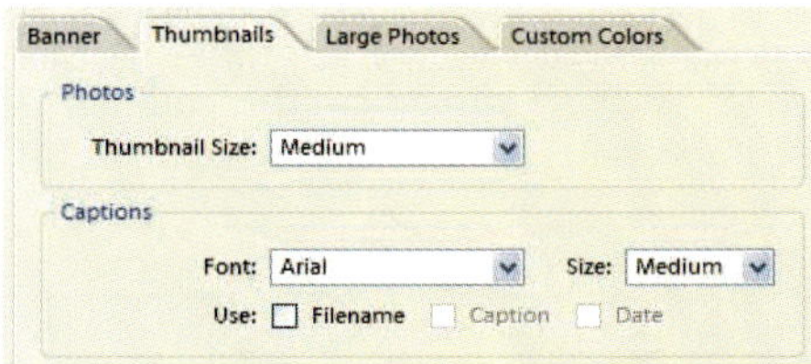

Figure 8.43 Select the thumbnail size on the Thumbnails tab; usually you'll want to use Small or Medium thumbnails and leave the caption off.

On the Thumbnails tab you choose how big you want the thumbnails to be (**Figure 8.43**). The smaller they are, the more will fit on a page and the faster the page will load. Larger thumbnails, on the other hand, make it easier for people to see the photos without enlarging any of them. You can also choose the caption font and size, and whether the caption is composed of the caption text from the catalog, the date, or the filename.

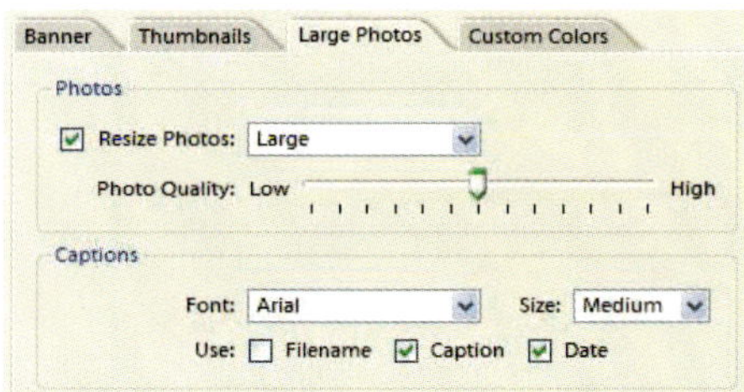

Figure 8.44 Set the photo size and quality on the Large Photos tab.

On the Large Photos tab you specify options for what is displayed when the user clicks one of the thumbnails (**Figure 8.44**). If you uncheck the Resize Photos box, the photos will appear in their full resolution. This is useful if you want viewers to be able to print the files, but it makes for very slow loading if you have high-resolution photos and is generally undesirable for Web viewing. If you check the Resize Photos box, you can choose the size to which you want the photos scaled, as well as the JPEG compression level, which you set with the Photo Quality slider. Here you have to make tradeoffs between how fast the Web pages will load and how good the photos will look.

Tip ***If you expect all the viewers to have broadband connections, use the X-Large size and set the quality level toward the High end. If some are likely to have dial-up connections, on the other hand, try the Medium size and a lower quality level.***

Use the Custom Colors tab if you want to modify the colors used in the gallery (**Figure 8.45**).

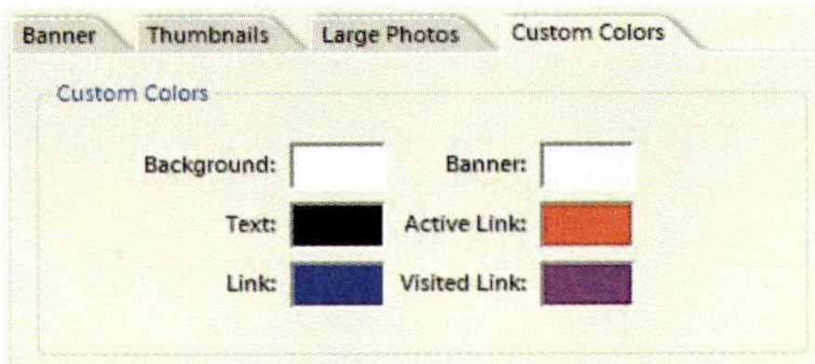

Figure 8.45 You can customize the colors of the gallery components on the Custom Colors tab.

When you've finished choosing options, click OK; the Web pages will be created and opened in a preview window, the Web Photo Gallery Browser (**Figure 8.46**). If you're happy with them, upload the files to your Web site using an FTP program or your Web authoring tool.

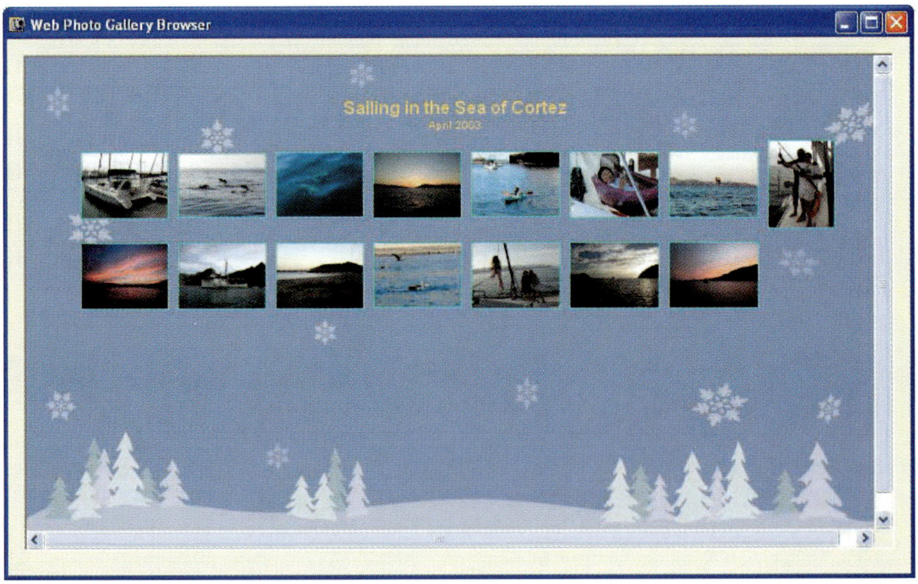

Figure 8.46 When you're done making the Web photo gallery, you can open it in a preview window.

Note *All your settings are saved, except the folder name. Be sure to edit the title and subtitle if you're making a different gallery.*

To overwrite the previous photo gallery, enter the same folder name. All previous photo gallery files in that folder will be erased, so if you want to save the previous gallery, be sure to enter a new name.

Atmosphere 3D Galleries

For a cool twist on a Web photo gallery, try the Atmosphere 3D Gallery. This feature creates a set of special Web pages that provide a simulated 3D viewing experience. Viewers of your site will virtually walk through a three-dimensional gallery with your pictures on the walls (**Figure 8.47**).

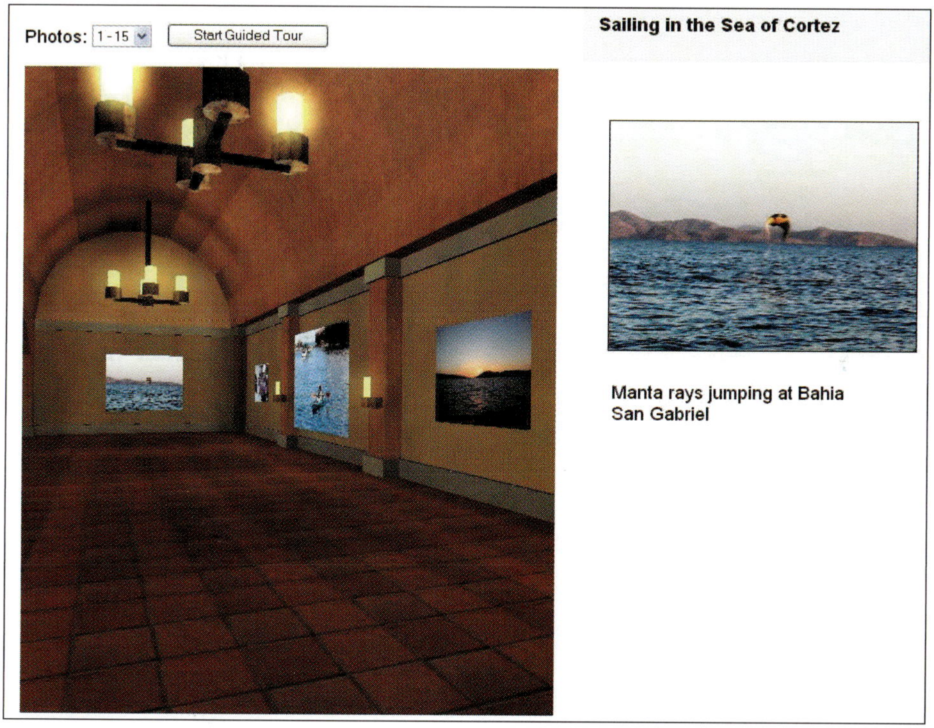

Figure 8.47 **Atmosphere 3D galleries are a novel way to show off your photos.**

When viewers access your Web site to view a 3D gallery, their browsers will automatically download the Adobe Atmosphere player plug-in required to view it.

Note *Atmosphere does not support the Macintosh or browsers other than Microsoft Internet Explorer, so some people will not be able to view your 3D gallery.*

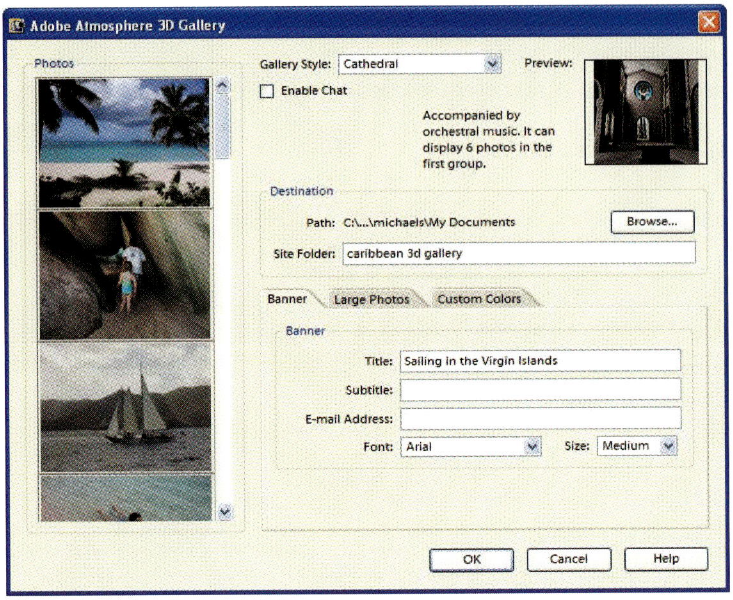

Figure 8.48 The options in the Adobe Atmosphere 3D Gallery dialog are much like those for Web photo galleries.

To create a 3D Gallery, select the photos in the photo well, just as if you were making a Web Photo Gallery, and choose Creations > Adobe Atmosphere 3D Gallery. You then choose options in the Adobe Atmosphere 3D Gallery dialog (**Figure 8.48**). The 3D galleries have an entirely different set of styles, listed in the Gallery Style pop-up menu (**Figure 8.49**). The rest of the options in the dialog are similar to those for Web photo galleries, with the exception that there are no thumbnails. The Atmosphere 3D Gallery has one additional option: you can enable a chat window as part of the gallery, allowing viewers to enter text comments that other viewers can read. This is a fun way to have an online dialog with people viewing your photos.

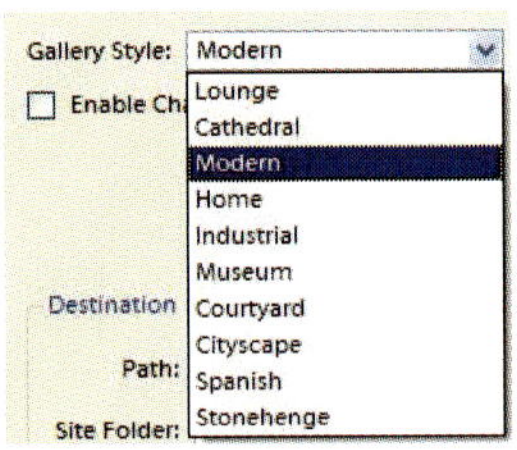

Figure 8.49 In the Gallery Style pop-up menu you select gallery styles that determine the environment in which the photos appear and the background music.

To create the gallery, choose your options and click OK. As with Web photo galleries, the files will be written to the folder you specify, and the 3D gallery will open in a preview window. These galleries are fun to play in the preview window even if you don't have a Web site to upload them to.

***Tip** If you want to view a 3D photo gallery after you've closed the preview window, open the folder that has the gallery pages and double-click the file called "index." The 3D gallery will open in your Web browser. (This procedure also works for regular Web photo galleries.)*

The 3D galleries take a while to load, especially over a slow connection. Once the gallery is loaded, you can navigate to a particular photo using the pop-up menu; or click and drag in the 3D gallery to move in 3D space. You can also click the Start Guided Tour button to automatically "walk through" the gallery.

For more information on the Atmosphere player authoring tool, see www.adobe.com/atmosphere.

Ordering Other Photo Merchandise

You can order many other products from online providers, ranging from different types of photo albums to coffee mugs, T-shirts, and cookies with photos in icing. You can't place orders for such creations from within Photoshop Album, however. There are two approaches you can take, depending on the provider.

Ordering Snapbooks and Greeting Cards from Shutterfly

Shutterfly (www.shutterfly.com) offers a couple of very attractive products that are not supported directly within Album: greeting cards and Snapbooks.

Shutterfly's greeting cards are printed on card stock and folded in half, so they look professional. They come with envelopes, and Shutterfly will even address and mail them for you if you provide the address list.

Shutterfly's Snapbooks are photo albums made by taking a stack of 4-by-6-inch or 5-by-7-inch prints and spiral-binding them with a plastic cover (**Figure 8.50**). These books are simpler and feel more casual than the My Publisher photo books, but they use smaller pages and put only a single photo on each page. They are printed on standard photo paper, whereas the My Publisher books use an inkjet-like process.

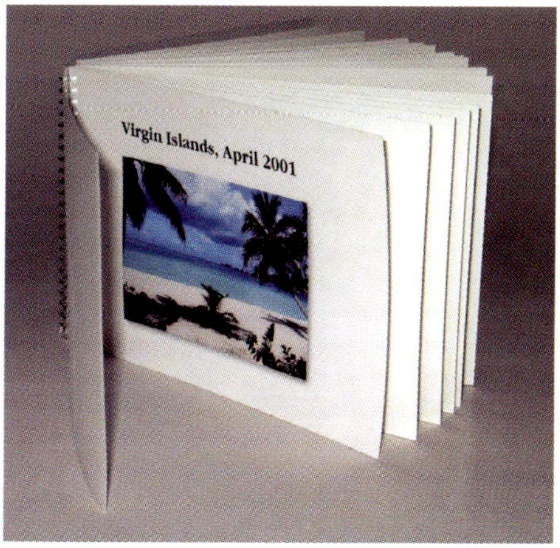

Figure 8.50 **Shutterfly's Snapbooks are sets of prints spiral-bound with a plastic cover.**

To order these Shutterfly products, you can use the online sharing mechanism to upload the photos to the Shutterfly site, and then access the site via the Web to order the products you want:

1. Select the photos you want to use in the photo well, and then choose Share > Share Online and follow the onscreen instructions. If it's the first time you've done this, you'll have to set up an account.

2. Shutterfly will insist that you have some recipient for your share, so you can enter yourself, and it will also insist on a subject, which can be anything.

3. Launch your Web browser, open www.shutterfly.com, and log in to your account. You should see a gallery with the photos you just uploaded (**Figure 8.51**).

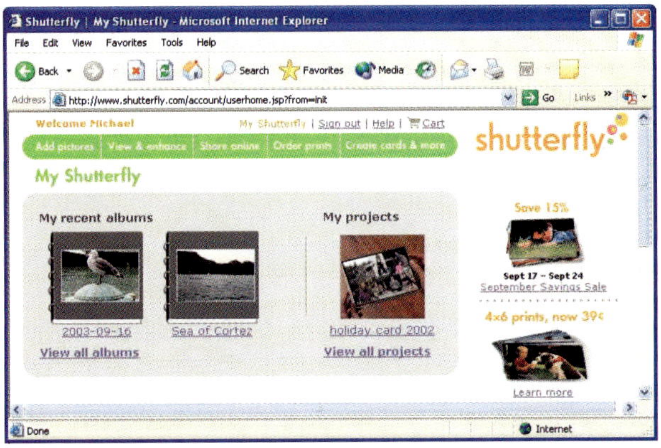

Figure 8.51 After uploading your photos to Shutterfly as if to share them, access www.shutterfly.com in your browser to view a gallery with your photos.

4. Click "Create cards & more" and follow the instructions to make greeting cards or Snapbooks (**Figure 8.52**).

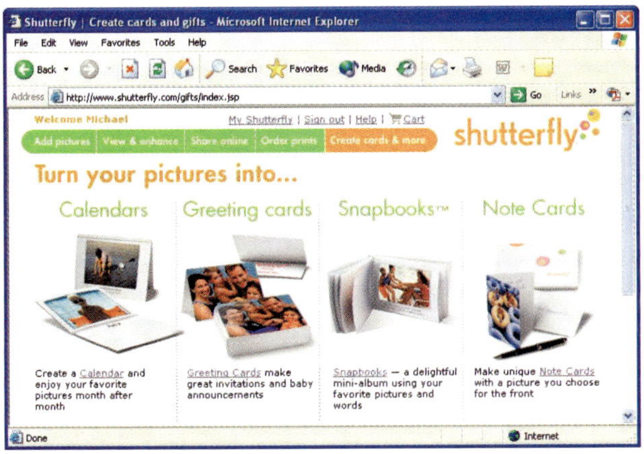

Figure 8.52 Click "Create cards & more" to make Snapbooks and other products.

***Note** The order of your photos may not be preserved when uploading them to Shutterfly, so if you're making a Snapbook, you'll have to use Shutterfly's Web-site tools to put the photos in the correct order.*

Ordering from Other Online Providers

To order a T-shirt, cookie, poster, or whatever from any of the multitude of other online providers, you'll need to use their software to upload photos to their Web site and then use their Web interface to order the product.

If you're just uploading a single file, such as for a T-shirt or a mug, first find the photo in Album. Then open its Properties palette (right-click the photo and choose Properties, or select it and press Alt-Enter) and write down the filename. Click the folder button next to the folder path to open the folder that includes this file (**Figure 8.53**). Now you can easily locate the file to transfer it to the Web site of the company you're ordering from.

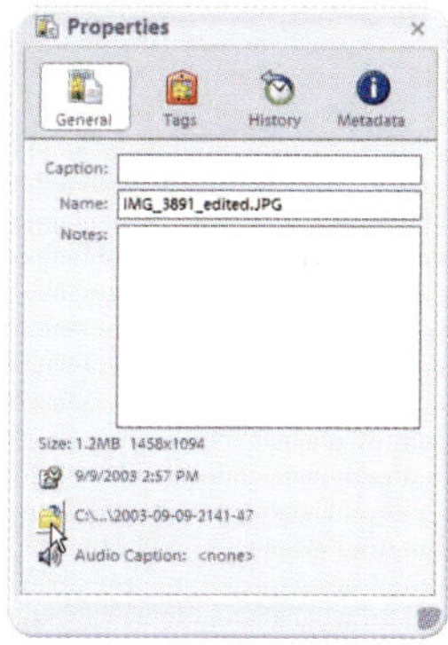

Figure 8.53 Open the Properties palette and click the folder button to open the folder that contains the photo.

You may also be able to drag and drop photos directly from Album's photo well to the Web site's uploader window, if it supports this.

If you're uploading multiple files, it is easier to export copies of the photos to a temporary location (see "Working with Windows," which follows Chapter 4).

Beyond Photoshop Album

Photoshop Album's creations are very easy to make because Album does all the work for you automatically. If you want more creative freedom, however, you'll need to use other programs in conjunction with Album.

Photoshop Elements makes a good complement to Photoshop Album for adding text to your photos, creating text-only pages, or even creating entirely customized pages, which you can still assemble using Album. You can also use Elements to join multiple photos seamlessly together into a panorama.

To go even further with your creations, you can use programs dedicated to making DVDs or laying out pages. The price you pay, of course, is the additional complexity of using multiple programs and learning the user interfaces of each.

Using Photoshop Elements to Supplement Creations

If you're chafing against the limits of Album's Creations Wizard, you can expand by using it along with Photoshop Elements.

If you want to put text on top of a photo, first duplicate the photo in the photo well, and then select the copy and choose Edit With > Photoshop Elements. In Elements you can use the text tool (see Chapter 7) to add text to the photo. You can also enter text below, above, or to the side of the photo by increasing the canvas size in Photoshop Elements (Image > Resize > Canvas Size) to create space around the photo into which you can place text.

You can even go so far as to create entire pages in Photoshop Elements and import those pages as "photos" into Album. Then you can use Album to organize and print the pages. If you're going this far, though, you'd probably be better off using a page layout program, such as Adobe PageMaker (see "Creating with Page Layout Programs," later in this chapter).

Making Panoramas with Photoshop Elements

If you want to create an image that is wider (or taller) than your camera can capture in a single photo, you can take multiple overlapping photos and combine them using Photoshop Elements' Photomerge function (**Figure 8.54**). For this to work well, you need a set of photos with considerable overlap (ideally at least a third of the frame), taken with the same exposure and from the same place.

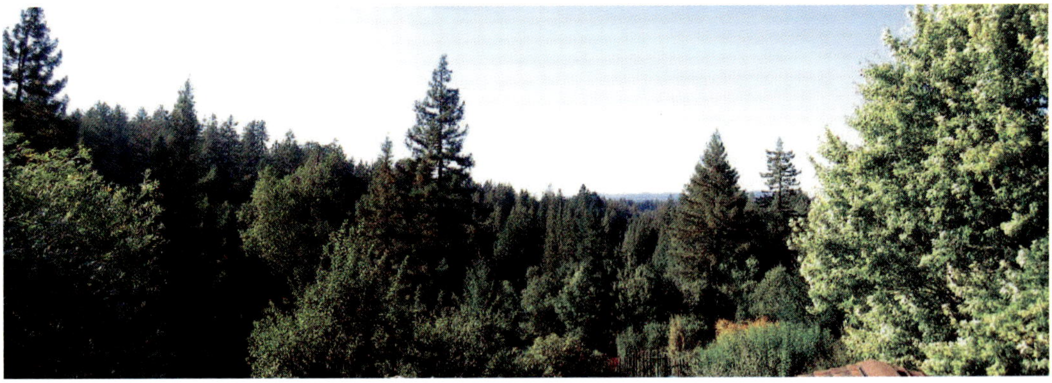

Figure 8.54 Using Photoshop Elements' Photomerge function, you can stitch multiple photos together to create a seamless panorama.

To create a Photomerge, first examine your photos and determine which ones you want to merge. Select all the photos you want to use and export them to a temporary folder by choosing File > Export. This makes them easy to find after you are in Photoshop Elements.

Launch Photoshop Elements from Windows and choose File > Create Photomerge. Click Browse in the dialog, navigate to the temporary folder in which you saved the photos, open that folder, press Ctrl-A to select all of them, and click Open. You should then be back in the Photomerge dialog with all the component photos listed (**Figure 8.55**).

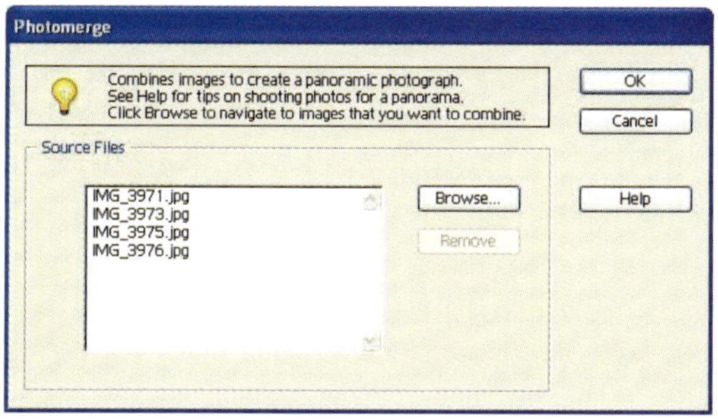

Figure 8.55 **In the Photomerge dialog click Browse to select the photos you want to include in the panorama.**

Click OK, and Photoshop Elements will open each of the files and then launch the Photomerge window (**Figure 8.56**).

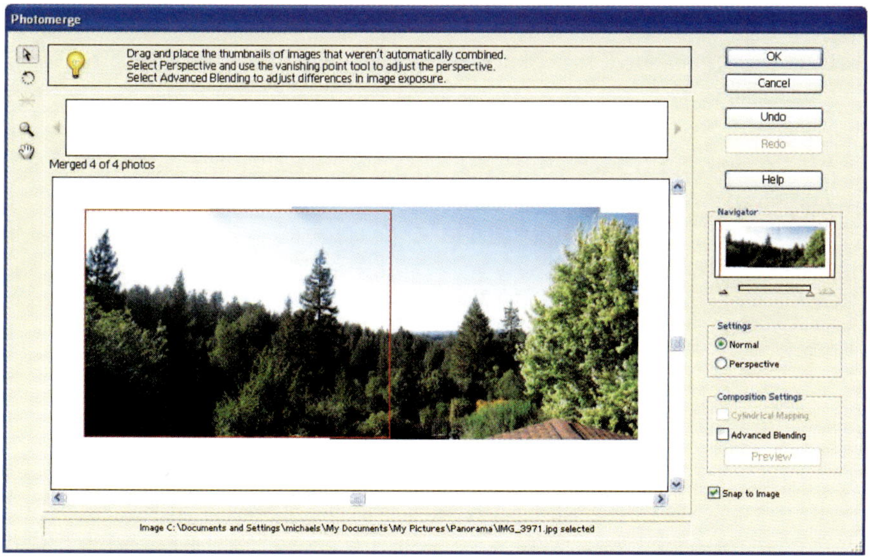

Figure 8.56 **Photomerge will try to align the photos automatically; click and drag to adjust.**

Photoshop Elements will attempt to align the photos; if there is not sufficient overlap between them, you may have to position them manually. Photos that Photomerge cannot position manually will be in the strip at the top; drag them down into the correct positions. Photomerge will snap them into alignment if you get them close.

You can try a few options to refine how the photos are merged. Click the Advanced Blending check box and then the Preview button to see how the merged images look. In many but not all cases, Advanced Blending will smooth the transitions between photos.

Another option to try is Perspective (in the Settings section on the right, choose it instead of Normal by clicking its radio button). With this mode enabled, Photomerge will adjust the geometry of each image to compensate for the images' different perspectives. In this mode, you can try the Cylindrical Mapping option (in the Composition Settings on the right). You can also move the vanishing point by selecting the Set Vanishing Point tool (the star-like icon, third from the top at the upper left) and clicking various spots in the panorama.

When you're happy with the panorama, click OK, the merge will be performed, and Elements will show the merged image in a standard photo window.

Typically there will be jagged edges at the top and bottom of the merged panorama, and if you've selected the Perspective mode, some of the edges will be angled. Select the Crop tool and crop the photo to a rectangular shape. Choose Layers > Flatten Image so that you can save it as a JPEG file (see Chapter 7 for information on layers); then choose File > Save, navigate to a folder where you want to save the file (My Pictures/Adobe/Other Photos is one good choice), choose JPEG as the file type, enter a filename, and click OK. Choose the quality level in the JPEG Options dialog that appears and click OK to save the file.

Finally, use Windows to locate the file you just created, right-click it, and choose Import into Adobe Photoshop Album. Alternatively, you can use Get Photos > From Files and Folders from within Album and choose the folder that contains the photo.

Making More Elaborate Slide Shows and DVDs

With Photoshop Album it's very easy to make slide shows and Video CDs, but Album doesn't provide as much flexibility as some programs that are dedicated to these tasks. Dozens of such programs are available; try searching on the Web for "slide show programs" to find reviews and download sites.

For making slide shows with synchronized audio and other features, two programs you can try are Photodex's ProShow, which will also make Video CDs (www.photodex.com), and SmoothShow Imaging's SmoothShow (www.smoothshow.com).

If you want to make Video CDs and DVDs with more options, there are many programs available, such as Ulead's DVD PictureShow (www.ulead.com), ArcSoft's ShowBiz DVD (www.arcsoft.com), Sonic's MyDVD (www.sonic.com), and VCDEasy.org's VCDEasy. If you want to go all out, try Encore DVD, Adobe's professional DVD-creation tool.

To use any of these programs, export the photos you want to use to a temporary folder and access them from there in the slide show or DVD program.

Creating with Page Layout Programs

If you want full control over your creations, use a page layout program such as Adobe PageMaker or Microsoft Publisher. You can drag and drop photos directly from Album to your document in the page layout program.

***Tip** You can drag and drop even if you can only fit one application at a time on your screen. Open both Album and the page layout program. Choose the photo in Album and drag it to the icon in the Windows task bar for the page layout program. Keep the mouse button down while the page layout program opens, drag the photo to the document window, and then release the mouse button.*

Alternatively, you can export to a temporary folder all the photos you want to use and then access the photos in that folder from the page layout program.

BEHIND THE SCENES: What to Look for in a Digital Camera

Since you're reading this book, you probably already have a digital camera. Cameras are improving so rapidly, however, that it's equally likely that you'll want to move up to a new model soon, especially now that you have a better idea of how much you can do with your photos. (Your spouse or child needs your current camera as a hand-me-down, anyway.)

Your best resource for information about specific cameras is the list of Web sites in Appendix A. Here are some general guidelines about features to look for.

Buy the Best Resolution You Can Afford

The first thing you need to decide is how much you're willing to spend. Anywhere in the range of $100 to $1,000, spending another $100 will generally get you a noticeably better camera.

Buy the highest-resolution camera you can afford (up to 5 or 6 megapixels), as long as it has the other features you want. Even if you don't plan to make large prints, it is great to be able to crop a small part of a photo—say, one person in a group shot—and still be able to make a decent print. You also never know when you're going to get that one-in-a-thousand shot from which you'll want to make a big print.

It is easy to reduce the resolution of the photos after you take them, if you need to save space, and you can always set the camera to shoot at a lower-than-maximum resolution if you want to fit more photos on the memory card. But details you didn't capture can never be recovered.

A 2 megapixel camera is adequate for many uses, but the additional resolution of a 3 or 4 megapixel camera will allow you to make great 8-by-10 prints and also to crop a smaller area and still produce a great 4-by-6 print.

Size, Quality, and Features

You'll also need to decide how important it is that the camera be compact. Being able to carry your camera in a pocket is great, and it increases the chances that you'll have the camera with you when a surprise opportunity arises. The very smallest cameras don't produce the same quality of images as the larger models, however, because of their very small lenses and other design compromises, and their small batteries tend to run out more quickly. But if small size is your priority, you can get some very nice, tiny cameras for $300 to $500.

The sweet spot for many people is the midsize compact camera—big enough for a high-quality lens, a decent-size battery, and easy-to-use controls, yet small enough to be carried in a pants or coat pocket (if a little bulky). You get the most bang for the buck in such cameras in the $400 to $500 range.

At the high end of the consumer camera range, roughly $500 to $1,000, you'll find cameras with larger lenses, bigger batteries, and more features. These cameras often have wide-angle and telephoto accessory lenses you can attach to the main lens, even though they don't have truly interchangeable lenses. Such cameras are typically too bulky to be pocketable, but they are often a little more comfortable to hold and use than smaller models, and they offer more options. If you're interested in exploring further what you can do with photography, these cameras are a great choice.

Digital SLRs

The next step up is to a single-lens reflex (SLR) camera, with several models in the $900–$1,500 range. These cameras use conventional interchangeable lenses, and this base price doesn't include a lens. With a modest collection of lenses you can easily double or triple the price of the camera. These cameras are also relatively bulky, and they often don't offer features like movie mode that less expensive models include. Furthermore, the SLR design means that you don't get a live preview on the LCD display; you have to use the optical viewfinder to frame the picture, and the display is just for reviewing what you've captured.

Nevertheless, if you're looking for top-quality images and are willing to deal with the bulk and make the financial investment, these are fantastic cameras. They are very much like 35 mm SLRs in terms of their controls, and they meet or exceed 35 mm image quality in most respects. They also respond to the shutter button more quickly than less expensive cameras, so it is easier to catch the perfect moment or expression.

If you do choose an SLR, you'll probably want a lower-cost point-and-shoot camera as well—after all, it's only the price of one more lens—so that you can carry a camera more easily at times when you're not on a photo expedition.

Assessing Camera Features

Here are a few other factors to consider when selecting a camera:

- Look for optical zoom, preferably 3X or more. The least expensive cameras, and the most compact, often lack a zoom lens or have only a 2X zoom. This can make it much harder to frame shots the way you'd like, and in these inexpensive cameras you won't have enough resolution to crop the picture to zoom in on an area. A few cameras are available with 4X, 7X, and even 10X zoom.

- Ignore digital zoom. All it does is crop the image for you before it is stored; you lose resolution as you zoom. You can do this cropping on the PC and achieve the identical result.

- Check the battery type and life. Some cameras use standard AA batteries, which is fine as long as you use the NiMH (nickel metal hydride) rechargeable type. If you travel a lot, the option to use standard alkaline AA batteries in a pinch is a great advantage—but it is both expensive and environmentally irresponsible to use disposable batteries on a regular basis. Most cameras now use special lithium ion batteries, which deliver the most power for a given size and weight, but you'll have to use the special charger that comes with the camera. You'll want to buy at least one spare battery (several if you travel or shoot lots of pictures), since you'll be utterly dependent on them and they take time to recharge. Check out how long the battery lasts, how long it takes to recharge, and what the cost is for extras—they are expensive.

- See how it feels. Go to a store where you can hold the camera and try it out. Make sure the controls feel good in your hands. See if you can quickly figure out how to navigate the menus. (If you find a store with great salespeople, buy there to support them, and they will support you! Don't exploit them by taking their advice and then buying from a discounter that provides no support.)

- Check the speed of response. The lag between the time when you push the shutter button and the time when the photo is captured can be infuriating. Pushing the button halfway should focus the image and set the exposure, and from that point the photo should be captured quickly after you push the button all the way down. Shutter delay is a huge problem and has been significantly improved, but it can still be frustrating. Older and cheaper models may still be quite slow. The expensive SLRs are the fastest.

- Decide whether manual controls are important to you. The least expensive cameras operate only in fully automatic mode. Better models give you the option to take over manual control of shutter speed and aperture, as well as white balance, flash brightness, and focusing. If you're strictly a point-and-shoot picture taker, these features won't matter, but if you enjoy having some creative control, you'll want these features. (Note that you can always ignore them and shoot in fully automatic mode.) Also look for advanced features like automatic exposure bracketing and burst mode.

- Consider models with a swiveling lens or display, especially if you take pictures of children or animals. These models allow you to hold the camera at your waist with the display pointing up. This makes you less intrusive and gets the camera at the eye level of little kids—or big dogs. It is also great in reverse; hold the camera up high to take pictures over a crowd or a fence.

- Look at the movie clips that the camera can capture. Check how much noise (random color variation) is in the clips, and what the resolution and frame rate are. Most cameras today can capture a maximum of 320 by 240 pixels at 15 frames per second (fps), but a few can capture a 640-by-480 video, and some can even capture at 30 fps.

- Consider your current collection of 35 mm lenses if you're looking at digital SLRs. You may be able to use your existing lenses, leveraging the investment you've already made, if you stick with the same manufacturer (typically Canon or Nikon). Note that older lenses may not be usable, however.

There are so many great cameras available today that it is hard to go too far wrong. As in most things, you generally get what you pay for, so stretch your budget and get the best camera you can afford. But don't pay for flexibility you won't ever use, and don't buy a bulky camera if you plan to carry it around a lot—unless you're planning to get two cameras.

9 Printing Your Photos

Printing your photos is one of the best ways to enjoy them. Back in the days of film, we all had plenty of prints—usually two for every picture; even all the bad ones. But in the digital world only a tiny fraction of photos is ever printed.

If you're not printing photos because you're perfectly happy viewing them onscreen, that's great. But if you're like most people, you're not making nearly as many prints as you'd like, either because it seems like too much trouble or because you're not happy with the results. If that's the case, read on, and I hope that by the end of this chapter you'll be making prints of great quality and enjoying your photos more.

Choosing How to Get Prints

There are four common ways you can get prints from your digital photos:

- Using a home printer
- Uploading photos to one of the Internet services, which mail prints back to you
- Uploading photos to a retailer's Web site and picking the prints up at the store
- Taking your memory card or a CD to a photo retailer and getting prints, usually while you wait

Photoshop Album will help you make prints in any of these ways. Let's look at home printing first, which is the most popular method. Printing at home is great for the immediacy it offers—before the birthday party is over, you can have a picture up on the wall of your kid blowing out the candles. You don't have to go anywhere or wait days for prints in the mail.

Ordering prints from online photofinishers, such as Shutterfly (www.shutterfly.com), is a great alternative to home printing. Your photos are printed using conventional photo paper, not printed on an inkjet printer, so they look just like film prints.

Online printing is most practical if you have a high-speed Internet connection, but that isn't essential unless you're printing a large number of photos. It takes a few days to get the prints back, but you don't need to spend any time feeding the printer, dealing with jams, replacing ink cartridges, or trimming prints. And when you take the cost of ink cartridges and photo paper into account, online photofinishing may actually be less expensive.

Many photofinishing retailers, from drug stores to camera stores, offer prints from digital photos. Taking this route saves you the trouble of printing at home without having to endure long uploads to online photofinishers or waiting for prints to arrive in the mail. The quality of prints from retailers varies, however, and prices tend to be higher.

If you're printing albums (or photo books) and calendars, you can get a professional-looking result by ordering from an online service that delivers a bound product (see "Creating Albums and Photo Books" in Chapter 8). Alternatively, you can print your project at home or at a retail photofinisher and use a copy shop (such as Kinko's) to bind it.

All the sources of printing are useful, each in different circumstances. I print at home when I'm making larger prints (typically 8.5 by 11 inches) or when I want the prints right away. I use online photofinishers when I want lots of prints, especially when I want to mail them to someone else (the photofinisher does the mailing for me), or when I'm printing albums and want them bound. And I use retail printing when I'm traveling and want to see prints right away.

Your preferences no doubt will vary, but you're likely to find some use for all three print sources once you give them a try.

Making Great Color Prints

Before we get into the specifics of the various kinds of prints you can make, it's important to understand the basics of getting great color prints. Many people end up frustrated with the quality they get, but rest assured: if you have a photo printer less than a couple of years old, it shouldn't be hard to get outstanding prints. (If you're totally satisfied with the quality of the prints you're getting already, feel free to skip this section.)

Start with Quality Images

First, make sure you aren't unintentionally damaging the color integrity of your photos when you edit them. If your display shows colors inaccurately, and you edit your photos so that they look right onscreen, they aren't going to look right when you print them, no matter how much you fuss with your printer. So if you're adjusting the colors in your photos, make sure your display is reasonably accurate (see the "Getting Accurate Colors on Your Monitor" sidebar in Chapter 6).

If your display isn't calibrated, avoid using Photoshop Elements (or any other editor) to make manual adjustments of hue, saturation, brightness, or contrast. Rely on the automatic adjustments that Photoshop Album can make for you—and keep the Correct Color slider toward the low end of its range and the Adjust Temperature slider near the middle (in the Fix Color area of the Fix Photo dialog). This won't give you complete control, but you'll be less likely to really mess things up!

Getting the color right in scanned photos can be challenging, because fading in the print and inaccuracies in your scanner change the colors. Digital camera images, on the other hand, generally have good color fidelity, though you may find a blue or yellow cast in photos from some cameras in some lighting conditions. The Fix Color feature will usually clean up such problems nicely.

Print with Adequate Resolution

If you print a photo at a size where there just aren't enough pixels in the image (there should be a minimum of 150 pixels per inch), there's no way the printer can create a sharp image. If you attempt to do so, Album warns you when you start printing. You can ignore the warning, but be aware that quality will be compromised.

To maintain full quality, you'll need to limit the size of prints you make if the resolution of your photos is not high enough. If you crop, keep in mind that what's important is the size of the section remaining after the crop, not the size of the full image. (You can see a photo's resolution in the General tab of the Properties palette.)

Table 9.1 shows the required resolution to achieve 150 pixels per inch for various print sizes.

Table 9.1 **Resolution Required for 150 Pixels per Inch**

Print Size (in Inches)	Minimum Dimension (in Pixels)
2.1 by 2.8	315 by 420
3.5 by 5	525 by 750
4 by 6	600 by 900
5 by 7	750 by 1050
8 by 10	1200 by 1500
8.5 by 11	1275 by 1650
13 by 17	1950 by 2550

Use the Right Printer, Ink, and Paper

You'll get the best results if you use an inkjet printer that is designed for photos and is no more than a couple of years old (see "Behind the Scenes: Choosing Your Printer," which follows this chapter). Such printers have more ink colors and can present photos more accurately.

Use new ink cartridges from the printer manufacturer. They're more expensive than recycled cartridges or those from independent suppliers, but they will usually deliver better color unless you do your own printer profiling—which is not for the faint of heart (see the sidebar "Printer Profiles").

***Tip** Don't refill the ink cartridges. Yes, it's painful to spend so much money for them and then throw them away, but do it anyway if you care about color. Refill inks won't have exactly the same colors, and they won't have the same chemistry, which could reduce the longevity of the prints. Replacing the ink cartridge also replaces parts that can clog or wear out.*

Use the printer manufacturer's photo paper. Paper from other manufacturers may be fine, but then again it might not, and it almost certainly will have at least slightly different color characteristics. You'll also get the best longevity (time before your photo fades) by using the photo paper designed for your printer.

You can't get good color without using good paper. It's expensive but not unreasonable, compared with the price of photographic prints. No printer will give you great

Printer Profiles

If you want to use inks and papers from various makers and keep the colors accurate, you'll have to create your own ICC (International Color Consortium) printer profiles. You can also improve results by using profiles with standard inks and papers.

Profiles describe the exact color characteristics of your printer, just as they can for your monitor (see Chapter 6). You can buy software, such as Monaco's EZcolor (www.monacosys.com), that will print a test pattern on your printer. You then scan this test printout with a scanner or a separate color-measuring device, and the software creates a profile.

If you're obsessed with getting great color and want more freedom in materials and greater color accuracy—and you're willing to invest some time and money pursuing it—check the color management references listed in Appendix A.

photos on plain copy paper. On inexpensive paper the ink soaks in and spreads out. On photo paper special coatings cause the ink to stay on the top, keeping it vibrant and sharp.

Tip ***You can save a little money with the lighter-weight papers, but the heavy papers give the best results, whether you choose a matte, semigloss, or glossy finish. Buy a selection of papers to start with and find the one you like best—before you make a ton of prints.***

Pay Attention to Printer Settings

Photo printers offer a range of settings to suit different paper types and to allow you to make speed-versus-quality tradeoffs. The default settings will generally be for fast printing on plain paper; you have to change them to get good-quality prints. It's also important to select the borderless printing option if your printer offers it and you want the image to go all the way to the edge of the paper.

Always set your printer settings from within Photoshop Album, because you're likely to want different settings when printing photos than when printing documents, and you may even want to use a different printer. Album maintains its own set of printer settings that aren't affected by changes you make in the default printer settings in Windows.

To access the printer settings when printing anything other than creations, first select the photos you want to print in the photo well, and then either press Ctrl-P, choose File > Print, or click the Print button in the shortcuts bar and choose Print from the drop-down menu.

Keeping Your Prints from Fading

You've probably seen inkjet prints that are a few years old and very faded, with only the palest of colors remaining. Different ink colors fade at different rates, so even modestly faded prints can have odd color casts.

In recent years, inkjet technology has made great strides, and the newer printers and inks produce prints that fade much, much more slowly. The more expensive printers, such as the Epson 2200, use pigment-based inks that fade far more slowly than the dye-based inks of lower-cost printers. Prints from this printer (and some others) are claimed to fade more slowly than traditional photo prints. But even low-cost printers have significantly improved their fade resistance.

Fading is caused primarily by the effect of ultraviolet light (UV), which is plentiful in sunlight and is also present in artificial light, on the inks. Moisture and heat also contribute to fading. Prints kept in the dark (such as in albums) generally will not fade if kept dry and cool. Prints that are displayed in the light will last longer if they are framed under glass and kept away from sunlight.

Studies have shown that most third-party inks tend to fade much more rapidly than the manufacturer's inks, providing another reason to avoid off-brand ink cartridges.

Of course, the best protection against fading is to preserve your photo files. As long as you can access your photo files, you'll be able to make brand-new prints whenever you want them.

From the Print Photos dialog you can access the printer settings in two ways (**Figure 9.1**):

- Click the Page Setup button. The first Page Setup dialog is pretty useless, because you can't set margins when printing from Album (**Figure 9.2**). Just click the Printer button to pass through to the second Page Setup dialog (**Figure 9.3**). Now you can choose the printer you want to use, if you have more than one, and then click Properties.
- Alternatively, you can just click the Continue button in Album's Print Photos dialog. You'll go directly to the Windows Print dialog, from which you can choose a printer and access its settings by clicking Preferences (**Figure 9.4**). (For some unfathomable reason, the same printer settings dialog is called Preferences instead of Properties if you access it in this way.)

The Printer Properties dialog will be different depending on what printer you have. Here you can set the paper type and other options, and then click OK in each of the dialogs until you're back in Album's Print dialog.

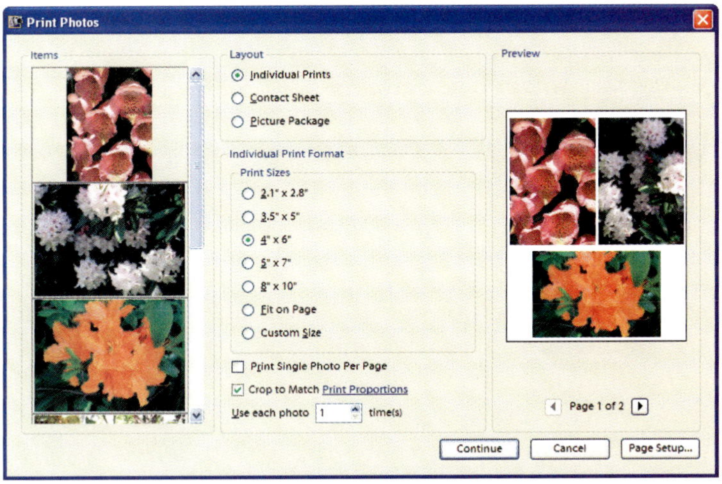

Figure 9.1 All of Album's home printing functions, except those used when printing creations, are accessed via this dialog.

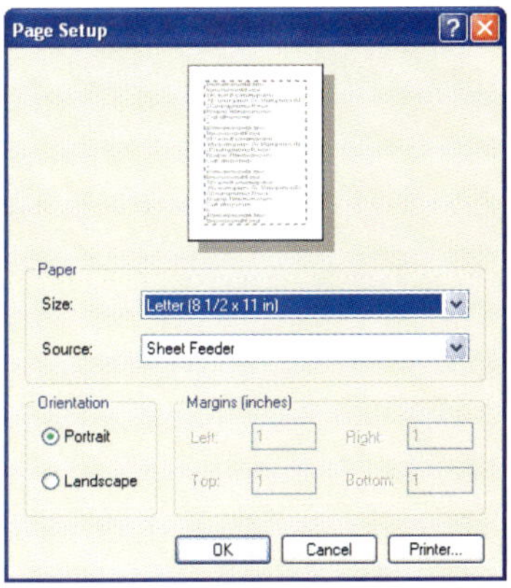

Figure 9.2 Just click the Printer button to pass right through this otherwise useless dialog.

Figure 9.3 Choose the printer from the Name pop-up menu and click Properties to access its settings.

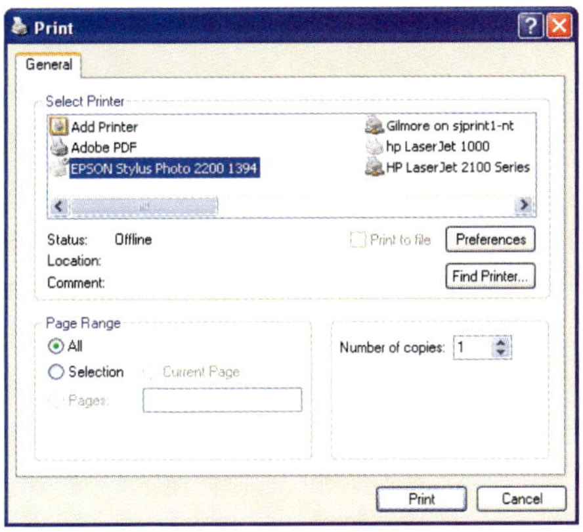

Figure 9.4 Click Preferences to access printer settings or Print to begin printing.

The second approach is the easiest if you're changing only the paper type and not the size or borderless-print settings. If you're making such changes, use the first approach so that the print preview will be accurate.

In either case, Album will remember these printer settings, even if you make changes to printer settings in Windows or in other applications.

Choose the right settings

The settings you see in Printer Properties (or Printing Preferences) are determined entirely by your particular printer driver, so they will vary from those shown in the figures (and if you have multiple printers, you'll see different properties for different printers). So I can't tell you exactly how to choose the settings for your printer but will give some general guidelines. **Figure 9.5** shows the settings for one printer, an Epson 2200.

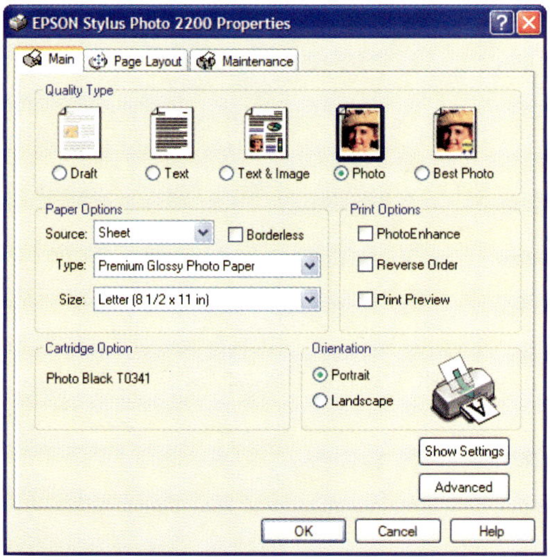

Figure 9.5 **Printing preferences for an Epson 2200 printer; this dialog varies according to the printer.**

One setting is universal and essential: picking the correct paper type. Other settings may require experimentation to find the ones whose results you like best for any particular printer and paper.

For most printers, if you set the paper type to the proper photo paper, the printer driver will automatically adjust all the other settings to their optimal values. There may still be a choice to emphasize speed or quality, and you'll have to experiment to see whether the higher speed setting produces good enough quality for you or if you'd rather wait for better prints at the lower speed.

Some printer drivers give you the option to enable or disable automatic color enhancement. In the Epson driver in Figure 9.5, for example, you can choose whether to enable PhotoEnhance.

Just what photo enhancements in the printer driver do is often unclear, but they typically deliver more saturated colors (since most people prefer colors that are more saturated than are strictly accurate). If you don't like the results you're getting from the default setting, you can try turning off any automatic enhancements (or turn them on if they are off).

Margins and borderless printing

Many newer, photo-oriented inkjet printers offer a borderless printing option, in which the print covers the paper all the way to the edges. I much prefer the look of borderless prints, which also allow you to make 8.5-by-11-inch prints on letter-size paper and avoid any need for trimming. Typically you must enable this option; **Figure 9.6** shows the setting for an Epson 2200.

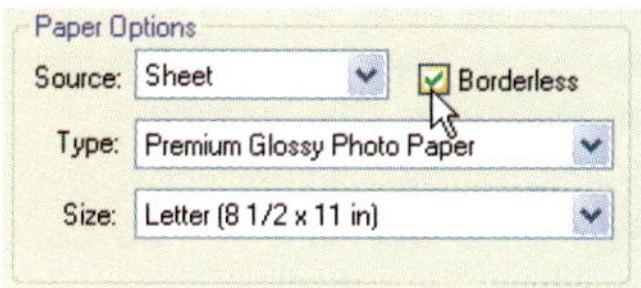

Figure 9.6 You can select the Borderless printing option on many photo printers to fill the page all the way to the edge.

Unless your printer is capable of borderless printing and you have enabled this feature, there are some nonprintable areas at each edge. The printer driver tells Album what these areas are; you cannot control them. When Album is laying out photos on the page, it uses as much of the printable area as it can. If borderless printing is enabled, Album will print on the entire page.

Printing Individual Photos

Printing photos is a simple process. First, select the photos you want to print, then bring up the Print Photos dialog by choosing File > Print, pressing Ctrl-P, or clicking the printer icon in the shortcuts bar. You'll then have the choice of making individual prints, picture packages, or contact sheets (Figure 9.1). Choose Individual Prints to print as many photos of the selected size as will fit on each sheet of paper. Also choose the size at which you want to print them. Click Continue, click Preferences in the Print dialog (to ensure that you have selected the proper paper and quality settings), and then choose Print from the Print dialog.

Note *Only the Contact Sheet option ensures that all photos are rotated to the same orientation as the photos in the photo well; the other print options assume you are going to cut apart multiple photos and will rotate photos as necessary to fit the most pictures on one page. Also, only the Contact Sheet allows you to optionally print the date, filename, or caption. If you want control over layout other than using contact sheets, make a creation and print that.*

Choosing the Print Size

If you want one of the standard sizes, just click the radio button for that size. If you want a different size, click the Custom Size radio button, and enter the dimensions you want in the Custom Size dialog (**Figure 9.7**). Custom sizes can't go above 8.5 by 11 inches, however.

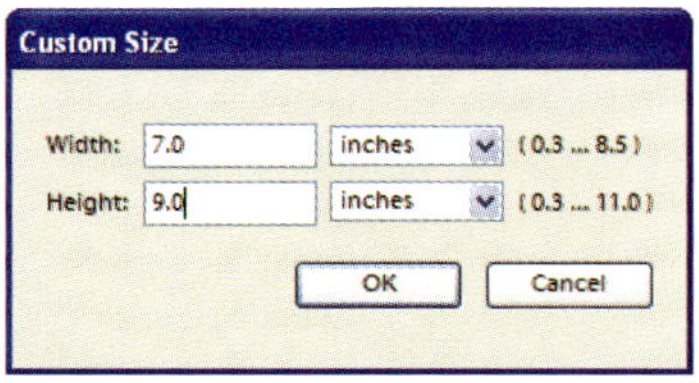

Figure 9.7 Use the Custom Size option to make prints to fit an odd-size mat or frame.

Note *Throughout this book, I've assumed you're using inch measurements. You can choose metric measurements instead in the General pane of Preferences.*

The remaining option, Fit on Page, does just that—it fills whatever paper size you have selected in your printer setup with one photo. If you want a borderless, page-filling print, choose Fit on Page for the print size, choose the Borderless printing option in Printer Preferences, and make sure that Crop to Match Print Proportions is checked (as described in the following section).

Tip *The only way to print a size larger than 8 by 10 inches (or 8.5 by 11 inches if you're using the Custom Size option) is with the Fit on Page mode. This only works if you want to fill each sheet with one photo. If you have a wide-carriage printer, for example, you can make 13-by-19-inch prints in this way.*

To fill any size paper your printer can handle with a single photo, click the Page Setup button in the Print Photos dialog, then the Printer button in the Page Setup dialog, and then the Properties button in the second Page Setup dialog. You can now choose the paper size in the printer's properties dialog. Click OK in each of the dialogs until you are back to Album's Print Photos dialog, and then choose Fit on Page.

Album normally fits as many photos on each page as it can. If you want instead to put only one photo on each page, regardless of how much empty space that will leave, check the box for Print Single Photo per Page in the Print Photos dialog.

To Crop or Not?

You have an important choice to make about whether to have the photos cropped automatically. If you leave the default setting of Crop to Match Print Proportions enabled, each photo will be cropped automatically (trimming equally from both sides, or from the top and bottom, as needed) unless its aspect ratio matches that of the chosen print size. Leave this option enabled if you want the prints to be the exact size you choose, which is generally what you want if you're using standard mats or frames.

If, on the other hand, you want all of your image to be printed, turn this option off by unchecking the box. Each photo will then be placed inside a rectangle of the specified print size, but if the aspect ratios don't match, there will be white space either above and below or to each side of the photo (**Figure 9.8**).

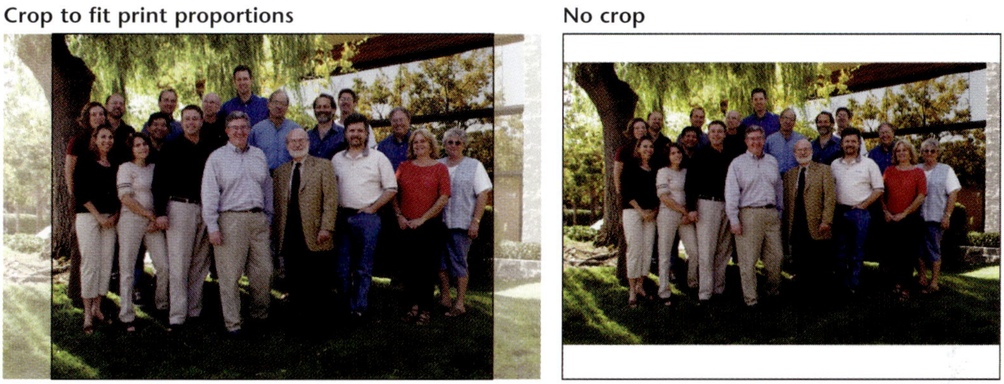

Figure 9.8 There are two ways to fit a photo with a 3:2 aspect ratio on a 4:3 aspect ratio print.

If you want to crop to fill the space but you want control over the cropping, crop using the Fix Photo window before you enter the print dialog (see Chapter 6).

Choosing Print Quantities

There are two places where you can choose the number of copies you want to print, and each has a different effect.

If you select the quantity in the "Use each photo ____ time(s)" field in Album's Print Photos dialog, then each photo will be repeated within the page layout that number of times. For example, if you enter 2, each photo will be placed twice, and then the next photo twice, and so on. If you've chosen a size that fits four photos per page, then the first page will have two copies of the first photo and two copies of the second photo.

Alternatively, you can leave this setting at 1 and change the quantity in the "Number of copies" field in the Windows Print dialog, which appears when you click Continue in the Print Photos dialog (Figure 9.4). In this case, if you select a quantity of 2, you'll get one set of pages with each photo included once, and then a second set of identical pages. So the result is two copies of each photo, as with the previous approach, but they are grouped differently.

If you're cutting the photos apart, it doesn't matter which approach you use. If you want a set of pages to give to someone, be sure to use the second approach.

Previewing the Print Layout

On the right side of the Print Photos dialog is a preview of the pages that will be printed. Click the arrows below the preview page to move from one page to the next.

The preview reflects the current page-size setting and whether borderless printing has been enabled. You can change these settings by clicking Preferences in the Windows Print dialog, but if you do so, the preview will not reflect the printed output. For an accurate preview, change the printer settings by clicking Page Setup in Album's Print Photos dialog, as described earlier.

Using Picture Packages

Picture packages fill each page with multiple copies of a single photo in various sizes. You aren't likely to use them very often, but when you have a favorite picture (or a few) that you want lots of copies of in different sizes, Picture packages are convenient.

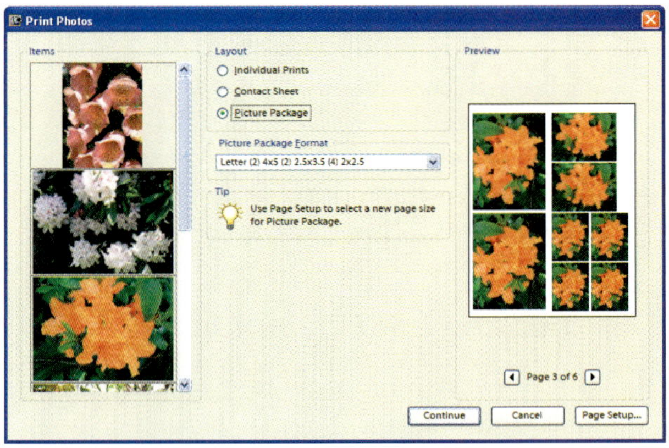

Figure 9.9 Picture packages combine an assortment of different print sizes on one page; to get them you select that option in the Print Photos dialog.

After selecting the photos and choosing File > Print (or one of the shortcuts), click the Picture Package radio button in the Print Photos dialog (**Figure 9.9**). In the same dialog, choose which sizes you want from the Picture Package Format pop-up menu. Note that this menu will show different layouts depending on the paper size you've chosen in your printer settings, so make sure the printer is set up first.

Photoshop Elements Picture Packages

Photoshop Elements also has picture packages, and its version offers more flexibility than Album's. You'll have to locate the photos you want to use in Windows' file system, and it's a bit more confusing to use than Album's equivalent, but it provides more options.

Open Photoshop Elements and choose File > Print Layouts > Picture Package (**Figure 9.10**). Elements provides a somewhat different collection of layouts and paper sizes (which are not, as in Album, drawn from the printer settings). It also allows you to overlay the filename, caption, date, or other text on each photo.

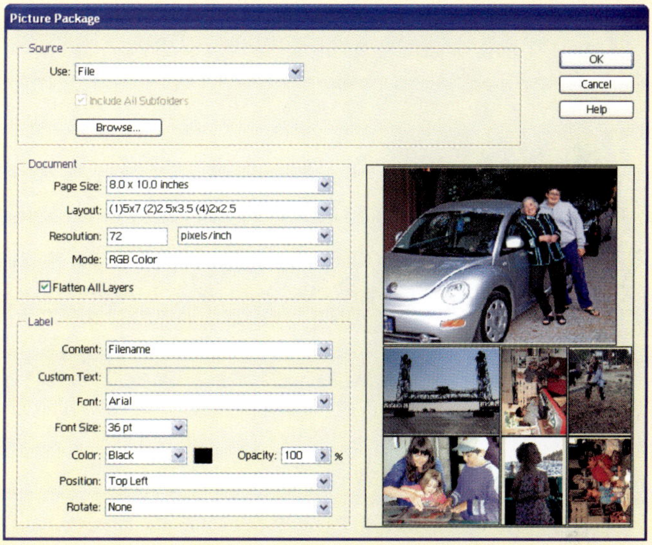

Figure 9.10 Photoshop Elements' picture package allows you to mix different photos on one page.

To choose which photos to use, go to the Use pop-up menu in the Source section of the dialog and choose File to select a single photo or Folder to select all the photos in a folder. Clicking Browse will open a standard file-browsing dialog where you can locate the file or folder.

Unlike Album's picture packages, Photoshop Elements' version lets you put different photos in each area of the page, instead of filling each page with copies of just one photo. To fill a page with copies of one photo, as Album does, click the Browse button and then navigate to the photo's file in the Select an Image File dialog. To change the photo in any location, click that location in the preview (on the right side of the Picture Package dialog). Elements will then display the Select an Image File dialog again and you can choose another photo (which Elements will place only in that one location).

To put a label on each photo, choose what text you want to use, the position in which you want it to appear, and the font and color from the pop-up menus in the Label section of the Picture Package dialog. Note that this text does not appear in the preview.

When you print picture packages, you'll get as many pages as the number of photos you selected, since Album fills each page with copies of one photo. If you want more than one page with each photo, increase the Number of Copies setting in the Windows Print dialog that appears after you click Continue.

Making Contact Sheets

If you've ever done any darkroom work or dealt with film labs, you'll remember contact sheets—made by laying the film strips down on a sheet of photo paper and exposing it. If you're more accustomed to one-hour photo shops, you'll probably think of these as index prints. By either name, it's a sheet of paper with lots of small photos and is useful for providing a printed overview of a set of photos.

To make a contact sheet, select the photos you want to include, choose File > Print or one of the shortcuts, and click the Contact Sheet radio button in the Print Photos dialog (**Figure 9.11**). To vary the size and number of photos per page, change the Columns setting in this same dialog. With six columns you'll get 72 photos per page; you probably won't want them any smaller than this.

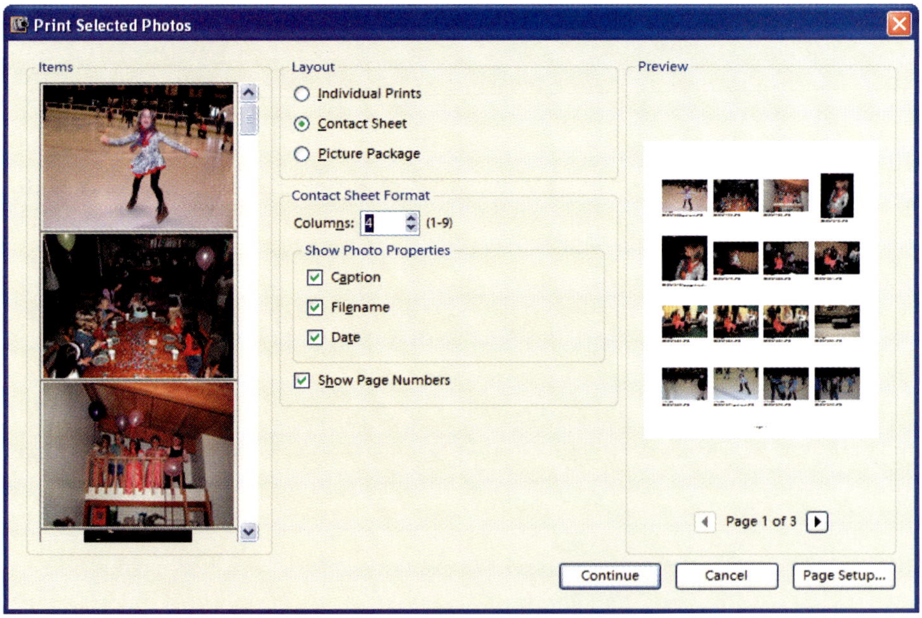

Figure 9.11 **Contact sheets provide a handy index to a set of photos; select Contact Sheet in the Print Selected Photos dialog.**

You can choose to show the filename, caption, or date—or any combination—below each photo. If you do, however, you should use relatively few columns. The text doesn't wrap on multiple lines; it's truncated if there isn't enough space within the width of the photo.

Tip *You can use a contact sheet with a setting of 1 column to produce printouts of one photo per page, with the caption, filename, or date printed beneath it.*

Printing Albums and Other Creations

When you make a creation (see Chapter 8), you can print it by simply clicking the Print button in step 6 of the Creations Wizard. You can also print a creation by selecting its icon in the photo well and choosing File > Print or one of the shortcuts. All the same printer-settings issues described earlier in this chapter apply.

You may also want to take a creation, such as an album, to a service bureau or copy shop (such as Kinko's) to be printed and possibly bound. To do so, click Save as PDF in step 6 of the Creations Wizard, choose Optimize for Printing in the next dialog, and then choose the location to store the PDF file in the File dialog. Copy this file to a CD, and take the CD to your service bureau for printing.

Tip *Check that the service bureau is using Adobe Acrobat 5.0 or later. If it uses an older version of Acrobat, some creations will not print properly.*

You can print slide shows as well as albums, but be aware of one issue. Slide shows generate (for mysterious reasons) PDFs with a page size of 10.67 by 14.22 inches. Acrobat or Adobe Reader can automatically scale this page to 8.5 by 11 inches, but you must ensure that this option is enabled by selecting Fit to Page in Acrobat's or Adobe Reader's Print dialog. If instead you choose one of the Tile options, the pages will be split across multiple sheets of paper.

You can also have albums, calendars, and photo books printed and bound by online photofinishers, as Chapter 8 describes.

Ordering Prints Online

Online photofinishing is a great alternative to home printing. If you don't have a top-notch printer at home, you can still get great prints this way. And you don't have to buy special paper, replace ink cartridges, or baby-sit your printer through a long print job. If you're making the prints for someone else, the online photofinisher will send them directly to the person you choose, so you never even have to handle or ship them. And when you take into account the cost of good-quality paper and ink cartridges, online photofinishing isn't expensive (as long as you have a big enough order so that the shipping cost doesn't add a lot to each print).

The first step, just as for printing at home, is to select the photos you want to print. Then click the Print button in the shortcuts bar and choose Order Prints from the drop-down list. If this is your first use of this feature or you haven't used it for a while, Album will access the Internet to check for an updated list of services. Then you'll see the initial online print dialog, which shows the photos you have chosen and lists the providers available in a pop-up list at the bottom (**Figure 9.12**).

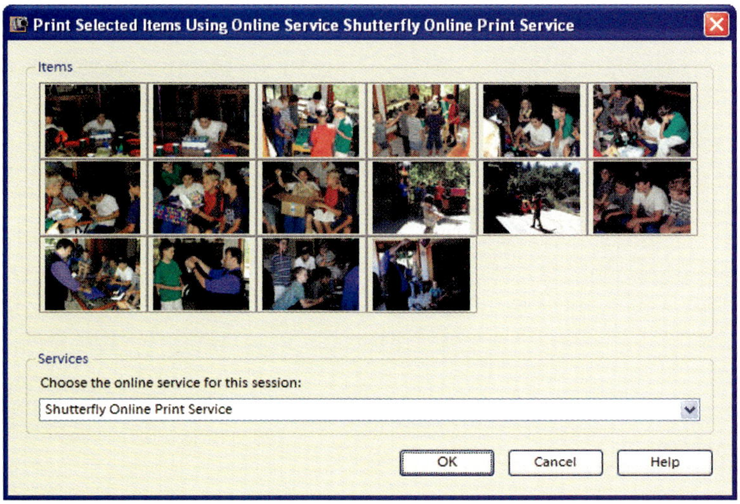

Figure 9.12 Choose the online service you want to use from the pop-up menu below the photos.

There are online photofinishing providers in various countries, so be sure to pick one that is in yours. (As of this writing, Shutterfly is the only provider in the United States, but others should be available before long.) The next time you use this feature, it will default to the provider you used most recently.

Setting Up Your Account

If this is the first time you've placed an order with this supplier, you'll next see the Create or Modify Online Service Accounts dialog (**Figure 9.13**). Click Select, and you'll see the Online Services user agreement. Click Agree to continue, and click OK in the next dialog that warns you to call the supplier, not Adobe, if you have problems with the service.

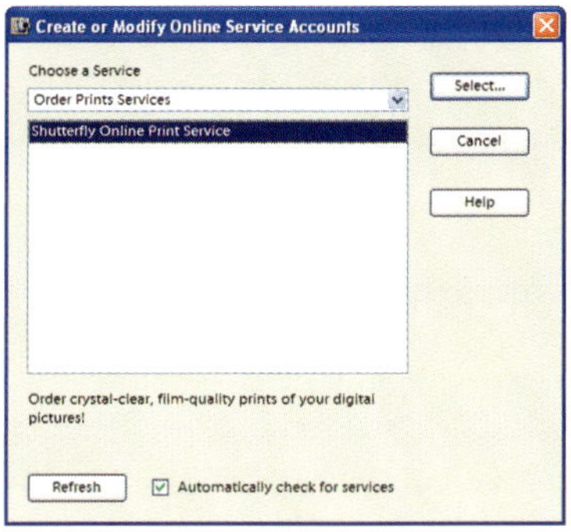

Figure 9.13 Click Select to set up your account for a particular service.

Next you must indicate in the Online Services Wizard dialog whether you have an account with this provider already (**Figure 9.14**). If you've already done business with the company via its Web site, you should be able to use the same account. If you have an account, just click Next; if you don't, click the "I do not yet have an account" radio button and then click Next. You'll then be able to set up an account (**Figure 9.15**).

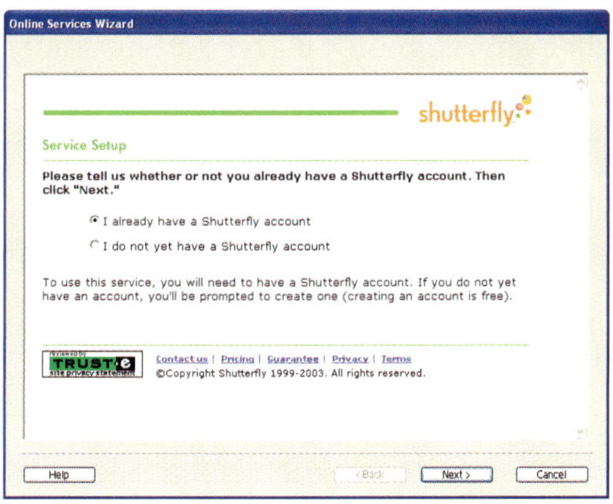

Figure 9.14 If you have an existing account, you can use it; otherwise, set up a new one.

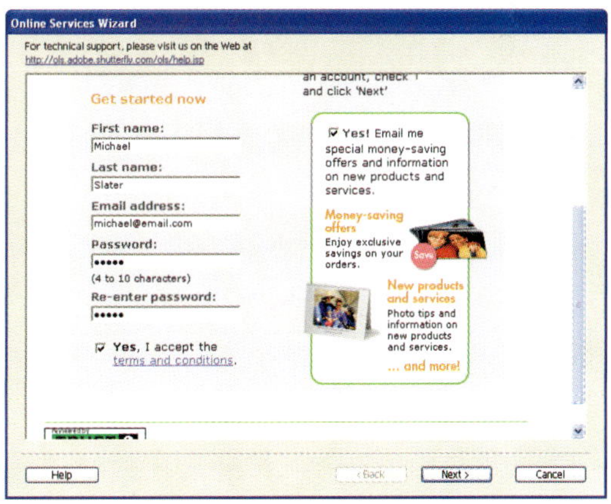

Figure 9.15 Provide some basic information in the Online Services Wizard to set up a new account.

Finally, you'll get to the log-in screen for the service (**Figure 9.16**). (In the future you'll get to this screen much more quickly, because you'll already have chosen your preferred service, agreed to the terms, and set up your account.) Enter your email address and password.

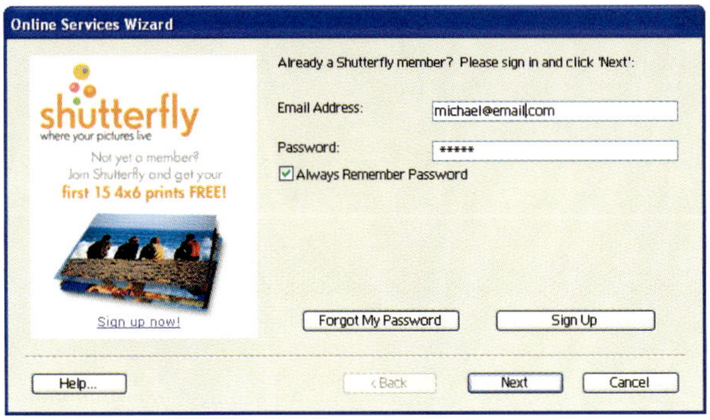

Figure 9.16 Enter your email address and password to log in to your account.

You need to decide whether you want your password to be stored; if you do, then leave the box next to Always Remember Password checked, and you won't have to enter it again. Keep in mind, however, that the service will store your credit card number, and if you have Album remember your password, anyone using your PC will able to order prints using your account and credit card.

Placing Your Order

Finally, click Next and you'll enter the Online Services Wizard ordering dialog. From this point on, these dialogs are actually driven by the online service partner's site, even though they appear within Photoshop Album. So even for the Shutterfly service, the screens may differ from those shown here as its offerings evolve, and for other services they are likely to be quite different.

Step through the ordering screens specifying the sizes and quantities of prints you want (**Figure 9.17**), where you want them shipped (**Figure 9.18**), and the credit card to which you want them billed (**Figure 9.19**). When you click Next on the order confirmation screen, Album will begin transferring your order to the online service (**Figure 9.20**).

This transfer may take quite a while, especially if you're making a lot of prints, have high-resolution photos, or have a slow Internet connection. Be sure not to interrupt your Internet connection while the transfer is occurring. If the transfer fails, Album will display an error dialog, and you'll have to restart it.

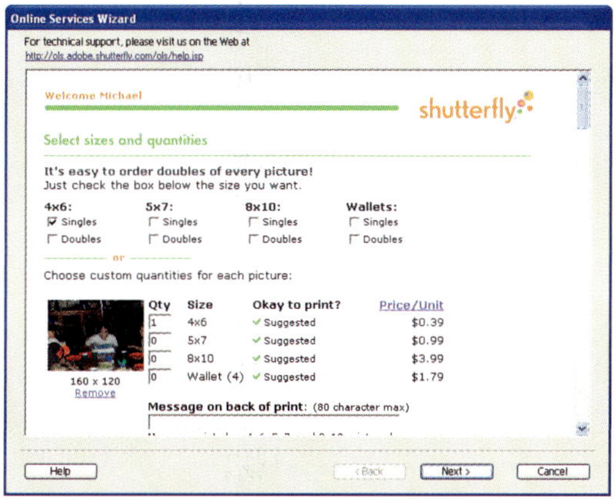

Figure 9.17 Choose sizes and quantities for each photo in the first pane of the Online Services Wizard.

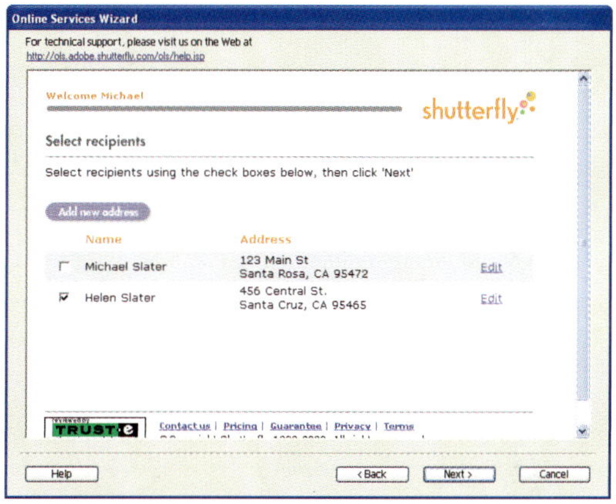

Figure 9.18 You can have the prints shipped to yourself or anyone else.

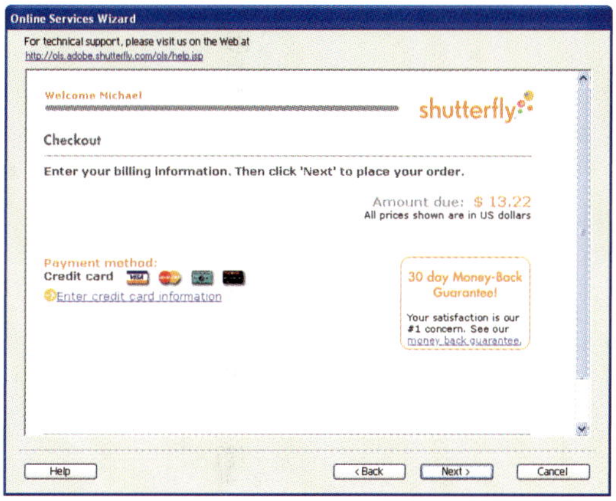

Figure 9.19 Enter your credit card information for billing; the service will remember it for future use.

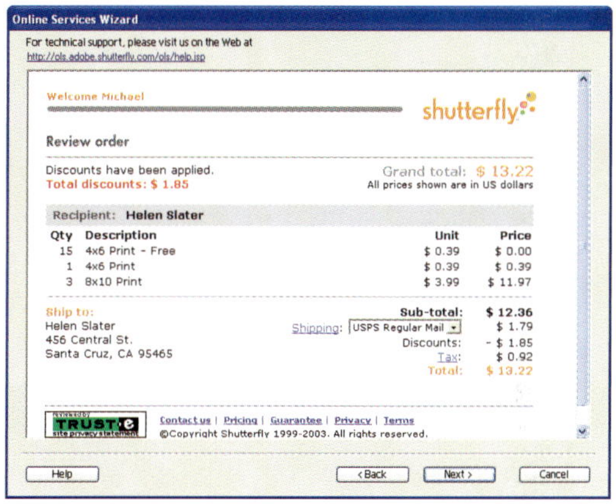

Figure 9.20 Review the order and click Next to start uploading the photos.

***Tip** You cannot use Album while the transfer is occurring, but you can switch to other applications and use them. You can even use other applications that access the Internet, but they will be more sluggish because Album is using much of your bandwidth, and using them will increase the time for Album to complete its transfer.*

You should receive an email from the online service provider when it has received your order, and generally you'll get another one when your order has shipped.

Using Other Online Photofinishers

Only a few of the many online photofinishers can be accessed from within Album. You may want to use a different supplier to get special print sizes or finishes, or to get the lowest prices. (As with anything, there is a range of prices, quality, and products among different suppliers.)

Most online photofinishers offer a small program, sometimes called an *uploader,* that you can download from their Web sites and then use to upload photos to their sites. Some of these programs provide a window into which you can drag and drop photos, and you may be able to drag photos right from Album's photo well into them (it works with some uploaders but not others). If not, you can always export photos to a temporary folder (see "Working with Windows," which follows Chapter 4) and browse to that folder from the uploader program.

Once the photos are uploaded, place your order at the service's Web site.

Making It Big

Every now and then, getting a poster-size print of a cherished photo can be great fun. For a few thousand dollars, you could buy a printer that would enable you to do this at home, but few people can justify such an investment. This is a perfect case for using an online service or a retail service to make the prints.

Shutterfly can make prints up to 20 by 30 inches (currently $22.99 each), but (as of this writing) you can't order such prints through Album, so you'll have to place the order on Shutterfly's Web site. These prints are made on conventional photo paper. You can upload the photo to Shutterfly from within Album by using Share > Online Share and sharing it with yourself; then go to the Web site to place the order.

Specialty providers offer even bigger prints using large-format inkjet printers. Sizes up to about 3 by 4 feet are readily available for under $50. If you really want to go all-out for a very special occasion, check out sign and banner printers; they can make huge prints, such as 12 by 15 feet, for $3 to $12 per square foot, depending on what material the photo is printed on (look in the yellow pages or do a Web search for *large-format printing*).

When making poster-size prints, you're unlikely to have enough resolution to achieve the 150-pixels-per-inch standard. This is OK, since these prints aren't designed to be viewed close up, and the companies that make these huge prints have special software that reduces the obvious pixellation at large sizes. But don't expect to look at these prints from 18 inches away and not see any graininess—they're intended to be viewed from several feet away.

Getting Prints at Retail

Most photofinishing shops, and an increasing number of drug stores, discount stores, and other retailers with one-hour photo services, now offer printing of digital photos. Check with your local stores, and you'll probably find several that offer this service.

This service can work in a variety of ways. Almost all stores accept photos from most common types of memory cards, and virtually all accept photos on CD.

In some stores you give the CD or memory card to the clerk, who transfers the photos and returns it to you, and in others you use a kiosk with a built-in printer in a completely self-service operation. Such systems take more of your time, however, since you have to wait there while the prints are made. They generally use dye-sub printers. In other stores, the printing is done by the same minilab used to make conventional photographic prints.

The types of printers and the quality of the prints vary, so try a small batch of photos first and see how you like them. If several stores are convenient to you, try each of them. You may also find a lot of variation in price.

Tip ***If you use a kiosk, you can choose which photos you want to print, and often you can crop, fix red-eye, and make other enhancements. These functions are generally easier and quicker to do with Album, however, and with Album you can do them in the privacy of your home, sitting down, and without any time pressure.***

Some retailers will allow you to upload photos to their Web sites to be printed. In this case, treat the retailer just like an online photofinisher (see "Using Other Online Photofinishers" earlier in this chapter)—except, of course, you can drive to the store to get your prints instead of waiting for them to be mailed and paying for shipping.

Putting Your Photos on a CD

To get prints from a retail photofinisher, first make a collection in Album of all the photos you want to print. You may want to use Auto Fix or edit them. If you want to control how they are cropped when they are printed, crop them in Album. (The 4-by-6-inch prints, which are the most common, have a 3:2 aspect ratio, whereas most consumer digital cameras create images with a 4:3 aspect ratio, so some cropping is required; see Chapter 6. Either you do it, or the store will do it for you.)

After you've collected and fixed all the photos you want to get printed, make an archive CD. Select all the photos and choose File > Burn. Choose Copy/Move Files in step 1 of the Burn/Backup dialog; in step 2, choose Copy/Move Edited Files Only and make sure the Move Files box is *not* checked.

Click Next to go to step 3, and click Done to burn the disc. (See Chapter 3 for more details on making archive discs.) Then just take the CD into the store.

Transferring Photos with a Memory Card

If you have a spare memory card and a card reader connected to your PC, you can use the memory card instead of a CD to bring photos to the store. This is a little faster than burning a CD if you don't have many photos.

Insert the memory card into the card reader, open My Computer, and double-click the drive letter that represents your memory card. Make sure there are no photos on it that you want to keep. Assuming that you've used this card in your camera, there will be some folders on it, but they should be empty or have only small, leftover files (such as .thm thumbnail files) that you don't need. After double-checking that the card doesn't have any photos you want, drag all the folders on the card to the trash so that the card is completely empty.

Select the photos you want to print in the photo well and choose File > Export. Leave the File Type setting at Use Original Format. Click the Browse button and navigate to the drive letter that represents your memory card (it will be within My Computer), and click OK in the Browse for Folder dialog. Then click OK in the Export dialog, and the photos will be written to the memory card. Now you can take the memory card to the store.

***Tip** If you later want to use this memory card in your camera, be sure to format it in the camera; you need to erase all the photos on it anyway, and some cameras have trouble with memory cards that have been modified by PCs.*

If you want to make great prints at home, and your printer is more than a couple of years old or is not designed for printing photos, consider buying a new printer. You can get a fantastic printer today for under $200 and a surprisingly good one for under $100. (Of course, the manufacturers make their money by selling you ink cartridges.)

Photo printers have come a long way in the past few years. Not only is the image quality better with the newer printers, but they are faster, and the inks don't fade nearly as quickly.

Inkjet printers are by far the most common type of home photo printer today. The leading manufacturers are Epson, Hewlett-Packard, and Canon. HP has the lion's share of the market overall, but Epson is the most popular among digital photographers and Canon is rising quickly in popularity.

Choosing an Inkjet Printer

You can get good-looking photos from any new inkjet printer, but photo-optimized printers will do an even better job. This is in large part because they typically use more inks.

General-purpose inkjet printers usually have only four colors of ink (cyan, magenta, yellow, and black). Photo-quality printers typically have more colors—six, seven, or eight—because this allows colors to be reproduced more exactly using a smaller cluster of dots. A photo printer may have light cyan, light magenta, and light black in addition to the basic four colors; some even have two shades of gray in addition to black. The light colors allow lighter shades to be reproduced more precisely, instead of depending on dark dots surrounded by white space to simulate the lighter color (see "Understanding Printer Resolution" later in this section).

Here are some other factors to consider:

- Number of inks per cartridge—Some printers combine all the colors of ink into one cartridge, which means that you have to replace the cartridge when any one of the colors runs out. Ink cartridges will be a major expense, so you'll be happier in the long run with a printer that has each color in a separate cartridge. Having to buy and keep on hand all the different colors is a pain, but it will save you money in the long run, because the various colors are used up at very different rates, depending on what you're printing.
- Printer width—Wide-carriage printers (which typically can take paper up to 13 inches wide instead of only 8.5 inches) cost more and take up more desk space, but they

give you the flexibility to make prints up to 13 by 19 inches (assuming that you have a 4 or 5 megapixel camera). They do fine with smaller paper, too, so if you can afford it (they're typically $300 and up) and have the space, look for a wide-carriage model.

- Roll paper—Some printers can take rolls of paper and include an internal paper cutter. This can be very convenient if you want to produce lots of 4-by-6 prints or long panoramas, but the prints tend to curl up.

- Longevity of prints—Different printers use different ink systems (sometimes even within a single vendor's lineup), and the amount of time before fading occurs varies tremendously. If you want your prints to last as long as possible, check the fading specs and read the reviews on the photo sites listed in Appendix A. Printers with pigment-based ink systems are at the high end of the price range (over $500) and provide the best longevity.

- Memory-card slot—Some printers include memory-card slots, allowing you to print directly from the memory card without involving the computer. Some even include displays so that you can preview and crop the photos on the printer. For most people, though, this is better done on the computer, and adding a card reader separate from the printer is easy and inexpensive. Spend the extra money on a printer with a better ink system instead, unless you want a printer you can keep in the living room to make quick prints while the PC is back in the office.

Understanding Printer Resolution

If you're looking at specifications for printers you're considering buying, the resolution claims can be really confusing. Only 200 pixels per inch are required for excellent prints. So why do photo-quality inkjet printers often tout resolutions of 2880 or more dots per inch? And how can other types of printers achieve the same quality with only 200 dots per inch?

The reason is that inkjet printers use only one pure color, out of a small number of choices, for each dot; they don't mix colors. **Figure 9.21** shows an enlarged section of a high-quality inkjet photo print, revealing the color dots. To make a particular shade, inkjet printers use a group of tiny adjacent dots, which our eyes perceive as being mixed together. The number of different colors of these dots is limited by the number of different inks in a printer. So an inkjet printer needs many dots for each pixel.

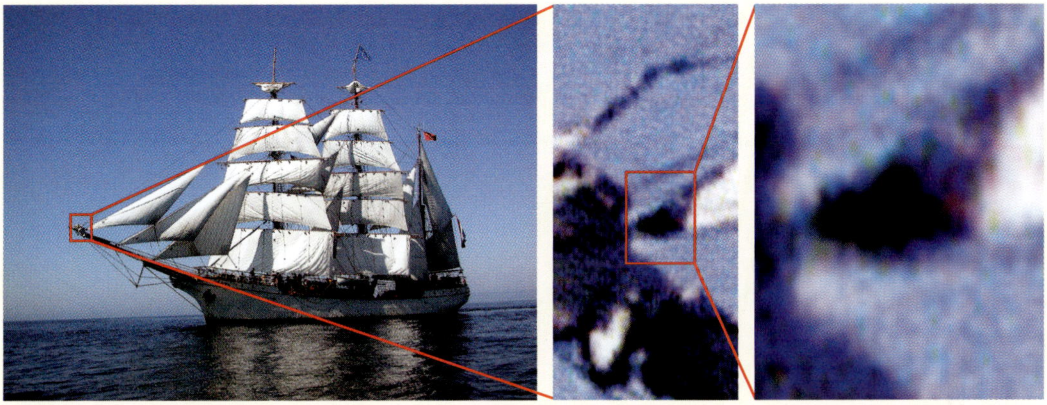

Figure 9.21 **Inkjet prints consist of nonoverlapping dots of a few pure colors, but you can't see that unless you magnify them.**

As a result, an inkjet printer's dots per inch (dpi) specification must be much higher than the pixels per inch (ppi) of the photo it is printing. So you don't have to worry about providing an image with 1440 ppi just because your inkjet printer says it has a 1440-dpi resolution; 200 ppi (or even 150 in a pinch) is perfectly adequate.

The technique of using a large number of fixed color dots to represent a smaller number of pixels with a much wider and more subtle color range is called *dithering*. The printer's software does it automatically, so you aren't aware of it (unless you look at your printouts through a powerful magnifying glass).

Continuous-tone printers, on the other hand, can make each dot any color, covering the full range and subtlety of shading. Inkjet printers are not continuous-tone printers, but dye-sublimation printers are, as are the photographic printers used by online photofinishers such as Shutterfly. These services use printers that project colored light, representing each pixel of your photo, onto conventional light-sensitive, silver-halide-based photo paper.

For a continuous-tone printer, the dpi and ppi are the same, because one dot can be any color and can therefore represent one pixel. Thus, a 200-dpi continuous-tone printer can deliver quality comparable to that of an inkjet printer, which may require 2800 dpi to deliver an effective 200 ppi. Such an inkjet printer would be using a cluster of dozens of dots to represent each pixel, whereas the continuous-tone printer uses only one.

The bottom line is that you can't compare dpi specifications among different printer types and come to any meaningful conclusions.

The Dye-Sub Alternative

Sony, Olympus, Kodak, and others sell small photo printers that use a technique called *dye sublimation* (often called *dye-sub*), in which a mix of colored dyes is applied to each dot. With this approach, which is fundamentally different from that used by inkjet printers, each dot can be any shade because the inks mix. (In an inkjet printer the dots sit side-by-side and don't mix, except in your eye.)

You'll also find dye-sub printers in the kiosks in many retail stores that allow you to make 4-by-6 prints from your memory cards or CDs. Larger dye-sub printers are available but are generally too expensive for home use. (You can buy a 4-by-6-inch dye-sub printer for $150–$300. An 8-by-10-inch model typically costs $400–$1000.)

Some people prefer the finish and color that a dye-sub printer provides, and it can be a good choice if you're adding a small printer just to make 4-by-6-inch prints. Dye-sub printers are pretty much just for photos, however, and the per-print cost tends to be higher than for inkjet printers. For all-around versatility and value, you can't beat today's inkjet printers.

10 Sharing Photos

Sharing photos is a powerful way to share experiences and memories. You've no doubt put photos on your refrigerator, brought out envelopes of photos (or maybe albums) when friends visited, taken packs of photos with you to visit a friend, and mailed extra copies of photos to family and friends.

With digital photos, you can share in all the ways you have in the past, plus lots of new ways. Making prints from digital photographs is a little more trouble, and you won't routinely have two prints of everything. But by sharing electronically, you can share photos instantly, even with friends and family members who live halfway across the world—and it costs virtually nothing.

You can share using conventional email, with photos attached as individual files or as a PDF slide show. If your friends or family members have photo-capable mobile phones, you can send photos right to their phones. And if you're sharing lots of photos with a group of people, putting the photos on the Web—either on a commercial site or your own—is a good way to go.

Electronic sharing isn't just for sending photos to people who are far away—it will also help you share face-to-face. Instead of carrying a couple of pictures of your spouse or kids in your wallet, you can carry dozens or even hundreds of photos in your PDA. And in addition to putting photos on your refrigerator, you can set up an electronic picture frame to display a slide show of your current favorites—and you can make an assortment of slide show discs to run on your DVD player.

You'll probably get a lot more enjoyment out of your photos if you remember to share them regularly, no matter what method you choose. I try to make it a habit to think about who would enjoy certain photos every time I import or organize a new batch. If I don't share them right away, it tends not to happen.

Sharing via Email

Often, the easiest way to share your photos is to email them. Photoshop Album will resize your photos appropriately, create a PDF slide show if you want, attach the files to an email message, and delete the files when they've been sent. It couldn't be easier!

Selecting Your Email Client

Before you can use Album to share via email, it needs to know which email program you want to use. Album can work directly with Microsoft Outlook and Outlook Express; Eudora; and Hotmail. You can use other email programs and Web-based email accounts indirectly, but the process is a little more cumbersome.

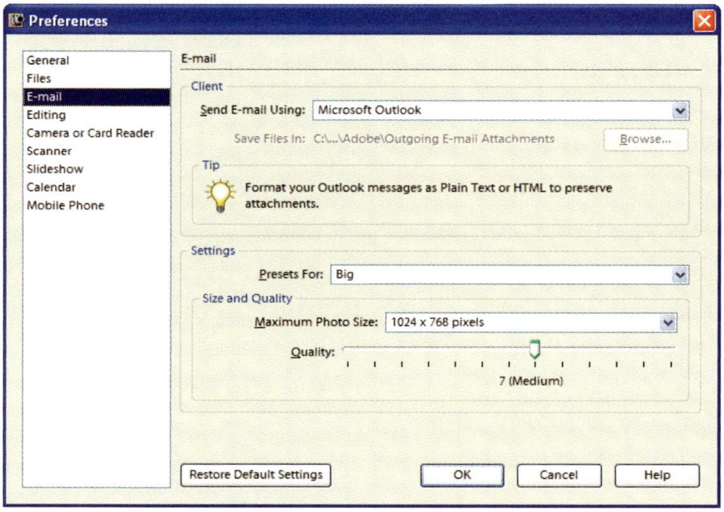

Figure 10.1 Set your preferred email client in the Preferences dialog.

To configure Album's email sharing, choose Edit > Preferences and select E-mail in the list on the left of the Preferences dialog (**Figure 10.1**). Choose your preferred email program in the Send E-mail Using pop-up menu, or choose "Other (save to disk)" if yours is not on the list (**Figure 10.2**).

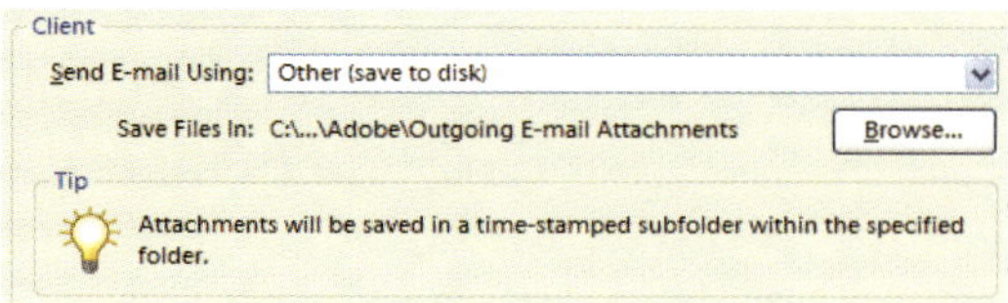

Figure 10.2 Use the "Other (save to disk)" setting if Album doesn't support your email program, or if you use Web-based email other than Hotmail.

If you use one of the supported email programs, Album will take care of attaching photo files to messages and deleting the files later. If you choose the "Other (save to disk)" option, Album creates the attachments and writes them to a folder, from which you can attach them to an email message. In this case, you'll have to delete the files using Windows after you've sent the email.

The Preferences dialog also gives you the opportunity to select resolution settings, but don't worry about that for now; I'll explain later in this chapter.

Sharing Photos

Select the photos you want to share in the photo well (if you're sharing a single photo, you can find it in calendar view), click the Share button in the shortcuts bar, and choose E-mail (**Figure 10.3**). (Alternatively, choose File > Attach to E-mail or press Ctrl-Shift-E.)

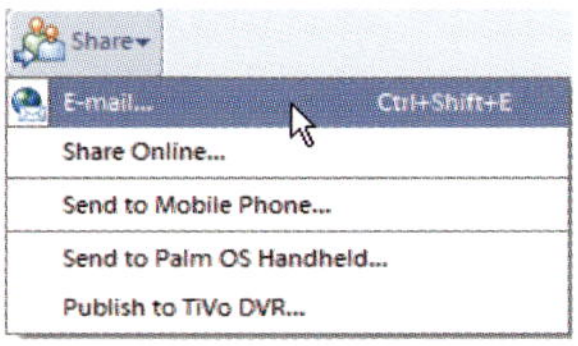

Figure 10.3 **You can access most sharing functions from the Share button in the shortcuts bar.**

In the Attach to E-mail dialog you can select recipients and how you want the photos prepared for sharing (**Figure 10.4**). If you are using the "Other (save to disk)" option for your email client, the recipient list will not appear in this dialog, and you'll have to address the message in your email program.

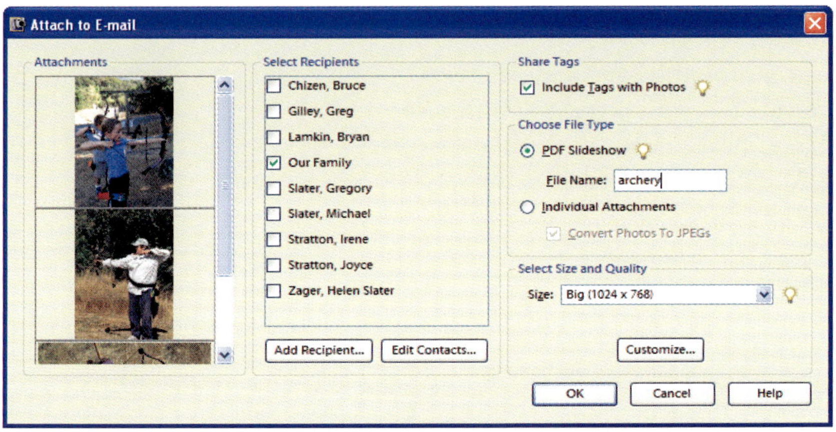

Figure 10.4 **In the Attach to E-mail dialog, choose the recipients of the photos, as well as the size and format you want, and you're done.**

Using the Contact Book

The potential recipients listed in the Attach to E-mail dialog are those you've entered in Photoshop Album's contact book. Once people are in your Album contact book, all you have to do is check the box next to their name to send them email.

You no doubt already have an address book in your email program, and entering these addresses again in Album is a pain—but it does have a payoff. If you address the emails in Album, you'll later be able to find photos based on whom you shared them with (Find > By History > E-mailed to; see Chapter 5 for details). You can ignore Album's contact book and just address messages in your email program, but then Album can't record who you sent photos to.

You can add people to the contact book from within the Attach to E-mail dialog by clicking Add Recipient. Enter the person's name and email address in the "Add a recipient" dialog, check the box next to Add to Contact Book, and he or she will be added to the contact book as well as to the list of recipients for these photos (**Figure 10.5**).

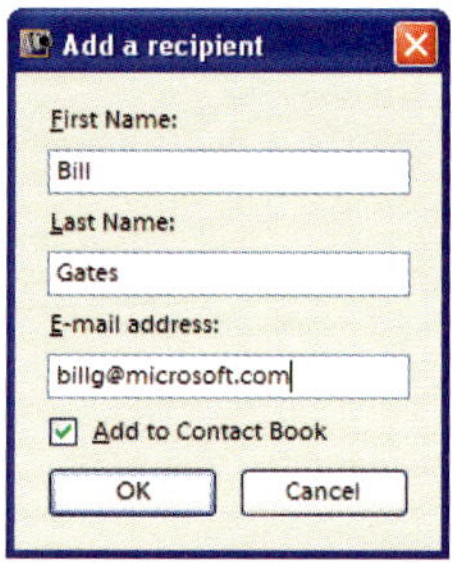

Figure 10.5 **In the "Add a recipient" dialog you can add someone not yet in your contact book.**

You can build your contact book gradually by adding recipients each time you share photos. You probably share mostly with the same relatively small group of people, so after a while you'll find that almost everyone is already in your contact book. But you can add to your contact book directly by clicking the Edit Contacts button in the Attach to E-mail dialog, or by choosing View > Contact Book.

In the Contact Book dialog you can add, delete, or modify contacts (**Figure 10.6**). Click New Contact to add another contact (**Figure 10.7**); to modify an existing entry, select it and click Edit. The only information you must enter is a first name and an email address.

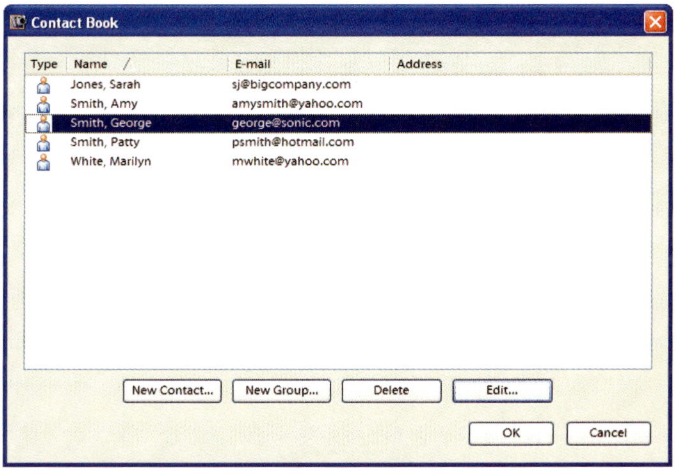

Figure 10.6 **In the contact book enter the names of those you've shared with to aid in searching later.**

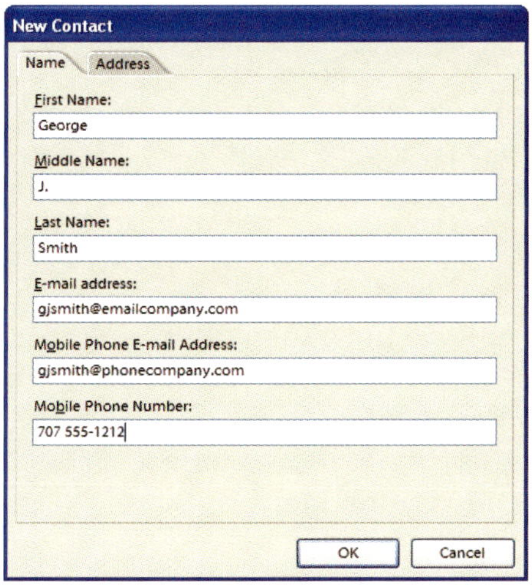

Figure 10.7 **In the Add Contact dialog, enter the name and E-mail address, and optionally, a mobile E-mail address for sharing to mobile phones.**

If you want to be able to send photos to someone's mobile phone, enter the person's mobile phone email address; see "Sharing to Mobile Phones," later in this chapter for details. You can also enter address information in the Address tab, but there's not much point, as Album doesn't use this information.

Making groups

You can also create groups in the contact book. Make a group for any set of people with whom you often share the same photos, such as your immediate family, your extended family, or members of the soccer team or the birding club. Like individuals, groups appear in the contact book (and the recipient list in the Attach to E-mail dialog).

To make a group, first enter all the members of the group as individual contacts in the Contact Book dialog, and then click the New Group button in the same dialog. In the New Group dialog enter a name for the group, select each member, and click the Add button (**Figure 10.8**).

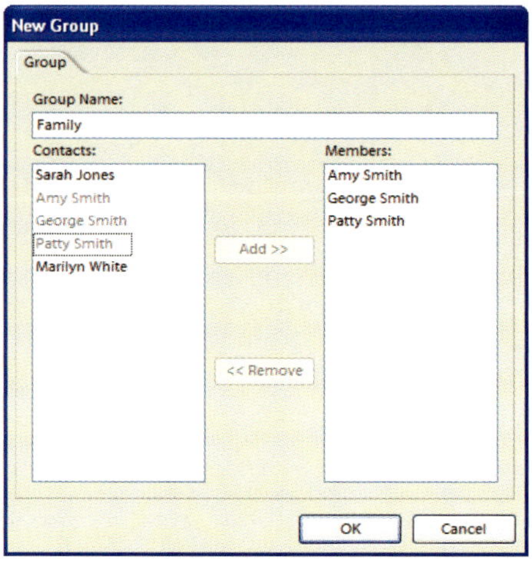

Figure 10.8 Create groups in the New Group dialog to make sharing easier.

Sharing Tags

If you're sharing photos you have tagged, you have the option of sharing those tags with recipients (if they have Photoshop Album 2.0). This enables people who receive photos from you to easily organize them in their catalogs, utilizing the tagging you've already done. If you do not want tags to be shared, uncheck the box next to Include Tags with Photos in the Attach to E-mail dialog.

***Note** Favorites and Hidden tags are not shared. Also, only the tag name itself (not the category or subcategory) is shared.*

People who receive photos or slide shows from you can import the shared tags into their catalogs along with the photos (see Chapter 2). Note that category and subcategory information is not shared—only the tag names. Recipients can move the shared tags into any category or translate the tags to others already in their catalogs.

Sharing Slide Shows

If you choose the Individual Attachments file-type option in the Attach to E-mail dialog, you'll be sharing photos just as you probably have in the past—as multiple JPEG files attached to the message.

***Note** If any of your files are not JPEGs, they'll automatically be converted to that format unless you uncheck the box next to Convert Photos To JPEGs. (Generally you don't want to share uncompressed formats such as TIFF and PSD because the files are large.)*

Album gives you an alternative to sharing a set of JPEG files: combining the photos into a PDF slide show. When you share a PDF slide show instead of a group of JPEGs, the people you're sharing with get a single file instead of lots of files, and they see your photos in the order you choose. They'll also see any captions you've included, and hear audio captions and background music if you've included them. They only need Acrobat Reader 5.1 or later, or the current version, now called Adobe Reader, to see the slide show. (Your friends can download Adobe Reader for free from www.adobe.com/reader; you already have it, because it is installed along with Album.)

The recipients of your slide show don't give up anything by getting a PDF instead of individual JPEG files. If they have Album 2.0 (or even the free Album 2.0 Starter Edition), they can import the PDF file and Album will extract the JPEGs from it. They can also extract the photos, or print them in various arrangements, using the free Adobe Reader software.

PDF slide shows you create for emailing are just like the instant slide shows you can view by clicking the Slideshow button at the bottom of the photo well. They use the same settings in Preferences for slide duration, transitions, captions, background music, audio captions, and video resizing. If you have background music enabled, you may want to turn it off, as it will substantially increase the size of the PDF files.

***Tip** You can use the instant slide show as a preview to see what the people you share with will see. The one difference will be in the resolution of the photos (see the next section). To preview exactly what they'll see, double-click the PDF attachment to the email message before you send the message; if you want to change something, just close the message without sending it.*

Sending photos as PDFs does impose a modest size premium, typically 150–250 KB, depending on the number of photos you're sharing. If you want to keep file size to a minimum and are sharing a few photos at a small size, then PDF is not a good choice. If you're sharing more photos or using a larger size, such as 1024 by 768, or if you and your recipients have high-speed Internet connections, then the size premium is insignificant.

Choosing Resolution for Sharing

Whether sharing photos as JPEG files or as a PDF slide show, you can choose the size at which you want to share them. To use one of the standard sizes, just select it from the Size pop-up menu in the Select Size and Quality section of the Attach to E-mail dialog (**Figure 10.9**). The larger the size, the better the photo will look for the people you're sharing with, but the larger the file will be.

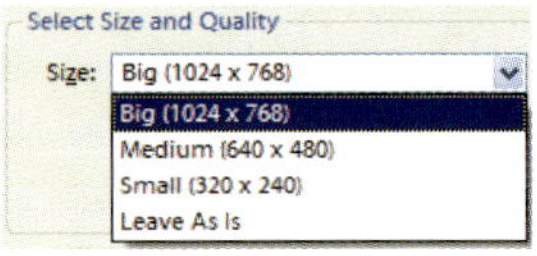

Figure 10.9 Choose the size to which you want to photos reduced for sharing in the Attach to E-mail dialog.

If I'm sharing with people who have high-speed Internet connections, I always use the Big size. For others I use Medium. I use the Small size only if I'm sending lots of photos to someone with a slow connection, and the details in the photos aren't important.

Choose Leave As Is for the size if you want to send the full-resolution photo. Keep in mind that this may be 1–3 MB per photo, depending on the resolution, so you might end up with very large email attachments. Use this option only if you want the recipient to be able to make a large print of the photo. The full resolution is unnecessary for viewing onscreen or for making small prints (1024 by 768 is fine for 4-by-6 prints).

Size and Resolution

Album's sharing dialogs use the term *size,* so I've used it here, too. This is not physical size, since the photo has no physical form—it is more properly called "pixel dimensions" and often referred to as "resolution."

Shared photos are usually viewed onscreen, and not printed, so there is usually no need to send files with a size larger than the recipient's screen. Most people with fairly new computers have displays of either 1024 by 768 or 1280 by 1024.

You can change these three standard sizes in the Settings section of the email Preferences dialog (**Figure 10.10**). You can access this dialog by clicking the Customize button in the Attach to E-mail dialog or selecting Edit > Preferences.

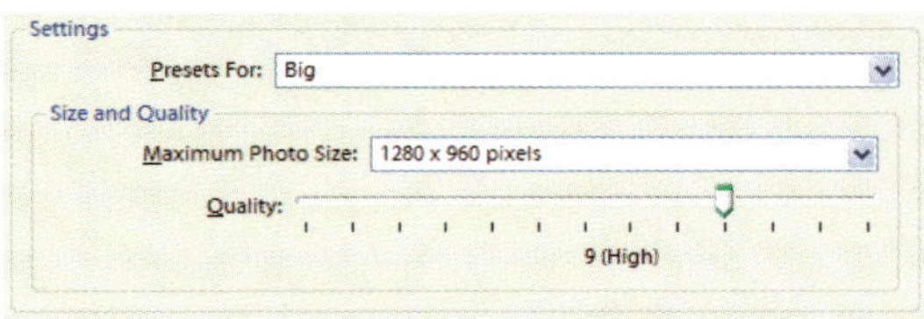

Figure 10.10 In the email Preferences dialog you can change the size and JPEG quality for Big, Medium, and Small settings.

In Preferences you can choose which resolutions correspond to Small, Medium, and Big. Choose the size from the Presets For pop-up menu and the dimensions you want to use in the Maximum Photo Size pop-up menu. I like to increase all the sizes, using "640 x 480 pixels" for Small, "800 x 600 pixels" for Medium, and "1280 x 960 pixels" for Big, so people who receive photos from me can see them filling more of their screen.

Tip *People with free email accounts from providers such as Hotmail and Yahoo might not be able to receive emails with attachments larger than 1 MB. Even some paid email accounts may be limited to attachments of a few megabytes. The email provider will also limit the total size of all email messages in the recipient's inbox. Furthermore, your email provider may limit the size of attachments you can send.*

Because of these limitations, check to see that your recipients all receive your emails if you use attachments larger than 1 MB. If you encounter problems, you'll have to limit the number or sizes of the photos you share. To avoid these restrictions, share via CDs or the Web (as described later in this chapter).

Table 10.1 shows typical file sizes for each photo size. Because the actual amount of compression depends on the content of the photo, the table shows a range of file sizes for each photo size. Note that a 1280-by-960 image is typically about ten times the file size of a 320-by-240 image.

Table 10.1 **Average File Sizes for Emailed Photos**

Photo Size (in Pixels)	Quality	File Size
320 by 240	5	14–26 KB
640 by 480	6	45–95 KB
800 by 600	6	65–145 KB
1024 by 768	5	75–140 KB
1024 by 768	7	100–170 KB
1024 by 768	8	125–200 KB
1280 by 960	5	100–210 KB
1280 by 960	7	130–260 KB
1280 by 960	8	170–340 KB
1280 by 960	9	220–450 KB

You can also adjust the JPEG quality for each size. The defaults are 7, 6, and 5 for Big, Medium, and Small, using more aggressive compression for the smaller sizes. If you're trying to keep file size down and get the best quality you can, however, you may find it better to use one of the largest photo sizes but with a lower Quality setting. Cutting the Quality level from 8 to 5 cuts the file size roughly in half while still giving a good image (though one that will not hold up as well to close scrutiny; see sidebar "Choosing JPEG Quality Level" in Chapter 7).

Tip ***The Presets For pop-up menu in the E-mail Preferences dialog has a second function that isn't immediately obvious. Whichever setting is selected when you close the dialog will be the default when you begin a new email share, so leave the menu set to the size you'll use the most.***

When you click OK in the Attach to E-mail dialog, Album will tell you the exact size of the attachment (**Figure 10.11**). If the size is bigger than you want to send, click Cancel and then either share fewer photos or reduce the photo size or Quality setting.

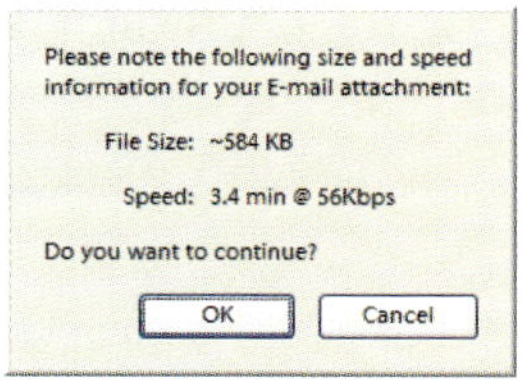

Figure 10.11 If the file is larger than you want to send, click Cancel and adjust the settings or number of photos.

If you've set your email client to Other in the Preferences dialog, Album will prepare the photo files to attach, make a folder for them, and tell you where the folder is located (**Figure 10.12**).

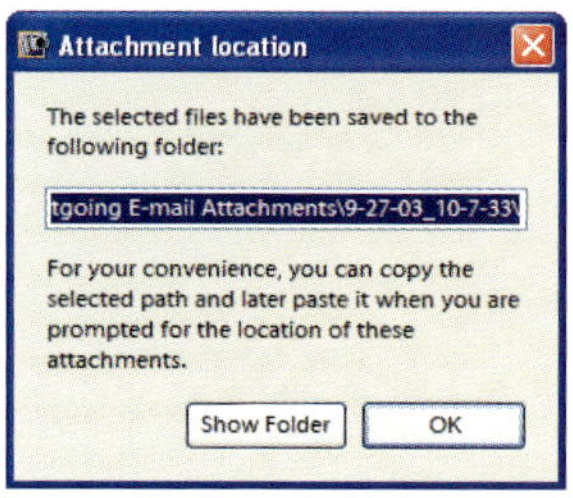

Figure 10.12 If you're not using one of the supported mail programs, the "Attachment location" dialog opens, telling you where the files you must attach to your email message have been saved.

Sharing Creations

If you want full control over the slide shows you share, make a slide show creation first instead of having Album make an instant slide show. (See Chapter 8 for details on making creations.) You can choose E-mail from step 6 of the Creations Wizard (click on the Create button in the shortcuts bar) or select the creation's thumbnail in the photo well and click Share > E-mail.

When you're sharing a creation (slide show, album, or eCard), you have different size options (**Figure 10.13**). It's generally best to use Optimize for Viewing Onscreen, which is roughly equivalent to the largest (1280 by 960) size option for instant slide shows.

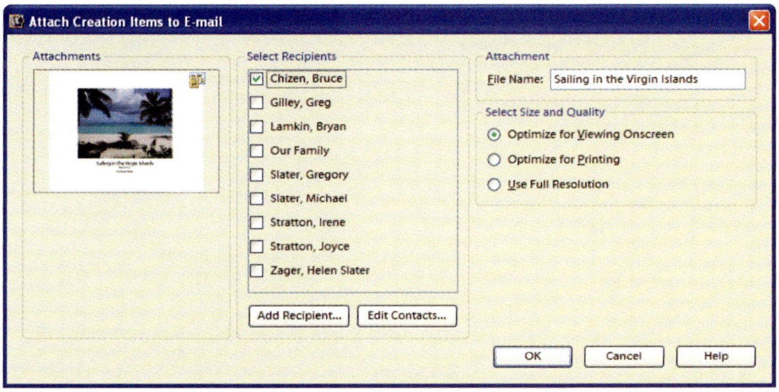

Figure 10.13 When you share a creation, you can choose from different sizing options.

Slide show creations, when viewed in Adobe Reader, always fill the screen. Because of this, they need bigger files to look crisp. Instant slide shows made via the Attach to E-mail dialog, on the other hand, fill only part of the screen unless you select the Large size, so their file size is smaller.

Sharing via CDs

Sharing through email is great for its immediacy, but it's best suited to small slide shows of modest resolution; otherwise the attachments can take a very long time to send and receive, and they may exceed the limits of your email provider or those of the recipients' provider.

A CD, on the other hand, with its 650 MB or 700 MB size, is capacious enough to deliver slide shows that will drive all but the most interested recipients to distraction. CDs are generally the only way to effectively share slide shows that contain video clips of more than a few seconds or lots of audio captions.

Tip *Send a CD slide show instead of just a photo with your holiday cards. A CD actually costs no more than a single photo, and you can send dozens of photos and video clips on one of them.*

CD Slide Shows for PC Viewing

There are two ways you can make a CD for sharing photos:

- Burn a CD with just the photo files using File > Burn (see Chapter 3)
- Make a slideshow creation and choose Burn in the last step of the Creations Wizard (see Chapter 8)

The first approach produces a disc with just the photo files, at their full resolution, but there is no slide show on the disc. Use this approach only if you are sharing with someone who just wants easy access to the photo files and you want to get the maximum number of photos on the disc.

The second approach provides a better experience for the recipient. To create a slide show on CD, use the Creations Wizard to make the slide show and click Burn in step 6. You can put only one slide show on a CD using this method.

***Tip** If you want to put more than one slide show on a CD, you can use Save as PDF in step 6 of the Creations Wizard to write each slide show to your hard disk, and then use a CD-burning utility to write the PDFs to CD.*

Slide shows on CD look sharper than those sent by email, because Album stores photos on the CD with a size of 1600 by 1200. Furthermore, the CD also includes a PDF slide show with full-resolution images, which recipients can use if they want to print the photos (see sidebar Making the Most of Slide Show Discs in Chapter 8). To print photos, they can either import the PDF into their copies of Album (or Album Starter Edition) or open it in Adobe Reader.

Video CD Slide Shows for TV Viewing

If you want to share a slide show with someone who doesn't have a PC or will prefer watching it on TV, then make a Video CD creation (see Chapter 8). These slide shows look great, within the limits of TV, when played on a DVD player.

***Note** Video CDs don't have nearly the resolution of a CD slide show for PC viewing, so even though a Video CD can be played on a PC (by recent versions of the Windows Media Player or the RealOne Player), it won't look nearly as good as a CD slide show made for PC viewing.*

Any time I make a slide show I especially like, I make a Video CD, even if I don't have an immediate need for it. This gives me a collection of slide shows I can play on the TV, for social occasions when sitting on the couch (instead of at the computer) is more important than having high resolution.

Sharing via the Web

Sharing photos by uploading to a Web site has unique advantages (and disadvantages). Most important, the people you share with don't need to have high-speed Internet connections or premium email services, even if you want to share dozens or hundreds of photos with them.

There are two ways you can share photos on the Web:

- Using a commercial site, such as Shutterfly (www.shutterfly.com)
- Creating Web photo galleries and uploading them to your own Web site

You don't need to know anything about creating Web sites to use a commercial sharing site, since everything is done for you automatically. People who view your photos there can order high-quality prints without having to download the high-resolution images.

Creating your own Web photo galleries is useful only if you have your own Web site, and it doesn't provide an easy way for viewers to make prints. But it does give you the maximum flexibility, and you don't have any commercial brands or sales pitches competing with your photos. See Chapter 8 for details on making Web photo galleries.

Using Online Services for Sharing

You can share online using any of Adobe's online partners that offer this service (only Shutterfly, as of this writing). Select the photos in the photo well and choose Share Online from the Share pop-up menu in the shortcuts bar. In the Share dialog you can choose which service to use (assuming more than one is available), as well as who the recipients are (**Figure 10.14**).

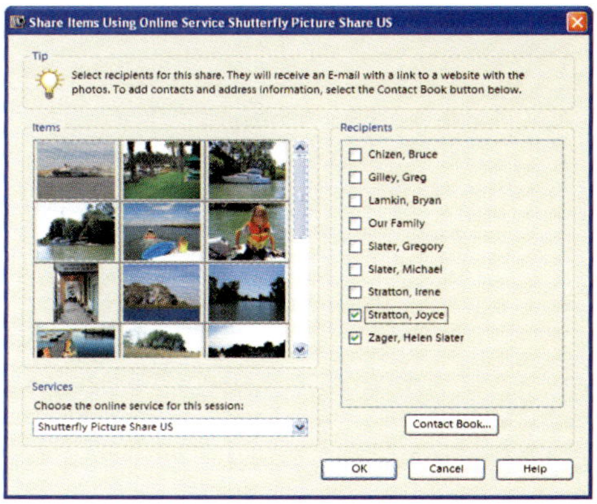

Figure 10.14 Sharing at an online photo site starts with the Share dialog, where you choose who you want the service to notify that the photos are available to be viewed.

Click the boxes next to the names of those with whom you want to share. To add names to the contact book, click the Contact Book button.

***Tip** As with sharing via email, you don't have to use Album's contact book; you can enter the email addresses of the share recipients later. But if you don't use the contact book, Album won't be able to record who you shared with.*

When you've selected all the recipients, click OK and log in to the sharing service in the Online Services Wizard (**Figure 10.15**). If you haven't used the service before, you'll have to create an account, just as for a printing-online service (see Chapter 9).

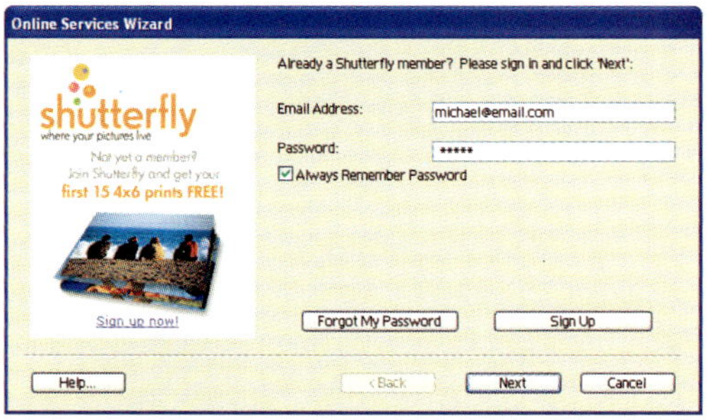

Figure 10.15 When logging in to the online sharing service in the Online Services Wizard, if you aren't concerned about others using your computer, click Always Remember Password and you won't have to enter it again.

Once you've logged in to the sharing service, the dialogs you're seeing are presented by the service, even though they appear within Album—so what you see may vary from what's shown in the figures here.

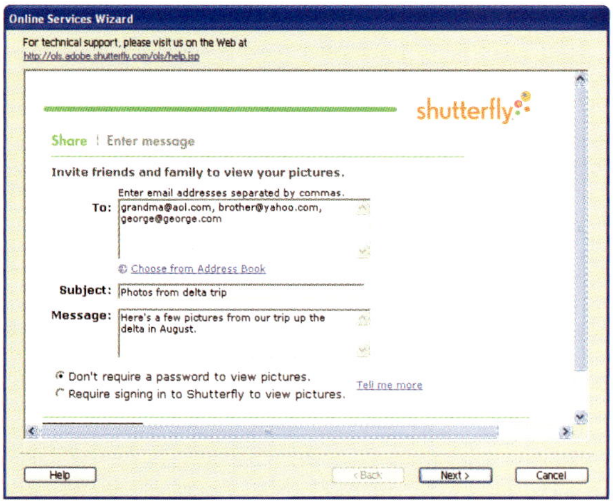

Figure 10.16 In the sharing service's dialog within the Online Services Wizard you can add to your recipient list when you enter the subject and message for the share-notification emails.

On the first screen you can add email addresses if you haven't used Album's contact book (**Figure 10.16**). Enter a subject for the message you want to send people notifying them of the new photos you've shared, and add a message for the text portion. Click Next, and Album will begin uploading the photos to the sharing service, displaying a Progress dialog (**Figure 10.17**).

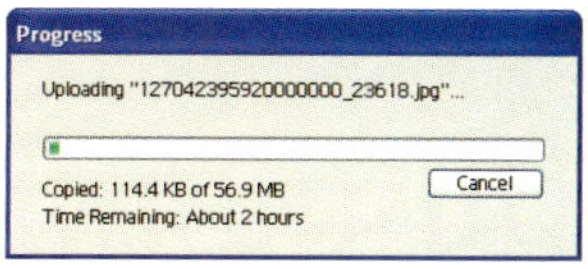

Figure 10.17 Album will show how much time is left to complete the upload; ignore the meaningless temporary filenames.

***Tip** You can't use Album while the upload is in progress, but you can switch to other programs and use them. Don't interrupt your Internet connection until the transfer is done.*

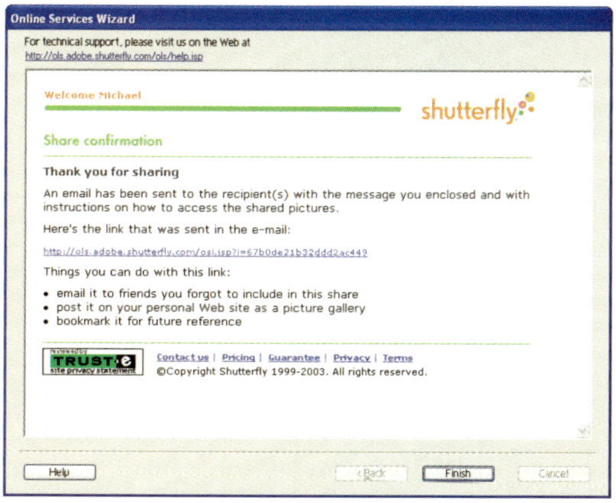

Figure 10.18 When the photos are uploaded, the service will display a confirmation and send notification emails.

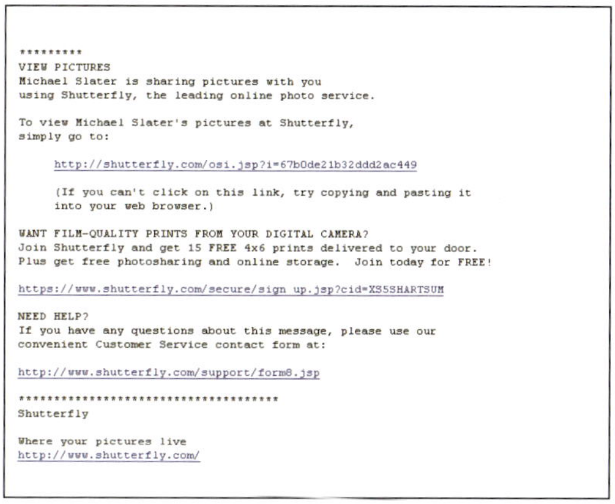
****
VIEW PICTURES
Michael Slater is sharing pictures with you
using Shutterfly, the leading online photo service.

To view Michael Slater's pictures at Shutterfly,
simply go to:

http://shutterfly.com/osi.jsp?i=67b0de21b32ddd2ac449

(If you can't click on this link, try copying and pasting it
into your web browser.)

WANT FILM-QUALITY PRINTS FROM YOUR DIGITAL CAMERA?
Join Shutterfly and get 15 FREE 4x6 prints delivered to your door.
Plus get free photosharing and online storage. Join today for FREE!

https://www.shutterfly.com/secure/sign up.jsp?cid=XS5SHARTSUM

NEED HELP?
If you have any questions about this message, please use our
convenient Customer Service contact form at:

http://www.shutterfly.com/support/form8.jsp

****
Shutterfly

Where your pictures live
http://www.shutterfly.com/

Figure 10.19 Shutterfly sends an email to every recipient you listed, with a link to the photos.

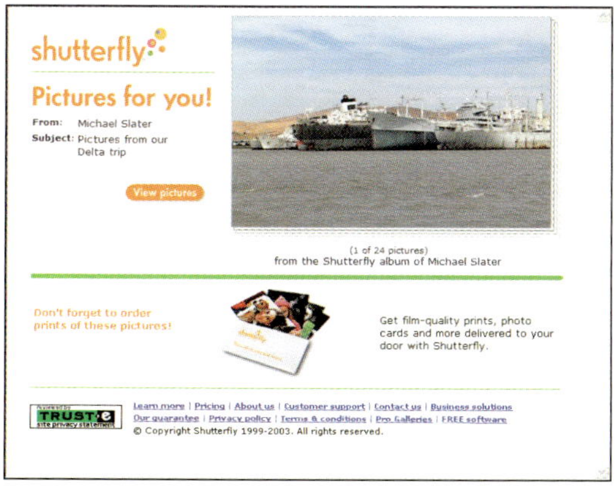

Figure 10.20 When recipients click on the link in the Email, they'll be taken directly to a Web page with your photos.

When the photos are all transferred, you'll see a confirmation dialog in the Online Services Wizard (**Figure 10.18**). Shutterfly will send an email message to all the people you selected (**Figure 10.19**). When the people you've shared with click the link in the email, their Web browsers will open and show the photos on the Web (**Figure 10.20**). On the Web site, people you've shared with can view a slide show or order prints.

There are other online sharing services that offer more flexibility to lay out pages as you'd like and include more text and graphics, but they charge for membership (typically about $30 per year). For example, you may want to take a look at www.funtigo.com and www.neptune.com. To use these services, export your photos from Album to a temporary folder, and then use the Web site's uploading tools to upload the photos.

Sharing on Your PDA

If you carry a PDA (personal digital assistant), you can keep lots of photos with you. When resized for the small screen of a PDA, photos don't take up much space, so you can carry dozens of them without occupying a lot of the device's precious memory.

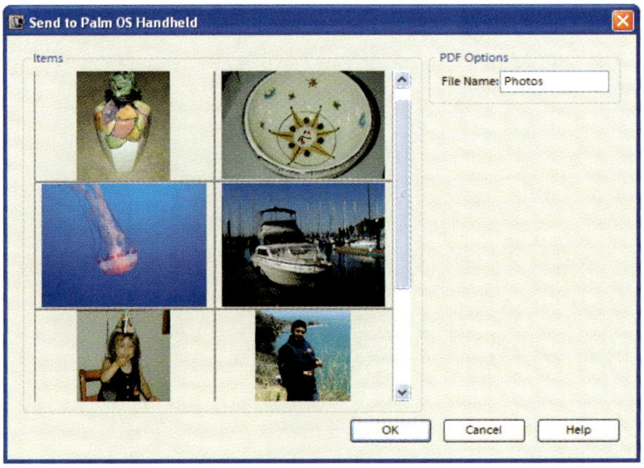

Figure 10.21 Just enter a name for the PDF slide show in the Send to Palm OS Handheld dialog and it will be created and sent to your Palm device.

If you have a recent Palm OS PDA (running Palm OS 4.0 or newer), Album can create PDF slide shows optimized for your PDA. Select the photos in the photo well, and choose Send to Palm OS Handheld from the Share pop-up menu in the shortcuts bar. In the Send to Palm OS Handheld dialog, just enter a name for the slide show in the File Name field and click OK (**Figure 10.21**). Album will create a PDF slide show and then pass the resulting file to the Adobe Reader for Palm OS program (**Figure 10.22**). (To use this feature, you must have Adobe Reader for Palm OS 3.0 or newer. If you don't, you can download it from www.adobe.com.)

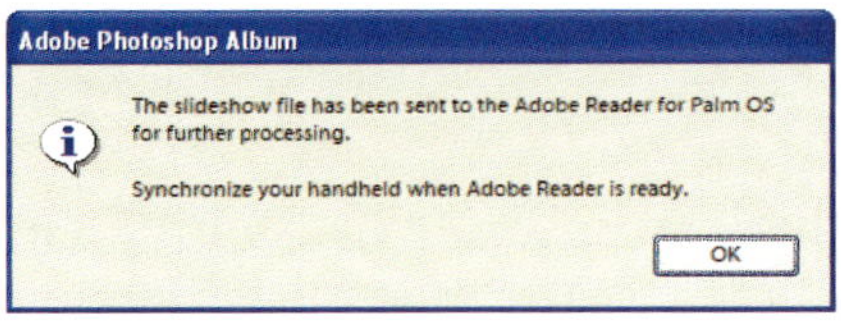

Figure 10.22 Album creates a PDF file and triggers Adobe Reader for Palm OS to prepare it to be sent.

Adobe Reader for Palm OS includes two programs: one that runs on your PC and another that runs on the Palm OS. After Album creates the PDF file, Adobe Reader for Palm OS should start on your PC and show the file it has ready to send to your PDA (**Figure 10.23**).

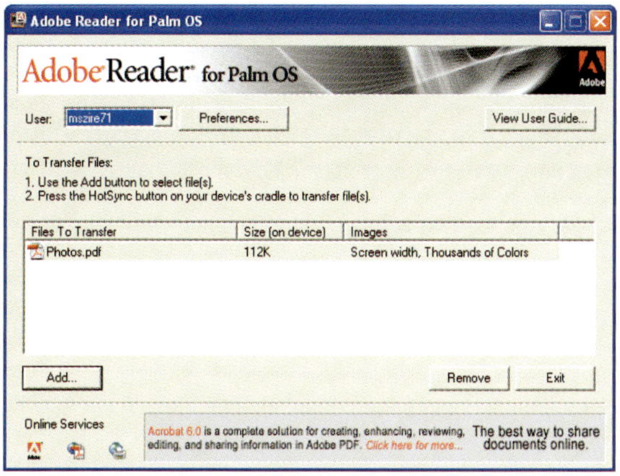

Figure 10.23 When Adobe Reader is ready, this dialog tells you that it is time to press the HotSync button on your Palm cradle.

To complete the transfer, press the HotSync button on your PDA's cradle. Palm's HotSync software takes over at this point and copies the PDF file to your handheld, displaying the HotSync Progress dialog (**Figure 10.24**).

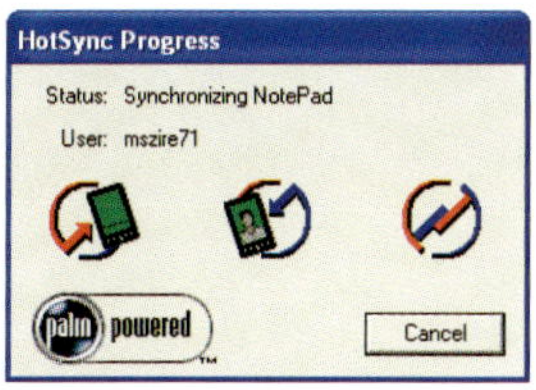

Figure 10.24 Palm's HotSync software transfers the file to your handheld device, and this dialog appears during the transfer.

To see the slide show on your PDA, just click Adobe Reader in your PDA's list of applications.

Sharing on Other PDAs

The send-to-PDA function in Photoshop Album works only with Palm OS handhelds. If you have a Pocket PC or other handheld, you can still share photos to it easily, but not in quite the same way.

Select the photos in the photo well and choose File > Export. Select JPEG for the file type from the Export dialog. Most Pocket PCs have 320-by-240 displays, so choose that size if you don't know the PDA's display dimensions.

Tip *If the size of your PDA's screen differs from the standard choices, choose Custom in the Photo Size pop-up list (of the Export Selected Items dialog). In the Custom Size dialog, enter the dimensions.*

Click the Browse button in the Export dialog, and navigate to the folder in which you want to save the photos to be sent to the PDA. Click the New Folder button to create a new folder for this set of photos, name the new folder, and click OK.

Album will place copies of the selected photos, reduced to the size of your PDA's screen, in the folder you created. You then must use your PDA's synchronization software to copy these files to the PDA.

Tip *You can also use this method to send photos to a Palm OS handheld instead of using the special Send to Palm OS Handheld feature if you'd rather not have the photos combined into a PDF slide show.*

Sharing to Mobile Phones

Even if you don't use a handheld device like a Palm, you probably have a cell (mobile) phone. If you have a phone that has a color display and can accept photos as attachments, you can email yourself photos to show on your phone (**Figure 10.25**). You can also send photos to other people's phones, if their phones are capable.

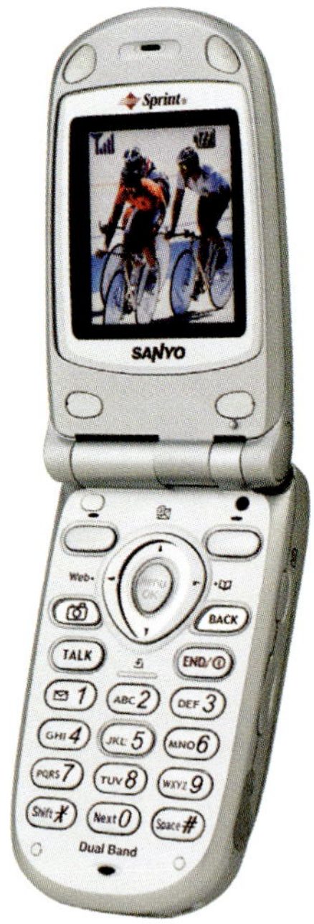

Figure 10.25
Mobile phones with color displays can show small photos.

Note *Some mobile phone services will not accept email with attachments. If the service won't accept attachments, this feature won't work.*

The receiver's experience on the phone varies depending on the particular carrier and phone. Messages generally arrive first as a text message, with a link to the attachment (your photo). When you select the link on the phone, the photo is downloaded and displayed. The details of this experience vary from phone to phone—but most are unreasonably complex and clumsy. As sharing photos on phones becomes more common, the phone makers and service providers no doubt will improve the experience.

Select the photos you want to share in the photo well, and choose Send to Mobile Phone from the Share pop-up menu. You can share to only one mobile phone at a time, so pick one name from the contact book in the Choose A Recipient For your Photos dialog (**Figure 10.26**). You can choose only names that have a valid mobile phone email address in the contact book. Select the name and click Continue.

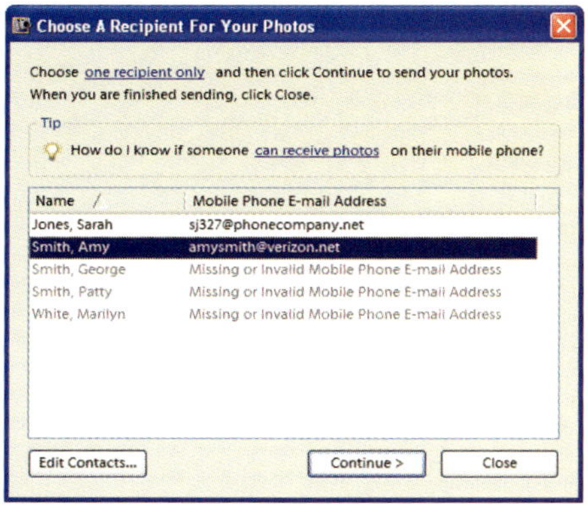

Figure 10.26 To use the Send to Mobile Phone feature, you must enter the mobile email address in the contact book.

In the Send to Mobile Phone dialog, choose a size for the photo you want to send (**Figure 10.27**). The Small (96 x 72 pixels) size makes a smaller file, of course, and if the phone's screen is small, it will be fine. For phones with bigger screens, the Big (120 x 90 pixels) size is better. If you know the size of the phone's screen, choose the size that matches, or click the radio button for Custom Size and enter the exact size in the Width and Height fields.

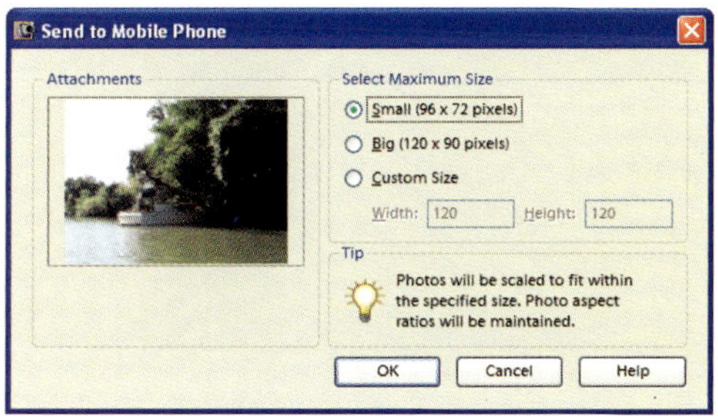

Figure 10.27 Pick the size of the photo you want to send in the Send to Mobile Phone dialog and you're done.

When you click OK, Album will create an email message in your email program. The photos are attached as JPEG files at the size you specified. Click Send in the email program to send the message.

Sharing on Your TV

Sharing photos on TV is great when you have a lot of people around. As mentioned earlier in this chapter (and in detail in Chapter 8), you can make a Video CD and play it on a DVD player.

There's another even more direct way, though, if you have the right setup. With this approach, you can browse photos stored on your PC—viewing them on TV. This approach works only for photos, however; you can't share video clips, slideshows, or other Album creations.

This feature works only with a TiVo Series2 DVR (digital video recorder) with the Home Media Option (an optional software upgrade you can order at www.tivo.com). You must have your TiVo connected to your PC's network, via an Ethernet cable or a wireless network (802.11b) adapter.

To make photos in your catalog visible on TiVo, you must "publish" them to TiVo, which tells the TiVo software that runs on your PC how to find them. You can publish as few, or as many, as you'd like.

If you haven't already installed and used the TiVo Home Media Option, you'll need to do that first. It includes TiVo server software that runs on your PC and an update to the software in your TiVo box, which allows you to view photos and play music from your PC on your TV. (See www.tivo.com/media to purchase the Home Media Option, or www.tivo.com/mediahelp if you have it and need help using it.)

Select the photos you want to share in the photo well, click on the Share button in the shortcuts bar, and choose Publish to TiVo DVR from the Share pop-up list. Then, in the Publish to TiVo DVR dialog, you must choose whether to make a folder for this set of photos, which is generally a good idea (**Figure 10.28**). Click Browse to make a new folder, or to choose an existing one.

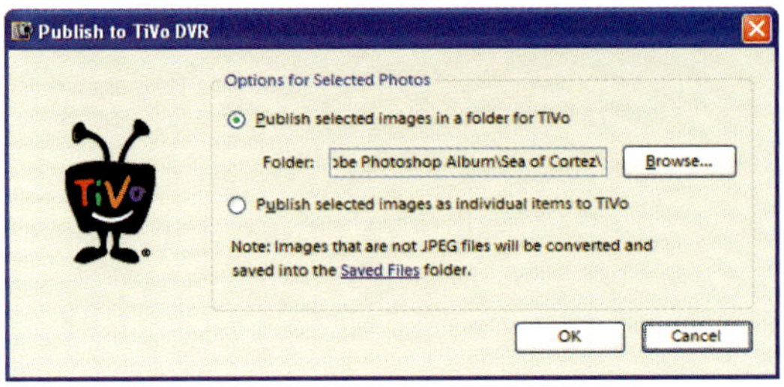

Figure 10.28 In the Publish to TiVo DVR, make a folder for each set of photos when sharing to TiVo.

When you click OK, Album will place shortcuts to the photos you selected in a folder on your PC. TiVo's PC software will then make this folder available on your TiVo.

***Note** Because Album only makes shortcuts to your photo files, and doesn't copy them, publishing photos to TiVo doesn't use up much disk space on your PC, or any on your TiVo—even if you publish many photos.*

If you publish photos to TiVo that are not in JPEG format, however, Album will make JPEG files, which take additional disk space.

When you have published the photos from Album, choose Music & Photos from the TiVo menu on your TV. If your TiVo network setup is working correctly and the TiVo server is running on your PC, you'll see your PC's name on the list that appears. Select it, and you'll see a grid that shows any photos or folders you've published to TiVo independently of Album, plus a folder called Adobe Photoshop Album. Select this folder, and you'll see the photos you published from Album (**Figure 10.29**). The photos that appear here were published without specifying a folder; those for which a folder was specified appear here as folders, which you select to view the photos in them.

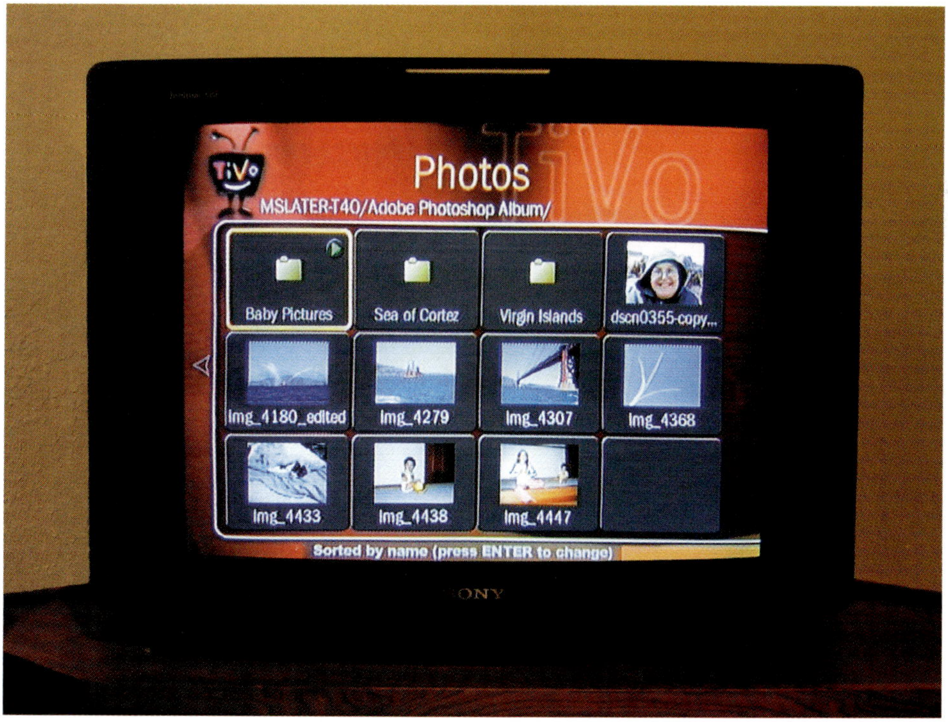

Figure 10.29 **TiVo's Home Media Option lets you see photos on your TV that are stored on your PC's hard disk.**

Unfortunately, Album doesn't give you any tools for rearranging or unpublishing photos once you've published them to TiVo. To do so, use Windows to navigate to C:/Documents and Settings/<your user name>/Local Settings/Application Data/TiVo Desktop/Photos/Adobe Photoshop Album, and delete or rearrange files there. (Local Settings is a hidden folder, so you'll have to enable display of hidden folders in Windows to be able to do this.) The items in this folder are just shortcuts to your photo files, so you can delete and move them without affecting your Album catalog.

Sharing with Digital Picture Frames

A digital picture frame is, in essence, an LCD monitor mounted in a picture frame, with just enough of a computer embedded in it to display slide shows (**Figure 10.30**). It's a wonderful means of enjoying many more of your photos without having to print them and find a way to display the prints.

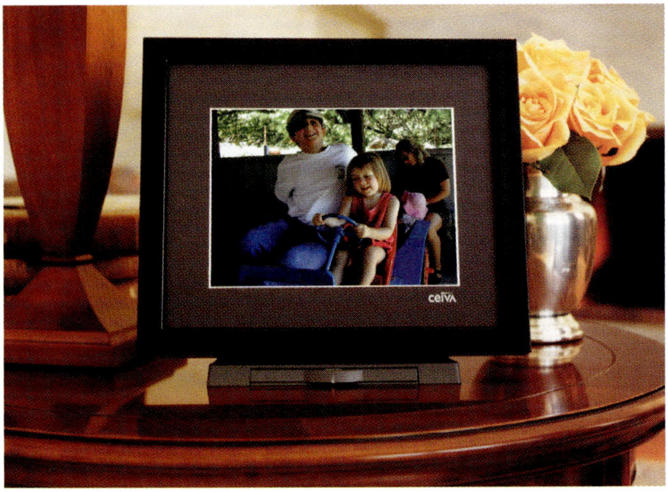

Figure 10.30 Digital picture frames, like this model from Ceiva, are a great way to enjoy more of your photos more often.

A digital picture frame can also be a great gift for friends or family members who would like to see more of your photos. Set them up with the frame and then regularly send them pictures to put in it.

Some frames have memory-card slots, so you can move the card right from your camera to the frame. With Photoshop Album, you can easily sort through all your photos and select ones to put in the picture frame. Use File > Export to write the photos to a memory card in a card reader connected to your PC. Set the file format to JPEG and the resolution to the size of the display in your picture frame. Export the photos to the card, and then remove the card and insert it in your picture frame.

A Home-Brew Digital Picture Frame

If you have an old PC and an LCD monitor—and a willingness to cut holes in your walls—you can make a great digital picture frame inexpensively (**Figure 10.31**). Cut a hole in the wall big enough for the LCD display, and buy a picture frame that will cover it. Put the PC (notebooks are best because of their small size and low power consumption) in a nearby closet. With a wireless network adapter, you can have your photo-display computer on your home network. Then just let it run the Windows screen saver, or leave it running an Album instant slide show (set to repeat) or a PDF slide show playing in Adobe Reader.

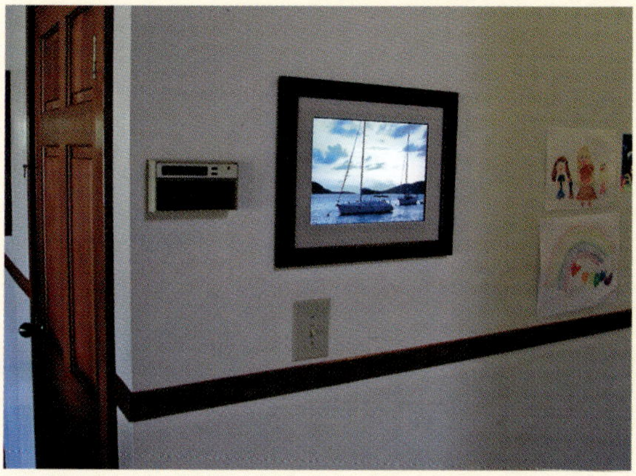

Figure 10.31 **This picture frame is a desktop LCD monitor mounted in a hole in the wall, connected to a PC in the closet behind.**

Some frames, such as Ceiva's Digital Photo Receiver (www.ceiva.com), don't have a memory-card slot or connect to your PC—they have a built-in modem and connect only to the phone line. To put photos in the frame, you upload them to the Ceiva service on the Web, and then each day the frame calls up the Ceiva service to see if new photos are waiting.

There's a monthly fee of about $8 for the service. The Ceiva frame itself is $149. They make great gifts, because the recipients can just plug them into the phone line, and then you can send photos to their frames without any action on their part.

Other companies that make digital picture frames include DigiFrame (www.digiframe.com), Pacific Digital (www.pacificdigital.com), and Wallflower Systems (www.wallflower-systems.com). The DigiFrame frames accept memory cards; Pacific Digital's have USB interfaces to connect to your PC; and Wallflower's frame has a built-in wireless network interface. Prices range from about $300 to $800 (and up to several thousand dollars for large displays). You can buy many of these at www.eframestore.com.

Making Desktop Backgrounds and Screen Savers

Using a favorite photo as your Windows desktop background is a great way to enjoy the photo more of the time—and it's very simple to do. Just select the photo in Album, in the photo well or calendar view, right-click it, and choose Set as Desktop Wallpaper. That's it! The photo is now your Windows background.

I like to change the desktop photo each time I import a new set of pictures, choosing one of my favorites from the group. Changing it is so quick that you can do so every day if you're so inclined.

Using the Windows XP Screen Saver

Having a slide show as your screen saver makes it easy to see lots of your pictures all the time. Album won't create one for you automatically, but it isn't hard to put together once you know how—especially if you're running Windows XP.

The process sounds complicated, but it is quite simple once you're familiar with it. First, you need to configure the Windows XP screen saver:

1. Create a new folder in your My Pictures folder and name it something like Slide Show Photos.
2. Right-click the Windows desktop and choose Properties.
3. Click the Screen Saver tab in the Display Properties dialog (**Figure 10.32**).

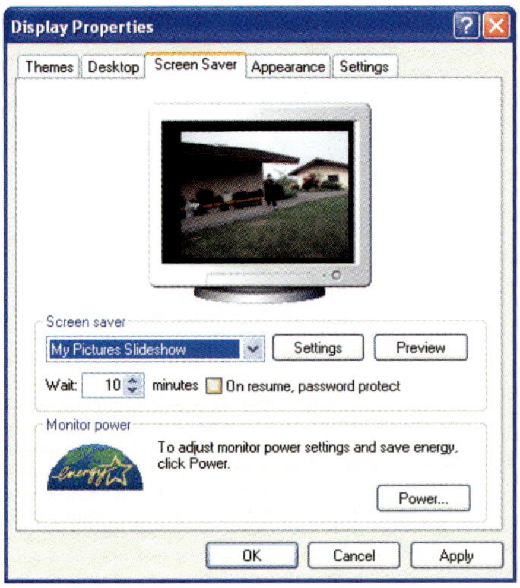

Figure 10.32 Choose My Pictures Slideshow in Windows' Display Properties dialog and click Settings.

4. Choose My Pictures Slideshow from the pop-up menu of screen saver choices.

5. Adjust the Wait time to the number of minutes of inactivity you want Windows to require before it starts the screen saver. Try 2 minutes if you want the screen saver coming on all the time, or 30 minutes if you want it to stay off until you've taken a substantial break.

6. Click Settings, and then click Browse in the My Pictures Screen Saver Options dialog (**Figure 10.33**).

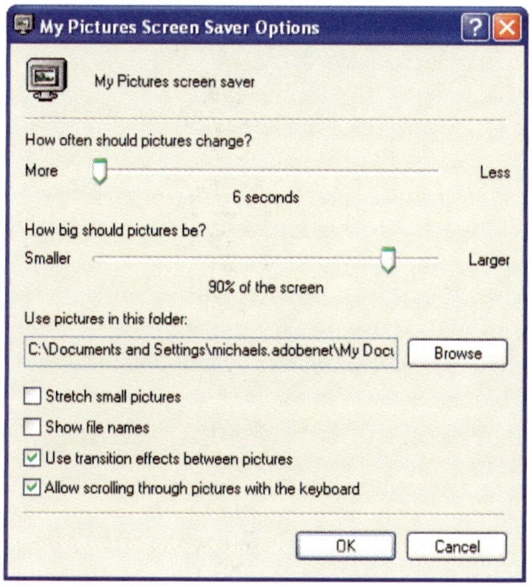

Figure 10.33 Set the amount of time you want each picture shown, and choose other slide show options, in the My Pictures Screen Saver Options dialog.

7. Navigate to the folder you created in step 1, select it, and click OK.

8. Change any of the options, such as the amount of time each photo is displayed, in the options dialog, and then click OK in the options dialog and in the Display Properties dialog.

Now, in Album, select the photos you want to include in the screen saver, and choose File > Export. From the Export dialog, select JPEG for the file type and set the size to the resolution of your display (as shown in Windows' Display Properties dialog). Click Browse, navigate to the new folder you created in step 1 of configuring the Windows XP screen saver, and click OK.

Album will now make appropriately sized copies of all the photos you included in your screen saver and put them in the new folder you created. The Windows XP screen saver will then read photos from this folder when it is activated.

Sharing Prints

As you're well aware of now, there's an abundance of ways to share your photos electronically. For many people, however, there's nothing like having prints in hand. You may get accustomed to the ease of electronic sharing and forget that many people would really like to have prints.

Online photofinishing is great for getting prints to your family and friends on a regular basis. The prints are easy to order, and they're shipped directly to the recipients. (See Chapter 9 for an in-depth discussion of printing options.)

You've Made It!

Congratulations! You've reached the end of *The Photoshop Album 2 Book*. You now have the tools and knowledge you need to enjoy your digital photos with a minimum of hassle.

Here are some final reminders for making the most of your photos:

- Always import your new photos, whether from your camera, scanner, or email, so you can find them in Album.
- Make sure your camera's clock is set correctly so your photos will have the right date and time.
- Tag photos each time you import a new batch, so you'll later be able to find them by subject, event, or special interest.
- Remember to email your favorite photos to friends and family.
- Make a collection of the best photos from each vacation, party, or other event. From these collections, make Album or Photo Book creations for printing, or Video CDs if you want to view them on your TV.
- If you haven't yet done so, try ordering prints and a Photo Book online. These are great ways to get more enjoyment from your photos.
- Pick out a dozen of your favorite photos and make a calendar. Keep one for yourself, and use them as gifts for friends and family.
- Back up regularly so you don't lose any of your precious photos.

Finally, if you have questions or comments about this book, or are looking for the latest tips and updates, visit www.enjoyingdp.com.

A APPENDIX A: Resources for Going Further

Photoshop Album

For the latest information on Photoshop Album, check these Web resources:

- Enjoying Digital Photography (www.enjoyingdp.com)—The Web site that supports this book. It includes an updated version of this appendix with live links, so the easiest way to use this appendix is to go directly to www.enjoyingdp.com/resources.
- Adobe Photoshop Album Support (www.adobe.com/support/products/photoshopalbum.html)—Adobe's support site for Photoshop Album. Here you can find links to tech notes on current issues and any program updates that may be available.
- Adobe User to User Forums (www.adobe.com/support/forums/main.html)— Read discussions of various issues and ask questions. You can also reach this page by clicking the "Forums" link on the Album Support page.

Photoshop Elements

You can learn about Photoshop Elements and download a trial version from the Adobe Photoshop Elements Web site (www.adobe.com/products/photoshopel).

There are many books available on Photoshop Elements. Here are a few of the ones I've found most useful. This is a good place to start if you don't have any experience with photo editing:

- *Photoshop Elements 2 For Dummies*, by Deke McClelland and Galen Fott (For Dummies, 2002; www.wiley.com)

The following books take you deeper but assume you know the basics of using Photoshop Elements:

- *Adobe Photoshop Elements 2.0 Idea Kit,* by Lisa Matthews (Adobe Press, 2002; www.adobepress.com)
- *The Photoshop Elements Book for Digital Photographers,* by Scott Kelby (New Riders Publishing, 2004; www.newriders.com)
- *Photoshop Elements 2 Solutions: The Art of Digital Photography,* by Mikkel Aaland (Sybex, 2002; www.sybex.com)
- *The Hidden Power of Photoshop Elements 2*, by Richard Lynch (Sybex, 2002)

Photoshop

You can learn about Photoshop at the Adobe Photoshop Web site (www.adobe.com/photoshop). I recommend that you seek out a class at a local community college or photo store; it takes a lot of reading to learn as much as you can from a few hours of live instruction.

It would take a whole book to list all the books and other resources for learning about Photoshop. Here's a small selection of the ones I've used.

Some introductory books:

- *Adobe Photoshop CS Classroom in a Book* (Adobe Press, 2004)
- *Photoshop CS for Windows and Macintosh: Visual QuickStart Guide,* by Elaine Weinmann and Peter Lourekas (Peachpit Press, 2004; www.peachpit.com)

More-advanced books on Photoshop as a creative tool:

- *The Photoshop Show Starring Russell Brown,* by Russell Brown (Adobe Press, 2004)
- *Real World Adobe Photoshop CS*, by David Blatner and Bruce Fraser (Peachpit Press, 2004)
- *Adobe Photoshop CS Artistry*, by Barry Haynes and Wendy Crumpler (New Riders Publishing, 2004)

These books are focused especially on photographer's needs (rather than those of graphic designers or Web designers):

- *The Adobe Photoshop CS Book for Digital Photographers,* by Scott Kelby (New Riders Publishing, 2004)

- *Photoshop Restoration and Retouching*, second edition, by Katrin Eismann (New Riders Publishing, 2004)
- *Adobe Photoshop 7.0 for Photographers*, by Martin Evening (Focal Press, 2002; www.focalpress.com)

To find plug-ins for Photoshop (or Photoshop Elements):

- The Plugin Site (http://thepluginsite.com)—Includes extensive lists of free and commercial plug-ins available for downloading.

If you become a serious Photoshop addict, join NAPP (National Association of Photoshop Professionals; www. photoshopuser.com) and get its *Photoshop User* magazine. Another excellent magazine for sophisticated users is *PEI* (Photo Electronic Imaging; www.peimag.com).

Digital Cameras

Books about digital cameras provide helpful background, but camera models and features are changing so rapidly that books aren't useful for learning about specific cameras. For general background on digital cameras, see

- *The Little Digital Camera Book*, by Cynthia L. Baron and Daniel Peck (Peachpit Press, 2003)

For details on specific cameras, check out these excellent Web sites, which provide detailed reviews of the latest cameras:

- Digital Photography Review (www.dpreview.com)
- The Imaging Resource (www.imaging-resource.com)
- Steve's DigiCams (www.steves-digicams.com)
- Digital Camera Resource Page (www.dcresource.com)
- megapixel.net (www.megapixel.net)

There are also several digital photo magazines, although their camera reviews generally don't have either the depth or the timeliness of those on the Web sites:

- *Digital Photographer* (www.digiphotomag.com)
- *Digital Camera* (www.digicamera.com)
- *PCPhoto* (www.pcphotomag.com)
- *Popular Photography & Imaging* (www.popphoto.com)

Printing, Scanning, and Color

Books on working with color:

- *Photoshop Color Correction,* by Michael Kieran (Peachpit Press, 2003).
- *Real World Color Management*, by Bruce Fraser, Chris Murphy, and Fred Bunting (Peachpit Press, 2003)
- *Understanding Color Management*, by Abhay Sharma (Delmar Publishers, 2003)

Books on scanning and printing:

- *A Few Scanning Tips*, by Wayne Fulton (www.scantips.com)
- *The Scanning Workshop,* by Richard Romano (Que, 2002)
- *Mastering Digital Printing*, by Harald Johnson (Muska & Lipman, 2002)

Other color management resources:

- International Color Consortium (www.color.org)—Standards organization that offers good articles about ICC profiles
- Inkjet Mall (www.inkjetmall.com)—Online store for inkjet ink, as well as color-management hardware and software
- Creative Pro (www.creativepro.com)—Site oriented toward graphic artists, which includes several good articles on color management

Digital Photography Techniques

For information about more advanced techniques, from color management to editing with Photoshop, check these Web sites:

- photo.net (www.photo.net)—One of the largest online communities for photographers
- Computer-Darkroom (www.computer-darkroom.com)—Lots of tutorials on Photoshop techniques and other subjects
- RetouchPRO (www.retouchpro.com)—Tutorials on photo retouching
- Scanning Basics 101 (www.scantips.com)—Lots of information on making better scans
- Photoshop Restoration & Retouching (www.digitalretouch.org)—The companion site for Katrin Eismann's *Photoshop Restoration and Retouching* book
- The Luminous Landscape (www.luminous-landscape.com)—Professional photographer Michael Reichmann's beautiful landscape and nature photos, and tutorials on the artistic and technical aspects of digital photography

APPENDIX B: Keyboard Shortcuts

No one can remember dozens of keyboard shortcuts, unless they use the combinations all the time. So I list here just the ones I have found most useful. These shortcuts are well worth memorizing if you use Photoshop Album often.

General

Undo	Ctrl-Z
Redo	Ctrl-Y
Help	F1

Photo-Display Controls

Make thumbnails bigger	Ctrl-+ (plus)
Make thumbnails smaller	Ctrl-– (minus)
Select All	Ctrl-A
Start slide show	Ctrl-spacebar
Show full screen	F11
Next photo	→ (right-arrow)
Previous photo	← (left-arrow)
Show (or hide) Properties palette	Alt-Enter
Find photos	Alt-1
Find video clips	Alt-2
Find audio clips	Alt-3
Find creations	Alt-4

Actions

Get photos from camera or card reader	Ctrl-G
Get photos from files or folders	Ctrl-Shift-G

(continues)

Apply Favorites tag	Alt-F1
Apply Hidden tag	Alt-F2
Rotate counterclockwise	Ctrl-← (left-arrow)
Rotate clockwise	Ctrl-→ (right-arrow)
Print	Ctrl-P
Fix photo	Ctrl-I
Duplicate photo or creation	Ctrl-Shift-D
Export	Ctrl-E
Attach to E-mail	Ctrl-Shift-E

Fix Photo Window

Fit to Window	Ctrl-0 (zero)
Show Actual Pixels	Alt-Ctrl-0 (zero)

C APPENDIX C: Using Multiple PCs with Photoshop Album

Photoshop Album is designed to run on a single PC. If you have multiple PCs and want to share the same photos and catalog among them, you have my sympathy. It can be done—but it can also be rather painful. Tread carefully if you go down this path, and be prepared to deal with a lot of issues.

Traveling with a Notebook PC

If you have a notebook PC that you travel with and a desktop PC at home, then you may want multiple copies of your catalog and photos. The simplest solution is to get a big hard disk for your notebook and keep everything there. You can update your home PC copy when you return, as described below—or, for minimum hassle and maximum reliability, just plug your notebook into a docking station and don't try to copy everything to your desktop system.

If you need to have your catalog and photos on a desktop PC and use a notebook when traveling, there are some workarounds, but none of them are very pretty. You can keep a small traveling catalog and import photos there to review them while you're traveling, but this won't provide you with access to your full catalog when you're using the notebook.

If you do any tagging in the temporary traveling catalog, you can't readily incorporate those tags into your desktop catalog. And if you edit photos while you're traveling, there will be no way to connect the originals and the edited copies when you import them into your main Photoshop Album catalog on your return.

You could travel with a full catalog but without all the photo files. If you were to access (even in single-image view) any photo for which the file was not on your notebook, you would get the

"Searching for missing files" dialog, which you'd have to cancel since it won't find the file on your notebook disk. This can get annoying. When you cancel (or let it search your entire hard disk and fail to find the photo), the photo would be marked as missing.

So unless you're not going to do anything but view your photos at thumbnail sizes while you're traveling, you need to keep the full catalog and all the photo files on your notebook (unless you've stored them on CDs or DVDs). Fortunately, you can now get replacement hard disks that are 80 MB and larger for most notebooks, so it is practical to carry even very large photo collections with you in their entirety.

Synchronizing Multiple PCs

You can copy a catalog and its photos from one PC to another by creating a backup from one and restoring to the other. If you keep copies of your catalog and your photos on more than one PC, however, you need to be very careful about how you use them. Photoshop Album does not have the capability to synchronize two catalogs, so if you make different changes in two copies of the same catalog, you will have no way to create a catalog with both sets of changes (other than manually making the changes again).

For example, I travel with my notebook PC, which has my catalog and all my photos on its hard drive. I keep a copy of all of it on my wife's PC at home so that she can share and print photos while I'm away. When I'm traveling with my notebook, I add photos to the catalog and will often tag and share them. Then, when I return, I back up my catalog and use Album's Restore function to copy it to my wife's PC.

This is a less-than-perfect system. Aside from the time it takes to do the backup and restore operation, if my wife makes any changes to the catalog on her system, those changes are lost when I restore the new version from my notebook. Even if all she has done is print or share photos, the history information associated with those operations is lost. Also, she can't add photos to her copy of the catalog, since her catalog gets overwritten when I update it from my notebook.

***Tip** You can tremendously speed up the transfer via backup and restore by backing up to a hard disk that both PCs can access, instead of to CDs or DVDs. For example, if the desktop PC's disk can be accessed by the notebook via the network, use it as the destination when backing up the catalog from the notebook. Then the copy of Album running on the PC can restore from its own disk.*

You can move files manually between the systems instead of using backup and restore, but this must be done very carefully. You must move all the items linked to the catalog, in addition to the catalog itself and its thumbnail cache. This only works if the paths on both systems are identical. If you do take this approach, the easiest way to move all your catalogs and their thumbnail caches is to move the folder Documents and Settings/All Users/Application Data/Adobe/Photoshop Album (and all the subfolders within it).

The bottom line is that Photoshop Album just doesn't support this mode of operation very well, and it's best to think of it—at least in this version—as a single-PC product.

Using Servers and Network Drives

Although Photoshop Album is designed for single-PC use, it is possible to keep your photos on a network drive (a disk drive connected to a server or another PC, or a stand-alone network-connected storage unit). Because Photoshop Album is not really designed for this type of use, however, some cautions are in order.

Change the Folders for Saved Files path in Edit > Preferences > Files to point to a folder (which you might want to name *Photoshop Album Files*) on your network drive. This will not move any files, but it will cause any new imports from a camera or scanner to be written to the network drive.

If you have photos on the network drive and have not yet imported them into Photoshop Album, just import them using the usual mechanism, navigating to the network drive as you would to a folder on the local drive. If you have photos already in the catalog and you want to move them to the network drive, either select them in Photoshop Album and use File > Move to move them to the network drive, or move them using Windows and then choose File > Reconnect All Missing Files in Photoshop Album to fix the links. (To ensure the reconnect function will search a netwrok drive, map it to a drive letter.)

Photoshop Album works best with network drives if the drive is always available. If you use Album when the network drive is not present, any photos stored there will appear as missing. When the drive becomes available again, the automatic reconnect logic will reconnect the files. (If your catalog is on a network drive and the network drive is unavailable, you cannot, of course, use Album at all.)

D APPENDIX D: Moving to a New PC

Eventually you'll want to replace your trusty old PC with a shiny new one, and of course you'll want all your photos, audio clips, video clips, and catalogs to be copied to your new system. The best way to do this is to use Photoshop Album's backup function to create a backup of your catalog and the items it references, and then restore this backup on the new system. With this method, any changes in file paths will be automatically corrected, and you'll be sure to catch all files that are linked to your catalog, no matter where they may be on your hard disk.

On your old PC, just select File > Backup from within Photoshop Album to start the backup process. (See Chapter 3 for more details on using the backup function.) If your collection is small, CD-Rs are a good backup choice; if it's large, writable DVDs are much more practical. You can also back up to an external hard disk, which is the most painless method if you have one with enough space. Then you can just connect the external hard disk to the new machine instead of having to burn a series of discs on the old PC and insert them one at a time in the new PC as the catalog is restored.

Once your backup is complete, install Photoshop Album on your new PC, and select File > Restore. Select the CD or DVD drive you want to use (or connect an external hard disk), and follow the instructions to insert each disc in turn.

Moving Files Without Album's Backup and Restore

If you instead use a systemwide backup and restore or a system migration utility to move from one system to another, you need to ensure that all the photos are properly linked to the catalog on the new system. If your new system uses a different operating system, or you use a different user name, or you are part of a different network domain, then the full path to My Pictures will be different on your new computer, and photos stored there will require their links to be corrected. Also, if you choose to rearrange your photo folders in any way when setting up the new system, the links will be broken.

As long as you don't use any software that changes the file-modification dates when copying the files, Album's File > Reconnect All Missing Files function should reconnect everything. It can take a long time to handle large numbers of files, however.

To move your catalogs, copy the entire folder at Application Data/All Users/Adobe/ Photoshop Album, and all its subfolders, to the new system. (In some cases the folder path may be Application Data/All Users.Windows/Adobe...)

Upgrading Your Operating System

If you are not changing PCs but just upgrading your operating system, you may encounter many of the same issues as when moving to a new PC. Upgrading the operating system can change the location of the My Pictures folder, and Album requires different support files for different operating systems. So to be safe, do a full backup using Photoshop Album's File > Backup command and uninstall Album before upgrading the OS. Then, after upgrading the OS, reinstall Photoshop Album and use File > Restore to restore the backup set. The restore routine will adjust for any changes in folder paths with the new OS.

E APPENDIX E: Understanding Image Quality

Why do some photos look great onscreen but poor when printed? What does *resolution* really mean, and how much do you need? Why does one camera produce better photos than another with the same resolution specifications? The answers lie in the fundamentals of the digital photo technology. The more you understand about how digital images work, the less mysterious image quality and resolution will seem. You'll be able to make better decisions about what size to print photos and what resolution to choose when you're making your camera settings.

Resolution: the Key to Detail

Resolution is the most touted specification of digital cameras: a 3 megapixel camera, for example, produces images that each have 3 million pixels. That sounds impressive, but how much resolution do you really need? It depends on what you plan to do with an image. Will you print the image or only view it on a computer screen? And at what size do you intend to view it (**Figure 1**)?

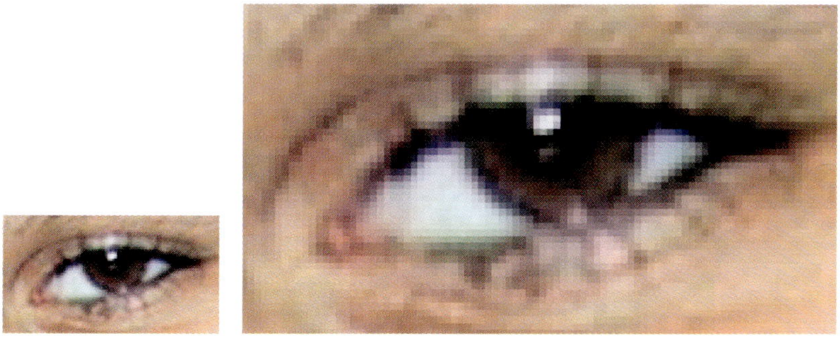

Figure 1 All digital photos are composed of individual pixels, each of which is a square of a single color. When the pixels are small, as in the image on the left, you don't see them. When enlarged, the pixels are obvious. (Both images have the same number of pixels.)

In terms of quality, when you're taking pictures it's always better to capture the highest-resolution image you can. It's also the safest bet, since you can easily create a lower-resolution version but you can't increase the resolution once you've captured the image. Higher-resolution images take more memory, however, so you'll be able to store fewer of them in the camera, they'll fill up your hard disk more quickly, fewer of them will fit on a CD, and the computer will take longer to process them.

Resolution for onscreen viewing

If your photos are destined only for Web pages, then camera resolution is virtually irrelevant; you'll have more than you need. That's because even low-end cameras deliver images with more than enough resolution for computer monitors. For instance, a 4-by-6-inch image onscreen requires about 240,000 pixels, which is about one-quarter of a megapixel. All digital cameras can take images with resolution higher than that.

For onscreen slide shows, you'll typically want images to fill the screen. Most 17-inch to 20-inch computer monitors operate at a resolution of 1024 by 768 (0.8 megapixel) or 1280 by 1024 (1.3 megapixels); the highest-resolution screens in common use are 1600 by 1200 (2 megapixels). So even a 2 megapixel camera will give you all the resolution you need for great slide shows.

One other important factor that affects the quality of images is *bit depth* (the number of colors that each pixel can represent). Set your monitor to a bit depth of at least 16 bits per pixel, and preferably to 32 bits per pixel (to see the full range of colors your camera can capture).

Resolution for good prints

For printing, you need a higher pixel density than for onscreen display, or the images won't look sharp. If you have a 4-megapixel-or-better camera, you're unlikely to run into any issues unless you make prints larger than 11 by 14 inches. But if you have a 2 megapixel camera, or if you crop a photo to use only a fraction of the image, or if you receive photos in email and want to print them, you need to be careful to have enough resolution for the size prints you're making, or the results will be disappointing.

A reasonable minimum for good-quality prints is 150 pixels per inch (ppi); 200 ppi makes for noticeably sharper images (**Figure 2**). (Album will warn you any time you are printing images with less than 150 ppi.) Above 200 ppi, however, the improvements are usually very subtle. If you are a real perfectionist, you'll want 300 ppi for the largest prints.

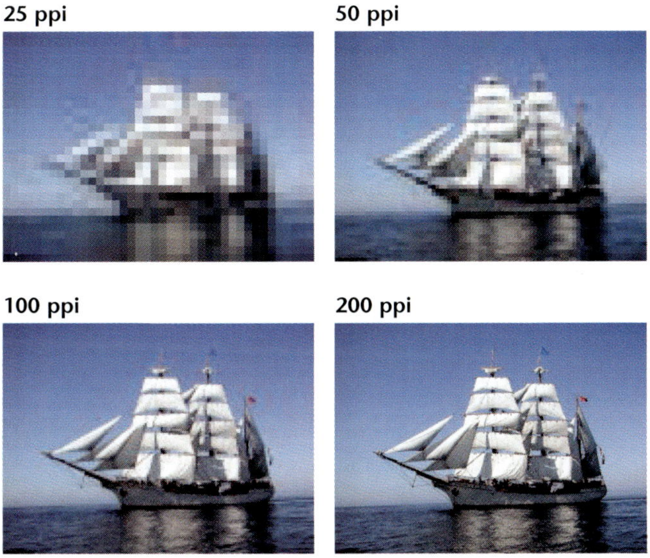

Figure 2 The number of pixels per inch determines how much detail you see. At 25 or 50 ppi, the pixels are obvious. At 100 to 150 ppi the pixels don't stand out but the image doesn't look sharp. At 200 ppi and above, images are crisp.

Table 1 shows the maximum-size print you can make with each of these pixel densities for various image resolutions. (Note that I'm using the term *ppi* here instead of *dpi* to be more precise; the term *dpi,* short for *dots per inch,* is often used interchangeably with *ppi,* though it means something slightly different if you're talking about inkjet printers, as described in Chapter 9.)

Don't make prints larger than those listed in the "150 ppi" column for a given resolution image, unless you're willing to accept noticeable graininess.

Table 1: **Typical Resolutions and Maximum Print Sizes**

Image Size	150 ppi (Good Quality)	200 ppi (Excellent Quality)	300 ppi (Maximum Quality)
1 megapixel 1024 by 768	5.1 by 6.8 inches	3.8 by 5.1 inches	2.6 by 3.4 inches
2 megapixels 1600 by 1200	8 by 10.7 inches	6 by 8 inches	4 by 5.3 inches
3 megapixels 2048 by 1536	10.2 by 13.7 inches	7.7 by 10.2 inches	5.1 by 6.8 inches
4 megapixels 2272 by 1704	11.4 by 15.1 inches	8.5 by 11.4 inches	5.7 by 7.6 inches
5 megapixels 2560 by 1920	12.8 by 17.1 inches	9.6 by 12.8 inches	6.4 by 8.5 inches
6 megapixels 3000 by 2000	13.3 by 20 inches	10 by 15 inches	6.7 by 10 inches

Other Image-Quality Influences

The resolution and bit depth determine the maximum quality image that a camera (or scanner) can produce, but other factors can reduce the quality and account for the differences in image quality between cameras with identical specifications. It's important to understand these factors, especially when choosing a camera, or you can end up with lots of resolution but still have mediocre image quality. Here are some sources of variation:

- A lens that doesn't deliver a perfectly focused image to the camera's image sensor
- An image sensor that doesn't convert light into perfectly accurate color, so the colors may be a little off
- Noise in the signals from the image sensor, causing random variation in each pixel's color or brightness

Index

D

G

H

I

J

K

L

M

Q

R

S